Securing the AWS® Cloud

Securing the AWS® Cloud

A Guide for Learning to
Secure AWS Infrastructure

Brandon Carroll

WILEY

To Celeste, Weston, and Logan:
Thank you for your unwavering support, cooperation, and encouragement.

And to every bookworm who carries around massive tomes and never stops learning—this book is for you.

Contents

Preface

When I decided to write this book, I noticed a gap in how people learn AWS security. Too often, they rely on screenshots and web-based dashboards without ever touching the command line. As more organizations adopt a developer mindset for managing infrastructure and security, it is important to move beyond the GUI. That is why this book explores AWS security from the command line, gradually transitioning to infrastructure as code—so you can master the hands-on, code-centric practices that real-world developers use.

This book is written with newcomers to AWS and network security in mind. Many of these individuals will soon be expected to adopt developer-like workflows. You will find a comprehensive tour of essential AWS security concepts, from Identity and Access Management (IAM) to DevSecOps and GitOps, all reinforced with live demos, code samples, and diagrams from my own AWS environment. Along the way, I share anecdotes from personal experience to show why these topics matter in day-to-day operations.

Throughout each chapter, you have the chance to follow along with practical examples, using the CLI and code stored in my GitHub repository. By the end, you will not only understand the fundamentals of securing the AWS cloud but also be comfortable applying a developer mindset to building, automating, and maintaining secure cloud deployments. My hope is that these hands-on exercises and real-world insights will help you confidently navigate the ever-evolving landscape of AWS security.

Acknowledgments

I want to thank Romain Jourdan for believing in me when I transitioned from running Global Config Technology Solutions to Riverbed as a tech evangelist, and later for bringing me into AWS as a Senior Developer Advocate. He always championed learning, staying on top of the latest tools, and finding creative, fun ways to reach more people.

I'm also grateful to my tech editor and colleague, Du'An Lightfoot, who started at AWS on the same day as me. He's been my sounding board, a true friend, and someone I can always rely on for support and honest feedback.

A big thanks to several others in DevRel whose encouragement helped me complete this project, often without even knowing it. Stephen Preston's support as I tried to fit this book into my 2024 plan was invaluable, even if that plan didn't quite go as expected. And Cobus Bernard, thank you for being there whenever I had a Terraform question or needed a second pair of eyes on a tricky GitHub Action (even if you didn't realize it was for my book).

Finally, I want to acknowledge the young learners like Elijah Ramirez and Max Cloninger, whose enthusiasm for these technical topics keeps me energized. Their curiosity reminds me why I love sharing knowledge, and why I believe there's always something new to discover.

Introduction to Cloud Security

Welcome to the fascinating world of cloud computing and, more specifically, to securing your journey in the cloud with Amazon Web Services (AWS). Whether you're just starting out or looking to deepen your existing knowledge, this chapter lays the foundation for a robust understanding of cloud security dynamics.

Understanding Cloud Computing

Cloud computing isn't just a buzzword, although you may feel that way since it's been thrown around as such for many years now. No, in reality, cloud computing represents a shift in how organizations manage and deploy IT resources. Traditionally, organizations had to invest heavily in physical infrastructure, including things like servers, data centers, and networking equipment. These resources required significant upfront capital investment, not to mention space to "rack and stack" them. They also needed expertise to be configured and maintained.

Cloud computing has changed that to a large degree. Instead of solely relying on purchasing and managing extensive physical hardware, organizations are increasingly turning to cloud service providers like AWS to access and utilize these resources over the Internet. This doesn't eliminate the need for all physical infrastructure since organizations are still investing in hardware to provide connectivity and to maintain some critical services locally. However, the bulk of computing workloads have been or are being moved to the cloud.

This hybrid approach not only reduces the upfront capital expenditure but also combines the security and reliability of on-premises assets with the scalability and flexibility of the cloud, and there are many benefits to this approach. With the cloud, you can scale your resources up or down based on demand, and you pay only for what you use. This model democratizes access to the latest technology, enabling both small startups and large corporations to leverage powerful computing resources that they otherwise could not access.

This section covers the basics of what cloud computing is, the different models available, and the advantages it brings to businesses and individuals.

Definition and Evolution of Cloud Computing

What exactly is cloud computing? Simply put, cloud computing refers to the delivery of computing services, servers, storage, databases, networking, software, analytics, and more, over the Internet. In the early 2000s, when I was working as a Cisco trainer, we would often draw diagrams that showed two routers with a connection to one another through a service provider's network. The service provider's network was drawn in the diagram as a cloud. There were other components of the connectivity between the two routers in that cloud, but we did not have ownership or access to that networking equipment. So the cloud represented resources that were managed by someone else. I think this has something to do with why "the cloud" is called "the cloud." Using AWS as an example, organizations can store files in an object storage service called S3, and it sits "in the cloud." This represents that there are other components of the connectivity that provide access to this service, but the organization does not have access, nor does it control these resources. I'll get into that a bit more. For now, you should understand that "the cloud" involves more resources that provide access to services and applications than what you have control over or even see on an architecture diagram.

But why is using the cloud beneficial to organizations today? Well, this model allows for flexible resource allocation, reduces costs, increases efficiency, and provides scalability. The shift from dedicated physical servers to virtualized resources is a significant technological evolution.

Types of Cloud Models (IaaS, PaaS, and SaaS)

As you've seen, cloud computing changes the way companies manage IT resources, giving them different levels of control and management. You can think of cloud services like different ways of getting a meal. First, you can cook from scratch, using traditional on-premises computing. Or you can order a complete meal from a third party. In cloud model terms, this is called Software as a Service (SaaS). In this model, everything is prepared for you. You show up and get your food. You eat.

But maybe you prefer to get a meal kit delivered and make the meal yourself. This most resembles the cloud model known as Platform as a Service (PaaS). With PaaS, you get all the components you need to build your applications in the cloud; however, you have to put them together yourself.

Taking this idea a step further, you can have the groceries delivered to you. This cloud model is called Infrastructure as a Service (IaaS). In this case, you order and prepare the ingredients, and then you cook the meal. You simply have access to the store—you do the rest on your own.

Each of these cloud models caters to different needs. They each provide varying degrees of control—from full (IaaS) to minimal (SaaS)—and they allow you to choose based on your specific requirements.

Benefits of Cloud Computing

The flexibility mentioned in these cloud models leads directly to some of the major benefits of cloud computing. These benefits extend beyond simple cost savings (which is one of the first benefits most people mention when asked). Taking advantage of the cloud can significantly change how businesses operate. The scalability allows companies to easily adjust their resource use in response to varying demand without the need for physical upgrades. In addition to that, flexibility and accessibility can increase operational efficiency. This is important because it provides remote access to resources, pretty much from anywhere, which in turn reduces IT management headaches and, of course, overall costs. The benefits are real, and many organizations are already taking advantage of these benefits. And likely, you will either work for one of these organizations or are already working for one. There are still many misconceptions and challenges that these organizations face, however. Let's briefly discuss these.

Common Misconceptions and Challenges

As mentioned in the prior section, along with the clear benefits of cloud computing come some common misconceptions. One of these common misconceptions is that with cloud computing comes inherent security. It's important to understand that, while cloud providers like AWS secure the infrastructure, the security of the resources you deploy and manage is your responsibility. This is called the *shared responsibility model*, and it's essential that you understand it. Years ago, I worked for the phone company. When I arrived at someone's home to fix an issue with their service, I had to explain to them that the connection on the outside of the house was a demarcation point. Anything up to that point was the phone company's responsibility, and if the problem was there, I could fix it at no charge. Anything from that box into the house, all the way up to the telephone, was the customer's responsibility, and although I might be able to fix it, there would be a cost involved. This represented a clear change of responsibility. The shared responsibility model is similar. Security "of" the cloud is AWS's responsibility. Security "in" the cloud is the customer's responsibility, which means "your" responsibility. If you don't understand this, you'll have a hard time avoiding risks that can undermine the convenience that cloud computing offers.

Now that I've talked about cloud computing models at a high level, and I've specifically mentioned AWS and the shared responsibility model, it's time to look at the role that AWS plays in cloud computing.

AWS's Role in Cloud Computing

I started working with AWS services in the late 2000s. I worked at a training company teaching Cisco certification classes. Some of the assets we shared with students, along with my personal blog, were stored in S3. S3 is the Amazon Simple Storage Service, one of AWS's first offerings in the cloud. I will get into more details on services later, but my point here is that AWS has been around for a long time. Although others also provided services in the cloud before AWS, AWS is considered one of the first and most successful providers of cloud computing services.

Given its comprehensive tools and services, AWS plays a huge role in how many organizations leverage cloud computing. AWS isn't just a set of tools: it's way more. AWS supports everything from the ability to host simple websites to building complex Generative AI projects. Having a sense of AWS's role reveals why it has become a leader in the cloud industry and how it supports such a diverse range of computing needs. The good news is that you're here to learn more about how to implement the networking and security services AWS offers, so you're going to become very familiar with them by the time you finish this book. With that said, the next section gives a high-level overview of AWS services and infrastructure.

Overview of AWS Services and Infrastructure

AWS provides an extensive array of services that cater to various IT needs, making it the Swiss Army knife of the tech world—ready for nearly any task. If you don't believe me, try this. First, make sure you sign up for an AWS account at aws.amazon.com. With this account, once you're logged in, click on the Services option, and then select All Services. You should see several areas that AWS supports, from Analytics to Robotics. In fact, AWS supports over 230 services, and you can see just a fraction of them in Figure 1.1.

Yes, from computing power with Amazon EC2, storage options with Amazon S3, and networking (Amazon VPCs), to machine learning and Generative AI (Amazon Bedrock), Amazon SageMaker, and more, AWS's infrastructure is designed to support scalable, flexible, and secure applications across multiple

Figure 1.1: Some AWS services.

industries. You're going to learn more about this as you progress, so I don't go into details right now. With that said, why choose AWS?

Why AWS and the Advantages of Adoption and Learning

AWS's popularity stems from its robust, flexible, and secure infrastructure, trusted by startups and large enterprises alike. That might be reason enough to spend the time looking at AWS and moving some of your workloads there. But I would be remiss if I didn't compare AWS to my early days at the phone company. We used Lucent switches, Fujitsu DSLAMs (DSL access multiplexers), and Redback routers. I could have taken the time to learn any of those technologies and probably would have had a pretty good career with whatever certifications followed. But at the time, Cisco was in its prime, and everyone knew it. Today, the competition in cloud providers is a bit more fierce, but there are a few outliers that just make sense. AWS is one of them. If you take the time to learn AWS now, my belief is that you are in for a long career in cloud technology. That comes with one caveat. This long career will be a career of constant learning, constant testing, and constant growth. If you're up for that challenge, you've already answered the question, "Why AWS?" Still, whatever your decision is, I trust that if you're here, you really want to learn how to secure your AWS cloud infrastructure. That's exactly what you learn in this book.

You can expand on the examples in this book. I stretch beyond just the standard security practices to areas that are adjacent, like networking, DevOps, DevSecOps, and GitOps. I certainly can't cover security in today's day and age without a consideration of Generative AI, including the many ways it intersects with cloud security.

This chapter has explored the essential concepts and advantages of cloud computing with AWS, so you can now transition to Chapter 2, which dives a bit deeper into AWS security fundamentals. Chapter 2 examines the specific security services and features that AWS offers and explains how these tools can be mapped to core security concepts that you'll find across providers and on-premises environments.

AWS Security Fundamentals

"Most of us forget the basics and wonder why the specifics don't work."

—Garrison Wynn

Welcome to the second chapter of your journey to securing your infrastructure on AWS. By now, you should have a good grasp of what cloud computing is and why AWS stands out as a top choice for cloud services. This chapter digs deeper into the fundamentals of AWS security and covers some of the basic concepts that apply to security today. You'll need to map these basics to AWS's security services, so this chapter looks at these core security concepts at a high level and then identifies how the security services that AWS has to offer solve or address these core concepts. Buckle up, and let's get started!

AWS Security Service and Features

AWS has many security services. If you've spent any time in the AWS console, you know it's packed with an array of services—over 206, the last time I checked. The services that provide security features are designed to protect your data, applications, and infrastructure. This section covers some of the key security services that AWS offers. The first service to discuss is AWS Identity and Access Management (IAM).

Core Security Concepts

There are four core concepts addressed in this chapter. They are

- Confidentiality, Integrity, and Availability (the CIA triad)
- Principle of least privilege
- Defense in depth
- Shared responsibility model

The CIA Triad

The CIA triad is a foundational concept in information security. It represents the three core principles that should guide your security efforts: confidentiality, integrity, and availability. Figure 2.1 provides a visual representation of the CIA triad, in which all three areas of the triad surround your data. I break these down and highlight AWS services that provide a way to address these areas:

- Confidentiality has to do with ensuring that sensitive information is accessed only by authorized individuals. There are various ways to do this, but this example applies it to AWS. One way to make sure your data remains confidential is to ensure that only those you deem authorized are allowed to access it. In AWS, this involves using Identity and Access Management (IAM). With IAM you can create users, groups, policies, and roles to control access. Another way to maintain confidentiality is to make sure that when your data is *at rest*, meaning it is stored somewhere, or when your data is *in transit*, meaning it is being passed along the network, it is encrypted. Encryption ensures that your data is unreadable to prying eyes. In AWS, companies use services like AWS Key Management Service (KMS) and AWS Certificate Manager (ACM) when they encrypt their data.

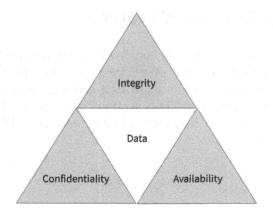

Figure 2.1: The CIA triad.

- Integrity is the act of protecting information from being altered by unauthorized parties. You can do this several ways. When you encrypt traffic, you can also use a one-way hash function to ensure integrity. The hashtag is like weighing a box before you ship it and then weighing it again at the destination. If the weight is different, you know something has changed without even opening the package. That's not the only way to ensure data integrity, though. AWS provides several tools to help maintain data integrity, including AWS CloudTrail for logging changes to your environment and Amazon Macie for monitoring and protecting sensitive data. I cover these in more detail later in this book.

- Availability is all about ensuring that information and resources are accessible when needed. This can be through providing redundancy for infrastructure equipment, or multiple paths for routing traffic to a destination. AWS offers various services to enhance availability, including Elastic Load Balancing (ELB) to distribute traffic across multiple instances and Amazon Route 53 for reliable DNS routing.

As you provision your resources in the cloud, you should always consider the CIA triad and apply these functions as you go.

The Principle of Least Privilege

The principle of least privilege (PoLP) is a security concept that promotes granting the minimal level of access or permissions that are necessary for users, programs, or systems to perform their tasks. The main idea is simple: the fewer permissions an entity has, the lower the risk of malicious or accidental damage.

In the context of AWS, this principle is particularly relevant. AWS provides a wide range of resources and services, from virtual machines (like EC2 instances) to storage solutions (like S3 buckets). As you build and manage your AWS infrastructure, applying the principle of least privilege ensures that each element (be it a user, service, or application) has only the permissions necessary to function correctly, and nothing more.

But you may wonder, why is applying the principle of least privilege important when working with resources in the cloud?

Implementing least privilege in AWS serves multiple purposes:

- *Security:* By limiting access, you reduce the potential impact of a security breach. If a user or service has minimal permissions, the scope for damage is significantly reduced.

- *Compliance:* Many regulatory frameworks require strict access controls. Adhering to the least-privilege principle helps in meeting these compliance requirements.

- *Operational simplicity*: Managing permissions can become complex. Applying the least-privilege principle keeps configurations as simple and as manageable as possible.

AWS offers various tools and features to help implement the least-privilege principle. Here are just a few of them:

- *Identity and access management (IAM):* Use IAM to create users, groups, roles, and policies that define permissible actions and resource access levels.
- *AWS IAM Access Analyzer:* This tool helps you identify and audit resources in your AWS environment that are accessible from outside your account, allowing you to detect unintended access and refine permissions to enforce least privilege.
- *AWS Policy Generator:* This tool helps you create security policies that grant only necessary permissions.
- *Access Advisor:* Within IAM, Access Advisor shows the services accessed by a user and provides information on the last access date. This can help in revising permissions to fit actual usage patterns.
- *Least-privilege Access Reviews:* Regularly review and adjust permissions to ensure they align with current needs and the principle of least privilege.
- *Automate Permissions Management:* Tools like AWS CloudTrail and AWS Config can help monitor and record compliance with your least-privilege policies.

As you progress through this book, you will learn more about some of these practices. Embracing the principle of least privilege is essential for maintaining a secure and efficient AWS environment. By granting only the necessary permissions, you not only bolster your security posture but also streamline your operations and compliance efforts.

One additional call-out here is to direct you to the AWS Well-Architected Framework, specifically the Security Pillar. The AWS Well-Architected Framework is a set of best practices and design principles for building secure, high-performing, resilient, and efficient infrastructure on AWS. Its Security Pillar focuses on protecting data, systems, and assets by implementing identity and access management, detection, infrastructure protection, data protection, and incident response. Within this pillar, least privilege is enforced through access control policies, and the CIA triad is addressed by securing data, ensuring data accuracy, and maintaining access to resources as needed.

As you can see, between the principle of least privilege and the CIA triad, there's much to consider when it comes to securing your resources. To help you with this, consider the defense-in-depth approach.

Defense in Depth

Defense in depth is a security strategy that uses multiple layers of defense to protect your data and resources. If one layer fails, other layers provide the needed protection. Oftentimes, this strategy is compared to that of a castle. Along the perimeter you have a moat. Then you have very high walls. Atop the walls are towers with lookouts and guards stationed at the ready. All of these layers of defense work together to keep the castle secure. This is illustrated in Figure 2.2.

Shared Responsibility Model

Security and compliance is a shared responsibility between AWS and the customer. By following this shared model, customers can reduce the operational burden, as AWS assumes responsibility for operating, managing, and controlling the components "of" the cloud. This leaves customers to focus on building their applications and implementing their services while assuming responsibility for securing those services "in" the cloud. You can see an example of this model in Figure 2.3.

There's an aspect of this model that I believe many fail to grasp. The model you see in Figure 2.3 does not apply to all services on AWS. In fact, the less customizable the service, the more responsibility AWS takes on. For example, Figure 2.4 illustrates the shared responsibility model as it applies to services like EC2.

With AWS foundational services, like compute, storage, networking, and physical infrastructure, AWS takes responsibility for all underlying security controls, including physical security. As a customer, you don't need to manage these aspects. However, for elements running on top of AWS services,

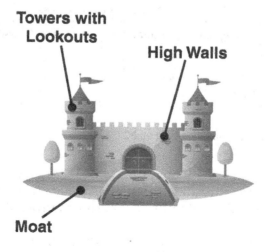

Figure 2.2: Defense in depth illustrated.

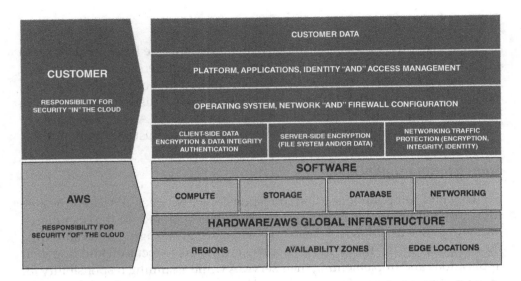

Figure 2.3: The shared responsibility model.

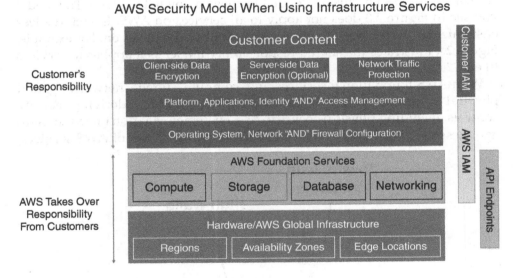

Figure 2.4: The shared responsibility model for EC2.

such as the operating system on an EC2 instance, firewall configurations, security rules, and identity and access management, you are responsible for implementing and maintaining these security controls. What about a more abstracted service?

Looking at Figure 2.5, you can see how the shared responsibility model applies to something like an RDS database. As you can see in the figure, AWS

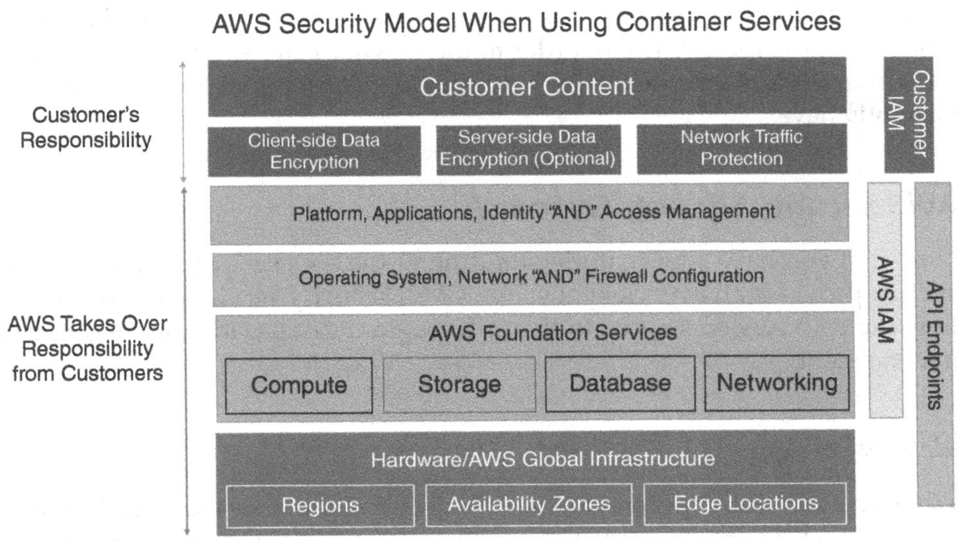

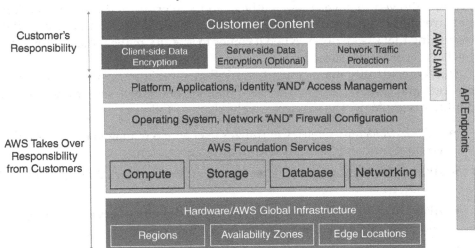

Figure 2.5: The shared responsibility model for RDS.

Figure 2.6: The shared responsibility model for DynamoDB, S3, and similar services.

provides the security all the way up to the platform, applications, and identity and access management.

To take it one step further, Figure 2.6 illustrates how AWS provides security for services like DynamoDB and S3, whereby network traffic protection and (optionally) server-side data encryption are provided by AWS as part of the shared responsibility model.

Why is this concept so important to understand? Because you need to know what is your responsibility in order to know what you need to secure, which tools and services are available to help you do so, and any gaps in security you currently have.

AWS Security Services Overview

Now that you have a basic understanding of the core security concepts, this section provides an overview of some AWS's security services and discusses how the core concepts apply to them. To begin, I discuss identity and access management.

Identity Services

What do you think of when you hear the term "identity services" or "identity management"? For me, I think back to my routing and switching days, and the first thing that comes to mind is authentication, authorization, and accounting (AAA). Authentication involves identifying a user and determining if they are supposed to have access to a resource. Once you know who a user is and that they are allowed to have access, authorization determines the specific actions they are allowed to take. And accounting involves keeping an audit trail of everything that's been done. When it comes to identity management with AWS, this isn't far from the same idea.

At its core, identity management on AWS involves managing identities, permissions, and resource access. There is more than one way to secure and manage identities with AWS. The services involved are as follows:

- *AWS IAM Identity Center:* Centralizes user access management across AWS accounts and applications within an organization.

- *AWS IAM:* Manages user access and permissions for AWS services and resources.

- *AWS Directory Service:* Provides managed directory services to integrate and manage user authentication for AWS resources.

- *AWS Resource Access Manager:* Shares AWS resources securely across accounts in your organization.

- *AWS Organizations:* Organizes and manages multiple AWS accounts centrally, enforcing policies and consolidating billing.

- *Amazon Cognito:* Enables secure user sign-up, sign-in, and access control for web and mobile apps.

- *Amazon Verified Permissions:* Offers fine-grained access control policies for custom applications, ensuring verified access permissions.

AWS identity and access management (IAM) is AWS's foundational service for controlling access to AWS resources. IAM allows you to manage users, groups, and roles within individual AWS accounts and apply specific permissions to secure access to AWS services. As the original service for access management on AWS, IAM provides the core features needed to control who has access to which resources. It's an essential part of the shared responsibility model.

Building on IAM's capabilities, the AWS IAM Identity Center is designed to help you manage the workforce access across your AWS accounts and applications. This is the AWS recommended service for doing so, but it's not the only one. The benefit of following this recommendation is that users get a consistent experience across all AWS applications. Prior to the use of the AWS IAM Identity Center, most workforce management was done with AWS IAM. So why choose Identity Center over IAM? Because Identity Center lets you manage access to all AWS accounts in an AWS organization, as well as access to other applications. IAM, on the other hand, lets you manage access to AWS services and resources within an AWS account. Chapter 3 goes into much more detail on identity management.

For now, it's important to understand that identity services on AWS allow you to manage users, groups, and roles as well as apply policies and permissions. This provides at least one layer of defense in the defense-in-depth approach, and it covers the confidentiality portion of the CIA triad. Regarding the shared responsibility model, the users and their permissions are part of your responsibility. When configuring user accounts, groups, and roles, you should follow the least-privilege principle.

Network Security

The next area of AWS security services is network security. There are several services to discuss in this area; however, the primary service is the Amazon Virtual Private Cloud (VPC). An Amazon VPC is a logically isolated section of the AWS cloud environment that allows you to define and control your own virtual networking environment, including IP address ranges, subnets, routing tables, and network gateways.

Within an Amazon VPC, you can create and configure various resources, including

- *Virtual Private Cloud (VPC):* The virtual network itself, where you can launch AWS resources like Amazon Elastic Compute Cloud (EC2) instances, Amazon Relational Database Service (RDS) instances, and others.

- *Subnet:* You can divide your VPC into multiple subnets, which are isolated segments within the VPC. These subnets can be public (accessible from the Internet) or private (accessible only from within the VPC or other connected networks).

- *Internet gateway:* A horizontally scaled, redundant, and highly available VPC component that allows communication between instances in your VPC and the Internet.

- *NAT gateway:* A Network Address Translation (NAT) gateway enables instances in a private subnet to connect to the Internet or other private subnets, or AWS services, but prevents the Internet from initiating connections with those instances.

- *Virtual private gateway:* This component establishes a secure and private connection between your corporate data center and your VPC, typically over an Internet Protocol Security (IPsec) virtual private network (VPN) connection.

By creating an Amazon VPC, you have control over your virtual networking environment, allowing you to customize it according to your specific security and infrastructure requirements. There are several security features within a VPC. For example, a VPC is a logically isolated network environment that is separate from other virtual networks in the AWS cloud. This isolation ensures that network traffic within your VPC is isolated by default from other VPCs or networks unless you allow that traffic, providing an additional layer of security.

Taking that a step further, subnet isolation could be considered another security feature of a VPC. Since public subnets are associated with route tables that have a route to an Internet gateway, while private subnets do not, you can isolate resources based on their accessibility needs. This setup helps ensure confidentiality when properly designed.

There is another feature within a VPC that is more clearly a security feature, and it's called a *security group*. Security groups act as virtual firewalls for your EC2 instances within a VPC. You can define inbound and outbound rules to control the traffic to and from your instances, allowing or denying specific IP addresses, protocols, and ports. You can specify other security groups, as well. Security groups offer you granular control at the instance level, and they are applied to the ENI of an instance (EC2 instances, RDS instances, etc.). Security groups are also stateful, meaning they track the state of a connection, and valid responses to a connection are allowed.

Another security construct at the network level is the Network Access Control List (NACL). NACLs are stateless firewalls that operate at the subnet level. They provide an additional layer of security (again, think defense in depth) by allowing or denying traffic based on inbound and outbound rules, including IP addresses, protocols, and port numbers. NACLs have a numerical order (lowest to highest) in which they are processed. By default, NACLs allow all inbound and outbound traffic, but you can modify the rules to restrict traffic.

VPCs fit into the integrity and availability sections of the CIA triad. And as you configure security groups and NACLs, you might keep the principle of least privilege in mind and allow only the necessary ports and protocols. Finally, the access into and out of your VPC is the customer responsibility of the shared responsibility model.

Before you move on from the network security section, there are a few other services and features that fall into this category. For the sake of brevity, I only mention these services briefly. A more in-depth discussion of these services comes when applicable, later in this book. These services include

- *Flow logs:* They capture information about the IP traffic going to and from network interfaces in your VPC. These logs can be analyzed to monitor and audit network traffic for security purposes. Flow logs can be applied at the VPC, subnet, and ENI levels.

- *AWS PrivateLink:* Allows you to securely access AWS services and resources from your VPC without traversing the public Internet. This reduces the exposure of your VPC resources to potential threats on the Internet.

- *AWS Network Firewall:* A managed network security service that enables you to deploy essential network protection across your VPCs. It provides stateful, managed firewalling capabilities to filter traffic at the perimeter of your VPC.

- *AWS Web Application Firewall (WAF):* A web application firewall that helps protect your web applications and APIs from common web exploits and bots. It operates at the application level, inspecting and filtering incoming HTTP/HTTPS traffic based on user-defined rules.

- *Amazon VPC Traffic Mirroring:* Enables you to capture and inspect network traffic from Amazon EC2 instances within your VPC, allowing for deep packet inspection and network analysis.

- *AWS Shield:* A managed DDoS (distributed denial-of-service) protection service that safeguards your applications from external threats, enhancing availability by mitigating large-scale attacks.

Data Protection

The data protection category in AWS security services covers a range of services and features designed to help protect and secure data in various states: at rest, in transit, and in use. These are not the traditional data protection services that some think of, like backup, disaster recovery, or data replication services. These services aim to prevent unauthorized access, ensure data integrity, and maintain data privacy and compliance. The data protection services to be aware of are as follows:

- *AWS Key Management Service (KMS):* A managed service that enables you to create, store, and manage cryptographic keys used for data encryption and decryption. It provides secure key management, including key rotation, key access control, and auditing capabilities, as well as integrating with other AWS services to enable encryption and decryption of data at rest and in transit.

- *AWS CloudHSM:* A cloud-based hardware security module (HSM) that provides secure key storage and cryptographic operations. It offers FIPS 140-2 Level 3 validated HSMs, ensuring high levels of security for cryptographic keys and operations. CloudHSM is often used for scenarios that require strict compliance requirements or additional control over key management.

- *AWS Certificate Manager (ACM):* A service that simplifies the provisioning, management, and deployment of public and private SSL/TLS certificates. It helps secure data in transit by enabling HTTPS connections between clients and web applications or services. ACM integrates with other AWS services, like Elastic Load Balancing, Amazon CloudFront, and API Gateway.

- *Amazon Macie:* A data security and privacy service that uses machine learning to discover and protect sensitive data stored in Amazon S3. It can identify and alert you to sensitive data, such as personally identifiable information (PII) or intellectual property. Macie helps you meet data privacy and compliance requirements by identifying and protecting sensitive data.

- *AWS Encryption Services:* AWS provides various encryption services and features, including server-side encryption for Amazon S3, Amazon EBS, and Amazon RDS, client-side encryption, and field-level encryption for specific services. These services enable data encryption at rest and in transit, helping protect data confidentiality and integrity.

- *AWS PrivateLink:* This provides private connectivity among AWS services, your VPC, and on-premises networks without exposing data to the public Internet. It helps secure data in transit and ensures that sensitive data remains within the AWS network or on your private network.

To conclude this section on data protection, I highlight how these services align with the core security principles and models covered at the onset.

AWS data protection services, such as AWS Key Management Service (KMS), AWS CloudHSM, AWS Certificate Manager (ACM), and Amazon Macie, directly contribute to the confidentiality and integrity aspects of the CIA (confidentiality, integrity, and availability) triad. They enable encryption, secure key management, and secure communication channels, protecting data at rest, in transit, and in use. Moreover, these services support the principle of least privilege by providing granular access controls and integrating with AWS identity and access management (IAM) for role-based permissions. Collectively, they form a defense-in-depth strategy, offering multiple layers of data protection through encryption, key management, certificate management, and sensitive data discovery. Finally, they align with the shared responsibility model, where AWS ensures the security of the underlying cloud infrastructure and you, the customer, are responsible for properly configuring and using these services to safeguard your data's confidentiality and integrity.

Now that you have fundamental knowledge of data protection, the next section explores AWS services focused on threat detection and monitoring.

Threat Detection and Monitoring

Threat detection and monitoring refers to the process of identifying, analyzing, and responding to potential security threats and risks within an organization's IT infrastructure and systems. It involves continuous monitoring of various sources, such as network traffic, system logs, user activities, and application events, with the goal of detecting any suspicious or malicious behavior that could compromise or otherwise impact the security of an organization's assets, data, and operations. This typically involves the use of various tools and technologies, such as security information and event Management (SIEM) systems, intrusion detection/prevention systems (IDS/IPS), log management solutions, vulnerability scanners, and security analytics platforms.

The key AWS services in this category include Amazon GuardDuty, AWS CloudTrail, and AWS Config. A brief overview of each of these and how they relate to the core security concepts already discussed is in order:

- Amazon GuardDuty is a threat detection service that continuously monitors for malicious activity and unauthorized behavior within your AWS accounts and workloads. I think of GuardDuty in a similar manner to a typical intrusion detection system. GuardDuty leverages machine learning, anomaly detection, and integrated threat intelligence to identify potential threats, such as compromised instances, suspected credential exposure, or suspicious network activity. GuardDuty helps organizations maintain the integrity and confidentiality of their data and systems by promptly alerting them to potential security incidents.

- AWS CloudTrail is a service that records API calls and related events across your AWS infrastructure. It provides a comprehensive audit trail of actions taken within your AWS accounts. This audit trail supports compliance efforts, security analysis, and operational troubleshooting. CloudTrail aligns with the principle of least privilege in that you can monitor and review the actions taken by different users, roles, and services and ensure that only authorized activities are performed. If actions are taken outside the scope of a user, role, or service, you can adjust the policies and permissions accordingly.

- AWS Config is a service that continuously monitors and records the configuration of your AWS resources and then assesses those resources against desired configurations and compliance rules that you select or define. It helps organizations maintain a secure and compliant infrastructure by identifying misconfigurations, deviations from best practices, and potential security risks. Config supports the defense-in-depth approach by providing a layer of continuous monitoring and assessment, complementing other security controls.

These threat-detection and monitoring services contribute to the CIA triad by supporting the confidentiality, integrity, and availability of your AWS resources and data. They align with the shared responsibility model, where AWS provides the secure service and you are responsible for configuring, enabling, and actively monitoring these services to detect and respond to potential threats effectively.

The threat detection and monitoring services discussed in this section are key services, and they play an important role in identifying potential security threats, monitoring user activities, and ensuring compliance with security best practices. However, in today's complex regulatory landscape, organizations must go beyond reactive threat detection and proactively ensure compliance with various industry standards, regulations, and internal governance policies.

This leads to the next category of AWS security services, focused on compliance and governance. The next section discusses services like AWS Artifact, AWS Config rules, and AWS Organizations and explains how they equip you with the tools and capabilities to streamline compliance efforts, enforce governance policies, and maintain a consistent security posture across your AWS environments.

Compliance and Governance

The next topic in this overview of AWS security services is compliance and governance. This category encompasses services designed to help organizations maintain compliance with industry standards, regulations, and internal policies within their AWS environments. The reason these services are important is that organizations operating in the cloud must adhere to various regulatory requirements and governance frameworks to ensure the security and integrity of their systems and data.

Although I can't provide an exhaustive list, the regulatory requirements and governance frameworks that many organizations need to comply with include

- PCI-DSS (Payment Card Industry Data Security Standard) for organizations handling credit card data
- HIPAA (Health Insurance Portability and Accountability Act) for healthcare organizations

- SOC 2 (Service Organization Control) reports for service providers
- ISO 27001/27017/27018 for information security management
- NIST 800-53 (National Institute of Standards and Technology) for federal agencies and contractors
- GDPR (General Data Protection Regulation) for handling personal data of EU citizens
- CCPA (California Consumer Privacy Act) for data privacy and consumer rights

That's not to mention that organizations often have their own internal governance frameworks, policies, and standards as well. These include

- Corporate security policies
- Data classification and handling procedures
- Access control and least privilege requirements
- Change management and configuration management processes
- Incident response and disaster recovery plans

Hopefully, seeing these two lists gives you an idea of what you're up against and helps you see why these AWS services I'm about to cover are important. With that said, here are the services that fall into this category, starting with AWS Artifact.

AWS Artifact

AWS Artifact is a centralized repository that provides on-demand access to AWS's security and compliance reports, including those related to industry standards and regulations such as PCI-DSS, HIPAA, and ISO. AWS Artifact lets an organization demonstrate compliance with these standards, helping users to expedite audits as well as make informed decisions about their cloud security posture.

AWS Config Rules

The previous section on threat detection and monitoring talked about AWS Config. Here, I want to drill down a bit deeper and specifically call out *AWS Config rules*. The rules that you can define in Config let you enforce desired configurations and compliance states for your AWS resources. Recall that Config records and continuously monitors and assesses your resource configurations. It assesses them against a set of predefined rules that are defined based on industry best practices and regulatory requirements. There are different rule sets you can enable based on various compliance or standards you want to enforce. Config rules support the defense-in-depth approach by providing an additional layer of continuous monitoring and enforcement, complementing other security controls.

AWS Organizations

The next service to talk about is AWS Organizations. AWS Organizations is a centralized management and governance service that allows you to control and manage multiple AWS accounts under one main account. When you create an organization, you can then apply service control policies (SCPs), which are JSON policies that define the maximum permissions for AWS services and actions across accounts within an organization. To simplify this, at the top-level account you can define a service control policy that says no organization can create or delete security groups.

By implementing SCPs, you can enforce consistent security and compliance policies across your entire AWS environment with your AWS Organization, ensuring adherence to the principle of least privilege and reducing the risk of misconfigurations or unauthorized activities.

AWS Security Hub

In addition to these services, AWS also offers *AWS Security Hub*. Security Hub provides a centralized view or dashboard of your security and compliance posture across your AWS accounts. Security Hub consolidates findings from various AWS services, such as GuardDuty, Inspector, and Config, as well as partner solutions, so that you can prioritize and remediate security issues more effectively.

Overall, these compliance and governance services contribute to the CIA triad by ensuring that AWS resources and data are configured and managed in a secure and compliant manner. They also align with the shared responsibility model, because AWS provides the services and tools and secures the service, while you are responsible for configuring, enabling, and actively monitoring the features in each of these services.

This list, although not exhaustive, should give you an idea of some of the most common security services and features you'll use on AWS. Now that you're armed with this knowledge, the next section talks a bit about best practices.

Security Best Practices

Throughout this chapter, I've discussed several core security concepts, including the CIA triad, the principle of least privilege, defense in depth, and the shared responsibility model. I've also explained various AWS security services categorized under identity services, network security, data protection, threat detection and monitoring, and compliance and governance. I go into further detail on many of these concepts and services throughout the remainder of this book. For now, I tie these concepts together and explain how they can be applied with best practices to AWS security services.

Applying Best Practices with the CIA Triad

I've talked quite a bit in this chapter about the CIA triad. Having an understanding of the triad should help you apply best practices in the AWS cloud. How so? Consider each of the three areas of the triad as they relate to the services overviewed in this chapter.

Recall that *confidentiality* is about ensuring that sensitive information is accessed only by authorized individuals. In AWS, you can maintain confidentiality through services like AWS Key Management Service (KMS) and AWS Certificate Manager (ACM), which enable data encryption and secure communication channels. Additionally, AWS PrivateLink allows you to securely access AWS services and resources from within your VPC without exposing traffic to the public Internet, therefore reducing exposure to potential threats.

To understand how services connect in AWS, it helps to know a bit about AWS's global networking structure. AWS resources are organized across geographic regions, each containing multiple Availability Zones. Some AWS services, like S3 and DynamoDB, operate outside of your VPC and require connections through public endpoints by default. However, to access these services securely without going over the public Internet, you can use VPC endpoints or AWS PrivateLink, which create private connections to these services directly within your VPC.

Integrity refers to protecting information from being altered by unauthorized parties. AWS CloudTrail provides auditing capabilities by recording API calls and related events across your AWS infrastructure, allowing you to monitor and review actions. AWS Config continuously monitors and records the configuration of your AWS resources, helping you identify misconfigurations or deviations from desired states. Moreover, Amazon GuardDuty uses machine learning and threat intelligence to detect unauthorized or malicious activities within your AWS accounts and workloads, helping to maintain data integrity.

Finally, availability is about ensuring that information and resources are accessible when needed. This can be accomplished through Route53, multiple routes in a VPC, load balancers in the VPC, and even being able to auto-scale your EC2 instances.

Applying Best Practices with the Principle of Least Privilege

Using IAM and Identity Center, you can apply the principle of least privilege. When you create users, groups, roles, and policies, whether it's in Identity Center or IAM, you should grant only the necessary permissions to perform specific actions or access specific resources. By following the least-privilege principle, you can reduce the risk of unauthorized access or accidental misconfigurations.

Applying Best Practices with Defense in Depth

AWS provides a wide range of security services that can be combined to create a multilayered defense strategy, also known as defense in depth. For example, you can use AWS WAF (Web Application Firewall) to protect your web applications, AWS Network Firewall to secure your VPC perimeter, AWS Config rules to enforce compliance, and AWS Security Hub to centralize and prioritize security findings. By implementing multiple layers of security controls, you can enhance your overall security posture and reduce the risk of a single point of failure.

Applying Best Practices with the Shared Responsibility Model

It's essential to understand the shared responsibility model when using AWS services. AWS is responsible for securing the underlying cloud infrastructure, while customers are responsible for securing their applications, data, and resources running on AWS. For example, AWS secures the physical infrastructure, while customers are responsible for configuring security groups, encrypting data, and managing access permissions.

The AWS Well-Architected Framework

This chapter wouldn't be complete if I didn't mention the AWS Well-Architected Framework, a set of best practices and guidelines that help you design and build secure, high-performing, resilient, and efficient systems in the cloud. It consists of six pillars:

- Operational excellence
- Security
- Reliability
- Performance efficiency
- Cost optimization
- Sustainability

Homing in on best practices, the security pillar of the Well-Architected Framework is particularly relevant. This pillar focuses on protecting information, systems, and assets while delivering business value through risk assessments and mitigation strategies. It provides guidance on implementing identity and access management, data protection, infrastructure protection, threat detection, and incident response capabilities. By following the security pillar's best practices, you can design and deploy AWS architectures that adhere to security principles such as the CIA triad, least privilege, and defense in depth. These best practices help you meet your security requirements, protect your data and systems, and maintain compliance with industry standards and regulations. Although I won't go into the specifics of the security pillar, I do recommend you get acquainted with it. You can find documentation for the security pillar at `https://docs.aws.amazon.com/wellarchitected/latest/security-pillar/welcome.html`.

Conclusion

This chapter explored the fundamentals of AWS security, covering core security concepts and their application to AWS services and best practices. It discussed the CIA triad, the principle of least privilege, defense in depth, and the shared responsibility model. Additionally, I provided an overview of key AWS security services across several categories, including identity services, network security, data protection, threat detection and monitoring, and compliance and governance.

As you wrap up this chapter, consider these key points:

- The CIA triad serves as a guiding principle for implementing security measures, ensuring the confidentiality, integrity, and availability of your data and resources in the AWS cloud.

- The principle of least privilege reduces the risk of unauthorized access and minimizes the potential impact of security breaches.

- The defense-in-depth approach leverages multiple layers of security controls, enhancing your overall security posture and reducing the risk of a single point of failure.

- Understanding the shared responsibility model is essential for delineating the security responsibilities between AWS and you, the customer. This helps you effectively secure your applications, data, and resources running on AWS.

- AWS offers a comprehensive suite of security services and tools that can be combined to address various security requirements and industry-specific compliance needs.

Although this chapter has provided a solid foundation in AWS security fundamentals, it's important to remember that security is an ongoing process—a moving target for certain. As you progress in your AWS journey, take time to explore the services and best practices discussed in this chapter in greater depth, especially during two key times of the year. The first is during the week of the AWS re:Inforce conference, AWS's annual security-focused conference.

It is designed specifically for cloud security professionals, providing them with the opportunity to learn about the latest security innovations, best practices, and strategies for securing their workloads on AWS. AWS re:Inforce typically takes place in June. This is a key time of year when many announcements are made and key security services are launched. The other time of year to be especially mindful of is during AWS re:Invent, AWS's largest and most comprehensive annual cloud-computing conference. You will typically get a lot of announcements and service launches during this time as well. AWS re:Invent typically happens in the first week of December.

Additionally, familiarize yourself with the AWS Well-Architected Framework, particularly the security pillar, which provides valuable guidance on designing and deploying secure AWS architectures. The framework's best practices can help you meet your security requirements, protect your data and systems, and maintain compliance with industry standards and regulations.

The next chapter dives deeper into identity and access management (IAM). Your journey toward mastering AWS security has just begun. I encourage you to keep exploring, learning, and applying the principles and best practices covered in this chapter.

Reference

Amazon Web Services, "Shared Responsibility Model," https://aws.amazon. com/compliance/shared-responsibility-model

Identity and Access Management on AWS

*"Why is identity so important? Identity forms
the basis for authorization and trust."*
—NIST draft publication 800-103

Welcome to the third chapter of your journey to securing your infrastructure on AWS. By now, you should have a good grasp of the AWS security fundamentals. This chapter dives into the specifics of identity and access management (IAM), which is critical for maintaining secure access control in your AWS environment. You'll explore IAM's core concepts and its various components, as well as best practices for configuration and management. The chapter starts by outlining what it aims to accomplish.

Overview

In today's world, where cloud computing is the backbone of modern IT infrastructure, securing access to resources is crucial. I won't patronize you: you know this, and that's why you're here. This chapter focuses on how identity and access management (IAM) in AWS forms the foundation of this security framework. As stated in NIST draft publication 800-103(retired), "Why is identity so important? Identity forms the basis for authorization and trust," this chapter aims to provide a comprehensive understanding of AWS IAM, emphasizing its critical role in maintaining a secure cloud environment.

In this chapter, I aim to

- Help you understand the various scenarios where IAM is essential
- Break down the core elements of IAM, such as users, groups, roles, and policies
- Show you how IAM policies work, their syntax, and how to evaluate and apply them
- Provide a detailed exploration of the creation and management of IAM identities, groups, roles, and policies
- Introduce you to AWS IAM Identity Center

By becoming well acquainted with these concepts, you will be equipped to enhance the security of your AWS infrastructure, ensuring strong identity and access management practices that align with best practices and compliance requirements.

Use Cases for IAM

This section reviews a few use cases where IAM fits in. Honestly, IAM fits everywhere, and you're going to use it a lot, sometimes without really thinking about it. As I begin, I want to make a delineation between *users* and *applications* from the standpoint of identity management on AWS.

Managing User Access

With IAM, you can manage AWS permissions for your users and applications. However, when it when it comes to users, AWS recommends that you use AWS IAM Identity Center. AWS IAM Identity Center is the successor to AWS Single Sign-On (SSO), and it is how you manage your user access to AWS accounts and permissions within those accounts. AWS IAM Identity Center makes it easier to provision and manage IAM roles and policies across your AWS organization, a concept I explain in a bit more detail at the end of this chapter. For application permissions, you should use IAM roles and policies. The following sections discuss a few more use cases for IAM.

Cross-Account Access

In many organizations, resources are spread across multiple AWS accounts. IAM roles facilitate secure cross-account access by allowing resources in one account to access resources in another. This is particularly useful for scenarios like centralized logging, where you might have a dedicated account for collecting and analyzing logs from various other accounts.

Temporary Security Credentials

IAM roles are also useful for granting temporary access to AWS resources. Instead of creating long-term credentials for users or applications, you can assign roles that provide temporary security credentials. This reduces the risk associated with long-term credential exposure and ensures that access is granted only for the necessary duration.

Automating Infrastructure Deployment

Automation is a key aspect of modern infrastructure management. IAM roles enable you to securely automate the deployment and management of AWS resources. For example, you can assign roles to AWS Lambda functions, EC2 instances, or ECS tasks, allowing them to interact with other AWS services without needing hard-coded credentials.

Fine-Grained Permissions for Applications

When it comes to application permissions, IAM roles and policies allow you to implement the principle of least privilege effectively. By granting only the necessary permissions required by an application to function, you minimize the risk of unauthorized access and potential security breaches. This ensures that applications can perform their tasks without having overly broad permissions that could be exploited.

These use cases illustrate the flexibility and power of IAM in managing access to your AWS environment. By leveraging IAM's features, you can enhance security, simplify administration, and ensure compliance with best practices and regulatory requirements.

The next section breaks down the core elements of IAM.

Understanding the Lingo

Understanding IAM starts with getting familiar with its terminology (lingo).

What Is AWS IAM?

AWS Identity and Access Management (IAM) is a web service that helps you securely control access to AWS resources. With IAM, you control who is authenticated (signed in) and authorized (has permissions) to use resources. You define who can access what by specifying fine-grained permissions, and IAM enforces those permissions for every request. By default, all requests are denied (except for the root user, which is allowed by default) unless an explicit "allow" is specified. An explicit "deny" overrides any allows.

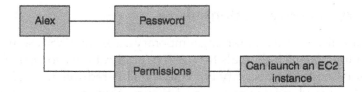

Figure 3.1: User and attributes.

What Are IAM Users?

An IAM user is an entity that you create in AWS to represent a person or application that interacts with AWS. A user in AWS consists of a name and credentials.

Imagine a user named Alex. When you create the IAM user Alex, you create a password for that user. You can also attach permissions to the IAM user that will allow Alex to launch a specific Amazon EC2 instance. You can see the relationship between the user Alex and the attributes in Figure 3.1.

What Are IAM User Groups?

An IAM user group is a collection of IAM users. User groups let you specify permissions for multiple users, making it easier to manage the permissions for those users.

For example, let's say you have a user group called Admins, and you give that user group the permissions that administrators typically need. Any user in that group automatically has the permissions assigned to the group. If a new user joins your organization and needs administrator privileges, you can simply add the user to the Admins group. Similarly, if someone changes roles within your organization, you can remove them from their old user groups and add them to the appropriate new groups.

Figure 3.2 shows a simple example of an AWS account with four groups. A *group* is a collection of users who have similar responsibilities. In this example, one group is for Administrators (called Admins), one for App Developers, one for Database Admins, and another for Infrastructure Admins. Each group has multiple users. Each user can be in more than one group, although the figure doesn't illustrate that. You can't nest groups within other groups.

You should also know that permissions from both user and group policies are combined to determine the final effective permissions for a user. If a user has a policy attached that explicitly allows an action, and a group policy they belong to denies it, the denial takes precedence. This is because an explicit deny in any policy (user or group) overrides any allows. Additionally, for all actions not explicitly denied, the permissions are additive. AWS evaluates all user policies, group policies, and any attached permissions boundaries or SCPs and grants the union of the allowed actions.

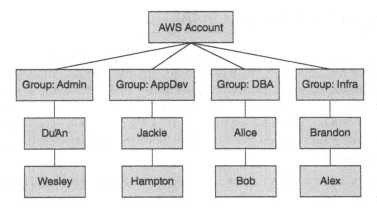

Figure 3.2: Simple AWS account IAM example.

What Are IAM Roles?

An IAM role is similar to a user, in that it is an AWS identity with permission policies that determine what the identity can and cannot do in AWS. The major difference is that, unlike users, IAM roles have no long-term credentials (i.e., passwords or access keys). You can use roles to delegate access to users, applications, or services that don't normally have access to your AWS resources.

For example, you might want to grant users in your AWS account access to resources they don't usually have or grant users in one AWS account access to resources in another account. Or you might want to allow a mobile app to use AWS resources without embedding AWS keys within the app, where they could be difficult to rotate and where users could potentially extract them.

What Is a Principal?

There's one more term I think you should know before I start talking about policies and permissions, and that's a *principal*. A principal is an entity in AWS that can perform actions and access resources. A principal can be an AWS account root user, an IAM user, or a role, and you can grant permissions to access a resource in one of two ways:

- *Identity-based policies:* You can directly attach a permissions policy to a user or to a role. You can indirectly attach a permission policy to a user through a group.

- *Resource-based policies:* For services that support resource-based policies, you can identify the principal in the Principal element of a policy attached to the resource.

Policies and Permissions in IAM

So far, you know what users, user groups, and roles are. For each of these entities, you can attach a policy. A *policy* is an object in AWS that defines the permissions that an identity or resource has. *Identity-based policies* and *resource-based policies* are the two most often used policies; however, there are others, including permissions boundaries, organizations SCPs, S3 bucket access control lists (ACLs), and session policies. For now, let's focus on identity-based policies and resource-based policies:

- *Identity-based policies* can be attached to users and groups. These policies grant permissions to an identity.

- *Resource-based policies* grant permissions to the principal that is specified in the policy. Principals can be in the same account as the resource or in other accounts.

Permissions in the policy define whether a request made by the identity or resource is allowed or denied. On AWS, most policies are stored as JSON documents.

IAM policy documents consist of one or more statements structured as shown in the following example:

```
{
 "Statement":[{
  "Effect":"effect",
  "Action":"action",
  "Resource":"arn",
  "Condition":{
   "condition":{
    "key":"value"
    }
   }
  }
 ]
}
```

Let's break down these statements. First, "allow" and "deny" are not actions. They are *effects* that can be applied to an *action*. The action will include a list of actions that the policy allows or denies. *Resources* are only required in some circumstances. For a resource-based policy, specifying resources is optional. If you don't specify a resource, the actions apply to the resource that the policy is attached to. Finally, the *condition* specifies the circumstances under which the policy grants permission.

Example Policy

Here is an example policy to illustrate how this fits together:

```
{
  "Version": "2012-10-17",
  "Statement": {
    "Sid": "1",
    "Effect": "Allow",
    "Action": "s3:ListBucket",
    "Resource": "arn:aws:s3:::my_s3_bucket"
  }
}
```

In this example policy, each element has a specific role in defining which actions are allowed and under what conditions:

- *Version:* The `"Version": "2012-10-17"` element specifies the policy language syntax version. AWS requires this date format for most policies, as it supports the latest IAM features and functionality. Using this version ensures that the policy is compatible with all current capabilities in AWS's policy language.

- *Statement:* The `"Statement"` element is the core component of the policy. It contains one or more individual permission statements. Each statement defines the effect, action, and resource for the permission. This example has a single statement.

- *Sid (Statement ID):* The `"Sid": "1"` element provides a unique identifier for this statement within the policy. Although optional, the Sid is helpful when multiple statements are present, as it makes the policy easier to read, reference, and troubleshoot by allowing each statement to have a distinct label.

- *Effect:* The `"Effect": "Allow"` element specifies whether the statement allows or denies the specified action(s). In this case, allow grants permission. AWS policies support two effects—allow and deny, where a deny will always override any allows for that action if both are present.

- *Action:* The `"Action": "s3:ListBucket"` element defines the AWS action(s) the policy permits or denies. Here, `s3:ListBucket` allows the principal to list the contents of the specified S3 bucket. Actions are always tied to a specific AWS service (in this case, s3) and must be explicitly listed to be allowed or denied.

- *Resource:* The `"Resource": "arn:aws:s3:::my_s3_bucket"` element specifies the AWS resource(s) the policy applies to. The ARN

(Amazon Resource Name) uniquely identifies the resource, in this case, an S3 bucket named `my_s3_bucket`. This restricts the policy so that the `s3:ListBucket` action applies only to this bucket, ensuring the principal cannot perform this action on other buckets.

Together, these elements form a policy that allows the principal to list the contents of the `my_s3_bucket` bucket. The `Version` element defines the syntax version, the Sid helps identify the statement, `Effect` grants or denies permission, `Action` specifies what can be done, and `Resource` restricts where it can be done.

This example is an identity-based policy, meaning it is attached to a user, group, or role to control what that identity can do. In contrast, a resource-based policy can be attached directly to resources, like S3 buckets, to control who can access them.

Now take a look at the following policy, which is a resource-based policy:

```
{
 "Version": "2012-10-17",
 "Statement": {
  "Sid": "1",
  "Effect": "Allow",
  "Principal": {"AWS": ["arn:aws:iam::account-id:root"]},
  "Action": "s3:*",
 }
}
```

You can attach this policy to an S3 bucket, and it allows members of a specific AWS account (`arn:aws:iam::account-id:root`) to perform any Amazon S3 actions (`"Action": "s3:*"`) in the bucket it's applied to. What's more interesting about this policy is that because the policy grants trust only to the account, individual users in the account still have to be granted permissions for the specified Amazon S3 actions they want to perform.

Policy Evaluation Logic

When a principal, such as a user or an application, attempts to interact with AWS services through the AWS Management Console, the AWS API, or the AWS Command Line Interface (CLI), it sends a request to AWS. When AWS receives the request, AWS enforcement code evaluates the request based on the applied policies. It then decides whether to grant or deny the requested action. Here is a summary of the evaluation logic for policies in a single AWS account:

1. AWS starts with a presumed denial, denying all requests by default.
2. It then evaluates all applicable identity-based and resource-based policies in the account.

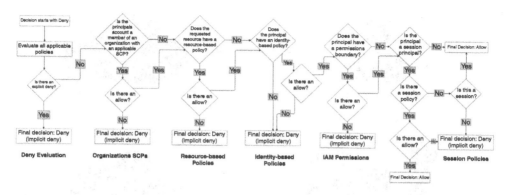

Figure 3.3: AWS policy evaluation logic.

3. If at least one policy explicitly allows the requested action, the request is permitted.

4. If no policy explicitly allows the request, but one or more policies have an explicit deny, the request is denied.

5. If no policies apply, the request is denied.

You can see this process in more detail in the Figure 3.3.

With this policy logic in mind, the chapter moves on to users, user groups, roles, and policies.

IAM Identities and Managing Access

When you first set up an AWS account, you start with a single sign-in identity that possesses full access to all the services and resources within that account. This identity is known as the *AWS account root user*, and it is accessed using the email address and password that were used during the account creation process.

While the root user holds the highest level of permissions in your AWS account, it should not be used for day-to-day activities, even if they are administrative in nature. Using the root user for routine tasks increases the risk of accidental or malicious changes that could impact your entire AWS environment. Instead, it is strongly recommended that you create an IAM Admin user, which you will use for all administrative tasks. The IAM Admin user can be granted the necessary permissions to manage AWS resources, while the root user is reserved for only the most critical account and service management activities. The difference in these types of accounts is shown in Figure 3.4.

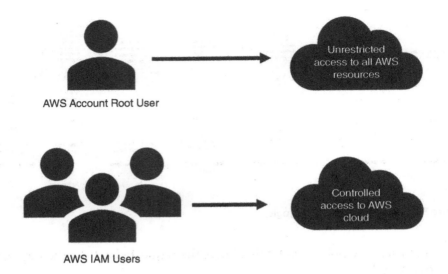

Figure 3.4: AWS user types.

This chapter guides you through the process of creating an IAM Admin user step by step.

Enable MFA for the Root User

As mentioned, it's not recommended to use the root user; however, there are certain situations where you'll need to. These include managing billing information, updating payment methods, changing AWS Support plans, enabling or disabling multifactor authentication (MFA) for the root account, and configuring IAM access to billing data. Additionally, only the root user can restore account access if all other administrative access is lost, accept compliance agreements for certain services, and request account-level quota increases. For these reasons, it's essential to secure the root account with MFA and use it only when absolutely necessary. Here are a few steps to secure your route user account.

The first step you should take is to enable a virtual MFA device for your AWS account root user. To do this, sign in as the root user and navigate to the IAM section in the AWS Console. On the IAM dashboard, you'll see some security recommendations, including one to set up MFA for the root user. Click on the MFA option in the security recommendations section. You can see this dashboard in Figure 3.5.

Next, give your device a name. For instance, if you're using 1Password as your authenticator app, you might name it "1Password." After naming your device, select Authenticator App as the type of MFA device, and then click Next. You can see this process in Figure 3.6.

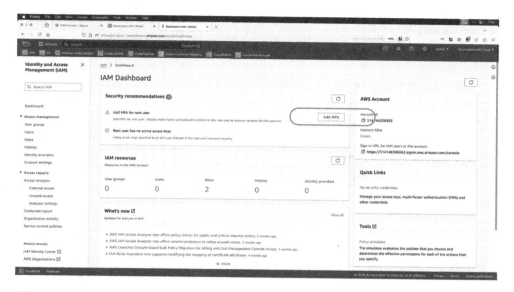

Figure 3.5: Security recommendations.

Figure 3.6: Using an authenticator app.

You'll then need to display the QR code by clicking Show QR Code. Scan this code with your authenticator app. The app will generate a code, which you should enter into the first form field in Step 3. Wait for the app to generate a second code, and then enter that into the second form field in Step 3. Once you have entered both codes, click Activate MFA. You can see part of this process in Figure 3.7.

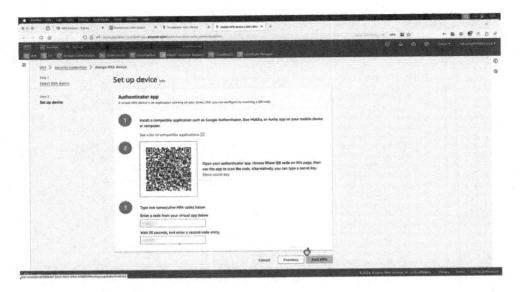

Figure 3.7: Setting up MFA.

Going forward, whenever you log in to your AWS account as the root user, you'll be required to enter your password along with the code generated by your authenticator app. This adds an extra layer of security to your account.

Configure Alternate Contacts

Another option you have is to configure alternate contacts in your account. This allows AWS to contact another person about issues with the account when you're unavailable. You can add these under the AWS account settings page, and your options are to enter a billing contact, operations contact, or security contact.

Periodically Change the Root User Password

You should periodically change the root user account password. To do this, use your user account to log in, provide your MFA code, and then, in the upper-right corner of the console, click on your account name or number and then click on My Account (they are on the right side of the page next to Account Settings). You may be required to log in again at this point. Once you're presented with the Update Account Settings page, you can edit the password. I recommend that you use a password manager, such as 1Password, to generate a strong password. I should also mention that providing detailed instructions like this is sometimes challenging because the AWS Console UI can, and does, change frequently. Therefore, this should give you a general idea of what you're looking for if the UI changes.

Configure a Strong Password Policy

One final tip to ensure that you have your accounts as secure as possible is to set up a strong password policy. To do so, navigate to IAM in the AWS Console and, under Access Management on the left side, select Account Settings. In the Password Policy section, click on Edit. Then select the custom option to define the password policy to your liking. Your organization may have a policy in place for this. If not, the default values will probably suffice. You can see the available options in Figure 3.8.

Now that your root user is secure, you can move on to creating IAM users. Once you create a few IAM users, you should no longer use the root user for day-to-day management.

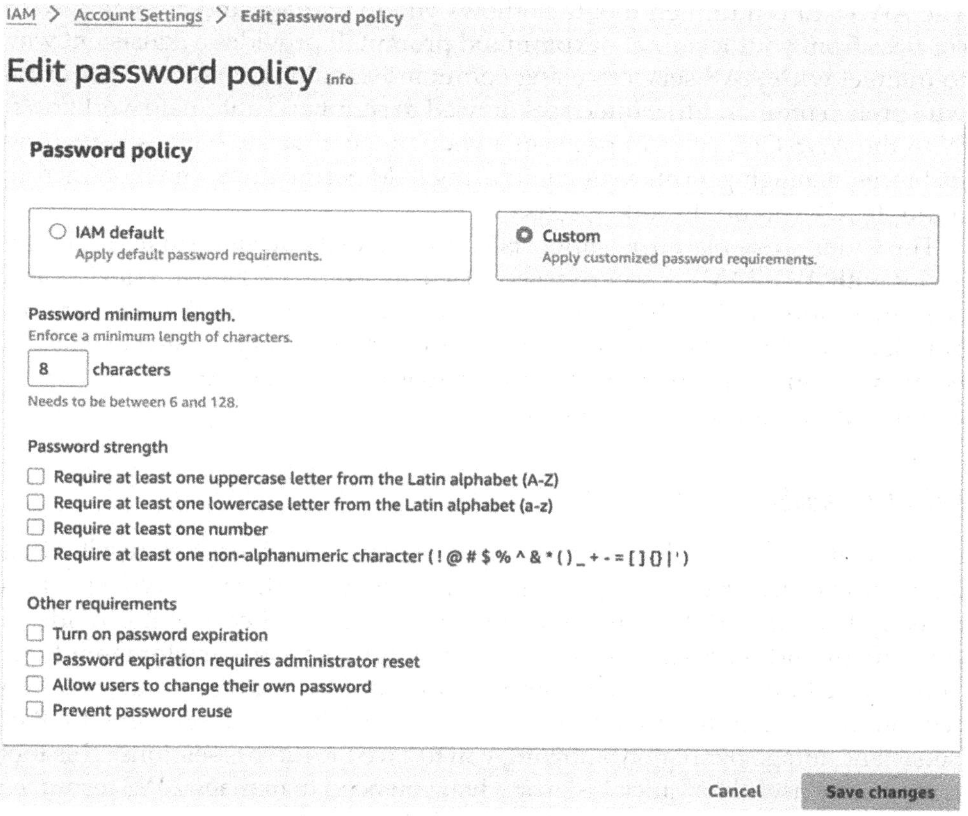

IAM > Account Settings > Edit password policy

Edit password policy Info

Password policy

○ **IAM default**
Apply default password requirements.

● **Custom**
Apply customized password requirements.

Password minimum length.
Enforce a minimum length of characters.

☐ 8 characters

Needs to be between 6 and 128.

Password strength

☐ Require at least one uppercase letter from the Latin alphabet (A-Z)
☐ Require at least one lowercase letter from the Latin alphabet (a-z)
☐ Require at least one number
☐ Require at least one non-alphanumeric character (! @ # $ % ^ & * ( ) _ + - = [ ] { } | ')

Other requirements

☐ Turn on password expiration
☐ Password expiration requires administrator reset
☐ Allow users to change their own password
☐ Prevent password reuse

Cancel   **Save changes**

Figure 3.8: Create a strong password policy.

Creating an IAM

In this book, I use the AWS Command Line Interface (CLI) for configurations whenever possible. The reason for this is twofold:

- The Console User Interface can change.
- Getting used to the CLI will help you later when you start to use Infrastructure-as-Code (IaC).

With that said, you can find everything you see in this book in the AWS documentation. Navigate to https://docs.aws.amazon.com/cli/latest/reference/iam/. I also perform these configurations in CloudShell when I can. I give you a brief overview of the AWS CLI and AWS CloudShell before beginning.

What Is the AWS CLI?

The AWS CLI is a unified tool that allows you to manage and automate AWS services from your terminal or command prompt. It provides a consistent way to interact with AWS services using commands, making it efficient for users who prefer command-line interfaces or need to script and automate workflows. With the AWS CLI, you can perform a wide range of tasks, such as launching instances, managing S3 buckets, configuring IAM permissions, and more, across multiple AWS accounts and regions.

The CLI is cross-platform, supports JSON and text output formats, and integrates with AWS IAM for secure access. It's truly a powerful tool for developers, administrators, and DevOps engineers that can streamline AWS operations. Your local machine likely does not include the AWS CLI, so you need to install it before you can use it. You can find instructions here: https://docs.aws.amazon. com/cli/v1/userguide/cli-chap-install.html.

What Is AWS CloudShell?

CloudShell is a browser-based, preconfigured command-line interface (CLI) that allows you to securely manage, explore, and interact with your AWS resources directly from the AWS Management Console. It's nice because it provides a convenient and ready-to-use environment with common development tools and AWS CLI installed, so you can run commands, scripts, and automation without needing to install anything locally. CloudShell also provides 1 GB of persistent storage per region, allowing you to save files across sessions. This tool is especially useful for quick tasks or when you need to manage AWS resources from environments where setting up the AWS CLI might be challenging. So, with that said, let's talk about IAM users.

Creating IAM Users from the AWS CLI

You will create two users:

- Administrator
- Bob

Bob will have very limited access, as you will see shortly. Now you will create IAM users from the AWS CLI.

In the top-right side of the AWS Console, select the CloudShell icon. You can see the location in Figure 3.9.

Using the CloudShell interface, create the first IAM user using the following command:

```
[cloudshell-user@ip-10-140-1-213 ~]$ aws iam create-user --user-name
Administrator
{
  "User": {
    "Path": "/",
    "UserName": "Administrator",
    "UserId": "AIDASCKEZRMU6ZC6YZYVX",
    "Arn": "arn:aws:iam::142415072041:user/Administrator",
    "CreateDate": "2024-08-30T16:55:33+00:00"
  }
}
[cloudshell-user@ip-10-140-1-213 ~]$
```

The resulting output will resemble Figure 3.10.

When you create an IAM user through the AWS CLI, the user doesn't automatically have console access to the AWS Management Console. To enable console access, you need to create a Login Profile for the user. A Login Profile allows you to set an initial password (or have AWS auto-generate one) so that the user can sign in to the console. Without a Login Profile, the IAM user is limited to programmatic access (e.g., through the AWS CLI or API) and cannot log in to the AWS Console directly. Creating a Login Profile with an auto-generated password simplifies the process of securely providing the new user with console access, as you can immediately share the generated password with them and require a password reset at first login for added security.

Figure 3.9: Access to AWS CloudShell.

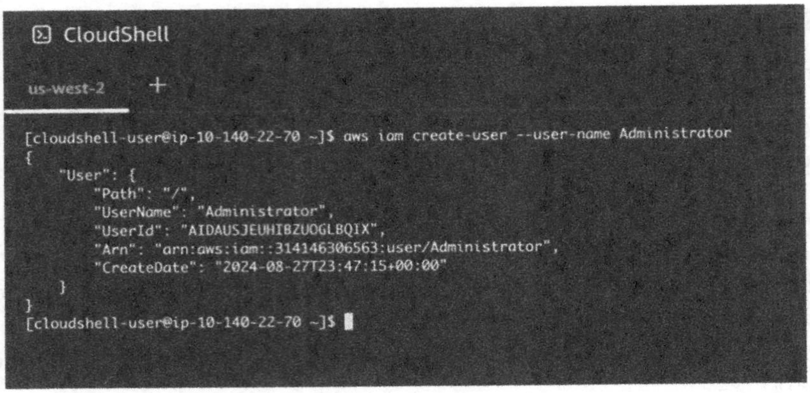

Figure 3.10: Output after adding an IAM user with AWS CLI.

Create a Login Profile with an auto-generated password:

```
[cloudshell-user@ip-10-140-1-213 ~]$ PASSWORD=$(openssl rand -base64 12)
```

Attach the AdministratorAccess policy:

```
[cloudshell-user@ip-10-140-1-213 ~]$ aws iam attach-user-policy --user-name
Administrator --policy-arn arn:aws:iam::aws:policy/AdministratorAccess
[cloudshell-user@ip-10-140-1-213 ~]$
```

When you create a user in the AWS Console, you see a link on the page to a login URL that can be shared with the user. This is not required but does make it easier to share the URL with the user. The next step is optional, but I want you to see how to get the URL using the AWS CLI.

Retrieve the login URL (optional):

```
[cloudshell-user@ip-10-140-1-213 ~]$ ACCOUNT_ID=$(aws sts get-caller-identity -
query "Account" --output text)
[cloudshell-user@ip-10-140-1-213 ~]$ LOGIN_URL=https://${ACCOUNT_ID}.signin.aws.
amazon.com/console
```

Using the previous output, open a new incognito window and paste the login URL.

Log in using the username and password that were generated. Once logged in, you have to set a new password.

Once logged in, note the user logged in on the top-right side of the console. You can now use this Administrator user to make any changes to your AWS resources. Only use the root user if you absolutely must.

At this point it's time to stop using the root user. Make sure you save the URL for your IAM user to log in, as well as the username and password, and log out of the root account. You will now remain in the AWS Console as the Administrator user and can use CloudShell in this account for CLI configurations.

Now, create one more user. Use the previous steps to create a user named Bob. Do not assign the Administrator policy to Bob. Instead, add the `AmazonVPCFullAccess` and `AmazonEC2FullAccess` policies:

```
[cloudshell-user@ip-10-140-1-213 ~]$ aws iam create-user --user-name Bob
{
  "User": {
    "Path": "/",
    "UserName": "Bob",
    "UserId": "AIDASCKEZRMUZZOC5TBQ6",
    "Arn": "arn:aws:iam::142415072041:user/Bob",
    "CreateDate": "2024-08-30T16:58:40+00:00"
  }
}
[cloudshell-user@ip-10-140-1-213 ~]$ PASSWORD=$(openssl rand -base64 12)
[cloudshell-user@ip-10-140-1-213 ~]$ aws iam create-login-profile --user-name
Bob --password "$PASSWORD" --password-reset-required
{
  "LoginProfile": {
    "UserName": "Bob",
    "CreateDate": "2024-08-30T16:58:42+00:00",
    "PasswordResetRequired": true
  }
}
[cloudshell-user@ip-10-140-1-213 ~]$ aws iam attach-user-policy --user-name
Bob --policy-arn arn:aws:iam::aws:policy/AmazonVPCFullAccess
[cloudshell-user@ip-10-140-1-213 ~]$ aws iam attach-user-policy --user-name
Bob --policy-arn arn:aws:iam::aws:policy/AmazonEC2FullAccess
[cloudshell-user@ip-10-140-1-213 ~]$
```

AWS provides two primary types of IAM policies: AWS managed policies and inline policies. Each is designed to control permissions in different ways. AWS managed policies are pre-built policies created and maintained by AWS that grant permissions for common use cases, such as full access to S3 or read-only access to RDS. These policies are reusable; can be attached to multiple IAM users, groups, or roles; and are automatically updated by AWS to incorporate best practices and new features. Inline policies, on the other hand, are custom policies that you create and embed directly within a single IAM user, group, or role, allowing you to tailor permissions specifically for that entity. Unlike managed policies, inline policies are tightly linked to the specific user, group, or role they're attached to, making them ideal for fine-grained, entity-specific permissions. Together, these policies provide flexibility, with managed policies offering convenience and inline policies offering precision.

Now that you have a few IAM users, you need to enable MFA for them. You see how to do that for the Administrator account in the next section. You can then do the user account Bob on your own.

Setting Up MFA for an IAM User

Assuming you are logged in to the Administrator IAM account, navigate to IAM in the AWS Console. There on the dashboard, you should see a security recommendation, just like you did for the root user. The difference is that the recommendation should say "Add MFA for myself." Click the Add MFA option, and follow the steps as you did with the root user.

Repeat this process for the user Bob by logging in to the Bob IAM user. The URL for Bob to log in is the same as the URL for Administrator.

With your newly created IAM users, you can now create some IAM user groups.

Types of Policies in AWS

AWS offers several types of policies that you can use to manage permissions for your resources:

- M*anaged policies:* Managed policies are standalone policies that you can attach to multiple users, groups, or roles in your AWS account. These are further divided:

  - *AWS managed policies:* Predefined policies created and managed by AWS. These are designed to provide permissions for common use cases, such as read-only access to S3 or full access to EC2.

  - *Customer managed policies:* Custom policies that you create and manage in your AWS account. These policies provide more flexibility and control compared to AWS managed policies. You can attach a customer managed policy to multiple IAM identities, making it reusable across your AWS environment.

  - *Inline policies:* Inline policies are embedded directly into a specific IAM identity (a user, group, or role). Unlike managed policies, inline policies are tightly coupled with the identity they are attached to and are not reusable. These are ideal when you want to define permissions that are specific to a particular identity.

  - *Resource-based policies:* Unlike identity-based policies, resource-based policies are attached directly to a resource, such as an S3 bucket, rather than to an identity. These policies specify which principals (users, roles, or accounts) can access the resource and what actions they can perform. Resource-based policies are always inline policies.

- *Permissions boundaries:* A permissions boundary is a way to set the maximum permissions that an identity-based policy can grant to an IAM user or role. Even if a policy attached to the identity allows an action, the action is allowed only if it is also allowed by the permissions boundary.

- *Service control policies (SCPs):* SCPs are used within AWS Organizations to set permission guardrails for all accounts in an organization. These policies control the maximum available permissions for all entities in the accounts to which the SCP is applied.

- *Access control lists (ACLs):* ACLs are service-specific policies that manage access to resources across AWS accounts. Unlike other policies, ACLs do not use the JSON format and are limited in their flexibility and capability.

- *Session policies:* These policies are passed when creating a temporary session for a role or federated user. They are useful for granting temporary permissions that are limited in scope and time.

I don't get deep into policy yet, but as you progress from here, I show you how to configure some policies, so having an overview should help you understand some of what you see from here.

IAM User Groups

An IAM user group is a way to organize IAM users into a single bundle for easier management. It's like creating a team. For example, you could have a group called Admins with all the permissions an admin needs. When you add a user to that group, they automatically inherit those permissions, saving you the trouble of assigning them individually. If a new admin joins your team, you just add them to the group, and they're ready to go. If someone's role changes, you don't have to adjust their permissions one by one. Instead, you can simply move them to a different group that matches their new responsibilities. It's a straightforward and efficient way to manage access.

Here are a few things to keep in mind about user groups:

- A user group can include multiple users, and a user can belong to more than one group.

- User groups can't contain other user groups. It's all about users directly.

- AWS doesn't provide a default group that includes all users in your account, so if you want one, you need to create it yourself and manually add users as needed.

The following sections walk through the steps to

- Create a user group
- Manage user groups

This includes how to add users to a group, attach permissions, and clean up old groups that are no longer needed. Let's go!

Creating a User Group

To set up a user group using the AWS CLI in CloudShell, you need to go through a few straightforward steps: creating the group, adding users to it, and assigning the appropriate permissions based on the tasks those users are expected to perform. This lab covers

- Creating a new user called PowerUser
- Creating a new user group called Developers
- Adding PowerUser to the Developers group, which will give PowerUser the permissions needed to manage the EC2 resources
- Verifying the effect of these permissions on PowerUser

First, you need to create a new user named PowerUser. You won't attach any policies at this stage, which means this user will initially have no permissions. If you already have a user that you want to repurpose, you can remove any existing policies to achieve the same effect.

Run the following command in CloudShell to create PowerUser:

```
[cloudshell-user@ip-10-140-1-213 ~]$ aws iam create-user --user-name PowerUser
{
  "User": {
    "Path": "/",
    "UserName": "PowerUser",
    "UserId": "AIDASCKEZRMUYHFH5UKTV",
    "Arn": "arn:aws:iam::142415072041:user/PowerUser",
    "CreateDate": "2024-08-30T16:59:31+00:00"
  }
}
[cloudshell-user@ip-10-140-1-213 ~]$
```

This command will generate a new user with the name PowerUser. If you need more details on creating users, refer to the section on creating IAM users earlier in this chapter.

Next, create a new user group called `Developers`. This group will eventually have permissions that allow all members to manage EC2 resources.

Use this command to create the `Developers` group:

```
[cloudshell-user@ip-10-140-1-213 ~]$ aws iam create-group --group-name Developers
{
  "Group": {
    "Path": "/",
    "GroupName": "Developers",
    "GroupId": "AGPASCKEZRMUXLDWSAWRT",
    "Arn": "arn:aws:iam::142415072041:group/Developers",
    "CreateDate": "2024-08-30T17:00:12+00:00"
  }
}
[cloudshell-user@ip-10-140-1-213 ~]$
```

This command sets up the `Developers` group, which is now ready to have users and permissions attached to it.

Now, add `PowerUser` to the `Developers` group. This action ensures that any permissions you assign to the `Developers` group will automatically apply to `PowerUser`.

Run the following command:

```
[cloudshell-user@ip-10-140-1-213 ~]$ aws iam add-user-to-group --user-name
PowerUser --group-name Developers
[cloudshell-user@ip-10-140-1-213 ~]$
```

The final step is to grant the `Developers` group the necessary permissions to manage EC2 resources. You do this by attaching the `AmazonEC2FullAccess` policy to the group.

Execute the following command:

```
[cloudshell-user@ip-10-140-1-213 ~]$ aws iam attach-group-policy --group-name
Developers --policy-arn arn:aws:iam::aws:policy/AmazonEC2FullAccess
[cloudshell-user@ip-10-140-1-213 ~]$
```

At this point, all users in the `Developers` group, including `PowerUser`, will have full access to EC2 services.

To verify that `PowerUser` now has the permissions you assigned to the `Developers` group, you can simulate the user's access. First, use the following command to generate temporary access credentials for `PowerUser`:

```
[cloudshell-user@ip-10-140-1-213 ~]$ aws iam create-access-key --user-name
PowerUser
{
  "AccessKey": {
    "UserName": "PowerUser",
```

```
        "AccessKeyId": "AKIASCKEZRMUYXW777M6",
        "Status": "Active",
        "SecretAccessKey": "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",
        "CreateDate": "2024-08-30T17:09:46+00:00"
    }
}
[cloudshell-user@ip-10-140-1-213 ~]$
```

This command will return an access key ID and a secret access key. Write these down (or save them securely in a password manager), as you'll need them to test the permissions.

Next, use the AWS CLI to configure a new profile for PowerUser using the temporary credentials:

```
[cloudshell-user@ip-10-140-1-213 ~]$ aws configure --profile PowerUserProfile
AWS Access Key ID [None]: AKIASCKEZRMUYXW777M6
AWS Secret Access Key [None]: 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
Default region name [None]:
Default output format [None]:
[cloudshell-user@ip-10-140-1-213 ~]$
```

You'll be prompted to enter the access key ID, secret access key, default region, and output format. Once the profile is set up, you can use it to run commands as PowerUser.

For example, let's check if PowerUser can list the VPCs:

```
[cloudshell-user@ip-10-134-77-19 ~]$ aws ec2 describe-vpcs --profile
PowerUserProfile
{
    "Vpcs": [
        {
            "CidrBlock": "172.31.0.0/16",
            "DhcpOptionsId": "dopt-0c977a08a152d7758",
            "State": "available",
            "VpcId": "vpc-0d0873987bc974310",
            "OwnerId": "314146306563",
            "InstanceTenancy": "default",
            "CidrBlockAssociationSet": [
                {
                    "AssociationId": "vpc-cidr-assoc-0260d98714a0241e1",
                    "CidrBlock": "172.31.0.0/16",
                    "CidrBlockState": {
                        "State": "associated"
                    }
                }
            ],
            "IsDefault": true
        }
    ]
}
```

That was successful. Now you can test something that should not be allowed. See if you can list your S3 buckets:

```
[cloudshell-user@ip-10-134-77-19 ~]$ aws s3 ls --profile PowerUserProfile
An error occurred (AccessDenied) when calling the ListBuckets operation:
User: arn:aws:iam::314146306563:user/PowerUser is not authorized to perform:
s3:ListAllMyBuckets because no identity-based policy allows the
s3:ListAllMyBuckets action
[cloudshell-user@ip-10-134-77-19 ~]$
```

Access was denied. So you know the permissions are working as expected and that PowerUser is correctly added to the Developers group.

If you're following along, you've successfully created a user group, added a user to it, and assigned permissions through the group. Additionally, you've verified that the permissions are correctly applied by simulating user actions. Making good use of groups can streamline access management and ensure that all members of a group have consistent permissions aligned with their roles. Before wrapping up this discussion of groups, let's take a look at how to manage groups.

Managing IAM User Groups

Now that you have created IAM user groups, you need to know how to manage them. First, you need to be able to look at the groups in your account. To do that, use the following command:

```
[cloudshell-user@ip-10-132-36-128 ~]$ aws iam list-groups
{
    "Groups": [
        {
            "Path": "/",
            "GroupName": "Developers",
            "GroupId": "AGPAUSJEUHIBUNOGVMGGU",
            "Arn": "arn:aws:iam::314146306563:group/Developers",
            "CreateDate": "2024-08-28T00:33:14+00:00"
        }
    ]
}
[cloudshell-user@ip-10-132-36-128 ~]$
```

This command will return a list of all the IAM user groups currently in your account. In the output, you can see the Developers group that you created earlier. This is excellent. Now let's say that PowerUser leaves the developer team and moves into management. You need to remove the user from the Developers group. To do that, use the following command:

```
[cloudshell-user@ip-10-132-36-128 ~]$ aws iam remove-user-from-group --user-
name PowerUser --group-name Developers
[cloudshell-user@ip-10-132-36-128 ~]$
```

Let's put that user back. We can do that with the following command:

```
[cloudshell-user@ip-10-132-36-128 ~]$ aws iam add-user-to-group --user-name
PowerUser --group-name Developers
[cloudshell-user@ip-10-132-36-128 ~]$
```

Now list the users in the group using the following command:

```
[cloudshell-user@ip-10-132-36-128 ~]$ aws iam get-group --group-name Developers
{
  "Users": [
    {
      "Path": "/",
      "UserName": "PowerUser",
      "UserId": "AIDAUSJEUHIBZJ2N55ISC",
      "Arn": "arn:aws:iam::314146306563:user/PowerUser",
      "CreateDate": "2024-08-28T00:33:05+00:00"
    }
  ],
  "Group": {
    "Path": "/",
    "GroupName": "Developers",
    "GroupId": "AGPAUSJEUHIBUNOGVMGGU",
    "Arn": "arn:aws:iam::314146306563:group/Developers",
    "CreateDate": "2024-08-28T00:33:14+00:00"
  }
}
:
```

You can see PowerUser in the group, but they moved into a management role.
Let's move that user over to their new group. First, create the Managers group:

```
[cloudshell-user@ip-10-132-36-128 ~]$ aws iam create-group --group-name
Managers
{
  "Group": {
    "Path": "/",
    "GroupName": "Managers",
    "GroupId": "AGPAUSJEUHIBRIFDDQTSB",
    "Arn": "arn:aws:iam::314146306563:group/Managers",
    "CreateDate": "2024-08-28T23:35:47+00:00"
  }
}
[cloudshell-user@ip-10-132-36-128 ~]$
```

Next, give the group AdministratorAccess:

```
[cloudshell-user@ip-10-132-36-128 ~]$ aws iam attach-group-policy --group-name
Managers --policy-arn arn:aws:iam::aws:policy/AdministratorAccess
[cloudshell-user@ip-10-132-36-128 ~]$
```

And finally, move the user to the new group. To do this, you need to remove them from `Developers` and add them to `Managers`:

```
[cloudshell-user@ip-10-132-36-128 ~]$ aws iam remove-user-from-group --user-
name PowerUser --group-name Developers
[cloudshell-user@ip-10-132-36-128 ~]$ aws iam add-user-to-group --user-name
PowerUser --group-name Managers
[cloudshell-user@ip-10-132-36-128 ~]$
```

You saw how to attach a policy to a group earlier. Let's add a policy to the `Developers` group to allow them access to `CodeCatalyst`:

```
[cloudshell-user@ip-10-132-36-128 ~]$ aws iam attach-group-policy --group-name
Developers --policy-arn arn:aws:iam::aws:policy/AmazonCodeCatalystFullAccess
[cloudshell-user@ip-10-132-36-128 ~]$
```

Now detach that policy:

```
[cloudshell-user@ip-10-132-36-128 ~]$ aws iam detach-group-policy --group-name
Developers --policy-arn arn:aws:iam::aws:policy/AmazonCodeCatalystFullAccess
```

So far, so good, right? But what if you want to change the name of a group? Currently, AWS CLI does not support directly renaming an IAM user group. If you need to rename a group, you have to create a new group with the desired name, attach the same policies to it, and move all users from the old group to the new one. Here's how to do it.

Create your new group:

```
[cloudshell-user@ip-10-132-36-128 ~]$ aws iam create-group --group-name
NewManagerGroup
{
  "Group": {
    "Path": "/",
    "GroupName": "NewManagerGroup",
    "GroupId": "AGPAUSJEUHIBUCD5ET5PI",
    "Arn": "arn:aws:iam::314146306563:group/NewManagerGroup",
    "CreateDate": "2024-08-28T23:53:30+00:00"
  }
}
[cloudshell-user@ip-10-132-36-128 ~]$
```

Next, add the users to the new group:

```
[cloudshell-user@ip-10-132-36-128 ~]$ for user in $(aws iam get-group --
group-name Managers | jq -r '.Users[].UserName'); do aws iam add-user-to-
group --user-name $user --group-name NewManagerGroup; done
[cloudshell-user@ip-10-132-36-128 ~]$
```

Now loop over the old group to remove the users:

```
[cloudshell-user@ip-10-132-36-128 ~]$ for user in $(aws iam get-group --group-
name Managers --query 'Users[].UserName' -output text); do
>  aws iam remove-user-from-group --user-name $user --group-name Managers
> done
[cloudshell-user@ip-10-132-36-128 ~]$
```

Next, remove all the policies:

```
[cloudshell-user@ip-10-132-36-128 ~]$ for policy in $(aws iam list-
attached-group-policies --group-name Managers --query 'AttachedPolicies[].
PolicyArn' --output text); do
>  aws iam detach-group-policy --group-name Managers --policy-arn $policy
> done

[cloudshell-user@ip-10-132-36-128 ~]$
[cloudshell-user@ip-10-132-36-128 ~]$
```

And finally delete the old group:

```
[cloudshell-user@ip-10-132-36-128 ~]$ aws iam delete-group --group-name
Managers
[cloudshell-user@ip-10-132-36-128 ~]$
```

Keep in mind that once a group is deleted, it cannot be restored. At this point you have two groups—Developers and NewManagerGroup. There is a user, called PowerUser, in NewManagerGroup. The Developers group has a policy called AmazonEC2FullAccess attached to it, and NewManagerGroup has the AdministratorAccess policy attached to it. You'll learn more about policies soon, but first you need to learn about roles.

IAM Roles

Now that you've explored IAM users and groups, it's time to move on to a more flexible and dynamic form of identity management in AWS: IAM roles. Unlike IAM users, which are uniquely associated with a person or an application and come with long-term credentials like passwords or access keys, IAM roles operate a bit differently. You can think of IAM roles as a way to delegate access without needing to manage individual credentials for every entity that needs access.

An IAM role is an AWS identity that has a set of permissions defining what it can and cannot do, but there's a key difference. IAM roles don't have any credentials directly associated with them. Instead, roles are designed to be assumable by trusted entities, whether they are IAM users within the same AWS account or users and applications from external identity providers. Roles are particularly useful for temporary access or cross-account access scenarios.

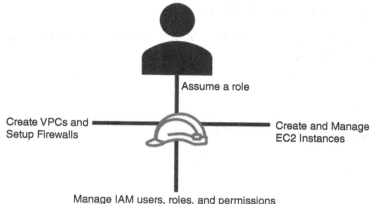

Create VPCs and
Setup Firewalls

Assume a role

Create and Manage
EC2 Instances

Manage IAM users, roles, and permissions

Figure 3.11: Assuming an IAM role.

Assuming an IAM Role

When a user, application, or service needs to perform a specific task, it can "assume" a role that grants it the necessary permissions for that task. For example, a developer in your organization might assume a role that grants access to create VPCs and set up firewalls, without permanently having the ability to perform these functions under their user credentials. You can see this in Figure 3.11. Similarly, federated users, those authenticated via an external identity provider like Google or Microsoft Active Directory, can assume roles in AWS. AWS will use the information provided by the external provider to determine which role to assign to these users, which simplifies access management across hybrid environments.

Creating an IAM Role

Now that you understand what IAM roles are and how they differ from users and groups, it's time to roll up your sleeves and create one. Roles in AWS are identities with permissions, similar to users, but they aren't tied to a specific individual and don't use long-term credentials. Instead, they provide temporary security credentials for a session, making them ideal for temporary or shared access scenarios.

In this exercise, you'll create a role that can be assumed by an EC2 instance, granting it trusted access to all S3 buckets in your account. By doing this, you allow the instance to perform actions on S3 without having hard-coded credentials, which aligns with best practices for security and access management.

Create a role for EC2 with S3 access

To create a new IAM role, you use the AWS CLI in CloudShell. Let's walk through the steps to set this up.

```
[cloudshell-user@ip-10-132-36-128 ~]$ nano trust-policy.json
```

Paste the following into CloudShell:

```
{
 "Version": "2012-10-17",
 "Statement": [
  {
   "Effect": "Allow",
   "Principal": {
    "Service": "ec2.amazonaws.com"
   },
   "Action": "sts:AssumeRole"
  }
 ]
}
```

Use Ctrl-O to save and Ctrl-X to exit nano.
Verify the file using cat:

```
[cloudshell-user@ip-10-140-1-213 ~]$ cat trust-policy.json
{
 "Version": "2012-10-17",
 "Statement": [
  {
   "Effect": "Allow",
   "Principal": {
    "Service": "ec2.amazonaws.com"
   },
   "Action": "sts:AssumeRole"
  }
 ]
}

[cloudshell-user@ip-10-140-1-213 ~]$
```

Create a role with the new trust policy

Use the following command to create the role with the trust policy you just defined. This command creates a role named EC2S3FullAccess and attaches the trust policy, allowing EC2 to assume the role:

```
[cloudshell-user@ip-10-140-1-213 ~]$ aws iam create-role --role-name
EC2S3FullAccess --assume-role-policy-document file://trust-policy.json
```

```
{
  "Role": {
    "Path": "/",
    "RoleName": "EC2S3FullAccess",
    "RoleId": "AROASCKEZRMU6LAMFZ37Y",
    "Arn": "arn:aws:iam::142415072041:role/EC2S3FullAccess",
    "CreateDate": "2024-08-30T17:21:12+00:00",
    "AssumeRolePolicyDocument": {
      "Version": "2012-10-17",
      "Statement": [
        {
          "Effect": "Allow",
          "Principal": {
            "Service": "ec2.amazonaws.com"
          },
          "Action": "sts:AssumeRole"
        }
      ]
    :
```

Attach a policy

You now need to attach a policy that grants access to all S3 buckets in the account. You will use the AmazonS3FullAccess policy, which is an AWS-managed policy that provides full access to Amazon S3. With this command, any EC2 instance assuming the EC2S3FullAccess role will have full access to all S3 buckets in the account. Run the following command:

```
[cloudshell-user@ip-10-140-1-213 ~]$ aws iam attach-role-policy --role-name
EC2S3FullAccess --policy-arn arn:aws:iam::aws:policy/AmazonS3FullAccess
[cloudshell-user@ip-10-140-1-213 ~]$
```

Verify your efforts

Use this command to verify that the role has been created and the policy has been attached successfully:

```
[cloudshell-user@ip-10-140-1-213 ~]$ aws iam get-role --role-name
EC2S3FullAccess
{
  "Role": {
    "Path": "/",
    "RoleName": "EC2S3FullAccess",
    "RoleId": "AROASCKEZRMU6LAMFZ37Y",
    "Arn": "arn:aws:iam::142415072041:role/EC2S3FullAccess",
    "CreateDate": "2024-08-30T17:21:12+00:00",
    "AssumeRolePolicyDocument": {
      "Version": "2012-10-17",
      "Statement": [
        {
          "Effect": "Allow",
          "Principal": {
```

```
          "Service": "ec2.amazonaws.com"
        },
        "Action": "sts:AssumeRole"
      }
    ]
  },
  "MaxSessionDuration": 3600,
  "RoleLastUsed": {}
  }
}
(END)
```

To check the attached policies, use the `list-attached-role-policies` command. You should see the trust policy and the `AmazonS3FullAccess` policy listed in the output:

```
[cloudshell-user@ip-10-140-1-213 ~]$ aws iam list-attached-role-policies --role-
name EC2S3FullAccess
{
  "AttachedPolicies": [
    {
      "PolicyName": "AmazonS3FullAccess",
      "PolicyArn": "arn:aws:iam::aws:policy/AmazonS3FullAccess"
    }
  ]
}
[cloudshell-user@ip-10-140-1-213 ~]$
```

Now that you have created an IAM role, take a quick look at some of the key attributes that define a role:

- *Role name:* The name you assign to your role will appear in various AWS interfaces when selecting a role to attach to a service.

- *Role ARN:* The Amazon Resource Name (ARN) is a unique identifier for the role across AWS. It's required when specifying the role in policies or API calls, or when referencing it in other AWS services.

- *Maximum session duration:* This setting determines how long the temporary credentials are valid when a role is assumed. It ranges from 15 minutes to 12 hours. By default, the maximum session duration is set to 1 hour.

- *Permissions policies:* These policies define which actions the role can perform. For example, attaching the `AmazonS3FullAccess` policy to the `EC2S3FullAccess` role allows it to perform any S3 action.

- *Trusted relationships:* A trust policy defines who or what can assume the role. In this example, the EC2 service is the trusted entity.

Let's talk about the trust policy you just created.

By understanding these attributes and how roles are created and managed, you can begin to design more secure and flexible AWS environments that leverage temporary credentials for enhanced security. Now that you have a working knowledge of how to create and manage roles, it's time to talk about policies.

IAM Policies

In AWS, policies are the core mechanism for managing access to resources. A policy is essentially a set of permissions that defines which actions an identity (like a user or role) or resource can perform, on which resources, and under what conditions. As you may have picked up on from the other sections, policies are written in JSON and provide the granularity needed to precisely control access in your cloud environment.

When an IAM principal (such as a user or role) makes a request, AWS evaluates all policies associated with that principal to determine whether the request is allowed or denied. These policies can be attached to users, groups, roles, or resources. This section covers different types of policies in AWS and explains how to create a custom policy. It also walks through an example of testing a policy's effectiveness.

Creating a Custom Policy with AWS CLI

To fully understand how policies work, you'll create a custom S3 policy using the AWS CLI in CloudShell. This policy will grant a new IAM user permissions that can list and download S3 objects but not delete them. This approach allows you to see how policies define and enforce specific actions for identities in AWS.

First, create a JSON file named S3ExamplePolicy.json in CloudShell that contains the custom policy:

```
[cloudshell-user@ip-10-132-36-128 ~]$  nano S3ExamplePolicy.json
```

The policy you are going to create allows any attached entity to list and download objects from any S3 bucket in the account. However, this policy does not allow actions like deleting objects.

Paste the following JSON into the file. Use Ctrl-O and Ctrl-X to save and exit nano:

```
{
 "Version": "2012-10-17",
 "Id": "04d02149-8a5d-489d-9315-1541fde69f1b",
 "Statement": [
```

```
    {
      "Sid": "1",
      "Effect": "Allow",
      "Action": ["s3:GetObject", "s3:ListBucket", "s3:ListAllMyBuckets"],
      "Resource": "*"
    }
  ]
}
```

Next, you'll create the policy. When you do, the command will output details about the newly created policy, including the ARN (Amazon Resource Name), which uniquely identifies the policy. Use the following AWS CLI command to create the custom policy in your AWS account:

```
[cloudshell-user@ip-10-140-1-213 ~]$ aws iam create-policy --policy-name
S3ExamplePolicy --policy-document file://S3ExamplePolicy.json
{
  "Policy": {
    "PolicyName": "S3ExamplePolicy",
    "PolicyId": "ANPASCKEZRMU7FZUU6IO3",
    "Arn": "arn:aws:iam::142415072041:policy/S3ExamplePolicy",
    "Path": "/",
    "DefaultVersionId": "v1",
    "AttachmentCount": 0,
    "PermissionsBoundaryUsageCount": 0,
    "IsAttachable": true,
    "CreateDate": "2024-08-30T18:32:22+00:00",
    "UpdateDate": "2024-08-30T18:32:22+00:00"
  }
}
[cloudshell-user@ip-10-140-1-213 ~]$
```

Now create a new IAM user named S3User:

```
[cloudshell-user@ip-10-140-1-213 ~]$ aws iam create-user --user-name S3User
{
  "User": {
    "Path": "/",
    "UserName": "S3User",
    "UserId": "AIDASCKEZRMUQ64VLF5EI",
    "Arn": "arn:aws:iam::142415072041:user/S3User",
    "CreateDate": "2024-08-30T18:36:10+00:00"
  }
}
[cloudshell-user@ip-10-140-1-213 ~]$
```

Next, you'll attach the custom S3 policy to S3User. You are going to do this using two commands. The first will get the account ID and store it as a variable. The second will use the account ID variable to attach the policy:

```
[cloudshell-user@ip-10-140-1-213 ~]$ ACCOUNT_ID=$(aws sts get-caller-
identity --query "Account" --output text)
```

```
[cloudshell-user@ip-10-140-1-213 ~]$ aws iam attach-user-policy --user-name
S3User --policy-arn arn:aws:iam::$ACCOUNT_ID:policy/S3ExamplePolicy
[cloudshell-user@ip-10-140-1-213 ~]$
```

To test the permissions, you need to generate temporary access credentials for S3User and configure a new profile in AWS CLI:

```
[cloudshell-user@ip-10-140-1-213 ~]$ aws iam create-access-key --user-name S3User
{
    "AccessKey": {
        "UserName": "S3User",
        "AccessKeyId": "AKIASCKEZRMUZKTKDQGR",
        "Status": "Active",
        "SecretAccessKey": "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",
        "CreateDate": "2024-08-30T18:49:52+00:00"
    }
}
[cloudshell-user@ip-10-140-1-213 ~]$
```

Next, configure the profile:

```
[cloudshell-user@ip-10-140-1-213 ~]$ aws configure --profile S3UserProfile
AWS Access Key ID [***]: AKIASCKEZRMUZKTKDQGR
AWS Secret Access Key [***]: 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
Default region name [None]:
Default output format [None]:
[cloudshell-user@ip-10-140-1-213 ~]$
```

Now, using the profile, you can list the S3 buckets. Based on the policy you created, this should be permitted.

> **note:** If you have not created any buckets, you will not see any. Also, if you have not created any buckets, you cannot delete any. You can either create a bucket using the root user and the AWS Console, or you can create a bucket beforehand using the AWS CLI aws s3api create-bucket --bucket your-bucket-name --region your-region command.

```
[cloudshell-user@ip-10-140-1-213 ~]$ aws s3 ls --profile S3UserProfile
2024-06-26 19:24:27 anycompany-travel-policy
2023-10-11 15:34:38 steelersblog70bb442c47054951a2b58cc320765fd375152-dev
2024-04-15 21:33:22 transcribe-jobs-west
2023-01-05 18:29:03 transcribebcrrl10123
[cloudshell-user@ip-10-140-1-213 ~]$
```

Now try to delete an object. This should not be allowed:

```
[cloudshell-user@ip-10-140-1-213 ~]$ aws s3 rm s3://steelersblog70bb442
c47054951a2b58cc320765fd375152-dev/IMG_2812.jpeg --profile S3UserProfile
delete failed: s3://steelersblog70bb442c47054951a2b58cc320765fd375152-
dev/IMG_2812.jpeg An error occurred (AccessDenied) when calling the
```

```
DeleteObject operation: User: arn:aws:iam::142415072041:user/
S3User is not authorized to perform: s3:DeleteObject on resource:
"arn:aws:s3:::steelersblog70bb442c47054951a2b58cc320765fd375152-
dev/IMG_2812.jpeg" because no identity-based policy allows the s3:
DeleteObject action
[cloudshell-user@ip-10-140-1-213 ~]$
```

So everything worked as expected. Before wrapping up this chapter, let's clean up a bit.

List the IAM access keys for S3User:

```
[cloudshell-user@ip-10-140-1-213 ~]$ aws iam list-access-keys --user-name S3User
{
  "AccessKeyMetadata": [
    {
      "UserName": "S3User",
      "AccessKeyId": "AKIASCKEZRMUZKTKDQGR",
      "Status": "Active",
      "CreateDate": "2024-08-30T18:49:52+00:00"
    }
  ]
}
[cloudshell-user@ip-10-140-1-213 ~]$
```

You can now delete the keys.

```
[cloudshell-user@ip-10-140-1-213 ~]$ aws iam delete-access-key --user-name
S3User --access-key-id AKIASCKEZRMUZKTKDQGR
[cloudshell-user@ip-10-140-1-213 ~]$
```

That's it! This section covered the fundamentals of IAM policies in AWS, the different types of policies, and how to create and manage them using AWS CLI. By understanding and leveraging IAM policies, you can ensure that your AWS environment adheres to the principle of least privilege, reducing the risk of unauthorized access and potential security breaches.

AWS IAM Identity Center

You've explored the various aspects of IAM and the core role it plays in securing your AWS environment. However, you still need to consider another service offered by AWS, called AWS IAM Identity Center. This service provides centralized management of user access across multiple AWS accounts and applications, enhancing the scalability and efficiency of permissions management in complex environments. If it sounds like there's overlap here, you're right, but that's okay. IAM doesn't make it easy to manage identity in complex environments. Identity Center aims to do that.

What Is Identity Center?

AWS IAM Identity Center was formerly called AWS Single Sign-On (SSO), and as mentioned, it's designed to simplify access management for AWS Organizations, allowing administrators to control user access across multiple AWS accounts from a single, unified console. Unlike AWS IAM, which operates on a per-account basis, IAM Identity Center integrates directly with AWS Organizations, providing a centralized way to manage your permissions across the entire organization. This is especially effective if you manage multiple AWS accounts or if you need integration with external identity providers (IdPs).

Identity Center lets you

- Set up user access to various AWS accounts within an organization from a single location.
- Automatically provision users and groups from external IdPs.
- Give end users access to all their assigned AWS accounts and cloud applications through a single user portal.
- Use permission sets for flexible access control. Define and manage permission sets that determine the level of access that users have within specific AWS accounts.

Similarities Between AWS IAM and AWS IAM Identity Center

AWS IAM and IAM Identity Center both give you a way to manage access to AWS resources and control users and applications permissions. They both support integration with external IdPs for federated authentication. However, the similarities largely end at this high level. Although both services manage access, IAM Identity Center is more focused on organizations managing multiple AWS accounts and applications, whereas AWS IAM focuses on managing access within a single AWS account.

Conclusion

As this chapter on AWS Identity and Access Management (IAM) comes to an end, it's clear that understanding and properly configuring IAM is foundational for maintaining a secure and well-managed AWS environment. This chapter covered the essential components of IAM, including users, groups, roles, and policies, providing you with hands-on examples to help you manage access and permissions efficiently. IAM is more than just access control, and when used properly, it can streamline operations, enforce security best practices, and simplify compliance management. Up next, you look at how to set up AWS Organizations and Identity Center.

References

AWS Command-Line Interface Documentation, `https://docs.aws.amazon.com/cli/`

AWS Identity and Access Management Documentation, `https://docs.aws.amazon.com/iam/`

NIST Draft Special Publication (SP) 800-103, "An Ontology of Identity Credentials, Part 1: Background and Formulation" (posted for public comment on October 6, 2006), `https://www.nist.gov/publications/ontology-identity-credentials-part-1-background-and-formulation`

AWS Identity Center: Centralizing Access Management

"Most of us forget the basics and wonder why the specifics don't work."
—Garrison Wynn

As I sat in my home office, reminiscing about my days working for the phone company, I couldn't help but draw parallels between the evolution of telecommunications and cloud computing. Back then, we had to manage individual phone lines and switchboards for each customer. Today, in the world of AWS, we face a similar challenge with Identity and Access Management (IAM) across multiple accounts and applications. This is where AWS Identity Center comes into play, offering a centralized solution that simplifies and streamlines access management, much like how modern telecom systems consolidated multiple phone lines into unified communication platforms.

Understanding AWS Identity Center

This chapter dives deep into AWS Identity Center, formerly known as AWS Single Sign-On (SSO). Identity Center is a powerful service that simplifies access management across your AWS accounts and applications, providing a centralized place to configure and control user access and permissions.

As you progress through this chapter, you learn what Identity Center is and why it's essential for managing access in your AWS environment. The chapter guides you through the step-by-step process of setting up AWS Identity Center in your AWS account. By the end of this chapter, you'll have a solid understanding of Identity Center!

What Is AWS Identity Center?

Before jumping into the setup process, take a moment to learn what Identity Center is and how it can benefit your organization.

Identity Center has the following key features:

- Centralized access management across AWS accounts and applications
- Integration with AWS Organizations for multi-account management
- Support for SAML 2.0-based identity providers
- Built-in identity store or integration with external directories (e.g., Active Directory)
- Fine-grained permission sets for access control
- AWS CLI and SDK support for programmatic access
- Attribute-based access control (ABAC) capabilities
- Automated user provisioning and deprovisioning

The following sections dive deeper into these features.

Centralized Access Management

Identity Center centralizes user access and permissions management for multiple AWS accounts and applications. It simplifies the process by giving you a single place to configure and control who has access to all the resources across your AWS environment.

Integration with AWS Organizations

It's important to note that Identity Center does not require AWS Organizations to be enabled. However, it is recommended. But don't worry, because enabling Organizations is a breeze. You can do it when you enable Identity Center from the AWS Console. In the following example, Organizations has already been enabled. This section walks you through enabling AWS Organizations and creating your member accounts so that they match the examples in this chapter.

First, create the organization from your management account. The CLI command for this is as follows:

```
~ $ aws organizations create-organization
{
    "Organization": {
        "Id": "o-10g6cxrcqh",
        "Arn": "arn:aws:organizations::120569608551:organization/o-10g6cxrcqh",
        "FeatureSet": "ALL",
        "MasterAccountArn": "arn:aws:organizations::120569608551:account/o-
10g6cxrcqh/120569608551",
```

```
        "MasterAccountId": "120569608551",
        "MasterAccountEmail": "brandon.carroll+wiley@globalconfig.net",
        "AvailablePolicyTypes": [
            {
                "Type": "SERVICE_CONTROL_POLICY",
                "Status": "ENABLED"
            }
        ]
    }
}
(END)
```

This creates an organization with all features enabled, which is what you want for security best practices.

Next, create some Organizational Units (OUs). These are kind of like folders that you can use to organize accounts. For this to work, you need to get the account ID first, then create the OUs:

```
~ $ ROOT_ID=$(aws organizations list-roots --query 'Roots[0].Id' --output text)
~ $ aws organizations create-organizational-unit \
>    --parent-id $ROOT_ID \
>    --name "Dev Accounts"
{
    "OrganizationalUnit": {
        "Id": "ou-2e19-yro4jfml",
        "Arn": "arn:aws:organizations::120569608551:ou/o-10g6cxrcqh/
ou-2e19-yro4jfml",
        "Name": "Dev Accounts"
    }
}
~ $ aws organizations create-organizational-unit \
>    --parent-id $ROOT_ID \
>    --name "Production Accounts"
{
    "OrganizationalUnit": {
        "Id": "ou-2e19-xucc2ebi",
        "Arn": "arn:aws:organizations::120569608551:ou/o-10g6cxrcqh/
ou-2e19-xucc2ebi",
        "Name": "Production Accounts"
    }
}
~ $
```

Next, you need to create the accounts that will be part of your organization. This example creates three accounts—Security 101 Dev, Security 101 Prod, and Security 101 Primary. The Dev account will go under the Dev OU and the Prod Account will go under the Prod OU:

```
~ $ # Create Security 101 Primary (stays in root)
~ $ aws organizations create-account \
>    --email brandon.carroll+primary@globalconfig.net \
>    --account-name "Security 101 Primary"
{
```

```
        "CreateAccountStatus": {
            "Id": "car-bf6a93b55a1446bab3a174655ca3c59f",
            "AccountName": "Security 101 Primary",
            "State": "IN_PROGRESS",
            "RequestedTimestamp": "2025-01-21T03:42:34.565000+00:00"
        }
    }
~ $
~ $ # Create Security 101 Dev
~ $ DEV_OU_ID=$(aws organizations list-organizational-units-for-parent \
>   --parent-id $ROOT_ID \
>   --query 'OrganizationalUnits[?Name=='Dev Accounts'].Id' --output text)
~ $
~ $ aws organizations create-account \
>   --email brandon.carroll+dev@globalconfig.net \
>   --account-name "Security 101 Dev"
{
    "CreateAccountStatus": {
        "Id": "car-66d7b4632f4d4997820045c0f6f88b4e",
        "AccountName": "Security 101 Dev",
        "State": "IN_PROGRESS",
        "RequestedTimestamp": "2025-01-21T03:42:38.087000+00:00"
    }
}
~ $
~ $ # Create Security 101 Prod
~ $ PROD_OU_ID=$(aws organizations list-organizational-units-for-parent \
>   --parent-id $ROOT_ID \
>   --query 'OrganizationalUnits[?Name=='Production Accounts'].Id' --output text)
~ $
~ $ aws organizations create-account \
>   --email brandon.carroll+prod@globalconfig.net \
>   --account-name "Security 101 Prod"
{
    "CreateAccountStatus": {
        "Id": "car-954788d5c6b84e2eb5df7316ff03a68a",
        "AccountName": "Security 101 Prod",
        "State": "IN_PROGRESS",
        "RequestedTimestamp": "2025-01-21T03:42:41.388000+00:00"
    }
}
~ $
```

Now you need to move the accounts into their OUs. You need the account numbers first, so here's a list of the accounts:

```
~ $ aws organizations list-accounts
{
    "Accounts": [
        {
            "Id": "586794451553",
            "Arn": "arn:aws:organizations::120569608551:account/o-
10g6cxrcqh/586794451553",
            "Email": "brandon.carroll+primary@globalconfig.net",
            "Name": "Security 101 Primary",
```

```
          "Status": "ACTIVE",
          "JoinedMethod": "CREATED",
          "JoinedTimestamp": "2025-01-21T03:42:36.408000+00:00"
      },
      {
          "Id": "557690592627",
          "Arn": "arn:aws:organizations::120569608551:account/o-
  10g6cxrcqh/557690592627",
          "Email": "brandon.carroll+prod@globalconfig.net",
          "Name": "Security 101 Prod",
          "Status": "ACTIVE",
          "JoinedMethod": "CREATED",
          "JoinedTimestamp": "2025-01-21T03:42:42.735000+00:00"
      },
      {
          "Id": "515966532362",
          "Arn": "arn:aws:organizations::120569608551:account/o-
  10g6cxrcqh/515966532362",
          "Email": "brandon.carroll+dev@globalconfig.net",
          "Name": "Security 101 Dev",
          "Status": "ACTIVE",
          "JoinedMethod": "CREATED",
          "JoinedTimestamp": "2025-01-21T03:42:39.807000+00:00"
      },
    ]
}
(END)
```

Once you have the account numbers, you can move the account under the correct OU:

```
~ $ aws organizations move-account \
>   --account-id 515966532362 \
>   --source-parent-id $ROOT_ID \
>   --destination-parent-id $DEV_OU_ID
~ $
~ $
~ $ aws organizations move-account \
>   --account-id 557690592627 \
>   --source-parent-id $ROOT_ID \
>   --destination-parent-id $PROD_OU_ID
~ $
~ $
```

Now that you have organizations set up so that they match the chapter examples, let's continue discussing Identity Center.

Identity Provider Support

Identity Center supports various identity providers, including a built-in identity store (which you will use in this chapter) and external providers like Microsoft Azure AD and Okta. This flexibility allows you to integrate with your existing identity management systems seamlessly.

Fine-Grained Permission Sets

With Identity Center, you can define fine-grained permission sets to control access at a granular level. Permission sets determine which actions users are allowed to perform on specific AWS resources.

Programmatic Access

Identity Center also works with the AWS CLI and SDKs, enabling programmatic access to your AWS accounts and applications. A common use case for Identity Center's programmatic access is in enterprise development environments where teams need to manage resources across multiple AWS accounts. For instance, a DevOps engineer working on a large-scale application might need to deploy infrastructure to the development, staging, and production environments, each hosted in separate AWS accounts. Instead of managing separate access keys for each account, the engineer can authenticate once through Identity Center and seamlessly switch between accounts using profile names in the automation scripts. This significantly reduces the security risks associated with managing multiple long-term credentials and simplifies the access management process while maintaining proper security controls and audit trails.

Now that you have a solid understanding of what Identity Center is and its key features, you're ready to dive into the setup process!

Setting Up AWS Identity Center

This section walks through the step-by-step process of setting up Identity Center in your AWS account. It covers enabling the service; configuring your identity source; creating users, groups, and permission sets; and assigning permissions to users.

Step 1: Enable Identity Center

First, navigate to the Identity Center service in the AWS Management Console. Click the Enable button to get started. It's that easy! You can see this in Figure 4.1.

It's important to note here that you can use all the Identity Center features including user management, permission sets, and access management across your AWS accounts without incurring any costs. However, you may still be charged for the AWS resources and services that your users access through Identity Center in your AWS accounts.

As you've been going through this book, I've been showing you how to enable these features using the AWS CLI. At this time, Identity Center can only be enabled via the AWS Console. Therefore, AWS CLI is not used in this chapter.

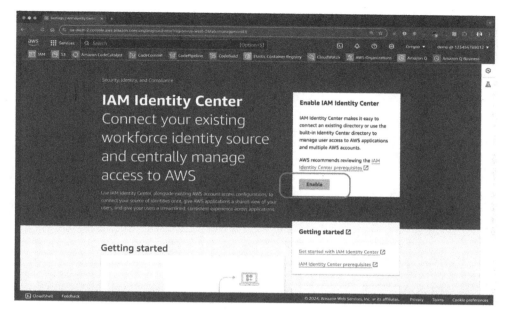

Figure 4.1: Enabling IAM Identity Center.

There are certain AWS CLI commands that do work once the EC2 instance has been created, but for sake of consistency, the remainder of this chapter uses the AWS Console only.

Step 2: Configure Your Identity Source

Identity Center supports various identity sources, including a built-in identity store and external providers like Active Directory. The examples in this chapter use the built-in identity store. To do this, in the AWS Console, navigate to Settings in the left menu. Scroll down the page and select the Identity Source tab. You can see this in Figure 4.2.

For the purposes here, this should say Identity Center Directory. If you wanted to use another directory, this is where you could select the Actions menu and change the directory. With the default set, you can now create your users, groups, and permission sets.

Step 3: Create Users, Groups, and Permission Sets

To grant access, you need to create users, groups, and permission sets. For the sake of this example, say you have two users, Admin Alice and Developer Dan. Admin Alice will have access to all three accounts in your organization.

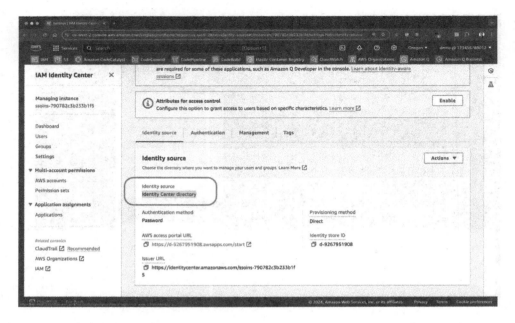

Figure 4.2: Selecting the identity source.

Developer Dan will have access only to Dev and Prod, and his permissions will be limited only to those needed to deploy his apps.

Let's start by creating the user named Alice.

Adding User Alice

1. Go to the Users section and click Add User.
2. Enter Alice's name and select the option to generate a one-time password.
3. Fill in Alice's email address and name, then click Next. This is shown in Figure 4.3.
4. Next, you can assign Alice to the appropriate group. Notice that this is "optional." You'll create groups in another step, so leave this page alone for now and click Next.
5. Review and click Add User.

At this point you are presented with the one-time password and other relevant information for Alice to log in later. Make sure to save the one-time password in a secure location, so you can share it with Alice later. You will see the popup window shown in Figure 4.4.

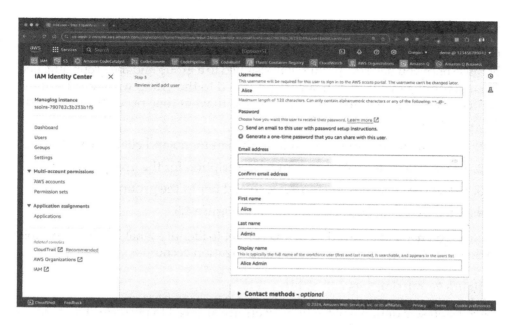

Figure 4.3: Creating the user Alice.

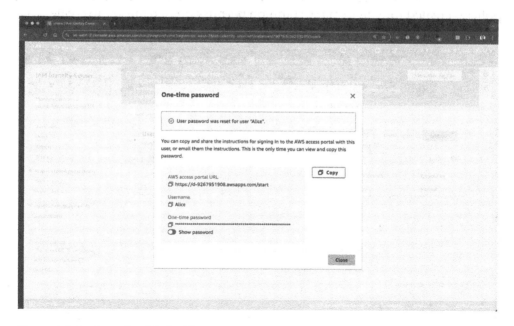

Figure 4.4: Login credentials for Alice.

Creating Groups

Groups allow you to assign permissions to multiple users at once. This is nice because once you have the permission assigned to a group and the group attached to an account, new users can simply be added to the group with no additional configurations needed to allow them access to what they need. To start, create an Administrators group for Alice:

1. Navigate to the Groups section in the left menu and click Create Group.
2. Enter a name (e.g., Admins) and a description for the group.
3. Select the checkbox next to Alice to add her to the group.
4. Click Create Group. This is shown in Figure 4.5.

Now you need to define the permission set to identity what Alice will be able to do once she logs in to one of your organization accounts.

Defining Permission Sets

Permission sets define what actions users are allowed to perform. The permissions are created or defined in a similar way to the permissions you saw in Chapter 3, on IAM. If you know how to define policy in IAM, you know how to define a policy in a permission set for Identity Center. However, there are some policies created for you to make common permissions a bit faster to create. You

Figure 4.5: Creating a group.

will use one of them in this example. For Alice, you'll create an Administrator Access permission set:

1. Go to Permission Sets in the left menu and click Create Permission Set.

2. You have two options for Permission Set Type—Predefined Permission Set or Custom Permission Set. The choice you make will be based on your access control needs. Predefined permission sets are ideal when you need common, standardized access levels like administrator access, read-only access, or power user access. These are prepackaged by AWS and ready to use. Custom permission sets, on the other hand, are your go-to choice when you need precise control over permissions, you want to implement the principle of least privilege, or you need to create specific combinations of permissions that don't align with the predefined options. Think of predefined sets as ready-made solutions for common scenarios, while custom sets allow you to tailor permissions exactly to your requirements. Select Predefined Permission Set if it's not already selected for you.

3. Choose the AdministratorAccess predefined permission set.

4. Click Next until you get to the Review and Create the Permission Set page and then click the button to review and create the permission set.

Figure 4.6 shows the AdministratorAccess selection for the permission set.

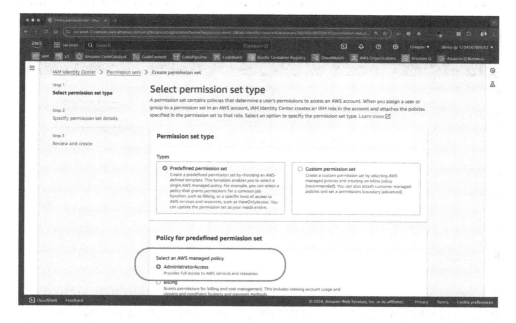

Figure 4.6: Selecting AdministratorAccess.

Step 4: Assign Permissions

Now it's time to bring everything together and assign permissions to Alice. In turn, anyone who is added to the same group Alice is in will also get the permissions of that group:

1. On the left menu, click AWS Accounts and select the accounts you want Alice to administer. In Figure 4.7, you can see that all three of the accounts are selected.

2. Click Assign Users or Groups and select the Admins group, as shown in Figure 4.8. Then click Next.

3. Choose the AdministratorAccess permission set and click Next. Then click Submit. You can see this in Figure 4.9.

Congratulations! Alice now has administrator access to the selected AWS accounts. The next step in the journey for Alice would be to log in. But before you do that, you'll create the Developers group and the Developer Dan user.

Adding More Users, Groups, and Permission Sets

Adding additional users, groups, and permission sets follows the same process you just went through with Alice and the Admins group. I recommend creating your group and permission set, and then attaching them to your AWS accounts

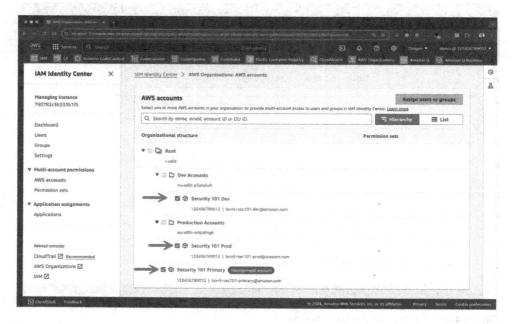

Figure 4.7: Selecting accounts for the Admins group permissions.

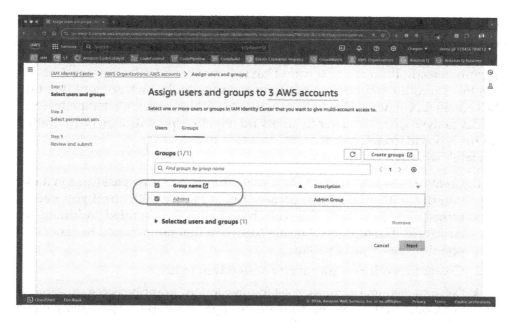

Figure 4.8: Assigning the Admins group to three accounts.

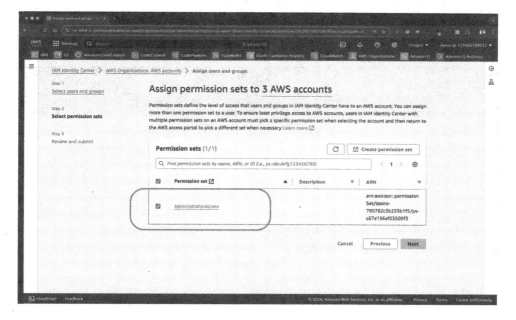

Figure 4.9: Selecting the permission set.

one at a time. This way, you can maintain a clear differentiation between which groups and permission sets are applied to each account.

Here, you'll walk through adding another user, Developer Dan, with different permissions. In this case, you want Dan to have access to the Dev account and the Prod account, but not the management account. In each account that Dan has access to, you want Dan to have access to EC2 instances, CodePipeline, and CodeCatalyst, since he currently uses CodePipeline but will soon be migrating all his repos to CodeCatalyst.

Here's what you need to do:

1. Create a new user named Dan, generating a one-time password just like you did with Alice. You can see this in Figure 4.10, but if you need a refresher on how to do this, turn back to the section titled "Adding User Alice" for the steps. Just be sure to switch that radio button to generate a one-time password for Dan.

2. Create a Developers group and assign Dan to it.

3. Define a custom permission set for developers, granting access to services like CodeCatalyst and EC2. I walk through this step-by-step since it's a bit different than what you did for Alice:

   a. First, as you did previously, go to Permission Sets and, from the left menu, choose Create Permission Set.

   b. Next, select the Custom Permission Set option shown in Figure 4.11. Then click Next.

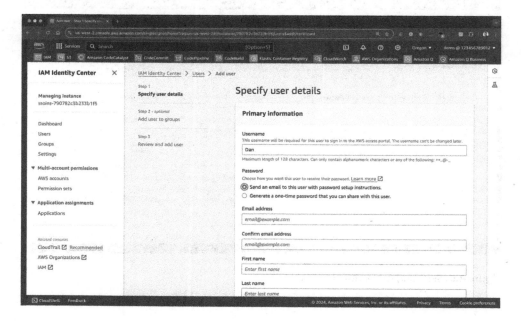

Figure 4.10: Creating the user Dan.

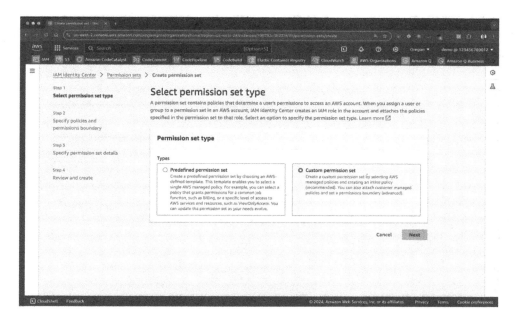

Figure 4.11: Selecting a custom permission set.

c. Select AWS Managed Policies and search for and select the AWSCodeCommitFullAccess, AmazonEC2FullAccess, and AmazonCodeCatalystFullAccess policies. Figure 4.12 shows the AWSCodeCommitFullAccess policy. Once you've selected the policies, click Next.

d. Name the permission set Developers, provide a description, and include any other necessary properties (this example uses the defaults). Click Next. See Figure 4.13.

e. Finally, review and create the permission set. When you do this, you should see the three policies attached to the permission set.

4. Assign the Developers group and permission set to the desired AWS accounts (e.g., Dev and Prod). This was done in a previous step for Alice, so if you need a refresher on how to do this, refer back to that section. Be sure to select only the two accounts that Dan should have access to, which are the Dev and the Prod accounts. This process is shown in Figures 4.14 and 4.15.

Dan can now access the Dev and Prod accounts with the specified permissions. The next step is to test the Alice and Dan users, which you do in the next section.

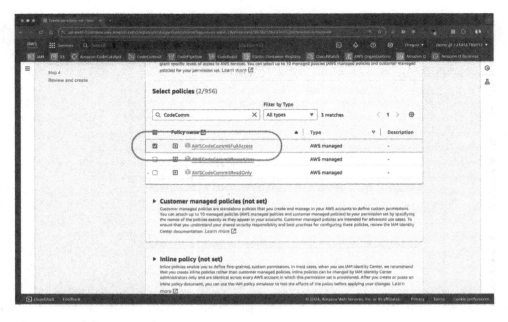

Figure 4.12: Selecting a policy.

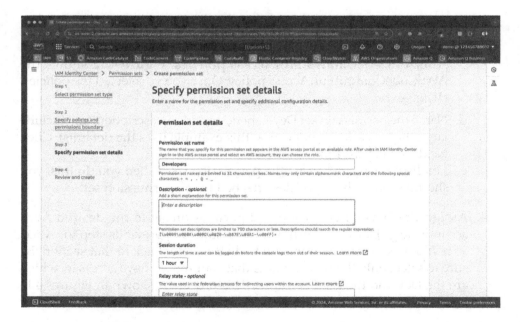

Figure 4.13: Naming the permission set.

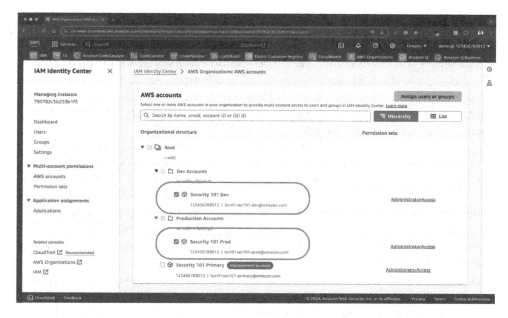

Figure 4.14: Selecting AWS accounts for the Developers group permissions.

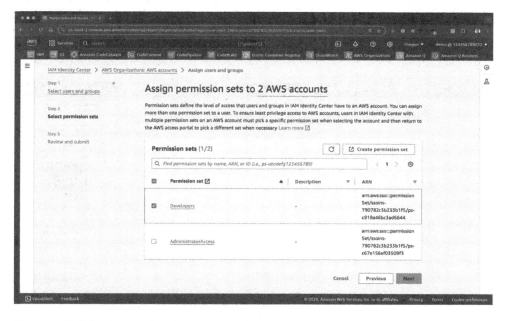

Figure 4.15: Selecting the Developers permission set to attach to two AWS accounts.

Testing Access for Alice and Dan

The URL for Alice and Dan to log in was provided with their one-time passwords when you created the users. You should have saved that information. If you didn't save the URL and you need to find it again, go to the Dashboard in the left menu of the AWS Console. Once you're on the Dashboard, you should see a section to the right of the page called Settings Summary. The AWS Access Portal URL can be found there.

First, test Alice. If you have MFA (multifactor authentication) enabled for the account, the first time you log in with Alice, you will need to set up MFA. Since this process may change, and you can decide which type of MFA you want to use, I don't cover it here. For reference, however, I used my preferred password manager to register an MFA device. If you are going to use the same method I use, you need to choose Authenticator App. There are many paid and free apps that do this, including 1Password, Microsoft Authenticator, and Google Authenticator.

Once you set up MFA for Alice and log in, you should see something similar to Figure 4.16. Here you can see that Alice has access to three AWS accounts. Expanding each account provides link access to the AWS Console as well as access keys for programmatic access.

Next, test Dan's login. Again, you may need to set up MFA. Once you are logged in as Dan, you should see something similar to Figure 4.17. Note that Dan only has access to two AWS accounts.

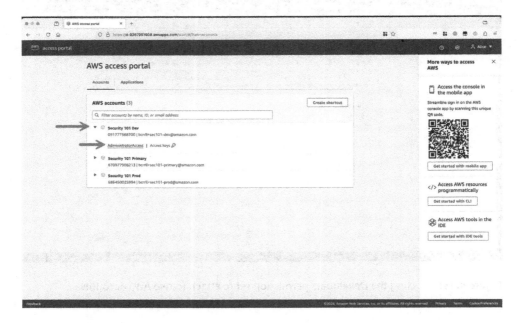

Figure 4.16: Logging in as Alice.

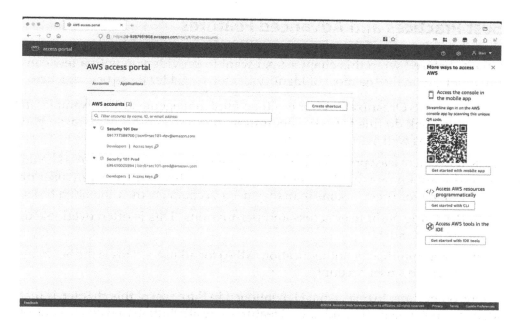

Figure 4.17: Logging in as Dan.

To further test this setup, access each account with Dan and Alice and see which services each of them have access to, based on the applied permission set. You should see that Alice has full access, while Dan's access is limited to fewer services.

Cleaning Up Your Work

Most of the time, as you work through various parts of this book, you'll want to clean up your configurations when you are done, so as to not incur any expected charges. In this case, IAM Identity Center is offered at no extra charge. However, if you still want to remove your instance of Identity Center, follow these steps:

1. In the AWS Console, Identity Center service, select Settings.
2. Next, select the Management tab and scroll to the bottom.
3. Click the Delete button in the Delete IAM Identity Center instance section and follow the subsequent prompts.

This will remove Identity Center, all the users you created, as well as the groups and permission sets.

Best Practices and Advanced Features

Finally, before I wrap this chapter up, I want to provide you with a few considerations to make the most of Identity Center. Consider these best practices:

- Use AWS Organizations for multi-account management. The examples in this book do this from the beginning. It doesn't cost any extra, so you might as well start out properly.

- Implement least privilege access with granular permission sets. You should already know what this means, but essentially, don't give any user or group more permissions than they need to complete their intended tasks.

- Regularly audit user access and permissions. This is often overlooked, but it's a must.

- Enable multifactor authentication (MFA) for all users. This is the best way to secure a user account.

One other thing to note, which I mentioned in the onset of this chapter, is that Identity Center also offers advanced features like attribute-based access control (ABAC) and automated user lifecycle management. These features allow you to scale permissions management based on user attributes and streamline the user provisioning and deprovisioning processes. While I don't cover them in this book, it's good to be aware of these features as you build on your knowledge of identity management and need to scale in the future.

Conclusion

And there you have it! This chapter covered the basics of setting up AWS Identity Center to simplify access management across your AWS accounts and applications. While traditional IAM works well for managing access within a single AWS account, Identity Center makes more sense when you need to manage user access across multiple accounts. Think of it this way—using IAM alone for multiple accounts would require you to create and manage separate IAM users in each account, maintain different sets of credentials, and repeatedly configure permissions. This is increasingly tough to manage as your organization grows.

Identity Center eliminates these challenges by providing a single place to manage all your users and their access across accounts. Users get one set of credentials to access all their assigned AWS accounts and applications, making the experience much simpler for administrators and end users. Plus, with its built-in identity store and support for external identity providers, Identity Center gives you the flexibility to integrate with your existing identity management systems while maintaining centralized control.

By following the examples and best practices outlined in this chapter, you are well on your way to managing access for your AWS accounts. Remember, Identity Center can grow with your organization's needs, and it's the recommended method of creating user accounts on AWS.

Reference

Amazon Web Services, "AWS IAM Identity Center, User Guide," `https://docs.aws.amazon.com/singlesignon/latest/userguide/ what-is.html`

Infrastructure Protection on AWS

"Most of us forget the basics and wonder why the specifics don't work."
—Garrison Wynn

In the early days of computing, successful security was a physical barrier. It was common to have locked server rooms, restricted access badges, and carefully guarded data centers. Today, infrastructure security has transformed into an intricate ecosystem where boundaries are much more fluid, and threats can emerge from anywhere around the globe.

For a moment, imagine a modern enterprise where a single misconfigured network setting can expose critical systems to potential attackers halfway across the world. No, this isn't fiction—it's the daily reality for cloud security professionals. Infrastructure security in AWS is no longer just about building walls. It's about creating intelligent, adaptive defense mechanisms that can anticipate and neutralize threats before they can cause damage.

When we talk about infrastructure security or infrastructure protection, we're not just talking about technical configurations. Twenty-first-century security is more complex than that because technology, strategy, and human decision-making all intersect here. For this reason, when we look at a network segment, a security group, or an access control policy, it tells us the story of risk management and strategic protection within our organization.

In this chapter, I want to go deep into AWS infrastructure protection and break down some of the more complex concepts. At the same time, I want to share some practical strategies and provide you with the knowledge you need to protect your cloud infrastructure.

Core Infrastructure Protection Concepts

Chapter 2 explored the foundational security concepts that underpin cloud computing. This chapter dives deeper into how these principles specifically apply to infrastructure protection in AWS.

A Guiding Framework

Remember the CIA triad—confidentiality, integrity, and availability? It remains our north star for infrastructure protection.

Confidentiality: Ensuring that sensitive infrastructure components and data remain accessible only to authorized entities. In AWS, this means:

- Implementing strict network segmentation
- Using encryption for data at rest and in transit
- Configuring granular access controls

Integrity: Protecting infrastructure from unauthorized modifications.

Availability: Ensuring infrastructure resources are accessible when needed. This involves:

- Designing redundant network architectures
- Implementing load balancing
- Creating disaster recovery strategies

Principle of Least Privilege

As discussed in previous chapters, the principle of least privilege isn't just a recommendation. It's a critical security strategy. In infrastructure protection, this means:

- Granting only the minimum necessary permissions for infrastructure components
- Regularly reviewing and auditing access rights
- Using IAM roles with specific, limited scopes
- Implementing fine-grained access controls

Understanding Your Role in the Shared Responsibility Model

Chapter 2 covered the shared responsibility model. Since this chapter covers infrastructure protection specifically, it's good to understand what AWS does and what the customer is responsible for so you have it fresh in mind. AWS provides the foundational infrastructure security, but you're responsible for:

- Configuring network access
- Managing identity and access
- Implementing security controls
- Monitoring and responding to potential threats

Much of this is explained in this chapter. But before you get into the configuration of your security controls for infrastructure protection, I want to cover some networking foundations as a starting point. This is important because your network architecture serves as the first line of defense in your cloud security strategy. When you're building cloud infrastructure, the VPC is where you define the boundaries and control the traffic flow—essentially establishing the perimeter of your cloud environment. Without a solid understanding of these networking fundamentals, it would be challenging to implement effective security controls or understand how they work together to protect your resources.

Before you start creating and configuring VPCs, it's important to understand how AWS structures its global network.

AWS Networking Foundations

Chapter 3 explored Identity and Access Management (IAM). This section dives into the network infrastructure that forms the backbone of your AWS environment. A Virtual Private Cloud (VPC) is more than just a network configuration. It's the fundamental framework that defines how your cloud resources—like ec2 instances—communicate, interact, and remain secure.

Before you start creating and configuring VPCs, you need to understand how AWS structures its global network. AWS operates in a global infrastructure. This consists of *regions, availability zones,* and *edge locations* spread across the world.

AWS currently spans 34 geographic regions, with 108 availability zones. Think of a region as a separate geographic area, like the eastern United States (Northern Virginia) or Europe (Ireland). Each region is independent and contains multiple availability zones (AZs).

Availability zones are physical data centers within each region. Each reach region has multiple AZs, usually at least three, and each AZ has its own power, cooling, and physical security. They're connected through high-speed, redundant networking. When you launch resources in AWS, you can select which availability zone you want your resources to be launched in a specific region.

This is important for infrastructure protection because when you create an AWS account, AWS automatically creates a default VPC in each region. This default VPC comes with a public subnet in each availability zone, making it easy to launch and access resources.

When you're building a cloud infrastructure, the VPC is one of the first lines of defense. It's where you define the boundaries and control the traffic flow.

With that said, the next section goes deeper into VPCs.

Core VPC Components

As mentioned, every VPC is built from key components that work together to create a network:

COMPONENT	PURPOSE
Subnets	Divide your network into isolated segments
Security groups	Act as virtual firewalls for individual resources
Network ACLs	Provide an additional layer of network protection
Route tables	Control how traffic moves between different network segments
Gateways	Enable communication between your VPC and other networks (Internet Gateway for public Internet access, Virtual Private Gateway for VPN connections, and NAT Gateway for private subnet Internet access)
VPC endpoints	Allow private connectivity to AWS services without traversing the public Internet, reducing exposure to potential threats

Creating a Secure VPC

This example uses the AWS CLI and CloudShell to do this, as you did back in Chapter 3. You'll want to be logged in to the Alice account that you created in Chapter 4.

To begin, I show you how to build a network foundation that will help protect your resources. As you move through the rest of this chapter, there are several resource values you need to take note of. You can use Table 5.1 to note these values. You can also find all the commands I use in this section in my GitHub repo, in the `https://github.com/8carroll/Securing-the-Cloud-with-Brandon-Carroll` folder. You'll find additional resources to help with cleanup after each chapter and initial configurations as well. One other thing you will find there is a complete list of all commands I used, so you can copy and paste with your own environment data.

Some of the values will be resource IDs, as is the case with your VPC. In other cases, you will need to note the Amazon Resource Number. An *Amazon*

Resource Name (ARN) is a unique identifier for AWS resources, ensuring you can pinpoint them accurately across your environment. Think of ARNs as the way AWS organizes and references everything, from S3 buckets to EC2 instances, in a clear and consistent format. ARNs are used whenever you need to specify a resource, whether it's in an API call, a permission policy, or a configuration.

Here's how an ARN is structured:

```
arn:partition:service:region:account-id:resource
```

You'll see ARNs everywhere when working in AWS. They make it easy to identify resources in your account.

An AWS account has a default VPC in each region. While you could use the default VPC, you are going to create your own in this example. This will help you see how things fit together. Before I discuss regions, I want to discuss the AWS Global Network.

Table 5.1: Resource Tracker

RESOURCE	PURPOSE	ARN/ID
VPC ID		
Subnet ID (Public)		
Subnet ID (Private)		
Internet Gateway ID		
Route Table ID (Public)		
Route Table ID (Private)		
Security Group ID (ALB)		
Security Group ID (EC2)		
Load Balancer ARN		
Target Group ARN		
IAM Role ARN (SSM)		
Instance Profile ARN (SSM)		
WebACL ARN (WAF)		
Certificate ARN (ACM)		
NAT Gateway ID		
Elastic IP Allocation ID		
Instance ID 1		
Instance ID 2		

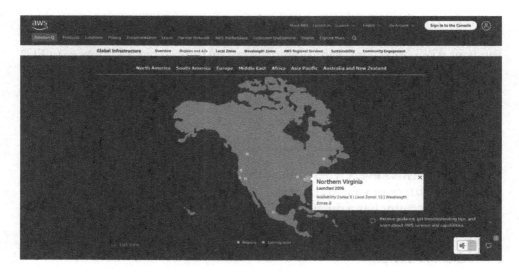

Figure 5.1: The AWS global network—North America.

The AWS Global Network

At the time of the writing of this book, the AWS website states that "The AWS Cloud spans 114 Availability Zones within 36 geographic regions, with announced plans for 12 more Availability Zones and four more AWS Regions in New Zealand, the Kingdom of Saudi Arabia, Taiwan, and the AWS European Sovereign Cloud." Figure 5.1 shows a North American map with regions indicated on it. I mentioned this already, but it bears repeating. Regions are located all around the world. Inside of a region, for example, us-east-1 or North Virginia, AWS clusters data centers. Each group of logical data centers is called an availability zone. Each region consists of at minimum three isolated and physically separate AZs within a geographic area. These AZs have independent cooling, power, networking, and so on. This makes the AWS Cloud a highly available, fault-tolerant network.

An Amazon Virtual Private Cloud (VPC) is a virtual network that resembles a traditional network that you would run in your own data center. It's located within a region, and you typically launch resources within a VPC. Figure 5.2 shows the example architecture of a VPC.

As you can see in Figure 5.2, the VPC is located in a region, in this case us-west-2. Recall that a region consists of at least three AZs. Figure 5.2 shows two AZs—AZ1 and AZ2. Inside the AZ are subnets, and Figure 5.2 shows a private and a public subnet in each AZ. Don't worry about that yet. These subnets are part of the overall CIDR range allocated to the VPC. From the subnet space, IP addresses can be allocated to the resources you launch in that AZ. Route tables determine where the network traffic from your subnet is directed.

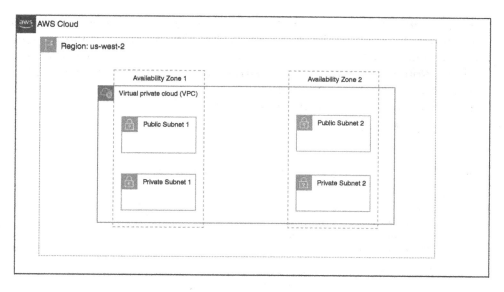

Figure 5.2: Example architecture of a VPC.

For traffic to be routed outside of your VPC, you need a gateway, and there are multiple gateway types. This chapter covers Internet Gateways (IGWs) and NAT Gateways. I explain those in more detail when you get to their deployment in the chapter examples. For now, though, you should have a basic understanding of the architecture. With that, the next section explains how to build a basic infrastructure. We begin by creating a new VPC and the corresponding subnets.

Creating VPCs and Subnets

First you'll create a VPC. You're also going to create a CIDR (Classless Inter-Domain Routing) block for your VPC. A CIDR block is a fundamental method for defining IP address ranges in an AWS VPC network. When you specify a CIDR block like 10.0.0.0/16, you're essentially creating a network that can host thousands of IP addresses. The notation consists of a base IP address (10.0.0.0) and a suffix (/16) that determines how many bits are fixed in the network portion. For example, a /16 suffix provides you with 65,536 IP addresses to work with, ranging from 10.0.0.0 to 10.0.255.255. When building your VPC infrastructure, you'll typically use private IP ranges (like 10.0.0.0/8, 172.16.0.0/12, or 192.168.0.0/16), which aren't directly accessible from the Internet. As you create subnets within your VPC, you'll divide this main CIDR block into smaller ranges—for instance, you might create a public subnet using 10.0.1.0/24 and a private subnet using 10.0.2.0/24, with each /24 subnet providing 256 IP addresses for your resources.

So, to create a VPC, you'll use the AWS `ec2 create-vpc` command. In this command, you are telling the VPC what CIDR block to use and adding tags. Tags will make it easier to identify later. The CIDR block is the top-level address block that you will then create subnets from. Issue the following command in `us-west-2`. If you decide to use a different region, be sure to change the region when it's called in any of the following commands.

```
[cloudshell-user@ip-10-144-118-61 ~]$ aws ec2 create-vpc \
>       --cidr-block 10.0.0.0/16 \
>       --tag-specifications
'ResourceType=vpc,Tags=[{Key=Name,Value=SecureInfraVPC}]'
{-
    "Vpc": {
        "OwnerId": "387974667323",
        "InstanceTenancy": "default",
        "Ipv6CidrBlockAssociationSet": [],
        "CidrBlockAssociationSet": [
            {
                "AssociationId": "vpc-cidr-assoc-0ebec9d7fdef4215f",
                "CidrBlock": "10.0.0.0/16",
                "CidrBlockState": {
                    "State": "associated"
                }
            }
        ],
        "IsDefault": false,
        "Tags": [
            {
                "Key": "Name",
                "Value": "SecureInfraVPC"
            }
        ],
        "VpcId": "vpc-0488a892d43711307",
        "State": "pending",
        "CidrBlock": "10.0.0.0/16",
        "DhcpOptionsId": "dopt-62d09d1a"
    }
}
(END)
```

Note the VPC ID in your output and add it to Table 5.1. You'll need this value for other commands.

When you create this VPC, you're using a private IP range (10.0.0.0/16). This is important because private IP ranges aren't directly accessible from the Internet. You should also know that you can bring your own public IP and IPv6 addresses to AWS and use them in a VPC as well.

You're also adding a tag to help identify and manage this resource later. To set up your subnets, you need to create public and private subnets to properly segment the network traffic. From the output, note the VPC ID. You need it in the following command to set up the public subnet.

```
[cloudshell-user@ip-10-144-118-61 ~]$ aws ec2 create-subnet \
> --vpc-id vpc-0488a892d43711307 \
> --cidr-block 10.0.1.0/24 \
> --availability-zone us-west-2a \
> --tag-specifications
'ResourceType=subnet,Tags=[{Key=Name,Value=PublicSubnet}]'
{
    "Subnet": {
        "AvailabilityZoneId": "usw2-az2",
        "OwnerId": "387974667323",
        "AssignIpv6AddressOnCreation": false,
        "Ipv6CidrBlockAssociationSet": [],
        "Tags": [
            {
                "Key": "Name",
                "Value": "PublicSubnet"
            }
        ],
        "SubnetArn": "arn:aws:ec2:us-west-2:387974667323:subnet/
subnet-0df6a70918521c6ac",
        "EnableDns64": false,
        "Ipv6Native": false,
        "PrivateDnsNameOptionsOnLaunch": {
            "HostnameType": "ip-name",
            "EnableResourceNameDnsARecord": false,
            "EnableResourceNameDnsAAAARecord": false
        },
        "SubnetId": "subnet-0df6a70918521c6ac",
        "State": "available",
        "VpcId": "vpc-0488a892d43711307",
        "CidrBlock": "10.0.1.0/24",
        "AvailableIpAddressCount": 251,
        "AvailabilityZone": "us-west-2a",
        "DefaultForAz": false,
        "MapPublicIpOnLaunch": false
    }
}
(END)
```

In this output, take note of the public subnet ID and add it to Table 5.1 for reference later.

Next, you'll create a private subnet:

```
[cloudshell-user@ip-10-144-118-61 ~]$ aws ec2 create-subnet \
> --vpc-id vpc-0488a892d43711307 \
> --cidr-block 10.0.2.0/24 \
> --availability-zone us-west-2b \
> --tag-specifications
'ResourceType=subnet,Tags=[{Key=Name,Value=PrivateSubnet}]'
{
    "Subnet": {
        "AvailabilityZoneId": "usw2-az1",
        "OwnerId": "387974667323",
        "AssignIpv6AddressOnCreation": false,
        "Ipv6CidrBlockAssociationSet": [],
        "Tags": [
```

```
                        {
                            "Key": "Name",
                            "Value": "PrivateSubnet"
                        }
                    ],
                    "SubnetArn": "arn:aws:ec2:us-west-2:387974667323:subnet/
            subnet-03b7ccdf1256e47b2",
                    "EnableDns64": false,
                    "Ipv6Native": false,
                    "PrivateDnsNameOptionsOnLaunch": {
                        "HostnameType": "ip-name",
                        "EnableResourceNameDnsARecord": false,
                        "EnableResourceNameDnsAAAARecord": false
                    },
                    "SubnetId": "subnet-03b7ccdf1256e47b2",
                    "State": "available",
                    "VpcId": "vpc-0488a892d43711307",
                    "CidrBlock": "10.0.2.0/24",
                    "AvailableIpAddressCount": 251,
                    "AvailabilityZone": "us-west-2b",
                    "DefaultForAz": false,
                    "MapPublicIpOnLaunch": false
                }
            }
            (END)
```

Again, in the output, note the subnet ID for the private subnet and add it to Table 5.1 for reference later.

You've created separate public and private subnets to isolate traffic and better control access patterns. The public subnet will host resources that need Internet access, while the private subnet will contain resources that should remain isolated from direct Internet access.

Internet Gateway and Route Tables

Now that you have the VPC and subnets set up, you can create an Internet Gateway (IGW). An Internet Gateway allows resources in your VPC to communicate with the Internet. Without it, even your public subnet remains isolated. To create an Internet Gateway, use the `aws ec2 create-internet-gateway` command as follows:

```
[cloudshell-user@ip-10-144-118-61 ~]$ aws ec2 create-internet-gateway \
>     --tag-specifications 'ResourceType=internet-gateway,Tags=
[{Key=Name,Value=SecureInfraIGW}]'
{
    "InternetGateway": {
        "Attachments": [],
        "InternetGatewayId": "igw-0b6e469e5f367bc49",
        "OwnerId": "387974667323",
        "Tags": [
            {
```

```
                    "Key": "Name",
                    "Value": "SecureInfraIGW"
                }
            ]
        }
    }
}
[cloudshell-user@ip-10-144-118-61 ~]$
```

In this output, note the IGW ID and add it to Table 5.1 for reference later.

Next, you need to attach the IGW to your VPC. To do this, you need the IGW ID from the output and your VPC ID. Once you have those, you can use the aws ec2 attach-internet-gateway command.

```
[cloudshell-user@ip-10-144-118-61 ~]$ aws ec2 attach-internet-gateway \
>     --vpc-id vpc-0488a892d43711307 \
>     --internet-gateway-id igw-0b6e469e5f367bc49
[cloudshell-user@ip-10-144-118-61 ~]$
```

Next, you need to set up the route tables. A route table contains statements that determine where network traffic is directed. You'll create separate route tables for the public and private subnets.

First, create a route table for the public subnet. You can do this by using the aws ec2 create-route-table command, as shown here:

```
[cloudshell-user@ip-10-144-118-61 ~]$ aws ec2 create-route-table \
>     --vpc-id vpc-0488a892d43711307 \
>     --tag-specifications 'ResourceType=route-table,Tags=[{Key=Name,Value=
PublicRT}]'
{
    "RouteTable": {
        "Associations": [],
        "PropagatingVgws": [],
        "RouteTableId": "rtb-0619d26fd5f74b369",
        "Routes": [
            {
                "DestinationCidrBlock": "10.0.0.0/16",
                "GatewayId": "local",
                "Origin": "CreateRouteTable",
                "State": "active"
            }
        ],
        "Tags": [
            {
                "Key": "Name",
                "Value": "PublicRT"
            }
        ],
        "VpcId": "vpc-0488a892d43711307",
        "OwnerId": "387974667323"
    },
    "ClientToken": "1cf66134-d1b8-4288-8c84-713a80b5c29f"
}
(END)
```

Next, you're going to add a route to the Internet through the Internet Gateway. For this, you need the route table ID from the output of the previous command. It's highlighted. Don't forget to add that value to Table 5.1. Once you have it, you can use the aws ec2 create-route command, as shown here:

```
[cloudshell-user@ip-10-144-118-61 ~]$ aws ec2 create-route \
>      --route-table-id rtb-0619d26fd5f74b369 \
>      --destination-cidr-block 0.0.0.0/0 \
>      --gateway-id igw-0b6e469e5f367bc49
{
    "Return": true
}
[cloudshell-user@ip-10-144-118-61 ~]$
```

Next, you need to associate the route table with the public subnet. For this, you need two IDs. You need the ID of the route table and the ID of the public subnet. Once you have those, you can use the aws ec2 associate-route-table command, as shown here:

```
[cloudshell-user@ip-10-144-118-61 ~]$ aws ec2 associate-route-table \
>      --route-table-id rtb-0619d26fd5f74b369 \
>      --subnet-id subnet-0df6a70918521c6ac
{
    "AssociationId": "rtbassoc-063cab584359f1cad",
    "AssociationState": {
        "State": "associated"
    }
}
[cloudshell-user@ip-10-144-118-61 ~]$
```

When you create this route table configuration, you're establishing clear traffic patterns. The public subnet can route traffic to the Internet through the Internet Gateway, while the private subnet remains isolated from direct Internet access. You can see how this VPC is coming together in Figure 5.3.

NAT Gateway and Private Subnet Routing

The private subnet needs a way to access the Internet for things like software updates and patches, but you want to do this securely. This is where a NAT Gateway comes in.

Before you create a NAT Gateway, you need an Elastic IP address. An Elastic IP is a static, public IPv4 address that can be assigned to your AWS resources. Unlike regular public IP addresses, which might change when you stop and start a resource, an Elastic IP remains constant until you release it.

You can allocate an Elastic IP using the aws ec2 allocate-address command, as shown here:

```
[cloudshell-user@ip-10-144-118-61 ~]$ aws ec2 allocate-address \
>      --domain vpc \
```

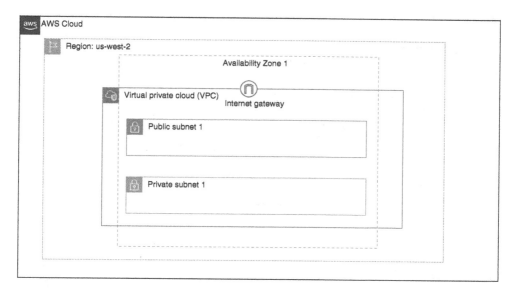

Figure 5.3: AWS Infrastructure with IGW.

```
>     --tag-specifications 'ResourceType=elastic-ip,Tags=[{Key=Name,
Value=NATGW-EIP}]'
{
    "AllocationId": "eipalloc-09674141fa5fb21b1",
    "PublicIpv4Pool": "amazon",
    "NetworkBorderGroup": "us-west-2",
    "Domain": "vpc",
    "PublicIp": "44.226.169.46"
}
[cloudshell-user@ip-10-144-118-61 ~]$
```

Note the AllocationId from the output. You'll need this to create the NAT Gateway.

Understanding NAT Gateway Placement

Before you create the NAT Gateway, it's important to understand why you place it in a public subnet even though it serves the private subnet. A NAT Gateway acts as an intermediary between your private resources and the Internet.

Here's how it works:

1. Resources in your private subnet need to make outbound connections (like software updates).

2. These requests go to the NAT Gateway in the public subnet.

3. The NAT Gateway then forwards these requests to the Internet through the Internet Gateway.

4. When responses come back, the NAT Gateway translates the traffic back to the private resources.

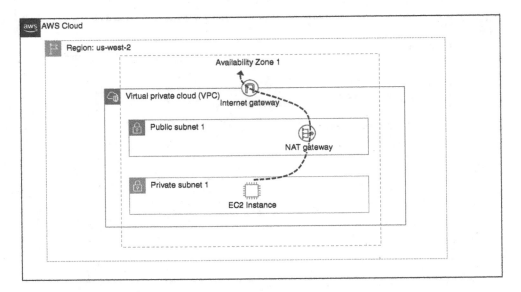

Figure 5.4: NAT Gateway placement.

Think of the NAT Gateway as a sort of proxy between the public and private subnets. You can see the architecture in Figure 5.4.

The NAT Gateway needs to be in a public subnet because it needs to communicate with your private resources and the Internet. However, it only allows outbound connections. This means that external services cannot initiate connections inbound to your private resources.

Now you can create the NAT Gateway in the public subnet. You'll use the `aws ec2 create-nat-gateway` command, which requires both the subnet ID of your public subnet and the allocation ID of the Elastic IP you just created:

```
[cloudshell-user@ip-10-140-19-93 ~]$    aws ec2 create-nat-gateway \
>    --subnet-id subnet-0df6a70918521c6ac \
>    --allocation-id eipalloc-09674141fa5fb21b1 \
>    --tag-specifications
'ResourceType=natgateway,Tags=[{Key=Name,Value=SecureInfraNATGW}]'
{
    "ClientToken": "e1ce5186-8cae-454d-9a2e-18cf77e8a731",
    "NatGateway": {
        "CreateTime": "2024-11-08T22:06:46+00:00",
        "NatGatewayAddresses": [
            {
                "AllocationId": "eipalloc-09674141fa5fb21b1",
                "IsPrimary": true,
                "Status": "associating"
            }
        ],
```

```
            "NatGatewayId": "nat-0df536d2774e09ccd",
            "State": "pending",
            "SubnetId": "subnet-0df6a70918521c6ac",
            "VpcId": "vpc-0488a892d43711307",
            "Tags": [
                {
                    "Key": "Name",
                    "Value": "SecureInfraNATGW"
                }
            ],
            "ConnectivityType": "public"
        }
    }
(END)
```

Note the NAT Gateway ID from the output. You'll need this when you set up the route table for the private subnet.

Next, create a route table for the private subnet. You can do this using the `aws ec2 create-route-table` command, as shown here:

```
[cloudshell-user@ip-10-140-19-93 ~]$ aws ec2 create-route-table \
>     --vpc-id vpc-0488a892d43711307 \
>     --tag-specifications 'ResourceType=route-table,Tags=[{Key=Name,Value=
PrivateRT}]'
{
    "RouteTable": {
        "Associations": [],
        "PropagatingVgws": [],
        "RouteTableId": "rtb-0181a4313f9a7f226",
        "Routes": [
            {
                "DestinationCidrBlock": "10.0.0.0/16",
                "GatewayId": "local",
                "Origin": "CreateRouteTable",
                "State": "active"
            }
        ],
        "Tags": [
            {
                "Key": "Name",
                "Value": "PrivateRT"
            }
        ],
        "VpcId": "vpc-0488a892d43711307",
        "OwnerId": "387974667323"
    },
    "ClientToken": "d58a5024-c665-41a3-8087-714c36c4ddcc"
}
(END)
```

Once again, note the route table ID and add it to Table 5.1.

You'll add a route that sends Internet-bound traffic through the NAT Gateway. For this, you'll need the route table ID from the output of the previous command

and the NAT Gateway ID you noted earlier. These values should be in Table 5.1. You can do this using the aws ec2 create-route command, as shown here:

```
[cloudshell-user@ip-10-140-19-93 ~]$    aws ec2 create-route \
>      --route-table-id rtb-0181a4313f9a7f226 \
>      --destination-cidr-block 0.0.0.0/0 \
>      --nat-gateway-id nat-0df536d2774e09ccd
{
    "Return": true
}
[cloudshell-user@ip-10-140-19-93 ~]$
```

Finally, you need to associate this route table with the private subnet. For this, you'll need both the route table ID and the ID of your private subnet. You can do this using the aws ec2 associate-route-table command, as shown here:

```
[cloudshell-user@ip-10-140-19-93 ~]$    aws ec2 associate-route-table \
>      --route-table-id rtb-0181a4313f9a7f226 \
>      --subnet-id subnet-03b7ccdf1256e47b2
{
    "AssociationId": "rtbassoc-040a7255095c2c326",
    "AssociationState": {
        "State": "associated"
    }
}
[cloudshell-user@ip-10-140-19-93 ~]$
```

At this point, you have successfully:

- Created an NAT Gateway in your public subnet
- Created a route table for your private subnet
- Added a route to send Internet traffic through the NAT Gateway
- Associated the route table with the private subnet

Your private subnet can now access the Internet securely through the NAT Gateway while remaining protected from inbound connections.

Testing the Network Configuration

Now that you have your network infrastructure set up, you can test it by launching two EC2 instances. To do this, you're going to use a CloudFormation template. CloudFormation is an Infrastructure-as-Code service in AWS that will build the resources that are defined by code in the template.

Before you deploy the template, you need to get your subnet IDs. You can do this using the AWS CL (although you may already have them in your table):

```
[cloudshell-user@ip-10-140-19-93 ~]$ aws ec2 describe-subnets \
>      --filters "Name=tag:Name,Values=PublicSubnet" \
```

```
>       --query 'Subnets[*].SubnetId' \
>       --output text
subnet-0df6a70918521c6ac
[cloudshell-user@ip-10-140-19-93 ~]$
[cloudshell-user@ip-10-140-19-93 ~]$ # Get the private subnet ID
[cloudshell-user@ip-10-140-19-93 ~]$ aws ec2 describe-subnets \
>       --filters "Name=tag:Name,Values=PrivateSubnet" \
>       --query 'Subnets[*].SubnetId' \
>       --output text
subnet-03b7ccdf1256e47b2
[cloudshell-user@ip-10-140-19-93 ~]$
```

Note both subnet IDs if you haven't done so already. You'll need these when deploying the CloudFormation template. You can get a copy of this CloudFormation template in my GitHub repo at `https://github.com/8carroll/Securing-the-Cloud-with-Brandon-Carroll`, in the Chapter 5 folder.

In the AWS Console, navigate to CloudFormation, select Create Stack (with new resources), and then select Upload a Template File. When prompted, provide a name for the stack and the subnet IDs you retrieved previously. You can see this process in Figure 5.5.

On the Configure Stack Options page, check the box next to "I acknowledge that AWS CloudFormation might create IAM resources" and then click Next. Finally, on the Review and Create page, click the Submit button.

Once the CloudFormation stack is complete, you can test your network configuration using AWS Systems Manager Session Manager. This allows you to connect to your instances without needing SSH access.

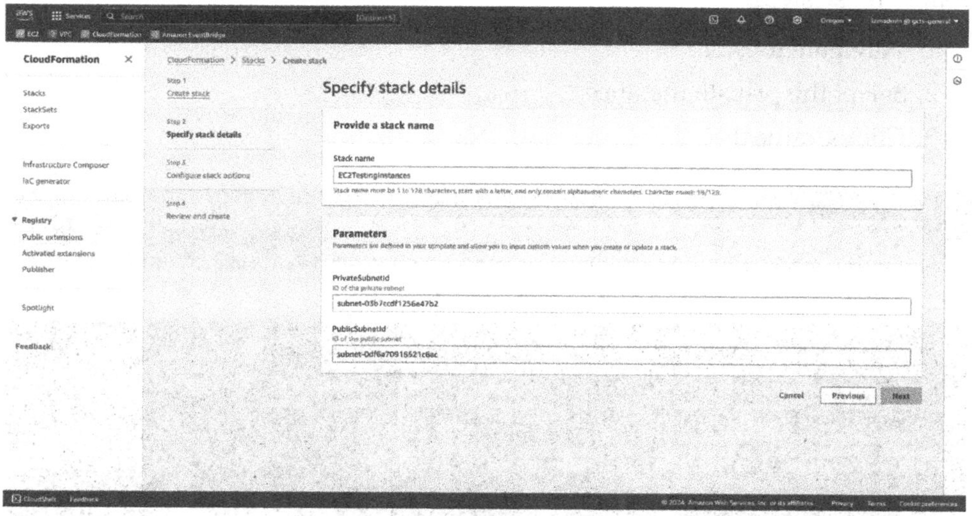

Figure 5.5: Subnet IDs for the CloudFormation template.

To connect to the instance in the AWS Console, follow these steps:

1. Navigate to EC2.
2. Select the public instance.
3. Click Connect.
4. Select the Session Manager tab.
5. Click Connect.

Session Manager may take a few minutes before it is ready for connections. If the Connect button is not immediately available, wait a few minutes and try again. Once the Connect button is there and you click it, the EC2 instance CLI will open in a new browser tab. Once you're on the CLI of the public instance, you can test connectivity using the ping and curl commands, as shown in Figure 5.6. The commands used here are ping amazon.com to test connectivity, followed by curl http://checkip.amazonaws.com, which returns the IP address of your EC2 instance. In this example, it's 52.39.22.106. This will differ in your output.

Once you've used curl and noted the public IP address, compare it to the public address shown on the EC2 instance page in Figure 5.7. These addresses should match. To find this information, go to EC2, then select the public instance. You'll find the address on the Details tab.

Remember, since this is a public instance, it has a public IP address. Also remember that the connectivity is from the instance, through the IGW. Now let's test the private instance. To connect to the instance in the AWS Console, follow these steps:

1. Navigate to EC2.
2. Select the private instance.
3. Click Connect.

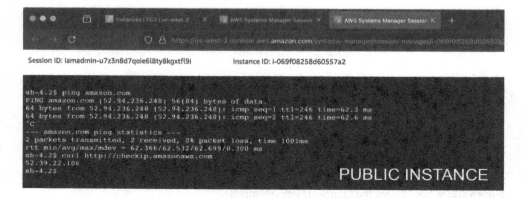

Figure 5.6: Public instance connectivity test.

4. Select the Session Manager tab.

5. Click Connect.

Once you're on the CLI of the private instance, you can test connectivity using the ping and curl commands, as shown in Figure 5.8, using the same ping and curl commands you just used for the public instance.

Notice the public IP address. You can compare this to what is shown on the EC2 instance page for the private instance in Figure 5.9. To find this information, go to EC2, select instances, then select the private instance. Note on the Details tab that there is no public IP address assigned.

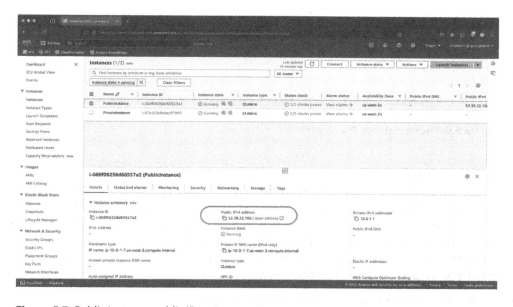

Figure 5.7: Public instance public IP assignment.

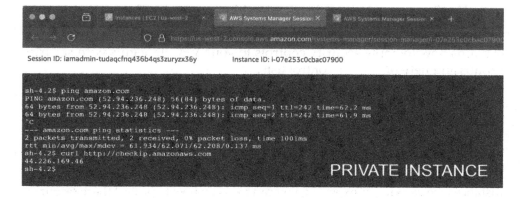

Figure 5.8: Private instance connectivity test.

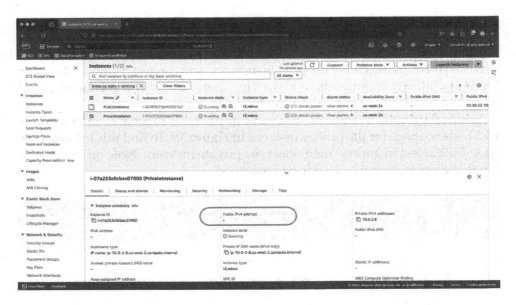

Figure 5.9: Private instance IP assignment.

Remember, since this is a private instance, it does not have a public IP address assigned. So how is it able to ping and why is a public IP address shown in the curl output? Recall that the connectivity is from the private instance in the private subnet, through the NAT Gateway that is in the public subnet. Therefore, the address you see in the curl output is the NAT Gateway.

Before moving on to security groups and network ACLs, let's summarize what you've accomplished in this section:

- Created your VPC network infrastructure
- Deployed test instances using CloudFormation
- Verified connectivity using Session Manager and curl

Now that you have the basic networking components set up, the next section explains how to apply security controls to your VPC. It begins with security groups and network access control lists.

Security Groups and Network Access Control Lists (NACLs)

Now that you have your basic infrastructure in place and can confirm your instances are working as expected, you can focus on how to protect these resources using security groups and NACLs.

Understanding the Differences

It's important to understand how these controls differ. The following table provides a high-level look at how security groups and NACLs differ.

FEATURE	SECURITY GROUPS	NETWORK ACLS
Scope	Instance level	Subnet level
State	Stateful	Stateless
Default action	Deny all inbound, allow all outbound	Allow all inbound and outbound
Rule processing	All rules evaluated	Rules processed in order
Rule types	Allow rules only	Allow and deny rules

Instance-Level Protection

Security groups act as instance-level virtual firewalls in AWS, controlling traffic through stateful inspection. More specifically, security groups are associated with Elastic Network Interfaces (ENIs), not just instances directly, and since an instance can have multiple ENIs, each interface can be associated with different security groups to provide granular network security control. Unlike traditional firewalls, they only contain allow rules, automatically denying anything not explicitly permitted. They also maintain state to allow return traffic without additional rules. A security group is stateful because it automatically remembers and tracks the state of network connections. Here's what this means in practice.

When you send a request from your instance:

- The security group remembers this outbound request.
- When the response comes back, it's automatically allowed in, regardless of inbound rules.
- This is because the security group knows this is a response to an earlier request.

Similarly, when allowed inbound traffic arrives:

- The security group remembers this inbound connection.
- The response is automatically allowed to go back out, regardless of outbound rules.
- This is because the security group knows this outbound traffic is just a response.

When you create a security group, you're essentially defining a set of firewall rules that will be applied to any instance associated with that group.

Here's an example of how this would work. Assume that your EC2 instance makes a request to amazon.com. The security group remembers this connection by creating an entry in a state table. When amazon.com responds, that traffic is automatically allowed back in because it matches a state table entry. This means you don't need to create a separate rule for the return traffic.

This is different from a stateless firewall (like a network ACL), where you need separate rules for the request and the response traffic. With stateless firewalls, each packet is evaluated independently, without any memory of previous connections.

When you first create a security group, it comes with

- No inbound rules (all inbound traffic denied)
- An outbound rule allowing all traffic to any destination (0.0.0.0/0)

Creating Security Groups

Now you need to create security groups for your instances. A security group needs to be associated with your VPC, and you'll create one that allows basic connectivity for testing.

The aws ec2 create-security-group command requires several parameters:

- group-name: A name for your security group (must be unique within the VPC)
- description: A text description of the security group's purpose
- vpc-id: The ID of your VPC where this security group will reside
- tag-specifications: Optional tags to help identify and manage your security group

Now you'll create your first security group:

```
[cloudshell-user@ip-10-132-50-171 ~]$ aws ec2 create-security-group \
>     --group-name InfraTestSG \
>     --description "Security group for infrastructure testing" \
>     --vpc-id vpc-0488a892d43711307 \
>     --tag-specifications 'ResourceType=security-group,Tags=[{Key=Name,Value=
InfraTestSG}]'
{
    "GroupId": "sg-06af9df1e8b9465b0",
    "Tags": [
        {
            "Key": "Name",
            "Value": "InfraTestSG"
        }
    ]
}
[cloudshell-user@ip-10-132-50-171 ~]$
```

Note the security group ID from the output and add it to Table 5.1. You'll need this when you add rules to the security group.

Adding Security Group Rules

Now that you have created a security group, you need to add rules to it. By default, a new security group has

- No inbound rules (all inbound traffic is denied)
- An outbound rule allowing all traffic (destination 0.0.0.0/0)

You'll add an inbound rule to allow HTTPS traffic since you are running a web server that's operating on port 443. The aws ec2 authorize-security-group-ingress command requires several parameters:

- --group-id: The ID of the security group you just created
- --protocol: The protocol type (tcp, udp, icmp, or -1 for all)
- --port: The port number to allow
- --cidr: The source IP range in CIDR notation

Go ahead and issue this command in your account:

```
[cloudshell-user@ip-10-132-50-171 ~]$ aws ec2 authorize-security-group-ingress \
>      --group-id sg-06af9df1e8b9465b0 \
>      --protocol tcp \
>      --port 443 \
>      --cidr 0.0.0.0/0
{
    "Return": true,
    "SecurityGroupRules": [
        {
            "SecurityGroupRuleId": "sgr-0379fced616ae8fb2",
            "GroupId": "sg-06af9df1e8b9465b0",
            "GroupOwnerId": "387974667323",
            "IsEgress": false,
            "IpProtocol": "tcp",
            "FromPort": 443,
            "ToPort": 443,
            "CidrIpv4": "0.0.0.0/0"
        }
    ]
}
(END)
```

Remember, because security groups are stateful, you don't need to create a specific rule for return traffic—it's automatically allowed.

For outbound traffic, while the default allows all traffic, you might want to be more restrictive following the principle of least privilege. You can modify the outbound rules using the aws ec2 revoke-security-group-egress and aws ec2 `authorize-security-group-egress` commands. You'll need the security-group ID for these commands.

First, remove the default allow rule:

```
[cloudshell-user@ip-10-132-50-171 ~]$ aws ec2 revoke-security-group-egress \
>     --group-id sg-06af9df1e8b9465b0 \
>     --protocol -1 \
>     --port -1 \
>     --cidr 0.0.0.0/0
{
    "Return": true
}
[cloudshell-user@ip-10-132-50-171 ~]$
```

Next, add a specific HTTPS outbound rule.

```
[cloudshell-user@ip-10-132-50-171 ~]$ aws ec2 authorize-security-group-egress \
>     --group-id sg-06af9df1e8b9465b0 \
>     --protocol tcp \
>     --port 443 \
>     --cidr 0.0.0.0/0
{
    "Return": true,
    "SecurityGroupRules": [
        {
            "SecurityGroupRuleId": "sgr-049f4e653d4a58c51",
            "GroupId": "sg-06af9df1e8b9465b0",
            "GroupOwnerId": "387974667323",
            "IsEgress": true,
            "IpProtocol": "tcp",
            "FromPort": 443,
            "ToPort": 443,
            "CidrIpv4": "0.0.0.0/0"
        }
    ]
}
(END)
```

Applying Security Groups to Your Instances

Now that you have configured a security group, you can apply it to your EC2 instances. The `aws ec2 modify-instance-attribute` command lets you modify an existing instance's security groups. This command requires the following parameters:

- `--instance-id`: The ID of the instance you want to modify

- `--groups`: One or more security group IDs to associate with the instance

First, get your instance IDs. You can use the `describe-instances` command with a filter for the instance names:

```
[cloudshell-user@ip-10-132-50-171 ~]$ aws ec2 describe-instances \
>      --filters "Name=tag:Name,Values=PublicInstance,PrivateInstance" \
>      --query 'Reservations[*].Instances[*].[InstanceId,Tags[?Key==`Name`].
Value]' \
>      --output table


------------------------
|   DescribeInstances  |
+----------------------+
|  i-069f08258d60557a2 |
|  PublicInstance      |
|  i-07e253c0cbac07900 |
|  PrivateInstance     |
+----------------------+
[cloudshell-user@ip-10-132-50-171 ~]$
[cloudshell-user@ip-10-132-50-171 ~]$
```

If you like, you can add these IDs to Table 5.1. Now apply the security group to both instances:

```
[cloudshell-user@ip-10-132-50-171 ~]$ aws ec2 modify-instance-attribute \
>      --instance-id i-069f08258d60557a2 \
>      --groups sg-06af9df1e8b9465b0
[cloudshell-user@ip-10-132-50-171 ~]$ aws ec2 modify-instance-attribute \
>      --instance-id i-07e253c0cbac07900 \
>      --groups sg-06af9df1e8b9465b0
[cloudshell-user@ip-10-132-50-171 ~]$
```

You now have the security group applied to both instances; you could just leave this as is and move on. However, the next section covers some best practices.

Security Group Best Practices

Looking at the current configuration, you've applied the same security group to both of the public and private instances. While this works, it's not following security best practices. This section explains why so you can make improvements.

The current security group allows

- Inbound HTTPS (port 443) from anywhere
- Outbound HTTPS (port 443) to anywhere

For the public instance, this makes sense because it needs to

- Accept inbound HTTPS traffic from the Internet
- Make outbound HTTPS requests for updates

However, the private instance should

- Never accept direct inbound traffic from the Internet
- Only allow outbound HTTPS for updates through the NAT Gateway

Now create a separate security group for your private instance:

```
[cloudshell-user@ip-10-132-50-171 ~]$ aws ec2 create-security-group \
>     --group-name PrivateInstanceSG \
>     --description "Security group for private instance" \
>     --vpc-id vpc-0488a892d43711307 \
>     --tag-specifications 'ResourceType=security-group,Tags=[{Key=Name,Value=
PrivateInstanceSG}]'
{
    "GroupId": "sg-0ded515da4cfd51a3",
    "Tags": [
        {
            "Key": "Name",
            "Value": "PrivateInstanceSG"
        }
    ]
}
[cloudshell-user@ip-10-132-50-171 ~]$
```

For this security group, you only need to allow outbound HTTPS traffic. Note the new security group ID from the previous output and use it to create the rule. You can add this to the table, but at some point, as you can tell, you're going to run out of room. Hopefully you understand that as you use the AWS CLI,. you will often need to note resource IDs and ARNs. As you prepare your configurations, start thinking about this ahead of time so you don't have to hunt for these values later.

```
cloudshell-user@ip-10-132-50-171 ~]$ aws ec2 authorize-security-group-egress \
>     --group-id sg-0ded515da4cfd51a3 \
>     --protocol tcp \
>     --port 443 \
>     --cidr 0.0.0.0/0
{
    "Return": true,
    "SecurityGroupRules": [
        {
            "SecurityGroupRuleId": "sgr-0def279d095cd948d",
            "GroupId": "sg-0ded515da4cfd51a3",
            "GroupOwnerId": "387974667323",
            "IsEgress": true,
            "IpProtocol": "tcp",
            "FromPort": 443,
            "ToPort": 443,
            "CidrIpv4": "0.0.0.0/0"
        }
    ]
}
(END)
```

Now update your private instance to use this new security group:

```
[cloudshell-user@ip-10-132-50-171 ~]$       aws ec2 modify-instance-attribute \
>       --instance-id i-07e253c0cbac07900 \
>       --groups sg-0ded515da4cfd51a3
[cloudshell-user@ip-10-132-50-171 ~]$
```

By using separate security groups for the public and private instances, you've implemented better security controls. This approach is better because it follows the principle of least privilege. The public instance has the rules it needs for Internet access. The private instance only has the rules it needs for updates through the NAT Gateway and there are no unnecessary permissions granted to either instance. Additionally, ping and the wget that you ran earlier will no longer work. This is by design as those commands are not required. Should you need to use those commands for testing, you would need to add a rule allowing ICMP and HTTP to the respective security group.

This approach is also better because it gives you better security visibility. When each security group clearly defines its purpose, it's easier to audit what type of traffic is allowed, and it's simpler to maintain and update rules for specific use cases.

Another important aspect that this practice lends itself to is a reduced attack surface since the private instance no longer has rules allowing inbound Internet traffic. Even if someone compromised the public instance, the private instance's security group provides an additional layer of protection.

This improved security group configuration also helps with compliance requirements, by providing clear separation of public and private resources. This makes it easier to demonstrate security controls to auditors and better aligns with security frameworks and compliance requirements.

You can now verify your configuration using the AWS CLI to see the difference in rules, as shown in Figure 5.10.

While security groups provide instance-level security, you also need to consider subnet-level security. This is where NACLs come into play.

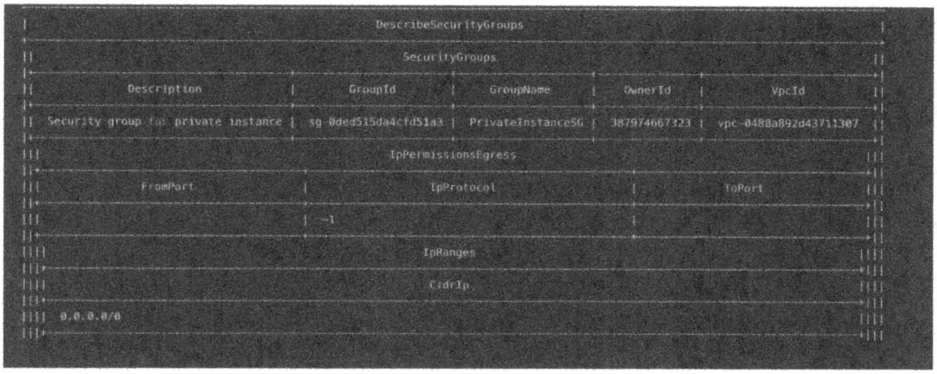

Figure 5.10: Verifying the configuration.

Network Access Control Lists (NACLs)

Unlike security groups, Network ACLs operate at the subnet level and are stateless. This means they require explicit rules for both inbound and outbound traffic, including return traffic. When you created your VPC, AWS automatically created a default NACL that allows all inbound and outbound traffic.

Now you'll create a custom NACL for your public subnet. The aws ec2 create-network-acl command requires the following:

- --vpc-id: The ID of your VPC

- --tag-specifications: Optional tags to help identify your NACL

```
[cloudshell-user@ip-10-132-50-171 ~]$ aws ec2 create-network-acl \
>    --vpc-id vpc-0488a892d43711307 \
>    --tag-specifications 'ResourceType=network-acl,Tags=[{Key=Name,Value=
PublicSubnetNACL}]'
{
    "NetworkAcl": {
        "Associations": [],
        "Entries": [
            {
                "CidrBlock": "0.0.0.0/0",
                "Egress": true,
                "IcmpTypeCode": {},
                "PortRange": {},
                "Protocol": "-1",
                "RuleAction": "deny",
                "RuleNumber": 32767
            },
            {
                "CidrBlock": "0.0.0.0/0",
                "Egress": false,
                "IcmpTypeCode": {},
                "PortRange": {},
                "Protocol": "-1",
                "RuleAction": "deny",
                "RuleNumber": 32767
            }
        ],
        "IsDefault": false,
        "NetworkAclId": "acl-0fafce26f095902e1",
        "Tags": [
            {
                "Key": "Name",
                "Value": "PublicSubnetNACL"
            }
        ],
        "VpcId": "vpc-0488a892d43711307",
        "OwnerId": "387974667323"
    },
    "ClientToken": "a4b11c79-6a7f-4622-b931-67daa6c3c13a"
}
[cloudshell-user@ip-10-132-50-171 ~]$
```

The aws ec2 create-network-acl-entry command requires several parameters:

- --network-acl-id: The ID of your NACL
- --rule-number: Lower numbers have higher priority. Valid numbers are 1–32766
- --protocol: The protocol type (tcp, udp, icmp, or -1 for all)
- --port-range: The range of ports to allow
- --cidr-block: The source IP range in CIDR notation
- --rule-action: Either allow or deny
- --egress: Whether this is an outbound rule (true/false)

Now you'll add rules to your NACL. Remember, NACLs are stateless, so you need rules for both inbound and outbound traffic. Also, NACLs evaluate rules in order, starting with the lowest numbered rule. You'll start with inbound rules. The first rule will be number 100 (remember that lower numbers take priority) and will allow inbound HTTPS.

```
[cloudshell-user@ip-10-132-50-171 ~]$ aws ec2 create-network-acl-entry \
>       --network-acl-id acl-0fafce26f095902e1 \
>       --rule-number 100 \
>       --protocol tcp \
>       --port-range From=443,To=443 \
>       --cidr-block 0.0.0.0/0 \
>       --rule-action allow \
>       --ingress
[cloudshell-user@ip-10-132-50-171 ~]$
```

Now add the second rule. This rule is number 140, and it will allow inbound ephemeral ports.

```
cloudshell-user@ip-10-132-50-171 ~]$ aws ec2 create-network-acl-entry \
>       --network-acl-id acl-0fafce26f095902e1 \
>       --rule-number 140 \
>       --protocol tcp \
>       --port-range From=1024,To=65535 \
>       --cidr-block 0.0.0.0/0 \
>       --rule-action allow \
>       --ingress
[cloudshell-user@ip-10-132-50-171 ~]$
```

Now add the outbound rules. Because NACLs are stateless, you need to explicitly allow both the outbound HTTPS traffic and the ephemeral ports for return traffic. First create rule number 100 and allow outbound HTTPS:

```
[cloudshell-user@ip-10-132-50-171 ~]$ aws ec2 create-network-acl-entry \
>       --network-acl-id acl-0fafce26f095902e1 \
>       --rule-number 100 \
```

```
>      --protocol tcp \
>      --port-range From=443,To=443 \
>      --cidr-block 0.0.0.0/0 \
>      --rule-action allow \
>      --egress
```

Next, create rule number 140 and allow outbound ephemeral ports:

```
[cloudshell-user@ip-10-132-50-171 ~]$ aws ec2 create-network-acl-entry \
>      --network-acl-id acl-0fafce26f095902e1 \
>      --rule-number 140 \
>      --protocol tcp \
>      --port-range From=1024,To=65535 \
>      --cidr-block 0.0.0.0/0 \
>      --rule-action allow \
>      --egress
[cloudshell-user@ip-10-132-50-171 ~]$
```

Finally, you need to associate this NACL with your public subnet. The `aws ec2 replace-network-acl-association` command requires the following:

- The current association ID of the subnet's NACL
- The ID of your new NACL

First, get the current association ID:

```
[cloudshell-user@ip-10-132-50-171 ~]$ aws ec2 describe-network-acls \
>      --filters "Name=association.subnet-id,Values=subnet-0df6a70918521c6ac" \
>      --query 'NetworkAcls[*].Associations[?SubnetId==`subnet-0df6a70918521c6ac`].
NetworkAclAssociationId' \
>      --output text
aclassoc-0463e9043eedeafe9
[cloudshell-user@ip-10-132-50-171 ~]$
```

In this output, you can see the current association ID. Once you have that, you can use the `aws ec2 replace-network-acl-association` command to associate your new NACL with the subnet. Let's do that next.

```
[cloudshell-user@ip-10-132-50-171 ~]$ aws ec2 replace-network-acl-association \
>      --association-id aclassoc-0463e9043eedeafe9 \
>      --network-acl-id acl-0fafce26f095902e1
{
    "NewAssociationId": "aclassoc-0ae0ec32c531dba21"
}
[cloudshell-user@ip-10-132-50-171 ~]$
```

Understanding Ephemeral Ports and Stateless NACLs

Ephemeral ports, also known as dynamic ports, are temporary ports that are automatically assigned by the operating system when a client initiates an outbound connection. These ports are used for the return traffic of a connection. The range is typically 1024-65535.

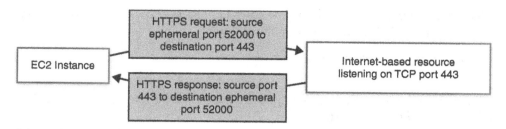

Figure 5.11: Ephemeral ports.

Here's a simple example of how ephemeral ports work: When your instance makes an HTTPS request to a website, it uses a random ephemeral port (let's say 52000) as the source port to connect to the website's destination port 443. When the website responds, the traffic flows from the website's port 443 back to your instance's ephemeral port 52000. This is depicted in Figure 5.11.

Because NACLs are stateless (unlike security groups), you need explicit rules for both directions. The configuration includes outbound rule 100, which allows outbound HTTPS on port 443, and outbound rule 140, which allows ephemeral ports for return traffic. Similarly, you have inbound rule 100, allowing inbound HTTPS on port 443, and inbound rule 140, allowing ephemeral ports for return traffic. Without these ephemeral port rules, return traffic would be blocked and the HTTPS connections would fail, even though you allowed the initial connection on port 443.

Now that you have configured both security groups and NACLs for your VPC, you should test the network security configuration. You can do this using the EC2 instances that you created earlier.

Verify the configuration by:

- Using Session Manager to connect to your public instance
- Testing outbound connectivity using the curl command to `checkip.amazonaws.com`
- Attempting the same from your private instance to verify NAT Gateway functionality

Verifying Your Network Configuration

Now that you have your security groups and NACLs configured, you can verify that everything is working as expected. First, connect to your public instance using Session Manager, as you did previously.

Once you are connected, test the outbound connectivity. First `curl` using HTTPS:

```
sh-4.2$ curl https://checkip.amazonaws.com
52.39.22.106
sh-4.2$
```

That was successful, as it should be since HTTPS is allowed. Now try changing the URL to HTTP. This attempt should fail:

```
sh-4.2$ curl http://checkip.amazonaws.com
^c
```

Since HTTP is not allowed, you got no response and had to use Control+C to break out of the command.

This tells you that your security group allows outbound HTTPS traffic, your NACL allows both the outbound request and inbound response, and your routing through the Internet Gateway is working.

Now test your private instance. Start a new session with the private instance and run the same commands to check both HTTPS and HTTP:

```
h-4.2$ curl https://checkip.amazonaws.com
44.226.169.46
sh-4.2$ curl http://checkip.amazonaws.com
^c
sh-4.2$
```

The results are exactly as expected. This tells you that the private instance can reach the Internet through the NAT Gateway, your security group and NACL rules are allowing the traffic, and your private subnet routing through the NAT Gateway is working.

While security groups and NACLs provide essential network security controls, modern applications often require additional layers of protection. As your applications scale and receive more traffic, you need a way to distribute that traffic securely while maintaining protection against threats. This is where Elastic Load Balancing (ELB) comes into play.

Elastic Load Balancing Security

An Elastic Load Balancer (ELB) serves as more than just a traffic distributor. By acting as a proxy between the Internet and your applications, an ELB helps protect your backend resources by:

- Providing a single-entry point for all incoming traffic
- Handling SSL/TLS termination, keeping private keys secure
- Integrating with AWS Shield for DDoS protection
- Operating from within your VPC's security controls
- Supporting health checks to ensure traffic only routes to healthy instances

The Application Load Balancer (ALB), in particular, adds an additional layer of security by operating at the application layer (Layer 7) of the OSI model.

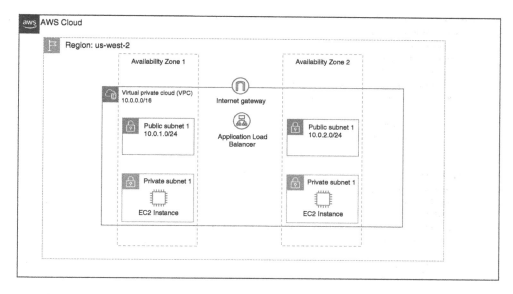

Figure 5.12: ALB infrastructure.

This allows it to understand and filter HTTP/HTTPS requests, providing more granular control over your application traffic. Let's enhance your infrastructure by adding an Application Load Balancer. You'll use CloudFormation to create all the necessary components. Once it's deployed, you'll have an infrastructure that looks like Figure 5.12.

The following code shows the CloudFormation template. You can get this from the GitHub repo at `https://github.com/8carroll/Securing-the-Cloud-with-Brandon-Carroll`, in the Chapter 5 folder. Look for the `ch5-elb-security.yml` file.

```
AWSTemplateFormatVersion: '2010-09-09'
Description: AWS Elastic Load Balancing Security with Auto Scaling Group
Parameters:
  LatestAmiId:
    Description: AMI for Instance (default is latest AmaLinux2)
    Type: 'AWS::SSM::Parameter::Value<AWS::EC2::Image::Id>'
    Default: '/aws/service/ami-amazon-linux-latest/amzn2-ami-hvm-x86_64-gp2

Resources:
  VPC:
    Type: AWS::EC2::VPC
    Properties:
      CidrBlock: 10.0.0.0/16
      EnableDnsSupport: true
      EnableDnsHostnames: true
      Tags:
        - Key: Name
          Value: ELB-Security-VPC
```

```yaml
PublicSubnet1:
  Type: AWS::EC2::Subnet
  Properties:
    VpcId: !Ref VPC
    CidrBlock: 10.0.1.0/24
    AvailabilityZone: !Select [ 0, !GetAZs "" ]
    MapPublicIpOnLaunch: true
    Tags:
      - Key: Name
        Value: PublicSubnet1

PublicSubnet2:
  Type: AWS::EC2::Subnet
  Properties:
    VpcId: !Ref VPC
    CidrBlock: 10.0.2.0/24
    AvailabilityZone: !Select [ 1, !GetAZs "" ]
    MapPublicIpOnLaunch: true
    Tags:
      - Key: Name
        Value: PublicSubnet2

InternetGateway:
  Type: AWS::EC2::InternetGateway
  Properties:
    Tags:
      - Key: Name
        Value: ELB-Security-IGW

AttachIGW:
  Type: AWS::EC2::VPCGatewayAttachment
  Properties:
    VpcId: !Ref VPC
    InternetGatewayId: !Ref InternetGateway

PublicRouteTable:
  Type: AWS::EC2::RouteTable
  Properties:
    VpcId: !Ref VPC
    Tags:
      - Key: Name
        Value: PublicRouteTable

PublicRoute:
  Type: AWS::EC2::Route
  Properties:
    RouteTableId: !Ref PublicRouteTable
    DestinationCidrBlock: 0.0.0.0/0
    GatewayId: !Ref InternetGateway

SubnetRouteTableAssoc1:
  Type: AWS::EC2::SubnetRouteTableAssociation
  Properties:
    SubnetId: !Ref PublicSubnet1
    RouteTableId: !Ref PublicRouteTable
```

```yaml
    SubnetRouteTableAssoc2:
      Type: AWS::EC2::SubnetRouteTableAssociation
      Properties:
        SubnetId: !Ref PublicSubnet2
        RouteTableId: !Ref PublicRouteTable

  SecurityGroupALB:
    Type: AWS::EC2::SecurityGroup
    Properties:
      GroupDescription: ALB Security Group
      VpcId: !Ref VPC
      SecurityGroupIngress:
        - IpProtocol: tcp
          FromPort: 80
          ToPort: 80
          CidrIp: 0.0.0.0/0
      SecurityGroupEgress:
        - IpProtocol: -1
          CidrIp: 0.0.0.0/0
      Tags:
        - Key: Name
          Value: ALB-SG

IAMRoleForSSM:
  Type: AWS::IAM::Role
  Properties:
    AssumeRolePolicyDocument:
      Version: "2012-10-17"
      Statement:
        - Effect: Allow
          Principal:
            Service: ec2.amazonaws.com
          Action: sts:AssumeRole
    ManagedPolicyArns:
      - arn:aws:iam::aws:policy/AmazonSSMManagedInstanceCore
    Path: /
    Tags:
      - Key: Name
        Value: SSMRole

InstanceProfileForSSM:
  Type: AWS::IAM::InstanceProfile
  Properties:
    Roles:
      - !Ref IAMRoleForSSM
    Path: /

ApplicationLoadBalancer:
  Type: AWS::ElasticLoadBalancingV2::LoadBalancer
  Properties:
    Name: ELB-Security-ALB
    Subnets:
      - !Ref PublicSubnet1
      - !Ref PublicSubnet2
```

```
      SecurityGroups:
        - !Ref SecurityGroupALB
      Scheme: internet-facing

  TargetGroup:
    Type: AWS::ElasticLoadBalancingV2::TargetGroup
    Properties:
      VpcId: !Ref VPC
      Protocol: HTTP
      Port: 80
      TargetType: instance
      HealthCheckPath: /
      HealthCheckIntervalSeconds: 30
      HealthCheckTimeoutSeconds: 5
      HealthyThresholdCount: 3
      UnhealthyThresholdCount: 3

  ALBListener:
    Type: AWS::ElasticLoadBalancingV2::Listener
    Properties:
      LoadBalancerArn: !Ref ApplicationLoadBalancer
      Protocol: HTTP
      Port: 80
      DefaultActions:
        - Type: forward
          TargetGroupArn: !Ref TargetGroup

  LaunchTemplate:
    Type: AWS::EC2::LaunchTemplate
    Properties:
      LaunchTemplateData:
        InstanceType: t2.micro
        ImageId: !Ref LatestAmiId
        SecurityGroupIds:
          - !Ref SecurityGroupALB
        IamInstanceProfile:
          Name: !Ref InstanceProfileForSSM
        UserData:
          Fn::Base64: !Sub |
            #!/bin/bash
            yum update -y
            yum install -y httpd
            systemctl start httpd
            systemctl enable httpd
            echo "<h1>Welcome to the Elastic Load Balancer Demo</h1>" >
/var/www/html/index.html

  AutoScalingGroup:
    Type: AWS::AutoScaling::AutoScalingGroup
    Properties:
      VPCZoneIdentifier:
        - !Ref PublicSubnet1
        - !Ref PublicSubnet2
      LaunchTemplate:
        LaunchTemplateId: !Ref LaunchTemplate
        Version: !GetAtt LaunchTemplate.LatestVersionNumber
```

```
      MinSize: 2
      MaxSize: 2
      DesiredCapacity: 2
      TargetGroupARNs:
        - !Ref TargetGroup
      Tags:
        - Key: Name
          Value: ELB-Demo-WebServer
          PropagateAtLaunch: true


# Output the ALB DNS Name
Outputs:
  ALBDNSName:
    Value: !GetAtt ApplicationLoadBalancer.DNSName
    Description: DNS Name of the Application Load Balancer
```

This template is a YAML file. Once you have that file, navigate to CloudFormation, load the template, and proceed once it is successfully deployed.

Follow these steps:

1. Save the provided CloudFormation template as `elb-security-stack.yaml`.

2. In the AWS Management Console, navigate to CloudFormation → Create Stack → Upload a Template File.

3. Upload the file and provide any required parameters. You'll find the values you need in Table 5.1, at the beginning of the chapter.

4. Once the stack creation is complete, note the Load Balancer DNS name from the Outputs section. This will serve as the public entry point for your application. You should be able to browse to this URL to confirm that the configuration is complete. If so, you should see Figure 5.13.

Default Security Posture

The security posture of this setup includes an ALB security group that initially allows all inbound HTTP (port 80) traffic from any IP range, and an EC2 instance security group that restricts inbound traffic to only what originates from the ALB's security group. Additionally, default health checks ensure that traffic is

Welcome to the Elastic Load Balancer Demo

Figure 5.13: ALB public-facing URL.

routed exclusively to healthy instances. While functional, this configuration needs some work to align with security best practices.

Securing the ALB involves enhancing its configuration to ensure it not only distributes traffic effectively but also protects your application and backend resources. This section takes a step-by-step approach to implement these security controls.

Here's what you'll do:

- Restrict inbound traffic to trusted sources.
- Enable HTTPS for encrypted communication.
- Implement AWS WAF to protect against web attacks.
- Enable access logging for auditing and monitoring.
- Leverage AWS Shield for DDoS protection.

As usual, you'll use the AWS CLI to do this. Let's go!

Restrict Inbound Traffic to Trusted Sources

Open access to port 80 (HTTP) is acceptable for testing, but not suitable for production environments. To secure your ALB, you need to update the security group to allow inbound traffic only from trusted IP ranges or CIDR blocks.

The aws ec2 authorize-security-group-ingress command requires the following parameters:

- --group-id: The ID of the security group to modify. In this case, it's the ALB security group sg-085cad5d162e3d8ea
- --protocol: The protocol for the rule; use TCP for HTTP traffic
- --port: The port to allow; for HTTP, this is 80
- --cidr: The trusted IP range in CIDR notation

Replace <TRUSTED-IP-RANGE> with your actual range. For a single IP address, append /32 to the address. For example, let's say that you are helping a developer build a new web app and they want to test the app live but not allow anyone else access. You can accomplish this by using their public IP address in the security group, denying all other traffic. The trusted IP range could also be a range of addresses owned by partners or customers that are granted exclusive access to this app.

Here's the command to update the existing ALB security group that was created with the CloudFormation template:

```
[cloudshell-user@ip-10-132-36-67 ~]$ aws ec2 authorize-security-group-ingress \
> --group-id sg-085cad5d162e3d8ea \
> --protocol tcp \
```

```
> --port 80 \
> --cidr 172.112.129.0/24

{
    "Return": true,
    "SecurityGroupRules": [
        {
            "SecurityGroupRuleId": "sgr-00c83a69d8f1afb28",
            "GroupId": "sg-085cad5d162e3d8ea",
            "GroupOwnerId": "387974667323",
            "IsEgress": false,
            "IpProtocol": "tcp",
            "FromPort": 80,
            "ToPort": 80,
            "CidrIpv4": "172.112.129.0/24",
            "SecurityGroupRuleArn": "arn:aws:ec2:us-west-
2:387974667323:security-group-rule/sgr-00c83a69d8f1afb28"
        }
    ]
}
(END)
```

You can find the security group ID by navigating to EC2 --> Load Balancers and then selecting the load balancer and the Security tab.

Command breakdown:

- --group-id: This is the security group ID for the ALB
- --protocol tcp: Restricts the rule to the TCP protocol used for HTTP
- --port 80: Specifies that only HTTP traffic will be allowed
- --cidr 172.112.129.0/24: Limits access to the IP range 203.0.113.0 to 203.0.113.255

Verifying the Rule

After running the command, confirm that the rule has been applied by checking the security group's inbound rules:

1. Open the AWS Management Console and navigate to EC2 → Security Groups.

2. Locate the security group in the list. It will look something like this: sg-085cad5d162e3d8ea.

3. Ensure that the new rule allows TCP traffic on port 80 from the IP address you specified. In my example, 203.0.113.0/24 appears under Inbound Rules.

This configuration ensures that only traffic from trusted IP ranges can access your ALB, adding an essential layer of security to your environment.

Enforcing HTTPS for Encrypted Communication

HTTP traffic is inherently insecure because it transmits data in plain text. To secure your ALB, you'll enforce HTTPS, ensuring that all communication between clients and the load balancer is encrypted. This involves adding an HTTPS listener to your ALB and configuring it to use an SSL/TLS certificate.

SSL/TLS certificates are used to encrypt data in transit, ensuring that communication between clients and servers remains private and secure. They verify the identity of a website or service, preventing attackers from impersonating trusted entities. When a browser or application connects to a server over HTTPS, the certificate enables secure encryption and authentication, protecting sensitive information from interception or tampering.

Since you don't have a certificate yet, you can use AWS Certificate Manager (ACM). ACM is a service that simplifies the provisioning, management, and renewal of SSL/TLS certificates. It eliminates the manual steps of creating, uploading, and renewing certificates for AWS services on your custom domains. The following example uses a custom domain that I own, that of gameonnetworks. com. You would replace this with a domain that you own, and the easiest way to obtain a domain in your AWS account and keep everything central is through the Route 53 service. To create the certificate, use the following command:

```
[cloudshell-user@ip-10-140-26-171 ~]$ aws acm request-certificate \
> --domain-name gameonnetworks.com \
> --validation-method DNS

{
    "CertificateArn": "arn:aws:acm:us-west-
2:387974667323:certificate/8aaef688-38e1-42b0-bb2f-b3a2e9fd4e9a"
}
[cloudshell-user@ip-10-140-26-171 ~]$
[cloudshell-user@ip-10-140-26-171 ~]$
```

Here's how that command breaks down:

- --domain-name gameonnetworks.com: Specifies the domain for which you're requesting the certificate. Do not use gameonnetworks.com, as that is the fictitious organization that I use for examples throughout this book. You must use a domain that you own and have control of the DNS records for.

- --validation-method DNS: Requires you to create a DNS record in your domain's DNS settings to validate ownership.

From the output, note the Certificate ARN and add it to Table 5.1.

The next step is to validate the DNS record. Using the certificate ARN, issue the following command, replacing the ARN with your own:

```
[cloudshell-user@ip-10-140-26-171 ~]$ aws acm describe-certificate --
certificate-arn arn:aws:acm:us-west-2:387974667323:certificate/8aaef688-38e1-42b0-
bb2f-b3a2e9fd4e9a
```

```
{
    "Certificate": {
        "CertificateArn": "arn:aws:acm:us-west-
2:387974667323:certificate/8aaef688-38e1-42b0-bb2f-b3a2e9fd4e9a",
        "CreatedAt": "2024-11-21T15:44:27.474000+00:00",
[cloudshell-user@ip-10-140-26-171 ~]$ aws acm describe-certificate --
certificate-arn arn:aws:acm:us-west-2:387974667323:certificate/8aaef688-38e1-42b0-
bb2f-b3a2e9fd4e9a
{
    "Certificate": {
        "CertificateArn": "arn:aws:acm:us-west-
2:387974667323:certificate/8aaef688-38e1-42b0-bb2f-b3a2e9fd4e9a",
        "DomainName": "gameonnetworks.com",
        "SubjectAlternativeNames": [
            "gameonnetworks.com"
        ],
        "DomainValidationOptions": [
            {
                "DomainName": "gameonnetworks.com",
                "ValidationDomain": "gameonnetworks.com",
                "ValidationStatus": "PENDING_VALIDATION",
                "ResourceRecord": {
                    "Name":
"_a86c0eff74b22e19c98796579225194d.gameonnetworks.com.",
                    "Type": "CNAME",
                    "Value": "_2508032b232c35090a9c214debef4124.zfyfvmchrl.
acm-validations.aws."
                },
                "ValidationMethod": "DNS"
            }
        ],
        "Subject": "CN=gameonnetworks.com",
        "Issuer": "Amazon",
        "CreatedAt": "2024-11-21T15:44:27.474000+00:00",
        "Status": "PENDING_VALIDATION",
        "KeyAlgorithm": "RSA-2048",
        "SignatureAlgorithm": "SHA256WITHRSA",
        "InUseBy": [],
        "Type": "AMAZON_ISSUED",
        "KeyUsages": [],
        "ExtendedKeyUsages": [],
        "RenewalEligibility": "INELIGIBLE",
        "Options": {
            "CertificateTransparencyLoggingPreference": "ENABLED"
:
```

In the resource record portion of this output, you will find the name and value for the CNAME record. At this point, you need to take that information and create a CNAME record with your DNS provider. I am using Amazon Route53. Amazon Route 53 is a scalable and highly available Domain Name System (DNS) web service designed to route end users to applications running in AWS or on-premises. It manages domain registration, DNS records, and health checks, allowing you to direct traffic based on policies such as latency, geolocation, or

Figure 5.14: Creating a CNAME record.

failover. Route 53 integrates seamlessly with other AWS services. It's perfect for managing DNS for cloud-based infrastructure.

Here's how to create the CNAME in Route 53:

1. Navigate to Route 53 in the AWS Console.

2. Select Hosted Zones.

3. Select your domain. In this case, I chose gameonnetworks.com. If you don't own a domain, you can get your own with the Amazon Route 53 service. You need one for these steps.

4. Click the Create Record button. You can see this process in Figure 5.14.

Once you are on the page to create the record, follow these steps, as shown in Figure 5.15:

1. Enter the record name that you copied from this output.

2. Using the drop-down, select CNAME.

3. Enter the value of the CNAME that you copied from this output.

4. Click the Create Record button.

At this point, you now wait for validation to complete. You can reissue the describe-certificate command to see when the validation is successful. When it is, you can continue. In the following output, you can see that my certificate has successfully been issued.

```
[cloudshell-user@ip-10-140-26-171 ~]$ aws acm describe-certificate
--certificate-arn arn:aws:acm:us-west-2:387974667323:certificate/8aaef688-38e1-
42b0-bb2f-b3a2e9fd4e9a
{
    "Certificate": {
```

        "CertificateArn": "arn:aws:acm:us-west-
2:387974667323:certificate/8aaef688-38e1-42b0-bb2f-b3a2e9fd4e9a",
        "DomainName": "gameonnetworks.com",
        "SubjectAlternativeNames": [
            "gameonnetworks.com"
        ],
        "DomainValidationOptions": [
            {
                "DomainName": "gameonnetworks.com",
                "ValidationDomain": "gameonnetworks.com",
                "ValidationStatus": "SUCCESS",
                "ResourceRecord": {
                    "Name":
"_a86c0eff74b22e19c98796579225194d.gameonnetworks.com.",
                    "Type": "CNAME",
                    "Value": "_2508032b232c35090a9c214debef4124.zfyfvmchrl.
acm-validations.aws."
                },
                "ValidationMethod": "DNS"
            }
        ],
        "Serial": "09:69:2d:3f:5a:dd:a6:a4:d4:92:d3:e0:82:ea:40:87",
        "Subject": "CN=gameonnetworks.com",
        "Issuer": "Amazon",
        "CreatedAt": "2024-11-21T15:44:27.474000+00:00",
        "IssuedAt": "2024-11-21T16:16:49.678000+00:00",
        "Status": "ISSUED",
        "NotBefore": "2024-11-21T00:00:00+00:00",
        "NotAfter": "2025-12-20T23:59:59+00:00",
        "KeyAlgorithm": "RSA-2048",
        "SignatureAlgorithm": "SHA256WITHRSA",
        "InUseBy": [],
        "Type": "AMAZON_ISSUED",
        "KeyUsages": [
:

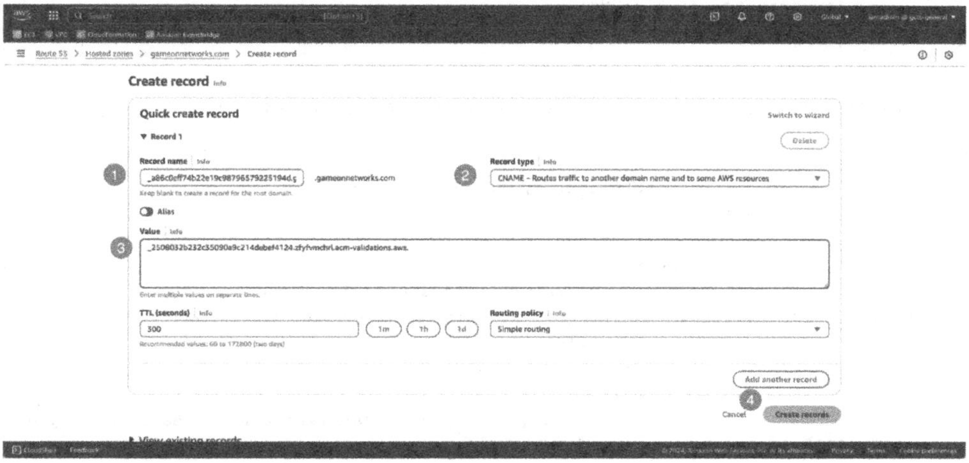

Figure 5.15: Entering the CNAME record information.

After the certificate status is ISSUED, you need to attach it to your ALB. The aws elbv2 create-listener command requires the following:

- --load-balancer-arn: The ARN of your ALB
- --protocol: Set this to HTTPS for encrypted traffic
- --port: The port to accept HTTPS traffic, typically 443
- --certificates: The ARN of the SSL/TLS certificate provisioned in AWS Certificate Manager (ACM)
- --default-actions: The action to perform when a request matches this listener. In this case, traffic is forwarded to the target group.

You'll need to replace the values in my output with your own values. Here's the command to add an HTTPS listener to your ALB:

```
[cloudshell-user@ip-10-140-26-171 ~]$ aws elbv2 create-listener \
>    --load-balancer-arn arn:aws:elasticloadbalancing:us-west-
2:387974667323:loadbalancer/app/ELB-Security-ALB/9f74e0e9b380c825 \
>    --protocol HTTPS \
>    --port 443 \
>    --certificates CertificateArn=arn:aws:acm:us-west-2:387974667323:certificate/
8aaef688-38e1-42b0-bb2f-b3a2e9fd4e9a \
>    --default-actions
Type=forward,TargetGroupArn=arn:aws:elasticloadbalancing:us-west-2:387974667323:
targetgroup/gpt7-TargetG-3IWNZYGZAXNJ/962ac76b25490ca8
{
    "Listeners": [
        {
            "ListenerArn": "arn:aws:elasticloadbalancing:us-west-
2:387974667323:listener/app/ELB-Security-ALB/9f74e0e9b380c825/
c5454c9fbbc14eb9",
            "LoadBalancerArn": "arn:aws:elasticloadbalancing:us-
west-2:387974667323:loadbalancer/app/ELB-Security-ALB/9f74e0e9b380c825",
            "Port": 443,
            "Protocol": "HTTPS",
            "Certificates": [
                {
                    "CertificateArn": "arn:aws:acm:us-west-
2:387974667323:certificate/8aaef688-38e1-42b0-bb2f-b3a2e9fd4e9a"
                }
            ],
            "SslPolicy": "ELBSecurityPolicy-2016-08",
            "DefaultActions": [
                {
                    "Type": "forward",
                    "TargetGroupArn": "arn:aws:elasticloadbalancing:us-
west-2:387974667323:targetgroup/gpt7-TargetG-3IWNZYGZAXNJ/962ac76b25490ca8",
                    "ForwardConfig": {
                        "TargetGroups": [
                            {
                                "TargetGroupArn": "arn:aws:elasticloadbalancing:us-
west-2:387974667323:targetgroup/gpt7-TargetG-3IWNZYGZAXNJ/962ac76b25490ca8",
                                "Weight": 1
                            }
```

```
                    ],
                    "TargetGroupStickinessConfig": {
                        "Enabled": false
                    }
                }
            ]
        }
    ]
}
(END)
```

One final step you need to take is to add a rule to your existing ALB security group that allows the listener on port 443. Use the following command to do this.

```
[cloudshell-user@ip-10-140-26-171 ~]$   aws ec2 authorize-security-group-ingress \
>    --group-id sg-085cad5d162e3d8ea \
>    --protocol tcp \
>    --port 443 \
>    --cidr 172.112.129.0/24
{
    "Return": true,
    "SecurityGroupRules": [
        {
            "SecurityGroupRuleId": "sgr-08b323895c9968268",
            "GroupId": "sg-085cad5d162e3d8ea",
            "GroupOwnerId": "387974667323",
            "IsEgress": false,
            "IpProtocol": "tcp",
            "FromPort": 443,
            "ToPort": 443,
            "CidrIpv4": "172.112.129.0/24",
            "SecurityGroupRuleArn": "arn:aws:ec2:us-west-
2:387974667323:security-group-rule/sgr-08b323895c9968268"
        }
    ]
}
(END)
```

With that completed, you can now test. The easiest way to do this without making any other modifications to DNS is to get the DNS name from the output of your CloudFormation template. You will have to accept the certificate since the certificate name is for your domain and the load balancer domain name is different; however, since you are testing, this is not an issue. To get the DNS name for the load balancer, follow these steps:

1. Navigate to EC2 in the AWS Console.

2. Select Load Balancers.

3. Select your load balancer.

4. Copy the domain name.

Figure 5.16: Load balancer URL.

This process can be seen in Figure 5.16.

Adding AWS WAF for Web Application Protection

While securing the ALB itself is important, protecting your applications from common web-based attacks such as SQL injection and cross-site scripting (XSS) is equally important. This is where AWS Web Application Firewall (WAF) comes into play.

AWS WAF is a managed web application firewall that allows you to create custom rules or leverage AWS Managed Rules to block malicious traffic before it reaches your application. By integrating WAF with your ALB, you add another layer of protection to your infrastructure.

Let's add WAF to your ALB. To do this, you first need to create a WebACL. The WebACL acts as a set of rules that determine which requests are allowed or blocked. You can use AWS Managed Rules to protect against common threats. This is a quick and easy way to implement WAF without having to write each rule on your own. To do this, use the following command:

```
[cloudshell-user@ip-10-140-26-171 ~]$ aws wafv2 create-web-acl \
>     --name ALBSecurityWebACL \
>     --scope REGIONAL \
>     --default-action Allow={} \
>     --visibility-config
SampledRequestsEnabled=true,CloudWatchMetricsEnabled=true,MetricName=TestWebAcl
Metrics \
>     --rules '[{
>     "Name": "AWS-AWSManagedRulesCommonRuleSet",
>     "Priority": 0,
>     "Statement": {
>       "ManagedRuleGroupStatement": {
>         "VendorName": "AWS",
>         "Name": "AWSManagedRulesCommonRuleSet",
```

```
>          "RuleActionOverrides":
>            {
>              "ActionToUse": {
>                "Count": {}
>              },
>              "Name": "NoUserAgent_HEADER"
>            }
>          ],
>          "ExcludedRules": []
>        }
>      },
>      "OverrideAction": {
>        "None": {}
>      },
>      "VisibilityConfig": {
>        "SampledRequestsEnabled": true,
>        "CloudWatchMetricsEnabled": true,
>        "MetricName": "AWS-AWSManagedRulesCommonRuleSet"
>      }
> }
>      ]' \
>      --region us-west-2

{
    "Summary": {
        "Name": "ALBSecurityWebACL",
        "Id": "26355319-25f8-47e7-900a-428811bd848b",
        "Description": "",
        "LockToken": "0f7ca968-782b-4393-8beb-46ee6bd97a51",
        "ARN": "arn:aws:wafv2:us-west-2:387974667323:regional/webacl/
ALBSecurityWebACL/26355319-25f8-47e7-900a-428811bd848b"
    }
}
```

The aws wafv2 create-web-acl command that you used previously requires several key parameters:

- --name: The name of your WebACL (e.g., ALBSecurityWebACL)

- --scope: Indicates whether the WebACL is regional (for ALBs) or global (for CloudFront)

- --default-action: Specifies the action to take when no rules match (Allow or Block)

- --rules: Defines the rules to include in your WebACL. Here, AWSManagedRulesCommonRuleSet is used to protect against common vulnerabilities

- --visibility-config: Enables logging and CloudWatch metrics for monitoring

Additionally, in the output, note the Web ACL ARN and add it to Table 5.1.

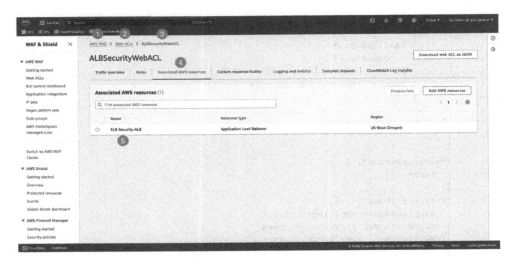

Figure 5.17: Verifying the ALB.

With your WebACL created, you now need to associate it with your ALB using the aws wafv2 associate-web-acl command. For this command, you'll need the ARN of the load balancer and the ARN of the WebACL from the previous output.

```
[cloudshell-user@ip-10-140-26-171 ~]$ aws wafv2 associate-web-acl \
>     --web-acl-arn arn:aws:wafv2:us-west-2:387974667323:regional/webacl/
ALBSecurityWebACL/26355319-25f8-47e7-900a-428811bd848b \
>     --resource-arn arn:aws:elasticloadbalancing:us-west-2:387974667323:
loadbalancer/app/ELB-Security-ALB/9f74e0e9b380c825
[cloudshell-user@ip-10-140-26-171 ~]$
```

You need to ensure that the WebACL is active. To do this, follow these steps:

1. Open the AWS WAF Console.
2. Navigate to Web ACLs.
3. Select your Web ACL.
4. Select the Associated AWS Resources tab.
5. Confirm the associated ALB is listed under Resources.

This process is shown in Figure 5.17.

Before this chapter wraps up, it introduces AWS Network Firewall and shows you how to set up a basic firewall inside your VPC.

Adding AWS Network Firewall to Your VPC

AWS Network Firewall is a managed security service that inspects network traffic using stateful filtering and intrusion prevention. While your security groups and network ACLs provide solid protection, Network Firewall allows you to go deeper by analyzing and filtering traffic at the packet level.

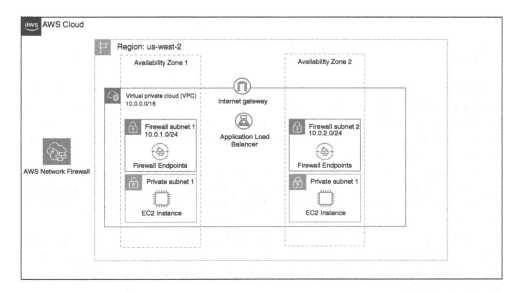

Figure 5.18: AWS network firewall architecture.

You'll create a simple firewall with a single firewall endpoint inside the public subnet. Right now, it will allow all traffic, but Chapter 12 builds on this by adding security rules to detect and block threats using GitOps practices. Figure 5.18 shows what the architecture will look like with AWS Network Firewall.

To get started, you need to create the firewall policy:

```
[cloudshell-user@ip-10-138-23-228 ~]$ aws network-firewall create-firewall-policy \
>     --firewall-policy-name AllowAllTrafficPolicy \
>     --firewall-policy '{
>         "StatelessRuleGroupReferences": [],
>         "StatefulRuleGroupReferences": [],
>         "StatelessDefaultActions": ["aws:pass"],
>         "StatelessFragmentDefaultActions": ["aws:pass"]
>     }' \
>     --region us-west-2
{
    "UpdateToken": "c6a9bf72-2c09-4d7f-aba7-fa2d8ac01610",
    "FirewallPolicyResponse": {
        "FirewallPolicyName": "AllowAllTrafficPolicy",
        "FirewallPolicyArn": "arn:aws:network-firewall:us-west-
2:387974667323:firewall-policy/AllowAllTrafficPolicy",
        "FirewallPolicyId": "6ffa6132-9653-4fbf-ad2a-b7c0ee788097",
        "FirewallPolicyStatus": "ACTIVE",
        "ConsumedStatelessRuleCapacity": 0,
        "ConsumedStatefulRuleCapacity": 0,
        "EncryptionConfiguration": {
            "KeyId": "AWS_OWNED_KMS_KEY",
            "Type": "AWS_OWNED_KMS_KEY"
        },
```

```
        "LastModifiedTime": "2025-02-03T02:44:47.389000+00:00"
    }
}
(END)
```

The `StatelessDefaultActions` parameter defines how AWS Network Firewall handles packets that don't match any stateless rules. Setting it to `aws:pass` allows all unmatched traffic to pass, while other options include `aws:drop` to block traffic and `aws:forward_to_sfe` to send packets to the stateful inspection engine for further evaluation.

Similarly, `StatelessFragmentDefaultActions` applies to fragmented packets that don't match any rules, with `aws:pass` permitting them to pass through. These defaults ensure that traffic is allowed, dropped, or processed further based on the security requirements of your network.

Next, the firewall needs to be associated with your VPC and at least one subnet where it will inspect traffic. Since this is a distributed firewall, it doesn't act like a traditional network appliance sitting in one place. It integrates directly into your VPC routing.

Run the following command to create the firewall:

```
[cloudshell-user@ip-10-138-23-228 ~]$ aws network-firewall create-firewall \
>     --firewall-name SecureInfraFirewall \
>     --firewall-policy-arn arn:aws:network-firewall:us-west-
2:387974667323:firewall-policy/AllowAllTrafficPolicy \
>     --vpc-id vpc-0488a892d43711307 \
>     --subnet-mappings SubnetId=subnet-064cd6599825d706d \
>     --region us-west-2
{
    "Firewall": {
        "FirewallName": "SecureInfraFirewall",
        "FirewallArn": "arn:aws:network-firewall:us-west-2:387974667323:firewall/
SecureInfraFirewall",
        "FirewallPolicyArn": "arn:aws:network-firewall:us-west-
2:387974667323:firewall-policy/AllowAllTrafficPolicy",
        "VpcId": "vpc-0488a892d43711307",
        "SubnetMappings": [
            {
                "SubnetId": "subnet-064cd6599825d706d",
                "IPAddressType": "IPV4"
            }
        ],
        "DeleteProtection": false,
        "SubnetChangeProtection": false,
        "FirewallPolicyChangeProtection": false,
        "FirewallId": "a9e387d0-6d5e-4f95-a175-5689bdf0f4d0",
        "EncryptionConfiguration": {
            "KeyId": "AWS_OWNED_KMS_KEY",
            "Type": "AWS_OWNED_KMS_KEY"
        }
    },
    "FirewallStatus": {
```

```
        "Status": "PROVISIONING",
        "ConfigurationSyncStateSummary": "PENDING"
    }
}
(END)
```

The output confirms that the AWS Network Firewall named SecureInfraFirewall has been successfully created and is currently in the provisioning state. The firewall is associated with the VPC (vpc-0488a892d43711307) and deployed in a subnet (subnet-064cd6599825d706d). It references the firewall policy (AllowAllTrafficPolicy) and is using an AWS-owned KMS key for encryption. The "FirewallStatus": "PROVISIONING" indicates that AWS is still setting up the firewall, and "ConfigurationSyncStateSummary": "PENDING" means the firewall policy and configurations are not yet fully applied. Once provisioning is complete, the status should change to "READY", indicating that the firewall is fully operational.

note When running this command in your own environment, replace the VPC ID, subnet ID, and firewall policy ARN with values specific to your AWS account.

After creating the firewall, you need to verify that it is fully provisioned before moving forward. AWS Network Firewall takes some time to set up, and while it starts in a provisioning state, it will eventually become active. To check its status, you can run the following command:

```
[cloudshell-user@ip-10-138-23-228 ~]$ aws network-firewall describe-firewall \
>    --firewall-name SecureInfraFirewall \
>    --region us-west-2

{
    "UpdateToken": "4c1b38d5-6fda-48cb-9cd6-91cc9b2a921d",
    "Firewall": {
        "FirewallName": "SecureInfraFirewall",
        "FirewallArn": "arn:aws:network-firewall:us-west-2:387974667323:firewall/
SecureInfraFirewall",
        "FirewallPolicyArn": "arn:aws:network-firewall:us-west-
2:387974667323:firewall-policy/AllowAllTrafficPolicy",
        "VpcId": "vpc-0488a892d43711307",
        "SubnetMappings": [
            {
                "SubnetId": "subnet-064cd6599825d706d",
                "IPAddressType": "IPV4"
            }
        ],
        "DeleteProtection": false,
        "SubnetChangeProtection": false,
        "FirewallPolicyChangeProtection": false,
        "FirewallId": "a9e387d0-6d5e-4f95-a175-5689bdf0f4d0",
        "Tags": [],
        "EncryptionConfiguration": {
```

```
                    "KeyId": "AWS_OWNED_KMS_KEY",
                    "Type": "AWS_OWNED_KMS_KEY"
                }
            },
            "FirewallStatus": {
                "Status": "PROVISIONING",
                "ConfigurationSyncStateSummary": "IN_SYNC",
                "SyncStates": {
                    "us-west-2b": {
                        "Attachment": {
                            "SubnetId": "subnet-064cd6599825d706d",
                            "EndpointId": "vpce-09607491bb0485abc",
                            "Status": "CREATING"
                        },
                        "Config": {
                            "arn:aws:network-firewall:us-west-2:387974667323:firewall-
policy/AllowAllTrafficPolicy": {
                                "SyncStatus": "IN_SYNC",
                                "UpdateToken": "c6a9bf72-2c09-4d7f-aba7-fa2d8ac01610"
                            }
                        }
                    }
                }
            }
        }
    }
(END)
```

The response will include a FirewallStatus field. Once the status changes from "PROVISIONING" to "READY", the firewall is fully operational. At this point, it exists inside your VPC, but traffic is not yet being inspected. By default, AWS Network Firewall does not automatically handle traffic. You need to update the VPC route tables to direct relevant traffic through the firewall. In the output, note the endpoint ID because you will need it to adjust the routing tables.

Since this firewall is meant to inspect Internet-bound traffic, you can modify the route table associated with the subnet. Updating the default route ensures that all outbound traffic flows through the firewall before reaching the Internet. The following command replaces the existing default route with one that sends traffic through the firewall:

```
[cloudshell-user@ip-10-134-93-86 ~]$     aws ec2 replace-route \
>     --route-table-id rtb-0619d26fd5f74b369 \
>     --destination-cidr-block 0.0.0.0/0 \
>     --vpc-endpoint-id vpce-09607491bb0485abc \
>     --region us-west-2
[cloudshell-user@ip-10-134-93-86 ~]$
```

Be sure to replace the values with the ones relevant to your own account.

With that, your Network Firewall is now handling traffic from your private subnet to the Internet. You will come back and add some rules in a later chapter. For now, you have successfully deployed AWS Network Firewall.

With these infrastructure security controls in place, it's a good time to do a little clean up.

Cleaning Up Your AWS Resources

Before you move on, it's important that you remove all the resources you created to avoid any lingering costs. Follow these steps to clean up your environment.

Delete CloudFormation Stacks

If you used CloudFormation to deploy any part of this lab (such as launching your EC2 instances, ALB, and other networking components), start by deleting the stack. You can do this from the AWS Console by navigating to CloudFormation, selecting your stack, and choosing Delete. Alternatively, run the following CLI command:

```
aws cloudformation delete-stack --stack-name <your-stack-name>
```

Deleting the stack will automatically remove all resources defined in the template.

Terminate EC2 Instances

Next, make sure to terminate any running EC2 instances. In the EC2 dashboard, select the instances created for this lab and choose Terminate. This prevents any compute charges from accumulating.

Delete NAT Gateway and Release the Elastic IP

First, delete the NAT Gateway using the AWS CLI or Console. Note that NAT Gateway deletion might take a few minutes to complete.

Once the NAT Gateway is deleted, release the associated Elastic IP to ensure you aren't billed for unused public IP addresses.

For example, using the CLI, you can run the following:

```
aws ec2 delete-nat-gateway --nat-gateway-id <nat-gateway-id>
aws ec2 release-address --allocation-id <allocation-id>
```

Detach and Delete the Internet Gateway (IGW)

If you created a custom IGW, first detach it from your VPC:

```
aws ec2 detach-internet-gateway --internet-gateway-id <igw-id> --vpc-id <vpc-id>
```

Then, delete the IGW:

```
aws ec2 delete-internet-gateway --internet-gateway-id <igw-id>
```

Remove Custom Route Tables and Associations

Identify and delete any custom route tables you created. If the route tables are still associated with subnets, disassociate them first using the AWS Console or CLI, then delete them:

```
aws ec2 delete-route-table --route-table-id <route-table-id>
```

Delete Subnets

With the route tables removed, you can now delete the subnets you created:

```
aws ec2 delete-subnet --subnet-id <subnet-id>
```

Delete the Custom VPC

Finally, delete the VPC you created once all associated resources (subnets, route tables, IGW, etc.) have been removed:

```
aws ec2 delete-vpc --vpc-id <vpc-id>
```

Remove Security Groups and Network ACLs

If you created any custom security groups or network ACLs (NACLs) specifically for this lab, make sure to delete them if they are no longer attached to any resources.

Delete the Firewall

Run the following command to delete your firewall. Replace <your-firewall-arn> with the ARN of your firewall (which was recorded when you created it):

```
aws network-firewall delete-firewall --firewall-arn <your-firewall-
arn> --region us-west-2
```

Delete the Firewall Policy

Next, delete the firewall policy using its ARN. Replace <your-firewall-policy-arn> with your policy ARN:

```
aws network-firewall delete-firewall-policy --firewall-policy-arn <your-firewall-
policy-arn> --region us-west-2
```

Restore the Route Table Modifications

If you modified your VPC route tables to direct traffic through the firewall, be sure to update or remove those custom routes to restore your previous routing configuration.

> **note** Double-check that all firewall-related resources are removed to prevent any ongoing charges.

Verify with the Resource Tracker

Refer back to Table 5.1 to verify that every resource, identified by its ID or ARN, has been removed. This helps ensure that nothing is overlooked.

By following these steps, you'll ensure that all the resources are properly cleaned up, and you won't incur any unnecessary charges.

Conclusion

This chapter explored the main components of infrastructure protection on AWS, focusing on the principles and best practices required to build a secure cloud network. It started by creating a secure Virtual Private Cloud (VPC) with isolated subnets and advanced routing configurations, ensuring proper segmentation between public and private resources. From there, you implemented security groups and network access control lists (NACLs) to enforce granular access controls at the instance and subnet levels. To enhance functionality and resilience, you added an Application Load Balancer (ALB) with optimized security configurations, integrating AWS WAF for advanced threat protection.

Throughout these exercises, I emphasized the importance of adhering to security best practices, such as the principle of least privilege, stateful versus stateless rules, and the proper application of defense-in-depth strategies. By testing configurations and validating connectivity, you can ensure that the infrastructure functions as intended while maintaining robust protection against unauthorized access.

The next chapter builds on this foundation by diving into threat detection and management on AWS. You'll learn how to identify, monitor, and mitigate potential threats using AWS-specific tools and services, enabling proactive defense strategies. This progression will solidify your ability to manage security across the entire lifecycle of your AWS resources, from infrastructure to operations.

References

Amazon Web Services, "AWS Global Network," https://aws.amazon.com/about-aws/global-infrastructure

Amazon Web Services, "Amazon VPC," https://aws.amazon.com/vpc/

Amazon Web Services, "AWS WAF," https://aws.amazon.com/waf/

Amazon Web Services, "AWS Network Firewall," https://aws.amazon.com/network-firewall/

Threat Detection and Management on AWS

*"There's no silver bullet solution with cybersecurity;
a layered defense is the only viable option."*

—James Scott

In cloud computing, threats are as dynamic as the technology itself. Just when you think you've locked down every possible vulnerability, a new attack vector emerges. This chapter looks at tools and services that help you stay one step ahead. You learn how to detect, analyze, and neutralize potential security risks in your AWS environment. With threat detection, you're not just waiting, you're constantly scanning, watching, and learning the subtle patterns that might signal something's not right. AWS provides you with a powerful tool kit to do exactly that. This chapter digs into how AWS services like GuardDuty, Security Hub, and CloudTrail work together to create a comprehensive threat-management strategy. By the end of this chapter, you'll understand how to build a proactive security approach that doesn't just react to threats but anticipates and prevents them before they can cause damage. Let's get started.

Introduction to Threat Detection

In the previous chapters, you built a robust security foundation. From understanding the CIA triad in Chapter 2 to implementing identity management in Chapter 3 and infrastructure protection in Chapter 5, you've systematically constructed layers of defense. Now it's time to transform those foundational principles into an active threat-detection strategy.

The Cloud Threat Landscape

Cloud security isn't a static environment: it's a dynamic, continuously shifting environment. The threat landscape is transforming at an unprecedented pace that continues to increase in complexity. As cloud architectures become more intricate, potential attack surfaces expand exponentially. Threat actors are also becoming more sophisticated. Cybercriminals are leveraging advanced technologies like AI and machine learning to develop more nuanced attack strategies. And the faster organizations migrate to the cloud, the more potential vulnerabilities emerge. The bottom line is that things move quickly.

AWS-Specific Threat Vectors

Much of what we face in cloud security is common between vendors and even applicable for cloud and on-prem environments. Still, AWS environments face some unique challenges that require specialized detection strategies.

Threat detection in AWS presents unique challenges that require a sophisticated and adaptive approach. The rapid scale and velocity of cloud environments mean that resources can be created and destroyed in minutes, demanding continuous active monitoring. This complexity is further amplified by the distributed architecture of AWS, where tracking potential threats across multiple services and regions requires advanced tooling and strategic oversight. At the heart of these challenges lies the nuanced shared responsibility model, which demands a clear understanding of where AWS's security responsibilities end and where your organizations begin. The key is not to strive for perfection because you'll never get there; rather, you need to develop a threat-detection strategy focused on three components:

- Gaining comprehensive visibility
- Enabling fast and decisive response mechanisms
- Cultivating a mindset of continuous learning and adaptation

If you embrace these principles, you can effectively navigate threat detection with AWS.

Diving into Threat-Detection Services with Amazon GuardDuty

GuardDuty is AWS's intelligent threat-detection service that continuously monitors your AWS environment for malicious activity. This section walks through a hands-on configuration that demonstrates its power.

Enabling GuardDuty is generally low risk and won't disrupt your existing infrastructure. The service operates passively, analyzing logs and network traffic without impacting performance. Check the GuardDuty pricing page at https://aws.amazon.com/guardduty/pricing/ for details on how Amazon bills for this service.

In addition to billing, here are a few additional items to be aware of:

- *False positives:* GuardDuty may generate some security findings that aren't actual threats.
- *Continuous monitoring:* It provides ongoing threat detection, so you'll want to set up proper alert mechanisms.
- *Configuration flexibility:* You can customize detection criteria to reduce unnecessary alerts.

Imagine a typical AWS environment where an EC2 instance unexpectedly starts communicating with a known malicious IP address associated with a botnet. In the past, this might have gone unnoticed until significant damage occurred. With GuardDuty and automated response mechanisms, however, you can create a proactive defense strategy.

First, you'll enable GuardDuty for the current region you are in (us-west-2) using the AWS CLI. You'll need your account ID for this. It's recommended that you enable GuardDuty in each region where you are operating workloads. Also, before you get started in this chapter, be sure to grab all the commands from my GitHub repo at https://github.com/8carroll/Securing-the-Cloud-with-Brandon-Carroll. Find the chapter that corresponds to this one and you'll find all the resources there.

All of the examples in this book are from the perspective of me typing them into my terminal or CloudShell. You will need to make some adjustments to match your environments with your account ID and your ARNs and resource IDs.

```
[cloudshell-user@ip-10-136-117-167 ~]$ aws guardduty enable-organization-admin-
account --admin-account-id 387974667323
[cloudshell-user@ip-10-136-117-167 ~]$
```

When you enable GuardDuty at the organizational level, it automatically sets up monitoring across all accounts in your AWS organization.

You've probably heard the cliche that one size fits all. That's not the case in cloud security: just like every organization is unique, so is its AWS environment. Out-of-the-box threat detection is a great starting point, but it's like using a generic alarm system in a complex, custom-built facility. While it might catch broad threats, it'll probably miss the nuanced risks specific to your infrastructure.

For this reason, custom threat-detection rules in GuardDuty give you a way of fine-tuning security monitoring to match your environment's exact characteristics and risk profile.

Why does this matter? Because your network architecture, application design, typical user behaviors, and compliance requirements create a unique landscape that generic threat detection might overlook. A financial institution's AWS environment will look dramatically different from a healthcare provider's or a tech startup's, and its threat-detection systems should reflect those differences. This section looks at how to create a custom rule.

First, get your Detector ID with the following command:

```
[cloudshell-user@ip-10-136-117-167 ~]$ aws guardduty list-detectors
{
    "DetectorIds": [
        "24c9ba318e0b9a9c48065c18cf0a9790"
    ]
}
[cloudshell-user@ip-10-136-117-167 ~]$
```

Note the DetectorID since you will need it later.

Next, create an S3 bucket to store the threat list. The threat list is a text file that contains CIDR addresses or IP addresses that your organization considers to be a threat. You can create the bucket with the following command:

```
[cloudshell-user@ip-10-136-117-167 ~]$ aws s3 mb s3://your-threat-intel-bucket-
${RANDOM}
\make_bucket: your-threat-intel-bucket-789
[cloudshell-user@ip-10-136-117-167 ~]$
```

Next, create a text file with those addresses. There are a few ways to do this, but this example uses the AWS CLI since it's fun. First, echo the two addresses into the threat-list.txt file.

```
[cloudshell-user@ip-10-136-117-167 ~]$ echo "192.168.1.100\n10.0.0.1" > threat-
list.txt
```

```
Next, copy the list to an S3 bucket.
[cloudshell-user@ip-10-136-117-167 ~]$ aws s3 cp threat-list.txt s3://your-
threat-intel-bucket-789/threat-list.txt
upload: ./threat-list.txt to s3://your-threat-intel-bucket-789/threat-list.txt
[cloudshell-user@ip-10-136-117-167 ~]$
```

The first command creates a file with two addresses in it. The second command uploads that file to the S3 bucket you created. Next, you will create a custom threat intel set using the following command:

```
[cloudshell-user@ip-10-136-117-167 ~]$ aws guardduty create-threat-intel-set \
>       --detector-id 24c9ba318e0b9a9c48065c18cf0a9790 \
>       --format TXT \
```

```
>      --location https://s3.amazonaws.com/your-threat-intel-bucket-789/threat-
list.txt \
>      --name "Custom IP Threat List" \
>      --activate
{
    "ThreatIntelSetId": "64c9ba42caf66e661ea39b19a0b0693c"
}
[cloudshell-user@ip-10-136-117-167 ~]$
```

note GuardDuty comes with built-in threat intelligence feeds that are automatically maintained and updated by AWS. These built-in feeds include known malicious IP addresses, domains, and other threat indicators that AWS continuously monitors and updates.

Now that you have your custom threat intel set configured, verify that it's working and explore how to manage findings. First, check the status of your threat intel set:

```
[cloudshell-user@ip-10-144-121-189 ~]$ aws guardduty list-threat-intel-sets --
detector-id 24c9ba318e0b9a9c48065c18cf0a9790
{
    "ThreatIntelSetIds": [
        "64c9ba42caf66e661ea39b19a0b0693c"
    ]
}
[cloudshell-user@ip-10-144-121-189 ~]$
```

Before you dive into managing findings, you need to generate some test data to work with. GuardDuty provides a built-in mechanism to create sample findings, which is invaluable for testing your response procedures and automation workflows.

```
[cloudshell-user@ip-10-144-121-189 ~]$ aws guardduty create-sample-findings \
>      --detector-id 24c9ba318e0b9a9c48065c18cf0a9790 \
>      --finding-types Recon:EC2/PortProbeUnprotectedPort
[cloudshell-user@ip-10-144-121-189 ~]$
```

This command simulates a port probe detection on an unprotected EC2 instance. The finding will be marked with "[SAMPLE]" to distinguish it from real threats. Now that you have some data to work with, you can examine your findings:

```
[cloudshell-user@ip-10-144-121-189 ~]$ aws guardduty list-findings --detector-
id 24c9ba318e0b9a9c48065c18cf0a9790
{
    "FindingIds": [
        "73f70904b0494d1a9aeb1c32e1d2d980"
    ]
}
[cloudshell-user@ip-10-144-121-189 ~]$
```

Managing GuardDuty Findings

Each GuardDuty finding contains detailed information about the potential security threat. Let's break down the anatomy of a finding. The finding severity levels are as follows:

- *High (7.0–8.9):* Indicates serious security issues requiring immediate attention
- *Medium (4.0–6.9):* Potential security issues that should be investigated
- *Low (1.0–3.9):* Suspicious but not immediately threatening activities

To get detailed information about a specific finding, use the following command:

```
[cloudshell-user@ip-10-144-121-189 ~]$ aws guardduty get-findings \
>     --detector-id 24c9ba318e0b9a9c48065c18cf0a9790 \
>     --finding-ids "73f70904b0494d1a9aeb1c32e1d2d980"
{
    "Findings": [
        {
            "AccountId": "387974667323",
            "Arn": "arn:aws:guardduty:us-west-
2:387974667323:detector/24c9ba318e0b9a9c48065c18cf0a9790/finding/73f70904b0494d
1a9aeb1c32e1d2d980",
            "CreatedAt": "2024-11-28T22:16:46.643Z",
            "Description": "An EC2 instance has an unprotected port which is
being probed by a known malicious host.",
            "Id": "73f70904b0494d1a9aeb1c32e1d2d980",
            "Partition": "aws",
            "Region": "us-west-2",
            "Resource": {
                "InstanceDetails": {
                    "AvailabilityZone": "generated-az-1a",
                    "IamInstanceProfile": {
                        "Arn":
"arn:aws:iam::387974667323:example/instance/profile",
                        "Id": "GeneratedFindingInstanceProfileId"
                    },
                    "ImageDescription":
"GeneratedFindingInstanceImageDescription",
                    "ImageId": "ami-99999999",
                    "InstanceId": "i-99999999",
                    "InstanceState": "running",
                    "InstanceType": "m3.xlarge",
                    "OutpostArn": "arn:aws:outposts:us-west-
2:123456789000:outpost/op-0fbc006e9abbc73c3",
                    "LaunchTime": "2016-08-02T02:05:06.000Z",
                    "NetworkInterfaces": [
                        {
                            "Ipv6Addresses": [],
                            "NetworkInterfaceId": "eni-abcdef00",
                            "PrivateDnsName":
"GeneratedFindingPrivateDnsName1",
                            "PrivateIpAddress": "10.0.0.1",
                            "PrivateIpAddresses": [
                                {
```

```
                                    "PrivateDnsName":
"GeneratedFindingPrivateName1",
                                    "PrivateIpAddress": "10.0.0.1"
                        },
                        {
<remainder of output omitted>
```

As you can see from the findings output, there is a lot to review. I've omitted a large portion of the output. For practical purposes, viewing your findings in the AWS Console is probably more appropriate. You can see what this looks like in Figure 6.1.

This list explains the key components of this GuardDuty findings and introduces some new concepts:

- Finding *overview*: The finding shows a port probe attempt (a type of reconnaissance activity) with several noteworthy elements.

- Severity and *timing*: The LOW severity indicates suspicious but not immediately threatening activity. The finding was created and last updated six minutes ago, showing real-time detection capabilities.

- Resource *details*: The target is an EC2 instance (i-99999999) running on an AWS Outpost. The instance is running on an m3.xlarge instance type with multiple product codes attached.

Notable new concepts:

- *AWS Outposts:* An Outpost ARN (arn:aws:outposts) is present, indicating that this instance is running on AWS Outposts. This is a service that extends AWS infrastructure to your on-premises data center. This is significant for security teams, as it represents a hybrid cloud scenario.

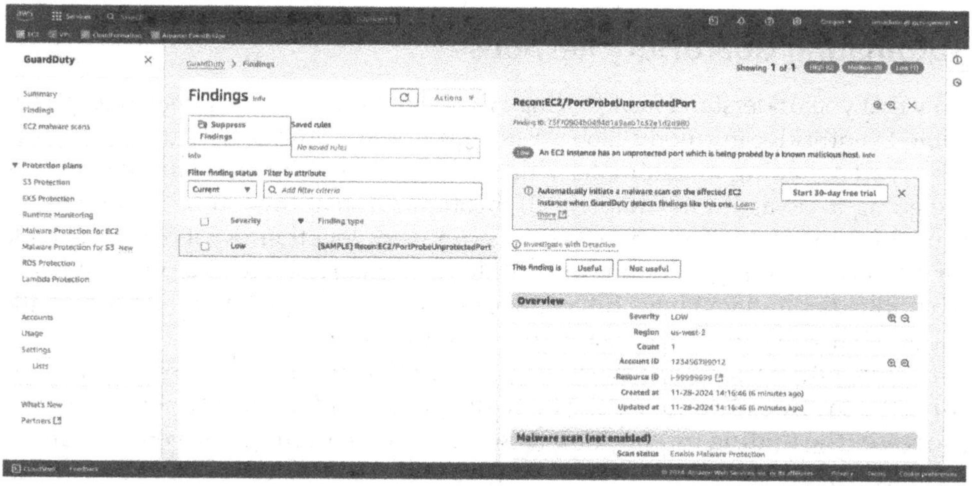

Figure 6.1: GuardDuty findings output.

- *Port Probe Analysis:* The finding detected probing activity on three critical ports:
  - Port 443 (HTTPS)
  - Port 22 (SSH)
  - Port 3306 (MySQL)
- This pattern suggests a systematic attempt to discover available services.
- *Network Configuration:* The instance has multiple network interfaces with private (10.0.0.x) and public (198.51.100.x) IP addresses. This dual-networking setup requires careful security consideration, especially for instances that shouldn't be publicly accessible.
- *Threat Intelligence Integration:* The finding includes threat intelligence details with multiple threat names, demonstrating GuardDuty's integration with threat intelligence feeds. The `"Sample: true"` indicator confirms this is a test finding.
- *Malware Protection Status:* The finding indicates that malware protection is not enabled—this is a newer GuardDuty feature that can scan EBS volumes and container images for malware. Consider enabling this for enhanced security coverage.
- *Security Implications:* The presence of multiple security groups (four in this case) and network interfaces suggests a complex network configuration that requires careful security review. The fact that port probing was detected on critical service ports (SSH, HTTPS, MySQL) indicates potential reconnaissance activity that should be monitored, even though this is a sample finding.

Automating GuardDuty Response

Now that you understand how findings work, you'll create an automated response using EventBridge (formerly CloudWatch Events) and Lambda. Figure 6.2 depicts what you are going to automate. This will be a good introduction to what you are going to do again in Chapters 10 through 12, so at this point I want you to start thinking about how these services can work together. A lot of people look for all-encompassing solutions and fail to recognize that AWS services already work together and you have full control of how they do that. I digress. Let's talk about what you can accomplish with the automation.

In this automation, you start with a GuardDuty finding event that is captured by an EventBridge rule. This rule triggers a Lambda function, which processes the finding by checking its severity. If the finding is severe (a score of 7 or higher), the function automatically isolates the affected instance and sends an SNS notification to alert you. For lower severity findings, no further action

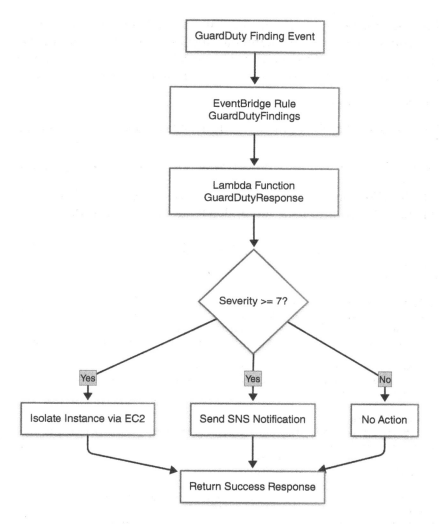

Figure 6.2: Automating GuardDuty.

is taken. This streamlined process ensures that high-risk threats are handled promptly and efficiently. Let's build it!

First, create a rule in EventBridge that captures GuardDuty findings:

```
[cloudshell-user@ip-10-144-121-189 ~]$ aws events put-rule \
>       --name GuardDutyFindings \
>       --event-pattern "{\"source\":[\"aws.guardduty\"],\"detail-
type\":[\"GuardDuty Finding\"],\"detail\":{\"severity\":[5,8]}}"
{
    "RuleArn": "arn:aws:events:us-west-2:387974667323:rule/GuardDutyFindings"
}
[cloudshell-user@ip-10-144-121-189 ~]$
```

This rule specifically captures medium- and high-severity findings.

Now you need to create the Lambda function. To do this from the AWS CLI requires multiple steps. First, you need to create your Lambda code and package it. Start by creating a new directory on your local machine:

```
[cloudshell-user@ip-10-144-121-`
```

Next, create the Lambda function code in a file named `lambda _ function.py`:

```
[cloudshell-user@ip-10-144-121-189 guardduty-response]$ nano lambda_function.py
```

Paste the following Python code into the `lambda _ function.py` file. I've included comments in the code to help you understand what the code does.

```python
# Import required AWS SDK for Python (boto3) and JSON handling library
import boto3
import json

def lambda_handler(event, context):
    # The main function that AWS Lambda will call when triggered
    # event: Contains the GuardDuty finding data
    # context: Contains information about the Lambda execution environment

    # Extract the finding details from the event object
    # The 'detail' key contains the actual GuardDuty finding information
    finding = event['detail']

    # Extract the severity score (1-8) and the type of finding
    # Example types: "UnauthorizedAccess:EC2/SSHBruteForce", "Recon:EC2/
PortProbeUnprotectedPort"
    severity = finding['Severity']
    finding_type = finding['Type']

    # Safely navigate the nested JSON structure to get the instance ID
    # Using .
get() method with default empty dict prevents errors if keys don't exist
    instance_id = finding.get('Resource', {}).get('InstanceDetails',
{}).get('InstanceId')

    # Check if this is a high severity finding (7.0 or higher)
    if severity >= 7.0:
        # If we have an instance ID and it's high severity,
        # isolate the instance by changing its security group
        if instance_id:
            isolate_instance(instance_id)

        # Send an SNS notification about the high severity finding
        send_notification(finding)

    # Return a success response
    # This tells Lambda the function executed successfully
```

```
        return {
            'statusCode': 200,
            'body': json.dumps('Processed GuardDuty finding')
        }

def isolate_instance(instance_id):
    # Create an EC2 client using boto3
    ec2 = boto3.client('ec2')

    # Create a new security group with the instance ID in its name
    # This security group will be empty, effectively blocking all traffic
    response = ec2.create_security_group(
        GroupName=f'ISOLATION-{instance_id}',  # Dynamic name based on instance ID
        Description='Isolation security group'
    )

    # Modify the instance to use only the newly created security group
    # This removes all other security groups and applies the empty one
    ec2.modify_instance_attribute(
        InstanceId=instance_id,
        Groups=[response['GroupId']]  # List containing only the new
security group ID
    )

def send_notification(finding):
    # Create an SNS (Simple Notification Service) client
    sns = boto3.client('sns')

    # Publish the finding to an SNS topic
    # The topic ARN needs to be updated with your actual ARN
    sns.publish(
        TopicArn='arn:aws:sns:region:account-id:GuardDutyAlerts',
    # Replace with your SNS topic ARN
        Message=json.dumps(finding, indent=2),
    #  Convert finding to formatted JSON string
        Subject='High Severity GuardDuty Finding Detected'
    #  Email subject if SNS is configured for email
    )
```

```
Create a ZIP package containing your function:
[cloudshell-user@ip-10-144-121-189 guardduty-response]$ zip -r function.zip lambda_
function.py
  adding: lambda_function.py (deflated 55%)
[cloudshell-user@ip-10-144-121-189 guardduty-response]$
```

Before creating the function, you need an IAM role with proper permissions:

```
[cloudshell-user@ip-10-144-121-189 guardduty-response]$ aws iam create-role \
>     --role-name guardduty-response-role \
>     --assume-role-policy-document '{"Version": "2012-10-17","Statement":
[{ "Effect": "Allow", "Principal": {"Service": "lambda.amazonaws.com"},
"Action": "sts:AssumeRole"}]}'
{
```

```
"Role": {
    "Path": "/",
    "RoleName": "guardduty-response-role",
    "RoleId": "AROAVUVIXTQ535JV35FZA",
    "Arn": "arn:aws:iam::387974667323:role/guardduty-response-role",
    "CreateDate": "2024-11-28T23:01:07+00:00",
    "AssumeRolePolicyDocument": {
        "Version": "2012-10-17",
        "Statement": [
            {
                "Effect": "Allow",
                "Principal": {
                    "Service": "lambda.amazonaws.com"
                },
                "Action": "sts:AssumeRole"
            }
        ]
    }
}
}
[cloudshell-user@ip-10-144-121-189 guardduty-response]$
```

Attach necessary policies to the role:

```
[cloudshell-user@ip-10-144-121-189 guardduty-response]$ aws iam attach-role-
policy \
>      --role-name guardduty-response-role \
>      --policy-arn arn:aws:iam::aws:policy/service-role/AWSLambdaBasicExecutionRole
[cloudshell-user@ip-10-144-121-189 guardduty-response]$
[cloudshell-user@ip-10-144-121-189 guardduty-response]$ aws iam attach-role-
policy \
>      --role-name guardduty-response-role \
>      --policy-arn arn:aws:iam::aws:policy/AmazonEC2FullAccess
[cloudshell-user@ip-10-144-121-189 guardduty-response]$
```

You might be wondering why you are attaching these policies specifically. AWSLambdaBasicExecutionRole gives permission to write logs to CloudWatch Logs, the ability to create log groups and log streams and permission to "put" log events (into the log stream). Without this policy, your Lambda function wouldn't be able to log its execution, making troubleshooting nearly impossible.

The AmazonEC2FullAccess policy is required because your Lambda function performs EC2-related actions like creating security groups and modifying instance attributes. However, this policy is actually too permissive for production use. Following the principle of least privilege, you should create a custom policy that only allows the specific actions the function needs.

One last thing you need to do is allow permission to create an SNS topic. For this, you need to create a policy:

```
[cloudshell-user@ip-10-144-121-189 guardduty-response] $ aws iam create-policy \
>      --policy-name lambda-sns-publish \
>      --policy-document '{
>          "Version": "2012-10-17",
>          "Statement": [{
>              "Effect": "Allow",
>              "Action": "sns:Publish",
>              "Resource": "arn:aws:sns:us-west-2:387974667323:GuardDutyAlerts"
>          }]
>      }'
{
    "Policy": {
        "PolicyName": "lambda-sns-publish",
        "PolicyId": "ANPAVUVIXTQ57W32NSYSN",
        "Arn": "arn:aws:iam::387974667323:policy/lambda-sns-publish",
        "Path": "/",
        "DefaultVersionId": "v1",
        "AttachmentCount": 0,
        "PermissionsBoundaryUsageCount": 0,
        "IsAttachable": true,
        "CreateDate": "2024-11-28T23:35:27+00:00",
        "UpdateDate": "2024-11-28T23:35:27+00:00"
    }
}
[cloudshell-user@ip-10-144-121-189 guardduty-response]$
```

note The SNS Topic ARN in this policy is a placeholder. The SNS topic referenced by this ARN is created in a later step, so replace it with your own SNS topic ARN once it's available.

Attach the policy to the Lambda role:

```
[cloudshell-user@ip-10-144-121-189 guardduty-response]$ aws iam attach-role-
policy \
>      --role-name guardduty-response-role \
>      --policy-arn arn:aws:iam::387974667323:policy/lambda-sns-publish
[cloudshell-user@ip-10-144-121-189 guardduty-response]$
```

Now you can create the Lambda function using your ZIP package. You'll need your account ID for this command.

```
[cloudshell-user@ip-10-144-121-189 guardduty-response]$ aws lambda
create-function \
>      --function-name GuardDutyResponse \
>      --runtime python3.9 \
>      --zip-file fileb://function.zip \
>      --handler lambda_function.lambda_handler \
>      --role arn:aws:iam::387974667323:role/guardduty-response-role \
```

```
>       --timeout 30 \
>       --memory-size 128
{
    "FunctionName": "GuardDutyResponse",
    "FunctionArn": "arn:aws:lambda:us-west-2:387974667323:function:
GuardDutyResponse",
    "Runtime": "python3.9",
    "Role": "arn:aws:iam::387974667323:role/guardduty-response-role",
    "Handler": "lambda_function.lambda_handler",
    "CodeSize": 829,
    "Description": "",
    "Timeout": 30,
    "MemorySize": 128,
    "LastModified": "2024-11-28T23:06:07.835+0000",
    "CodeSha256": "KedM9ILiGaGBoAVIf65dn21ng0x7ZpS/vGSpFqDFb6E=",
    "Version": "$LATEST",
    "TracingConfig": {
        "Mode": "PassThrough"
    },
    "RevisionId": "2ce2853d-0772-409f-98ec-0cf0bb9239f6",
    "State": "Pending",
    "StateReason": "The function is being created.",
    "StateReasonCode": "Creating",
    "PackageType": "Zip",
    "Architectures": [
        "x86_64"
    ],
    "EphemeralStorage": {
        "Size": 512
    },
    "SnapStart": {
        "ApplyOn": "None",
        "OptimizationStatus": "Off"
    },
    "RuntimeVersionConfig": {
        "RuntimeVersionArn": "arn:aws:lambda:us-west-
2::runtime:57e9dce4a928fd5b7bc1015238a5bc8a9146f096d69571fa4219ed8a2e76bfdf"
    },
    "LoggingConfig": {
        "LogFormat": "Text",
        "LogGroup": "/aws/lambda/GuardDutyResponse"
    }
}
(END)
```

Now you need to create the SNS topic and confirm the email address. First, create the SNS topic:

```
[cloudshell-user@
ip-10-144-121-189 guardduty-response]$ aws sns create-topic --name GuardDutyAlerts
{
    "TopicArn": "arn:aws:sns:us-west-2:387974667323:GuardDutyAlerts"
}
```

Next, create an email subscription (replace with your email address):

```
[cloudshell-user@ip-10-144-121-189 guardduty-response]$ aws sns
subscribe \
>     --topic-arn arn:aws:sns:us-west-2:387974667323:GuardDutyAlerts \
>     --protocol email \
>     --notification-endpoint brandon.carroll@gameonnetoworks.com
{
    "SubscriptionArn": "pending confirmation"
}
[cloudshell-user@ip-10-144-121-189 guardduty-response]$
```

And finally, confirm your email, as shown in Figure 6.3. If you don't see the email in your inbox, be sure to check your spam folder.

To test the function, create a test event in JSON format that simulates a GuardDuty finding. You're going to use one of the instances that you created in a previous chapter. If you deleted the CloudFormation stack from Chapter 5, you need to load it again. You need the instance ID from one of the instances that's created in Chapter 5.

```
[cloudshell-user@ip-10-144-121-189 guardduty-response]$      aws lambda
invoke \
>     --function-name GuardDutyResponse \
>     --cli-binary-format raw-in-base64-out \
>     --payload '{"detail": {"Type": "PortProbe", "Severity": 8.0, "Resource":
{"InstanceDetails": {"InstanceId": "i-069f08258d60557a2"}}}}' \
>     response.json
{
    "StatusCode": 200,
    "ExecutedVersion": "$LATEST"
}
[cloudshell-user@ip-10-144-121-189 guardduty-response]$
```

AWS Notification - Subscription Confirmation External ▷ Inbox ×

AWS Notifications <no-reply@sns.amazonaws.com>
to me ▾

You have chosen to subscribe to the topic:
arn:aws:sns:us-west-2:387974667323:GuardDutyAlerts

To confirm this subscription, click or visit the link below (If this was in error no action is necessary):
Confirm subscription

Please do not reply directly to this email. If you wish to remove yourself from receiving all future SNS subscription confirmation requests please send an email to sns-opt-out

↩ Reply   ↪ Forward

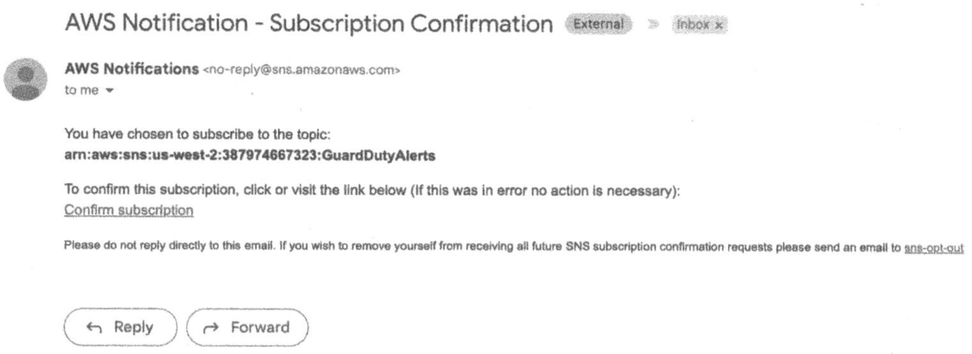

Figure 6.3: Confirming subscription to the SNS topic.

Let's break down the Lambda invocation response:

- `StatusCode: 200`: This indicates a successful synchronous invocation of the Lambda function.
- For the `RequestResponse` invocation type (the default), a 200 status code means the function executed and returned a response.
- `ExecutedVersion: "$LATEST"`: This shows which version of the Lambda function was executed. `$LATEST` indicates that the most recent version of the function code was used.

The command itself is performing a synchronous invocation of the `GuardDutyResponse` function with a test payload that simulates a high-severity (8.0) port probe finding. The `--cli-binary-format raw-in-base64-out` parameter is used to properly handle the JSON payload formatting.

Since there's no `FunctionError` field in the response, this indicates that the function executed without throwing any errors, successfully processing the simulated GuardDuty finding.

And you probably already guessed it: you will not get an email for these events, as shown in Figure 6.4.

After successfully implementing and testing your GuardDuty automation, you might be wondering, "What happens to all these security findings over time? How do I maintain visibility across multiple accounts and integrate findings from other security tools?" This is where AWS Security Hub comes into play. While GuardDuty excels at threat detection, Security Hub serves as your central command center for security findings, compliance monitoring, and security posture management.

Figure 6.4: SNS notification of a high-severity event.

AWS Security Hub Implementation

Think of Security Hub as the security dashboard you've always wanted. It aggregates, organizes, and prioritizes security findings from multiple AWS services, including GuardDuty, Amazon Inspector, Amazon Macie, and even third-party security tools. The findings you just generated from GuardDuty would automatically appear in Security Hub (if enabled), alongside other security insights from across your AWS organization. In this section, you enable Security Hub and explore how it complements your GuardDuty implementation.

Enabling Security Hub

Before learning about Security Hub's features, you need to enable it in your AWS environment. Since you're building on your GuardDuty implementation, Security Hub will automatically begin collecting those findings. First, enable Security Hub with the default security standards:

```
[cloudshell-user@ip-10-144-121-189 guardduty-response]$ aws securityhub enable-
security-hub \
>     --enable-default-standards \
>     --tags '{"Department": "Security"}'
[cloudshell-user@ip-10-144-121-189 guardduty-response]$
```

When you enable Security Hub, it automatically begins monitoring your security posture and collecting findings from integrated services like GuardDuty. The integration between GuardDuty and Security Hub happens automatically, and any findings generated by GuardDuty will appear in Security Hub within about five minutes. While you wait, get your detector ID and create a few more events that you can see:

```
[cloudshell-user@ip-10-144-121-189 guardduty-response]$ aws securityhub enable-
security-hub \
>     --enable-default-standards \
>     --tags '{"Department": "Security"}'
[cloudshell-user@
ip-10-144-121-189 guardduty-response]$ aws guardduty list-detectors
{
    "DetectorIds": [
        "24c9ba318e0b9a9c48065c18cf0a9790"
    ]
}
```

Now generate a few more findings to show in Security Hub:

```
[cloudshell-user@ip-10-144-121-189 guardduty-response]$ aws guardduty create-sample-
findings \
>     --detector-id 24c9ba318e0b9a9c48065c18cf0a9790 \
>     --finding-types \
```

```
>        "UnauthorizedAccess:EC2/SSHBruteForce" \
>        "UnauthorizedAccess:EC2/RDPBruteForce" \
>        "Trojan:EC2/PhishingDomainRequest!DNS" \
bash: !DNS: event not found
>        "UnauthorizedAccess:EC2/MetadataDNSRebind" \
>        "Execution:EC2/MaliciousFile"
[cloudshell-user@ip-10-144-121-189 guardduty-response]$
```

Viewing GuardDuty Findings in Security Hub

Now that you've generated several test findings in GuardDuty, you can explore them in the Security Hub console. Navigate to AWS Security Hub in the AWS Management Console. The Security Hub dashboard provides a comprehensive view of your security findings, but this section focuses on the GuardDuty findings.

When you navigate to Security Hub in the AWS Console, you see the Summary page shown in Figure 6.5.

You can now filter things down in the findings page:

1. In the left navigation pane, click on Findings.
2. Look for the Product Name filter in the search bar.
3. Select GuardDuty to view only GuardDuty-generated findings.

You can see the GuardDuty findings in Figure 6.6.
Here's what you're seeing in the Findings view:

- Each finding shows a severity level, indicated by color.
- The Title column provides a quick description of the finding.
- The Resource ID column shows which AWS resource was involved.

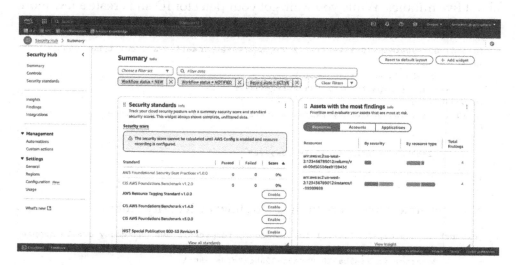

Figure 6.5: Security Hub Summary page.

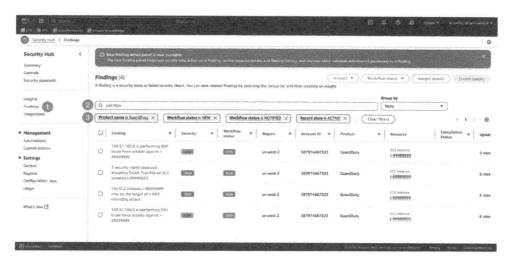

Figure 6.6: GuardDuty findings in Security Hub.

■ The Status column indicates whether the finding is still active or has been resolved.

When you click on a specific finding, the Details pane opens on the right side of the screen. Pay special attention to:

■ The Finding Details section, which provides comprehensive information about the security issue

■ The Resource Affected section, showing details about the impacted AWS resource

■ The Evidence section, containing information that triggered the finding (not shown)

You can see an example of the Details pane in Figure 6.7.

What you'll notice is that Security Hub standardizes these findings using the AWS Security Finding Format (ASFF), making it easier to understand security issues across different AWS services. Notice how the findings generated earlier appear with consistent formatting and severity ratings, regardless of their source within GuardDuty.

Another thing that is helpful in Security Hub is that it allows you to manage the workflow of findings:

■ Change the workflow status to In Progress when you're investigating

■ Mark findings as Resolved once addressed

■ Set findings to Suppressed if they're known and accepted risks

You can see an example of this process in Figure 6.8.

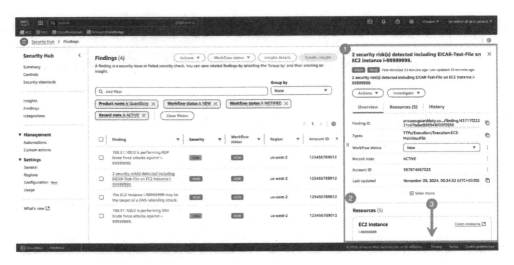

Figure 6.7: Finding details in Security Hub.

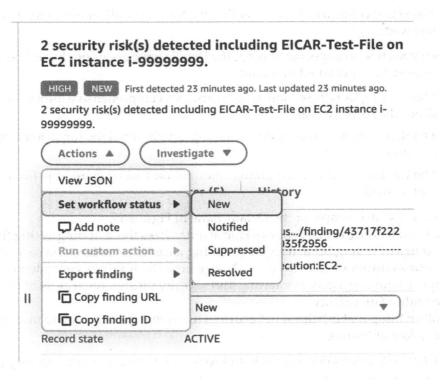

Figure 6.8: Workflow management.

This console view provides a more intuitive way to monitor and respond to security findings compared to using the CLI, especially when dealing with multiple findings across your AWS environment.

Setting Up Automated Responses in Security Hub

While the GuardDuty automation focused specifically on EC2 instance isolation and notifications for GuardDuty findings, Security Hub's automation capabilities offer a broader scope. Security Hub can trigger responses based on findings from multiple security services, not just GuardDuty. This means you can create unified response workflows that handle threats detected by GuardDuty, Amazon Inspector, AWS Config, and other integrated services.

For example, you can create a rule that handles high-severity findings across all security services:

```
[cloudshell-user@ip-10-144-121-189 guardduty-response]$ aws securityhub create-
automation-rule \
>      --rule-name "HighSeverityFindings" \
>      --rule-order 1 \
>      --description "Automatically send high severity findings to EventBridge" \
>      --criteria '{"SeverityLabel": [{"Value": "HIGH", "Comparison": "EQUALS"}]}' \
>      --actions '{"Type": "FINDING_FIELDS_UPDATE", "FindingFieldsUpdate": {"Note":
{"Text": "High severity finding detected", "UpdatedBy": "automation-rule"}}}' \
>      --no-is-terminal
{
    "RuleArn": "arn:aws:securityhub:us-west-
2:387974667323:automation-rule/3c4d31e3-5d56-45cc-8724-b31e8c51f383"
}
[cloudshell-user@ip-10-144-121-189 guardduty-response]$
```

This command creates an automation rule that:

- Identifies findings with high severity
- Adds a note to the finding
- Has a rule order of 1 (will be processed first)
- Is not terminal (will allow other rules to process after this one)

The `--no-is-terminal` parameter is important, as it allows other rules to process the finding after this rule completes.

This automation differs from the GuardDuty-specific automation in several ways:

- It processes findings from all integrated security services, not just GuardDuty.
- It can trigger different response playbooks based on the finding source.
- It provides a centralized way to manage security responses across your entire AWS security toolset.

Think of GuardDuty automation as your specialized response team for threat detection, while Security Hub automation serves as your security operations center, coordinating responses across all security tools.

Now that you've established the core threat-detection capabilities with GuardDuty and centralized your security findings management with Security Hub, you're ready to dive deeper into the methodologies that power effective threat detection. Understanding how AWS uses machine learning to identify potential threats will help you better interpret and respond to security findings.

Threat-Detection Methodologies

At the heart of AWS's threat-detection capabilities lies a sophisticated combination of machine learning algorithms and behavioral analytics. These technologies work together to establish what's normal in your environment and flag anomalous activities that could indicate security threats. The following sections explore how these methodologies work and how you can leverage them effectively.

Machine-Learning-Driven Detection

AWS's threat-detection services employ sophisticated machine learning models that continuously analyze patterns across billions of events. First, create some sample findings that demonstrate different ML detection patterns:

```
[cloudshell-user@ip-10-144-121-
189 guardduty-response]$ aws guardduty create-sample-
findings \
>       --detector-id 24c9ba318e0b9a9c48065c18cf0a9790 \
>       --finding-types \
>       "UnauthorizedAccess:EC2/RDPBruteForce" \
>       "Trojan:EC2/PhishingDomainRequest!DNS" \
bash: !DNS: event not found
>       "UnauthorizedAccess:EC2/MetadataDNSRebind"
[cloudshell-user@ip-10-144-121-189 guardduty-response]$
```

Each of these findings demonstrates different aspects of AWS's machine learning capabilities. The RDPBruteForce finding shows how GuardDuty's ML models analyze:

- Connection attempt frequency
- Source IP reputation
- Time-based patterns
- Geographic anomalies

The `PhishingDomainRequest` finding demonstrates ML analysis of:

- Domain reputation scoring
- DNS request patterns
- Communication frequency
- Data exfiltration attempts

The `MetadataDNSRebind` finding showcases ML detection of:

- Instance metadata service (IMDS) abuse
- Unusual DNS resolution patterns
- Potential credential theft attempts

Monitoring and Logging Strategies

Both GuardDuty and Security Hub leverage AWS's native logging capabilities to provide comprehensive threat detection, but they process this data differently.

GuardDuty's Data Sources

- CloudTrail management events (automatically analyzed when enabled)
- CloudTrail S3 data events (requires manual configuration)
- VPC Flow Logs for network traffic analysis
- DNS logs from Route 53 queries

Security Hub's Integration Points

- Aggregates findings from GuardDuty
- Integrates with AWS Config for compliance monitoring
- Processes CloudTrail Logs for security best practices
- Combines data from multiple security services, including Amazon Inspector and Amazon Macie

The key difference is that GuardDuty actively analyzes these logs for threat detection, while Security Hub aggregates and standardizes security findings from multiple sources, including GuardDuty's analysis. This creates a layered approach where GuardDuty performs the deep analysis of logs for threats, and Security Hub provides the central dashboard for all security findings.

Conclusion

Throughout this chapter, you've built a comprehensive threat-detection strategy using AWS's native security services. Starting with GuardDuty's intelligent threat-detection capabilities, you implemented automated responses to security findings using Lambda functions and EventBridge rules. You then expanded the security posture by integrating Security Hub, creating a centralized command center for security findings across your AWS environment.

Key takeaways from this chapter include the following:

- The importance of automated threat response in cloud environments
- How GuardDuty and Security Hub work together to provide comprehensive security coverage
- The value of testing your security controls using sample findings
- Implementing proper IAM permissions for security automation

Remember that threat detection is not a "set it and forget it" solution. As your AWS environment grows, you'll need to continuously refine your threat-detection strategy, update your automation rules, and adjust your response procedures. The next chapter explores how to implement comprehensive logging and monitoring strategies that complement the threat-detection capabilities you've established here.

References

Amazon Web Services, "Amazon GuardDuty—Intelligent Threat Detection," https://aws.amazon.com/guardduty/

Amazon Web Services, "Cloud Security Posture Management—AWS Security Hub," https://aws.amazon.com/security-hub/

## CHAPTER 7

Data Security and Cryptography on AWS

"The mantra of any good security engineer is: 'Security is not a product, but a process.' It's more than designing strong cryptography into a system; it's designing the entire system such that all security measures, including cryptography, work together."

—Bruce Schneier

Data protection in AWS requires more than just enabling encryption. What it demands is a comprehensive understanding of how data flows through your systems and which tools are available to secure it at every stage. This chapter explores AWS's data security and cryptography services, showing you how to implement encryption, manage keys, and protect sensitive information throughout its lifecycle. Building on the identity and infrastructure protection concepts from previous chapters, you learn how to use services like AWS KMS, CloudHSM, and Certificate Manager to create a robust data security strategy. Whether you're securing data at rest in S3 buckets, protecting information in transit between services, or managing encryption keys across your organization, you discover practical approaches that align with AWS best practices and compliance requirements.

As you work through this chapter, you can copy and paste the commands from the GitHub repo at `https://github.com/8carroll/Securing-the-Cloud-with-Brandon-Carroll`. You will find several resources in each chapter folder. Additionally, be sure to replace all the IDs, ARNs, and other unique data used in my examples with your own values from your own account.

Introduction to Data Security and Cryptography

AWS has many security services. If you've spent any time in the AWS console, you know it's packed with an array of services—over 206, last time I checked. The services that provide security features are designed to protect your data, applications, and infrastructure. This section covers some of the key security services AWS offers. The first service to discuss is AWS Identity and Access Management (IAM).

Understanding the Data Security Landscape

In your journey through AWS security, you've built a strong foundation with identity management, infrastructure protection, and threat detection. Now it's time to tackle one of the most critical aspects of cloud security: protecting your data.

The Evolution of Data Protection

Let me tell you how I think about data protection in AWS. It's like having a massive warehouse filled with valuable stuff—it could be anything. But some of it is sitting on shelves, some is moving on conveyor belts, and some is being actively worked on by your team. Chapter 5 explained how to build strong walls and security checkpoints around your infrastructure, but your data needs even more careful handling.

Remember when you could just lock the server room door and hand out access badges to trusted employees? People still do that. But the days of that being the only method of securing the data are long gone. Now data is flowing through multiple AWS services, crossing regions, and being accessed by applications and users from anywhere in the world. You need much more sophisticated tools. You need encryption that follows your data wherever it goes, automated systems watching for suspicious access patterns, and smart classification tools that know which data needs extra protection.

This approach aligns perfectly with what you learned about the CIA triad in Chapter 2. You're not just protecting data, you're ensuring it remains confidential, maintains its integrity, and stays available to authorized users. This section explains how AWS helps you achieve this.

Understanding Data States

Let's talk for a bit about how data exists in your AWS environment. Just like you need different security controls for different types of infrastructure, you also need specialized protection mechanisms for data in each of its three states:

- *Data at rest* refers to information stored in AWS services like S3 buckets, Elastic Beanstalk (EBS) volumes, and Amazon Relational Database Service (RDS) databases. Think of your sensitive customer records sitting in an RDS database or confidential documents stored in S3. This data needs strong encryption and careful access controls to maintain its confidentiality.

- *Data in transit* covers information moving between services or to users outside AWS. When your application sends data from an EC2 instance to an S3 bucket, or when users connect to your application through HTTPS, that's data in transit. You need to ensure this data is encrypted during its journey to prevent interception.

- *Data in use* is perhaps the most complex state to protect. This is your data while it's being processed in memory, such as when an EC2 instance is analyzing customer information or when Lambda functions are handling sensitive data. Protection here often involves secure enclaves and memory encryption.

The Role of Cryptography in AWS

To illustrate the role of cryptography in AWS, imagine you're running a health-care application on AWS that processes patient records. Figure 7.1 illustrates each of these states:

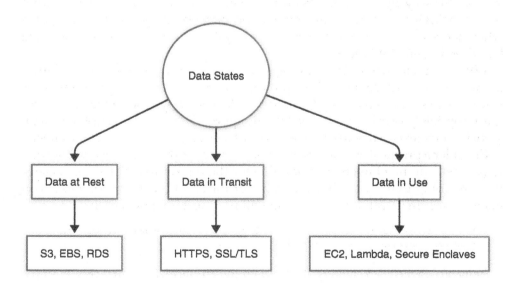

Figure 7.1: The three states of data.

- When patients' medical images are uploaded, they're encrypted in transit using TLS.
- The images are stored in S3 with KMS encryption at rest.
- When a doctor needs to view an image, it's decrypted in memory for processing, with the application running in a secure enclave.

This multilayered approach ensures that patient data remains protected in all three states, meeting both security best practices and HIPAA compliance requirements. As you move through this chapter, you'll explore each AWS service that helps protect data in these states, including practical implementations using the AWS CLI.

Core Data Security Concepts

This section discusses how data security builds on what you've learned about identity and infrastructure protection. Chapter 2 discussed the CIA triad (Confidentiality, Integrity, and Availability), and this section explains how it directly applies to protecting your data.

Data Classification

Data classification is your first line of defense in protecting information. Think back to our discussion of least privilege and remember that you can't protect what you don't understand. In AWS, you use tags to classify data sensitivity levels. This way, by using tags to classify data, you gain a clear understanding of its sensitivity level, allowing you to apply appropriate encryption measures when necessary. By doing this, you create a systematic way to protect your data based on its sensitivity level.

When you classify data using tags, you create a foundation for defining automated security controls. For example, you can enforce encryption policies based on these tags, ensuring that sensitive data is always encrypted and access is appropriately restricted. This systematic approach simplifies compliance with security standards and helps maintain consistency across your AWS environment.

Consider a practical example where you create an S3 bucket with classification tags. First, you need to create a variable for the bucket name. This is because you are going to need the bucket name for the second command, and if you generate it using a random value, you will need to somehow get that name"

```
[cloudshell-user@ip-10-132-35-185 ~]$ BUCKET_NAME="secure-customer-data-${RANDOM}"
[cloudshell-user@ip-10-132-35-185 ~]$
```

Now create the bucket using the following command. Note that this example uses the LocationConstraint=us-west-2, which is only necessary if you are creating a bucket in a region other than us-east-1:

```
[cloudshell-user@ip-10-132-35-185 ~]$ # Create an S3 bucket with classification
tags
[cloudshell-user@ip-10-132-35-185 ~]$ aws s3api create-bucket \
>       --bucket ${BUCKET_NAME} \
>       --region us-west-2 \
>       --create-bucket-configuration LocationConstraint=us-west-2
{
    "Location": "http://secure-customer-data-13148.s3.amazonaws.com/"
}
[cloudshell-user@ip-10-132-35-185 ~]$
```

I created the bucket in the us-west-2 region because regional placement can impact compliance and latency requirements. For example, certain regulations may require data to reside within specific geographic boundaries, and placing resources closer to users can reduce latency. By specifying LocationConstraint=us-west-2, you ensure that your bucket meets these needs.

With the bucket created, next add classification tags to the bucket using the following command:

```
[cloudshell-user@ip-10-132-35-185 ~]$ aws s3api put-bucket-tagging \
>       --bucket ${BUCKET_NAME} \
>       --tagging
'TagSet=[{Key=DataClassification,Value=Confidential},{Key=Department,
Value=Finance}]'
[cloudshell-user@ip-10-132-35-185 ~]$
```

Adding classification tags allows you to categorize your data based on sensitivity and organizational needs. These tags enable automated workflows, such as applying stricter access controls or encryption policies to sensitive data like financial records. This approach ensures consistent security practices across your AWS environment.

Now that you've classified your bucket, you can enforce the classification controls. To do so, apply the following bucket policy:

```
[cloudshell-user@ip-10-132-35-185 ~]$ aws s3api put-bucket-policy \
>       --bucket ${BUCKET_NAME} \
>       --policy '{
>           "Version": "2012-10-17",
>           "Statement": [{
>               "Sid": "EnforceEncryptionOnConfidentialData",
>               "Effect": "Deny",
>               "Principal": "*",
>               "Action": "s3:PutObject",
>               "Resource": "arn:aws:s3:::'"${BUCKET_NAME}"'/*",
>               "Condition": {
>                   "StringNotEquals": {
>                       "s3:x-amz-server-side-encryption": "aws:kms"
>                   }
>               }
>           }]
>       }'
[cloudshell-user@ip-10-132-35-185 ~]$
```

Let's break down what this bucket policy is doing. The policy uses a `Deny` effect, which means it will prevent any action that matches the conditions. The action `s3:PutObjec` refers to uploading objects to the bucket. The interesting part is in the `Condition` block. Notice that it uses `StringNotEquals` with "`s3:x-amz-server-side-encryption`": "`aws:kms`". This means that if someone tries to upload an object without KMS (Key Management Service) encryption, the upload will be denied.

When a bucket is labeled as `Confidential`, you do not necessarily need to specify the actual AWS KMS key in your bucket policy unless your use case requires granular control over which key is used. Instead, you can enforce encryption by ensuring that all uploaded files are encrypted using server-side encryption with AWS KMS (`aws:kms`). This approach simplifies management while maintaining strong security.

AWS KMS, which you'll explore in detail later in this chapter, is AWS's service for creating and managing encryption keys. When you specify `aws:kms` as the encryption method, you're telling S3 to use KMS keys for encrypting the data. KMS acts as a secure key vault where it stores and manages the keys used to encrypt and decrypt your data. At the same time, KMS ensures that only authorized users and services can use these keys.

So now you have a complete system in place. The tags identify this bucket as containing confidential finance data, and your bucket policy ensures that any data uploaded to this bucket must be encrypted using AWS KMS. If someone tries to upload an unencrypted file, or a file encrypted with a different method, the upload will be denied. This is a practical example of implementing the confidentiality piece of the CIA triad discussed in Chapter 2.

Now that you understand how data classification and protection work together, the next section looks at some key management fundamentals.

Key Management Fundamentals

In AWS, encryption is only as secure as the keys that protect your data. Proper key management ensures that sensitive data is encrypted and can only be accessed by authorized entities. AWS provides a centralized service, the AWS Key Management Service (KMS), to simplify the creation, storage, and management of encryption keys.

Key management is critical for cloud security for the following reasons:

- **Data protection:** Encryption keys are the foundation of protecting sensitive information across services like S3, EBS, and RDS.

- **Access control:** Keys can be tied to policies that enforce least privilege, ensuring that only specific users or roles can access them.

- **Regulatory compliance:** Many compliance frameworks, such as HIPAA and PCI DSS, require strong encryption and proper key management.

Types of Keys in AWS

AWS supports two types of keys for encryption:

- *Symmetric keys:* A single key is used for both encryption and decryption. These are commonly used for data at rest (e.g., S3 and EBS).

- *Asymmetric keys:* A pair of keys (public and private) is used. These are used for digital signatures or secure key exchanges.

Key Management Best Practices

Follow these practices for best results:

- **Rotate keys regularly:** Regular key rotation reduces the risk of key compromise. AWS KMS supports automatic rotation for customer-managed keys.

- **Apply least privilege:** Use policies to restrict who can create, manage, and use keys.

- **Monitor key usage:** Enable AWS CloudTrail to log key usage and detect unauthorized access.

Encryption Algorithms in AWS

Encryption in AWS is primarily based on two key methodologies: *symmetric encryption* and *asymmetric encryption*. Symmetric encryption uses the same key for both encryption and decryption, making it straightforward but requiring secure sharing of the key between parties. Its simplicity and efficiency make it the preferred choice for encrypting large datasets and securing data at rest in AWS services like S3, EBS, and RDS. The most common algorithm for symmetric encryption is AES-256, which offers a strong balance of security and performance.

Asymmetric encryption, by contrast, involves a pair of keys: a *public key* for encryption and a *private key* for decryption. This separation of keys makes asymmetric encryption ideal for establishing secure communications and verifying digital signatures. For example, in a TLS/SSL connection, asymmetric encryption is used during the initial handshake to exchange a symmetric session key securely. Once the key exchange is complete, symmetric encryption takes over for the actual data transfer to optimize speed.

Asymmetric encryption is commonly used for encrypting small data payloads, signing digital documents, and ensuring secure key exchanges. These use cases highlight its versatility in scenarios requiring both confidentiality and authenticity. AWS KMS allows you to generate both symmetric and asymmetric keys, enabling you to choose the right approach for your workload. Understanding the strengths of each type of encryption helps you design systems that are both secure and efficient.

AWS Key Management Service (KMS)

AWS Key Management Service (KMS) provides a centralized and fully managed solution for creating, storing, and managing encryption keys. Its architecture is designed to simplify encryption workflows while maintaining strong security practices. The following sections explore the key components of KMS and how they work together.

KMS Architecture

First, at the heart of KMS are *KMS keys*. These keys act as the primary resources for managing encryption and decryption processes. KMS keys can be customer-managed, providing full control over key policies, or AWS-managed, allowing AWS to handle key lifecycle management. For those with strict compliance requirements, KMS also supports keys backed by CloudHSM for added control and security.

Another important concept is *envelope encryption*, which enhances scalability and security. In this model, KMS generates and manages data keys that encrypt the actual data. These data keys are encrypted by the KMS keys and can be securely distributed for use in applications or other AWS services. This layered approach reduces exposure of sensitive key material and ensures consistent performance for large-scale encryption needs.

Lastly, KMS is deeply integrated with a variety of AWS services, including S3, RDS, and Lambda. This integration streamlines encryption workflows, allowing developers to enable encryption at rest or in transit with just a few configuration steps. Whether you're encrypting database snapshots, securing sensitive files in S3, or handling event-driven workloads in Lambda, KMS provides a seamless and consistent interface.

By combining robust key management capabilities with tight integration across AWS, KMS helps you secure your data and meet compliance requirements without adding complexity to your workflows.

KMS Keys

At the core of AWS Key Management Service (KMS) are KMS keys, which enable secure encryption and decryption across AWS services. These keys come in three types: AWS-managed keys, customer-managed keys, and AWS-owned keys. AWS-managed keys are automatically created and rotated by AWS for services like S3, EBS, and RDS, offering a low-maintenance solution for encryption. They are ideal for users who want simplicity without worrying about key management. Customer-managed keys provide greater control and flexibility, allowing you to define access policies, enable automatic rotation, and manage key deletion timelines. These are well-suited for compliance-driven workloads or scenarios requiring granular access control. AWS-owned keys, on the other hand, are fully managed by AWS and used internally for encryption-by-default workloads. While convenient, they lack visibility into usage and cannot be customized or audited.

The choice of KMS key type depends on your specific needs. For minimal overhead, AWS-managed keys are a great option since AWS handles their lifecycle. However, customer-managed keys are recommended when compliance or advanced security requirements demand precise control over access policies or auditability. They also integrate seamlessly with monitoring tools like AWS CloudTrail to track usage. For organizations with stringent regulatory requirements or custom cryptographic needs, CloudHSM-backed KMS keys offer enhanced control by storing key material in dedicated hardware security modules (HSMs). These keys comply with FIPS 140-2 Level 3 standards and support custom algorithms. By selecting the appropriate type of KMS key, you can balance convenience, security, and compliance while ensuring your data remains protected throughout its lifecycle.

Key Policies and Permissions

Key policies are essential to managing who can access and control Customer Master Keys (CMKs) in AWS KMS. These policies are JSON documents that function similarly to IAM policies but are specific to the management of encryption keys. Properly configured key policies ensure adherence to the principle of least privilege, restricting access to only those users or roles that need it.

Key policies offer the following capabilities:

- **Fine-grained access control:** You can specify detailed permissions for different actions, such as creating, encrypting, or deleting keys. This allows precise control over who can manage or use a CMK.

- **Role-based permissions:** By assigning specific permissions to IAM roles, you can enable key administration by dedicated teams while restricting usage to other roles, such as application services.

- **Integration with IAM policies:** Key policies work seamlessly with IAM policies, allowing you to define broader access controls across multiple AWS services. For example, an IAM policy might allow a user to call `kms:Encrypt` on a specific CMK, while the key policy enforces additional restrictions.

A well-constructed key policy should always enforce the principle of least privilege and explicitly define actions and roles. Combining these policies with IAM permissions provides a robust mechanism for securing access to your keys and the data they protect.

KMS Practical Example

For this example, you'll create a KMS key to see how it works. First you create a new KMS key with a description and tags to help identify its purpose. The command will output several details about the key. This section focuses on two key pieces of information—KeyId, which you'll use in subsequent commands, and AWSAccountId, which is necessary for the key policy.

Run the following command:

```
[cloudshell-user@ip-10-140-9-192 ~]$ aws kms create-key \
>     --description "Key for processing payroll data" \
>     --tags TagKey=Department,TagValue=Payroll

{
    "KeyMetadata": {
        "AWSAccountId": "387974667323",
        "KeyId": "a24d73e1-3e3c-4e87-b788-96bf08446957",
        "Arn": "arn:aws:kms:us-west-2:387974667323:key/a24d73e1-3e3c-4e87-
b788-96bf08446957",
        "CreationDate": "2024-12-08T01:12:26.303000+00:00",
        "Enabled": true,
        "Description": "Key for processing payroll data",
        "KeyUsage": "ENCRYPT_DECRYPT",
        "KeyState": "Enabled",
        "Origin": "AWS_KMS",
        "KeyManager": "CUSTOMER",
        "CustomerMasterKeySpec": "SYMMETRIC_DEFAULT",
        "KeySpec": "SYMMETRIC_DEFAULT",
        "EncryptionAlgorithms": [
            "SYMMETRIC_DEFAULT"
        ],
        "MultiRegion": false
    }
}
[cloudshell-user@ip-10-140-9-192 ~]$
```

Note the following values:

- KeyId: 4543a25c-d840-4436-85d7-9906d5e463e5

- AWSAccountId: 387974667323

You'll need these values in the next steps. Let's move on to creating a key policy. Now that you have the KeyId and AWSAccountId, you can define a policy that follows the principle of least privilege, ensuring that only specific roles can manage or use this key. Since you are going to be using some specific roles, you need to create them before you can reference them in a key policy. Create a trust policy to attach to the two new roles you are going to create:

```
[cloudshell-user@ip-10-132-36-220 ~]$ cat << EOF > trust-policy.json
> {
>     "Version": "2012-10-17",
>     "Statement": [
>         {
>             "Effect": "Allow",
>             "Principal": {
>                 "Service": "ec2.amazonaws.com"
>             },
>             "Action": "sts:AssumeRole"
>         }
>     ]
> }
> EOF
[cloudshell-user@ip-10-132-36-220 ~]$
```

At this stage, the trust policy is stored in a JSON file for later use. The next step involves attaching this policy when creating IAM roles that will assume the permissions defined within it.

You may recall that you did this back in Chapter 3. First create the PayrollKeyAdmin role:

```
[cloudshell-user@ip-10-132-36-220 ~]$ aws iam create-role \
>     --role-name PayrollKeyAdmin \
>     --assume-role-policy-document file://trust-policy.json
{
{
    "Role": {
        "Path": "/",
        "RoleName": "PayrollKeyAdmin",
        "RoleId": "AROAVUVIXTQ56QDVH7MID",
        "Arn": "arn:aws:iam::387974667323:role/PayrollKeyAdmin",
        "CreateDate": "2024-12-14T03:08:17+00:00",
        "AssumeRolePolicyDocument": {
            "Version": "2012-10-17",
            "Statement": [
                {
                    "Effect": "Allow",
                    "Principal": {
                        "Service": "ec2.amazonaws.com"
                    },
                    "Action": "sts:AssumeRole"
                }
            ]
        }
    }
}
[cloudshell-user@ip-10-132-36-220 ~]$
```

Then create the `PayrollKeyUser` role:

```
[cloudshell-user@ip-10-132-36-220 ~]$ aws iam create-role \
>     --role-name PayrollKeyUser \
>     --assume-role-policy-document file://trust-policy.json
{
    "Role": {
        "Path": "/",
        "RoleName": "PayrollKeyUser",
        "RoleId": "AROAVUVIXTQ56H4VOPTCX",
        "Arn": "arn:aws:iam::387974667323:role/PayrollKeyUser",
        "CreateDate": "2024-12-14T03:08:45+00:00",
        "AssumeRolePolicyDocument": {
            "Version": "2012-10-17",
            "Statement": [
                {
                    "Effect": "Allow",
                    "Principal": {
                        "Service": "ec2.amazonaws.com"
                    },
                    "Action": "sts:AssumeRole"
                }
            ]
        }
    }
}
```

You can list the roles to verify that they are there:

```
[cloudshell-user@ip-10-132-36-220 ~]$ aws iam list-roles -- query
'Roles[?RoleName==`PayrollKeyAdmin` || RoleName==` PayrollKeyUser`].RoleName' --
output text

PayrollKeyAdmin PayrollKeyUser
```

Now you'll move on to the key policy. A key policy is a JSON document that defines who can access the key and what actions they can perform. Use the following commands to create and apply the policy. You'll dynamically insert the account ID directly into the policy to ensure accuracy.

Run this to create the policy file:

```
[cloudshell-user@ip-10-140-9-192 ~]$ cat << EOF > key-policy.json
> {
>     "Version": "2012-10-17",
>     "Statement": [
>         {
>             "Sid": "Enable IAM User Permissions",
>             "Effect": "Allow",
>             "Principal": {
>                 "AWS": "arn:aws:iam::387974667323:root"
>             },
>             "Action": "kms:*",
>             "Resource": "*"
```

```
>          },
>          {
>               "Sid": "Allow Access for Key Administrators",
>               "Effect": "Allow",
>               "Principal": {
>                   "AWS": "arn:aws:iam::387974667323:role/PayrollKeyAdmin"
>               },
>               "Action": [
>                   "kms:Create*",
>                   "kms:Describe*",
>                   "kms:Enable*",
>                   "kms:List*",
>                   "kms:Put*",
>                   "kms:Update*",
>                   "kms:Revoke*",
>                   "kms:Disable*",
>                   "kms:Get*",
>                   "kms:Delete*",
>                   "kms:ScheduleKeyDeletion",
>                   "kms:CancelKeyDeletion"
>               ],
>               "Resource": "*"
>          },
>          {
>               "Sid": "Allow Use of the Key",
>               "Effect": "Allow",
>               "Principal": {
>                   "AWS": "arn:aws:iam::387974667323:role/PayrollKeyUser"
>               },
>               "Action": [
>                   "kms:Encrypt",
>                   "kms:Decrypt",
>                   "kms:ReEncrypt*",
>                   "kms:GenerateDataKey*",
>                   "kms:DescribeKey"
>               ],
>               "Resource": "*"
>          }
>      ]
> }
> EOF
[cloudshell-user@ip-10-140-9-192 ~]$
```

Here's what the policy does:

- The first statement ensures that the root user has emergency access to manage the key.

- The second statement allows the PayrollKeyAdmin role to perform administrative tasks like creating, deleting, or managing the key.

- The third statement grants the PayrollKeyUser role permissions to use the key for encrypting and decrypting data, but restricts administrative actions.

Now, attach this policy to the key using the `put-key-policy` command. Use the `KeyId` you noted earlier:

```
[cloudshell-user@ip-10-132-36-220 ~]$ aws kms put-key-policy \
>     --key-id 4543a25c-d840-4436-85d7-9906d5e463e5 \
>     --policy-name default \
>     --policy file://key-policy.json
```

Next, verify that it has been applied:

```
[cloudshell-user@ip-10-132-36-220 ~]$ aws kms get-key-policy \
>     --key-id 4543a25c-d840-4436-85d7-9906d5e463e5 \
>     --policy-name default{     "Policy": "{\n  \"Version\" : \ "2012-10-17\",\n
\"Statement\" : [ {\n    \"Sid\" : \"Enable  IAM User Permissions\",\n
\"Effect\" : \"Allow\",\n      \"Principal\" : {\n        \"AWS\" :
\"arn:aws:iam:: 387974667323:root\"\n       },\n    \"Action\" : \"kms:*\ ",\n
\"Resource\" : \"*\"\n  }, {\n    \"Sid\" : \"Allow Access for  Key
Administrators\",\n     \"Effect\" : \"Allow\ ",\n     \"Principal\" : {\n
\"AWS\" : \"arn:aws :iam::387974667323:role/PayrollKeyAdmin\"\n      },\n
\"Action\" : [ \"kms:Create*\", \"kms:Describe*\", \"kms :Enable*\",
\"kms:List*\", \"kms:Put*\", \"kms:Update*\ ", \"kms:Revoke*\",
\"kms:Disable*\", \"kms:Get*\", \"kms:Delete*\", \"kms:ScheduleKeyDeletion\",
\"kms:CancelKeyDeletion\" ],\n      \"Resource\" : \"*\"\n  }, {\n    \"Sid\" :
\"Allow Use of the Key\",\n      \"Effect\" : \"Allow\",\n     \"Principal\" : {\n
\"AWS\" : \"arn:aws:iam::387974667323:role/PayrollKeyUser\"\n      },\n
\"Action\" : [ \"kms:Encrypt\", \"kms:Decrypt\", \"kms:ReEncrypt*\",
\"kms:GenerateDataKey* \", \"kms:DescribeKey\" ],\n      \"Resource\" : \"*\"\n  }
]\n}",
    "PolicyName": "default"
}
```

Now that the key and policy are set up, you can test if the key works as expected by encrypting and decrypting some data.

First, create a test file with sensitive data and encrypt it using the KMS key:

```
[cloudshell-user@ip-10-132-36-220 ~]$ echo "Sensitive payroll data" > payroll.txt
```

You can `cat` to see what's in it:

```
[cloudshell-user@ip-10-132-36-220 ~]$ cat payroll.txt
Sensitive payroll data
```

Since that looks good, now encrypt it using the `aws kms encrypt` command. Using this command, you can encrypt the `payroll.txt` file using a specified KMS key and save the encrypted data to a new file called `payroll.encrypted`:

```
[cloudshell-user@ip-10-132-36-220 ~]$ aws kms encrypt \
>     --key-id 4543a25c-d840-4436-85d7-9906d5e463e5 \
>     --plaintext fileb://payroll.txt \
>     --output text \
>     --query CiphertextBlob | base64 --decode > payroll.encrypted
[cloudshell-user@ip-10-132-36-220 ~]$
```

You can make sure it's encrypted by trying to view the encrypted file:

```
[cloudshell-user@ip-10-132-36-220 ~]$ cat payroll.encrypted
00d0_<C `He.0u0s        *H
```

As you can see, the file is not readable since you encrypted it. You can now decrypt the file to verify that the key works for decryption. For this, use the aws kms decrypt command. This command decrypts the contents of the payroll. encrypted file and saves them to the payroll.decrypted file:

```
[cloudshell-user@ip-10-132-36-220 ~]$ aws kms decrypt \
>     --ciphertext-blob fileb://payroll.encrypted \
>     --output text \
>     --query Plaintext | base64 --decode > payroll.decrypted
```

Now verify that the decryption command worked:

```
[cloudshell-user@ip-10-132-36-220 ~]$ cat payroll.decrypted
Sensitive payroll data
[cloudshell-user@ip-10-132-36-220 ~]$
```

Because the content matches, you know the KMS encryption is working. The next section briefly covers AWS CloudHSM.

AWS CloudHSM

At this point, you understand key management and the role KMS plays. AWS CloudHSM takes key management to another level by offering dedicated hardware security modules (HSMs) for cryptographic operations. Before you dive into the details, it's important to understand how CloudHSM fits into AWS's broader encryption ecosystem. While KMS simplifies encryption with a managed service model, CloudHSM provides a hands-on approach, giving you direct control over the hardware and keys. This distinction makes CloudHSM appealing for organizations with compliance-driven requirements or custom encryption needs.

Hardware Security Modules

CloudHSM provides dedicated HSM devices that allow you to securely generate and manage encryption keys. Unlike KMS, where the key material is abstracted and managed by AWS, CloudHSM gives you control over the keys and cryptographic operations.

Each HSM instance is isolated and dedicated to your account, which gives you the highest level of data sovereignty and security. These devices meet FIPS

140-2 Level 3 compliance, making them suitable for industries with stringent security requirements, such as finance, healthcare, and government sectors.

Some key features of the Cloud HSM include:

- **Dedicated hardware:** Each CloudHSM instance operates as a single-tenant device, so you have cryptographic isolation and performance tailored to your workloads.

- **Full customer control:** With CloudHSM, you maintain full control over the encryption keys and cryptographic operations. AWS does not have access to your keys.

- **Custom encryption algorithms:** CloudHSM allows you to implement and use custom encryption algorithms, unlike AWS KMS, which is limited to predefined options. This flexibility is ideal for applications requiring specialized cryptographic approaches.

- **Scalability:** CloudHSM supports horizontal scaling by allowing you to add multiple HSMs to a cluster.

CloudHSM vs. KMS

While KMS and CloudHSM both provide encryption solutions, their use cases differ significantly. KMS is optimized for general-purpose encryption and is deeply integrated with AWS services. It's best used in scenarios where you want simplicity and seamless service integration.

In contrast, CloudHSM is designed for workloads that require granular control. Since CloudHSM gives you direct access to cryptographic operations, you get full visibility and control over your encryption keys. CloudHSM is also ideal when you want to use custom, or nonstandard, cryptographic algorithms, or in cases where you must meet FIPS 140-2 Level 3 compliance.

Integration Patterns

CloudHSM can be integrated into a wide range of cryptographic workflows. You can think of things like database encryption, where you want to manage Transparent Data Encryption (TDE) for Oracle or Microsoft SQL. You can also use CloudHSM for the creation and management of private certificate authorities. And finally, CloudHSM can be integrated into your application-level security and be used for secure key storage and advanced cryptographic operations.

CloudHSM isn't the right choice for every situation, and often KMS will suit your needs. However, when you need to design an encryption solution that's tailored to the use cases discussed in this section, CloudHSM is your AWS solution, and you should be aware of its existence.

With an understanding of KMS and CloudHSM, you'll now turn your attention to another AWS service that provides necessary data security and cryptography services on AWS—AWS Certificate Manager.

AWS Certificate Manager

AWS Certificate Manager (ACM) is a fully managed service that makes it easier to provision, deploy, and manage SSL/TLS certificates. These certificates play an important role in securing data in transit by encrypting the communication between clients and servers. Whether you're securing a website, an API, or internal endpoints, ACM removes much of the complexity associated with certificate handling by automating key processes like creation, deployment, and renewal.

At its core, ACM supports two types of certificates: public and private. *Public certificates* are used for Internet-facing applications and can be provisioned directly through ACM for free, while *private certificates* are designed for internal workloads and require *ACM's Private Certificate Authority (PCA)*. It's worth noting that ACM operates on a regional basis. Certificates are specific to the region where they are created, though services like CloudFront can use ACM certificates globally.

One of ACM's most important features is automation. Public certificates managed through ACM are renewed automatically, preventing the risk of downtime due to expired certificates. This is something many developers have dealt with when managing certificates manually. This seamless automation allows you to focus on your applications rather than worrying about certificate lifecycles.

Certificate Lifecycle Management

Managing the lifecycle of SSL/TLS certificates typically involves several stages: requesting, deploying, renewing, and revoking certificates. With ACM, this process is simplified because much of the heavy lifting is automated.

The process begins with the creation of a certificate. If you're working with a public-facing application, you can request a certificate directly through ACM. This can be done in the AWS console, using the AWS CLI, or through IaC. Once requested, ACM will validate domain ownership using DNS or email validation, depending on the method you choose. For DNS validation, ACM provides you with a CNAME record that you add to your domain's DNS configuration. If you're using Amazon Route53, this process is also simplified. However, you can use any DNS provider you choose. Once ownership is confirmed, ACM issues the certificate.

After a certificate is issued, the next step is deployment. ACM integrates with AWS services like Elastic Load Balancers (ELB), Amazon CloudFront, and API Gateway, making it easy to attach certificates to secure applications. For instance, deploying a certificate to an Application Load Balancer (ALB) only requires selecting the certificate from ACM during configuration.

Renewal is where ACM truly shines. For public certificates, ACM handles renewals automatically, so you know your certificates are always valid, and your services will remain available. This automation eliminates the risk of human error that often leads to expired certificates disrupting critical applications.

When a certificate must be revoked, ACM allows manual revocation to invalidate the certificate and ensure that it can no longer be trusted. While manual steps like revocation are sometimes necessary, ACM minimizes the effort required to manage certificates throughout their lifecycle, making it an ideal tool for maintaining secure communications.

Private Certificate Authority

While public certificates are ideal for Internet-facing applications, many organizations need private certificates for internal services like internal APIs, private networks, and device communications. AWS Certificate Manager Private Certificate Authority (ACM PCA) extends ACM's capabilities by allowing you to create and manage private certificates.

With ACM PCA, you can build a private certificate authority hierarchy that fits your organizational needs. This might include issuing certificates for internal endpoints, securing connections between IoT devices, or enabling mutual TLS authentication in private networks. Unlike public certificates, private certificates are not trusted outside your organization, making them ideal for internal use cases where you have full control over the trust chain.

ACM PCA provides flexibility and scalability for private certificates. You can issue an unlimited number of certificates and manage them across your workloads, and what's cool is that they still integrate seamlessly with other AWS services. This flexibility is valuable for organizations that have strict compliance or governance requirements. It's these use cases where a private certificate authority is the perfect choice.

As mentioned, one of the benefits of ACM PCA is its ability to integrate with AWS services and workloads. For example, you can use it to secure workloads running on EC2 instances, Kubernetes clusters, or serverless applications where private certificates might be required or even preferred. Additionally, ACM PCA combines automation with control, allowing you to issue and manage private certificates while still meeting your security and compliance requirements.

Integration with AWS Services

As mentioned, ACM integrates seamlessly with several AWS services. This section walks through the configuration of a certificate for an Elastic Load Balancer configuration with ACM. This way you can enable HTTPS on your load balancers, ensuring secure communication between clients and backend services. Similarly, Amazon CloudFront can use ACM certificates to encrypt content delivered globally, while API Gateway relies on ACM to secure API endpoints. The generation of the certificate in ACM will be similar for each of these use cases. These integrations make ACM a central part of your AWS security strategy when it comes to securing data in transit.

To see how ACM works in practice, you'll walk through creating a public certificate and deploying it on an Application Load Balancer (ALB) in the us-west-2 region, using the AWS CLI. This example will help you understand how ACM integrates with AWS services and how you can use it to secure an application.

To follow along, you can use the following CloudFormation template to create the basic resources. You can find this template in my GitHub repo at https://github.com/8carroll/Securing-the-Cloud-with-Brandon-Carroll, in the Chapter 7 folder. You'll also find additional resources in that folder that you can use to cut and paste the commands I use (be sure to replace the IDs, ARNs, and account numbers I use in this section):

```
AWSTemplateFormatVersion: '2010-09-09'
Description: >
  CloudFormation template to create prerequisites for the ACM  and ALB
integration example.
  This template creates a VPC, two public subnets (in us-west-2a  and us-west-
2b), an Internet Gateway,
  a public route table with associations, and a security group for the
Application Load Balancer.

Resources:
  DemoVPC:
    Type: AWS::EC2::VPC
    Properties:
      CidrBlock: 10.0.0.0/16
      EnableDnsSupport: true
      EnableDnsHostnames: true
      Tags:
        - Key: Name
          Value: ch7-demo-vpc

  DemoIGW:
    Type: AWS::EC2::InternetGateway
    Properties:
      Tags:
        - Key: Name
          Value: ch7-demo-igw

  AttachIGW:
    Type: AWS::EC2::VPCGatewayAttachment
    Properties:
      VpcId: !Ref DemoVPC
      InternetGatewayId: !Ref DemoIGW
```

```
    PublicRouteTable:
        Type: AWS::EC2::RouteTable
        Properties:
            VpcId: !Ref DemoVPC
            Tags:
                - Key: Name
                  Value: ch7-demo-public-rt

    PublicRoute:
        Type: AWS::EC2::Route
        DependsOn: AttachIGW
        Properties:
            RouteTableId: !Ref PublicRouteTable
            DestinationCidrBlock: 0.0.0.0/0
            GatewayId: !Ref DemoIGW

    PublicSubnet1:
        Type: AWS::EC2::Subnet
        Properties:
            VpcId: !Ref DemoVPC
            CidrBlock: 10.0.1.0/24
            MapPublicIpOnLaunch: true
            AvailabilityZone: us-west-2a
            Tags:
                - Key: Name
                  Value: ch7-public-subnet-1

    PublicSubnet2:
        Type: AWS::EC2::Subnet
        Properties:
            VpcId: !Ref DemoVPC
            CidrBlock: 10.0.2.0/24
            MapPublicIpOnLaunch: true
            AvailabilityZone: us-west-2b
            Tags:
                - Key: Name
                  Value: ch7-public-subnet-2

    Subnet1RouteTableAssociation:
        Type: AWS::EC2::SubnetRouteTableAssociation
        Properties:
            SubnetId: !Ref PublicSubnet1
            RouteTableId: !Ref PublicRouteTable

    Subnet2RouteTableAssociation:
        Type: AWS::EC2::SubnetRouteTableAssociation
        Properties:
            SubnetId: !Ref PublicSubnet2
            RouteTableId: !Ref PublicRouteTable

    AlbSecurityGroup:
        Type: AWS::EC2::SecurityGroup
        Properties:
            GroupDescription: Security group for ALB to allow HTTPS traffic
            VpcId: !Ref DemoVPC
```

```
        SecurityGroupIngress:
          - IpProtocol: tcp
            FromPort: 443
            ToPort: 443
            CidrIp: 0.0.0.0/0
        SecurityGroupEgress:
          - IpProtocol: -1
            FromPort: 0
            ToPort: 0
            CidrIp: 0.0.0.0/0
        Tags:
          - Key: Name
            Value: alb-sg

Outputs:
  VpcId:
    Description: VPC ID for the demo VPC
    Value: !Ref DemoVPC
  PublicSubnet1Id:
    Description: Public Subnet 1 ID
    Value: !Ref PublicSubnet1
  PublicSubnet2Id:
    Description: Public Subnet 2 ID
    Value: !Ref PublicSubnet2
  InternetGatewayId:
    Description: Internet Gateway ID
    Value: !Ref DemoIGW
  RouteTableId:
    Description: Public Route Table ID
    Value: !Ref PublicRouteTable
  AlbSecurityGroupId:
    Description: Security Group ID for the ALB
    Value: !Ref AlbSecurityGroup
```

Once you have the template loaded, you can start setting this up.

The first step is to request a public certificate for your domain. For this you need to have your own domain, and it's easiest to host it in Route53. I'm not going to cover how to get a domain in Route53, but you can read more about it at https://aws.amazon.com/getting-started/hands-on/get-a-domain/. Once the domain is registered, you can run the following command to initiate the request. (Note that gameonnetworks.com is my personal domain and you need to replace this with your own.)

```
[cloudshell-user@ip-10-140-18-175 ~]$ aws acm request-certificate \
>     --domain-name chapter7.gameonnetworks.com \
>     --validation-method DNS \
>     --region us-west-2
{
    "CertificateArn": "arn:aws:acm:us-west-2:387974667323:certificate/59c23fec-
4fce-42ec-a0c4-d65a46510d1d"
}
[cloudshell-user@ip-10-140-18-175 ~]$
```

Here, `--domain-name` specifies the domain for which you're requesting the certificate, and `--validation-method DNS` means domain ownership will be validated using DNS records. The output will include a `CertificateArn`, which you'll use in subsequent steps.

ACM will provide a CNAME record for DNS validation. Retrieve it using the following command:

```
[cloudshell-user@ip-10-140-18-175 ~]$ aws acm describe-certificate \
>     --certificate-arn arn:aws:acm:us-west-
2:387974667323:certificate/59c23fec-4fce-42ec-a0c4-d65a46510d1d
{
    "Certificate": {
        "CertificateArn": "arn:aws:acm:us-west-
2:387974667323:certificate/59c23fec-4fce-42ec-a0c4-d65a46510d1d",
        "DomainName": "chapter7.gameonnetworks.com",
        "SubjectAlternativeNames": [
            "chapter7.gameonnetworks.com"
        ],
        "DomainValidationOptions": [
            {
                "DomainName": "chapter7.gameonnetworks.com",
                "ValidationDomain": "chapter7.gameonnetworks.com",
                "ValidationStatus": "PENDING_VALIDATION",
                "ResourceRecord": {
                    "Name":
"_5a03db9220a5d56409fbb01c09e3260c.chapter7.gameonnetworks.com.",
                    "Type": "CNAME",
                    "Value": "_37b90757346ec6cf66138a6dcb8c76ac.zfyfvmchrl.
acm-validations.aws."
                },
                "ValidationMethod": "DNS"
            }
        ],
        "Subject": "CN=chapter7.gameonnetworks.com",
        "Issuer": "Amazon",
        "CreatedAt": "2024-12-17T16:00:12.946000+00:00",
        "Status": "PENDING_VALIDATION",
        "KeyAlgorithm": "RSA-2048",
        "SignatureAlgorithm": "SHA256WITHRSA",
        "InUseBy": [],
        "Type": "AMAZON_ISSUED",
        "KeyUsages": [],
        "ExtendedKeyUsages": [],
        "RenewalEligibility": "INELIGIBLE",
        "Options": {
            "CertificateTransparencyLoggingPreference": "ENABLED"
        }
    }
}
(END)
```

You'll see a DNS record that needs to be added to your domain's DNS configuration. Once you add the CNAME record, ACM will automatically validate

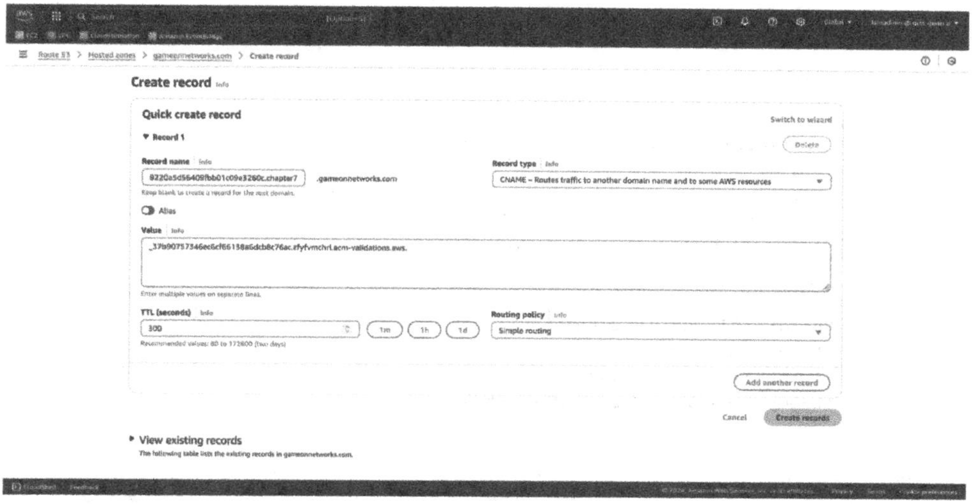

Figure 7.2: CNAME record.

the domain and issue the certificate. I don't cover that here since you already did this in Chapter 5; however, Figure 7.2 shows the CNAME record.

You can continue to run the `aws acm describe-certificate` command until the certificate has been issued. Once the certificate is issued, you can deploy it to an ALB. Although you can use a CloudFormation template to do this, for the sake of practice, you do it manually here. Before you can create and configure an ALB, you need to ensure the following resources exist:

- A VPC to house the ALB and resources
- Two public subnets in separate availability zones (required for the ALB)
- A security group to allow inbound HTTPS traffic

Let's start by creating these prerequisites.

You'll create a VPC named `demo-vpc` with a CIDR block of `10.0.0.0/16` in `us-west-2`:

```
[cloudshell-user@ip-10-140-18-175 ~]$ aws ec2 create-vpc \
>     --cidr-block 10.0.0.0/16 \
>     --tag-specifications 'ResourceType=vpc,Tags=[{Key=Name,Value=ch7-demo-vpc}]'
{
    "Vpc": {
        "OwnerId": "387974667323",
        "InstanceTenancy": "default",
        "Ipv6CidrBlockAssociationSet": [],
        "CidrBlockAssociationSet": [
            {
                "AssociationId": "vpc-cidr-assoc-005993ba18ffc46dd",
                "CidrBlock": "10.0.0.0/16",
```

```
                      "CidrBlockState": {
                           "State": "associated"
                      }
                  }
            ],
            "IsDefault": false,
            "Tags": [
                  {
                      "Key": "Name",
                      "Value": "ch7-demo-vpc"
                  }
            ],
            "VpcId": "vpc-0b26d205ba2bbd91b",
            "State": "pending",
            "CidrBlock": "10.0.0.0/16",
            "DhcpOptionsId": "dopt-62d09d1a"
      }
  }
  (END)
```

Note the VPC ID returned in the output. You can create your own table of this information, like Chapter 5 did, if that works for you. You need that information because you'll use it in the next steps. Now, you'll create two public subnets in separate availability zones within the VPC. Replace the VPC ID you see here with the ID of the VPC you created earlier. If you try to use mine, it won't work:

```
[cloudshell-user@ip-10-140-18-175 ~]$ aws ec2 create-subnet \
>      --vpc-id vpc-0b26d205ba2bbd91b \
>      --cidr-block 10.0.1.0/24 \
>      --availability-zone us-west-2a \
>      --tag-specifications 'ResourceType=subnet,Tags=[{Key=Name,Value=ch7-
public-subnet-1}]'
{
    "Subnet": {
        "AvailabilityZoneId": "usw2-az2",
        "OwnerId": "387974667323",
        "AssignIpv6AddressOnCreation": false,
        "Ipv6CidrBlockAssociationSet": [],
        "Tags": [
            {
                "Key": "Name",
                "Value": "ch7-public-subnet-1"
            }
        ],
        "SubnetArn": "arn:aws:ec2:us-west-2:387974667323:subnet/
subnet-05cb57c3045617a31",
        "EnableDns64": false,
        "Ipv6Native": false,
        "PrivateDnsNameOptionsOnLaunch": {
            "HostnameType": "ip-name",
            "EnableResourceNameDnsARecord": false,
            "EnableResourceNameDnsAAAARecord": false
        },
```

```
            "SubnetId": "subnet-05cb57c3045617a31",
            "State": "available",
            "VpcId": "vpc-0b26d205ba2bbd91b",
            "CidrBlock": "10.0.1.0/24",
            "AvailableIpAddressCount": 251,
            "AvailabilityZone": "us-west-2a",
            "DefaultForAz": false,
            "MapPublicIpOnLaunch": false
        }
}
(END)


[cloudshell-user@ip-10-140-18-175 ~]$ aws ec2 create-subnet \
>     --vpc-id vpc-0b26d205ba2bbd91b \
>     --cidr-block 10.0.2.0/24 \
>     --availability-zone us-west-2b \
>     --tag-specifications 'ResourceType=subnet,Tags=[{Key=Name,Value=ch7-
public-subnet-2}]'
{
    "Subnet": {
        "AvailabilityZoneId": "usw2-az1",
        "OwnerId": "387974667323",
        "AssignIpv6AddressOnCreation": false,
        "Ipv6CidrBlockAssociationSet": [],
        "Tags": [
            {
                "Key": "Name",
                "Value": "ch7-public-subnet-2"
            }
        ],
        "SubnetArn": "arn:aws:ec2:us-west-2:387974667323:subnet/
subnet-0cc3cbf934fbb1c69",
        "EnableDns64": false,
        "Ipv6Native": false,
        "PrivateDnsNameOptionsOnLaunch": {
            "HostnameType": "ip-name",
            "EnableResourceNameDnsARecord": false,
            "EnableResourceNameDnsAAAARecord": false
        },
        "SubnetId": "subnet-0cc3cbf934fbb1c69",
        "State": "available",
        "VpcId": "vpc-0b26d205ba2bbd91b",
        "CidrBlock": "10.0.2.0/24",
        "AvailableIpAddressCount": 251,
        "AvailabilityZone": "us-west-2b",
        "DefaultForAz": false,
        "MapPublicIpOnLaunch": false
    }
}
(END)
```

Note the subnet IDs returned in the output.

Next, you'll create a security group named alb-sg to allow inbound HTTPS traffic (port 443) and all outbound traffic:

```
[cloudshell-user@ip-10-140-18-175 ~]$ aws ec2 create-security-group \
>       --group-name alb-sg \
>       --description "Security group for ALB to allow HTTPS traffic" \
>       --vpc-id vpc-0b26d205ba2bbd91b \
>       --tag-specifications 'ResourceType=security-
group,Tags=[{Key=Name,Value=alb-sg}]'
{
    "GroupId": "sg-05daee71a0f98d360",
    "Tags": [
        {
            "Key": "Name",
            "Value": "alb-sg"
        }
    ],
    "SecurityGroupArn": "arn:aws:ec2:us-west-2 :387974667323:security-group/sg-
05daee71a0f98d360"
}
[cloudshell-user@ip-10-140-18-175 ~]$
```

Note the security group ID. Next, add an inbound rule to allow traffic on port 443 (HTTPS):

```
[cloudshell-user@ip-10-140-18-175 ~]$ aws ec2 authorize-security-group-ingress \
>       --group-id sg-05daee71a0f98d360 \
>       --protocol tcp \
>       --port 443 \
>       --cidr 0.0.0.0/0
{
    "Return": true,
    "SecurityGroupRules": [
        {
            "SecurityGroupRuleId": "sgr-07767adc6072627e7",
            "GroupId": "sg-05daee71a0f98d360",
            "GroupOwnerId": "387974667323",
            "IsEgress": false,
            "IpProtocol": "tcp",
            "FromPort": 443,
            "ToPort": 443,
            "CidrIpv4": "0.0.0.0/0",
            "SecurityGroupRuleArn": "arn:aws:ec2:
us-west-2:387974667323:security-group-rule/sgr-07767adc6072627e7"
        }
    ]
}
[cloudshell-user@ip-10-140-18-175 ~]$
```

This rule allows any IP to access the ALB over HTTPS.

Before creating the ALB, you need to ensure the subnets have a route to the Internet. This requires an Internet Gateway (IGW) and appropriate route tables. Run the following command to create the IGW:

```
[cloudshell-user@ip-10-140-18-175 ~]$ aws ec2 create-internet-gateway \
>       --tag-specifications 'ResourceType=internet-
gateway,Tags=[{Key=Name,Value=ch7-demo-igw}]'
```

```
{
    "InternetGateway": {
        "Attachments": [],
        "InternetGatewayId": "igw-0d9975f39b218ebeb",
        "OwnerId": "387974667323",
        "Tags": [
            {
                "Key": "Name",
                "Value": "ch7-demo-igw"
            }
        ]
    }
}
[cloudshell-user@ip-10-140-18-175 ~]$
```

The output will include the Internet Gateway ID. Copy this value for the next step. Now attach the Internet Gateway to the VPC you created earlier:

```
[cloudshell-user@ip-10-140-18-175 ~]$ aws ec2 attach-internet-gateway \
>       --internet-gateway-id igw-0d9975f39b218ebeb \
>       --vpc-id vpc-0b26d205ba2bbd91b
[cloudshell-user@ip-10-140-18-175 ~]$
```

Now that the IGW is attached, you need to ensure the public subnets have a route to the Internet. This involves creating or modifying the route table to include a default route through the IGW. Create a route table and associate it with the VPC:

```
[cloudshell-user@ip-10-140-18-175 ~]$ aws ec2 create-route-table \
>       --vpc-id vpc-0b26d205ba2bbd91b \
>       --tag-specifications 'ResourceType=route-table,Tags
=[{Key=Name,Value=ch7-demo-public-rt}]'
{
    "RouteTable": {
        "Associations": [],
        "PropagatingVgws": [],
        "RouteTableId": "rtb-085731c5a54d36109",
        "Routes": [
            {
                "DestinationCidrBlock": "10.0.0.0/16",
                "GatewayId": "local",
                "Origin": "CreateRouteTable",
                "State": "active"
            }
        ],
        "Tags": [
            {
                "Key": "Name",
                "Value": "ch7-demo-public-rt"
            }
        ],
```

```
        "VpcId": "vpc-0b26d205ba2bbd91b",
        "OwnerId": "387974667323"
    },
    "ClientToken": "fbd9390e-71cc-4a92-b249-8d2f7018321a"
}
[cloudshell-user@ip-10-140-18-175 ~]$
```

The output will include the Route Table ID, and you will need to copy this value as well. Next, add a route to the IGW for all outbound Internet traffic (0.0.0.0/0):

```
[cloudshell-user@ip-10-140-18-175 ~]$ aws ec2 create-route \
>      --route-table-id rtb-085731c5a54d36109 \
>      --destination-cidr-block 0.0.0.0/0 \
>      --gateway-id igw-0d9975f39b218ebeb
{
    "Return": true
}
[cloudshell-user@ip-10-140-18-175 ~]$
```

And now you need to explicitly associate this route table with both public subnets you created earlier:

```
[cloudshell-user@ip-10-140-18-175 ~]$ aws ec2 associate-route-table \
>      --subnet-id subnet-05cb57c3045617a31 \
>      --route-table-id rtb-085731c5a54d36109
{
    "AssociationId": "rtbassoc-0e17d4ec6a1949df9",
    "AssociationState": {
        "State": "associated"
    }
}
[cloudshell-user@ip-10-140-18-175 ~]$ aws ec2 associate-route-table \
>      --subnet-id subnet-0cc3cbf934fbb1c69 \
>      --route-table-id rtb-085731c5a54d36109
{
    "AssociationId": "rtbassoc-0d21e59fb83eb52c1",
    "AssociationState": {
        "State": "associated"
    }
}
[cloudshell-user@ip-10-140-18-175 ~]$
```

At this point, the subnets are configured as public subnets, with routes to the Internet. With the IGW and route tables in place, you can proceed to create the ALB. Use the subnet IDs and security group ID from the earlier steps:

```
[cloudshell-user@ip-10-140-18-175 ~]$ aws elbv2 create-load-balancer \
>      --name demo-alb \
>      --subnets subnet-05cb57c3045617a31 subnet-0cc3cbf934fbb1c69 \
>      --security-groups sg-05daee71a0f98d360 \
>      --scheme internet-facing \
>      --type application \
>      --tags Key=Name,Value=ch7-demo-alb
```

```
{
    "LoadBalancers": [
        {
            "LoadBalancerArn": "arn:aws:elasticloadbalancing:us-west-
2:387974667323:loadbalancer/app/demo-alb/563466163988716b",
            "DNSName": "demo-alb-1147590996.us-west-2.elb.amazonaws.com",
            "CanonicalHostedZoneId": "Z1H1FL5HABSF5",
            "CreatedTime": "2024-12-17T18:00:25.791000+00:00",
            "LoadBalancerName": "demo-alb",
            "Scheme": "internet-facing",
            "VpcId": "vpc-0b26d205ba2bbd91b",
            "State": {
                "Code": "provisioning"
            },
            "Type": "application",
            "AvailabilityZones": [
                {
                    "ZoneName": "us-west-2b",
                    "SubnetId": "subnet-0cc3cbf934fbb1c69",
                    "LoadBalancerAddresses": []
                },
                {
                    "ZoneName": "us-west-2a",
                    "SubnetId": "subnet-05cb57c3045617a31",
                    "LoadBalancerAddresses": []
                }
            ],
            "SecurityGroups": [
                "sg-05daee71a0f98d360"
            ],
            "IpAddressType": "ipv4"
        }
    ]
}
(END)
```

Note the load balancer ARN. You'll need it in the next step. As a frame of reference, creating the IGW and updating the route table ensures that the ALB can communicate with the Internet. Without these configurations, the ALB and resources in the public subnets will not have a route to external traffic, leading to errors during creation or testing.

With the ALB now successfully created, you can move on to attaching the ACM certificate and completing the setup. To do this, you need to create an HTTPS listener and associate the ACM certificate. Before you attach the HTTPS listener, you need to create a target group. A target group specifies where the ALB should route incoming traffic, such as EC2 instances, IP addresses, or Lambda functions. For this example, you'll create a target group that routes traffic to EC2 instances as its targets. This setup allows the ALB to distribute incoming requests to specific EC2 instances based on the load-balancing algorithm.

Run the following command to create the target group:

```
[cloudshell-user@ip-10-134-67-220 ~]$ aws elbv2 create-target-group \
>       --name ch7-demo-tg \
>       --protocol HTTP \
>       --port 80 \
>       --vpc-id vpc-0b26d205ba2bbd91b \
>       --target-type instance \
>       --tags Key=Name,Value=demo-tg
{
    "TargetGroups": [
        {
            "TargetGroupArn": "arn:aws:elasticloadbalancing:us-west-
2:387974667323:targetgroup/ch7-demo-tg/ae4bb9d05b11b17b",
            "TargetGroupName": "ch7-demo-tg",
            "Protocol": "HTTP",
            "Port": 80,
            "VpcId": "vpc-0b26d205ba2bbd91b",
            "HealthCheckProtocol": "HTTP",
            "HealthCheckPort": "traffic-port",
            "HealthCheckEnabled": true,
            "HealthCheckIntervalSeconds": 30,
            "HealthCheckTimeoutSeconds": 5,
            "HealthyThresholdCount": 5,
            "UnhealthyThresholdCount": 2,
            "HealthCheckPath": "/",
            "Matcher": {
                "HttpCode": "200"
            },
            "TargetType": "instance",
            "ProtocolVersion": "HTTP1",
            "IpAddressType": "ipv4"
        }
    ]
}
[cloudshell-user@ip-10-134-67-220 ~]$
```

This command creates a target group named demo-tg that listens for HTTP traffic on port 80. Note the target group ARN returned in the output—you'll need it in the next step.

Once the target group has been created, you can add an HTTPS listener to the ALB. The listener directs traffic to the target group and uses the ACM-managed certificate for encryption.

Run the following command, replacing the LoadBalancerArn, CertificateArn, and TargetGroupArn with the values obtained from your output:

```
[cloudshell-user@ip-10-134-67-220 ~]$ aws elbv2 create-listener \
>       --load-balancer-arn arn:aws:elasticloadbalancing:us-west-
2:387974667323:loadbalancer/app/demo-alb/563466163988716b \
>       --protocol HTTPS \
>       --port 443 \
```

```
>      --certificates CertificateArn=arn:aws:acm:us-west-
2:387974667323:certificate/59c23fec-4fce-42ec-a0c4-d65a46510d1d \
>      --default-actions Type=forward,TargetGroupArn=arn:aws:
elasticloadbalancing:us-west-2:387974667323:targetgroup/ch7-demo-
tg/ae4bb9d05b11b17b
{
    "Listeners": [
        {
            "ListenerArn": "arn:aws:elasticloadbalancing:us-west-
2:387974667323:listener/app/demo-alb/563466163988716b/197c2b542ccb796a",
            "LoadBalancerArn": "arn:aws:elasticloadbalancing: us-west-
2:387974667323:loadbalancer/app/demo-alb/563466163988716b",
            "Port": 443,
            "Protocol": "HTTPS",
            "Certificates": [
                {
                    "CertificateArn": "arn:aws:acm:us-west-
2:387974667323:certificate/59c23fec-4fce-42ec-a0c4-d65a46510d1d"
                }
            ],
            "SslPolicy": "ELBSecurityPolicy-2016-08",
            "DefaultActions": [
                {
                    "Type": "forward",
                    "TargetGroupArn": "arn:aws:elasticloadbalancing:us-west-
2:387974667323:targetgroup/ch7-demo-tg/ae4bb9d05b11b17b",
                    "ForwardConfig": {
                        "TargetGroups": [
                            {
                                "TargetGroupArn": "arn:aws:elasticloadbalancing:
us-west-2:387974667323:targetgroup/ch7-
demo-tg/ae4bb9d05b11b17b",
                                "Weight": 1
                            }
                        ],
                        "TargetGroupStickinessConfig": {
                            "Enabled": false
                        }
                    }
                }
            ]
        }
    ]
}
(END)
```

Here's what the command does:

- --load-balancer-arn: Specifies the ALB you created.

- --protocol HTTPS and --port 443: Set up an HTTPS listener on port 443.

- --certificates CertificateArn: Attaches the ACM certificate for SSL/ TLS termination.

■ `--default-actions Type=forward,TargetGroupArn`: Routes incoming traffic to the specified target group.

Once the listener is created, the ALB is fully configured and ready to handle HTTPS traffic. Use the following command to retrieve the DNS name of the ALB:

```
[cloudshell-user@ip-10-134-67-220 ~]$ aws elbv2 describe-load-balancers \
>      --names demo-alb \
>      --query 'LoadBalancers[0].DNSName' \
>      --output text

demo-alb-1147590996.us-west-2.elb.amazonaws.com
```

Copy the DNS name and access it in your browser using `https://`. If everything is set up correctly, you should see a secure HTTPS connection. From there, you can view the certificate to ensure that it is in fact the one you created in this section. At this point, the ALB is configured with an ACM-managed certificate, enabling secure HTTPS connections.

With AWS Certificate Manager providing automated management for SSL/TLS certificates, you now have a powerful tool to secure data in transit across your AWS environment. The next section covers Amazon Macie, a service that helps you discover, classify, and protect sensitive data stored in AWS.

Amazon Macie

Amazon Macie is a managed data security and privacy service that uses machine learning to help you discover, classify, and protect sensitive data stored in AWS. It's included in this chapter because data protection isn't just about encryption or access controls—it's also about understanding *what* data you have, *where* it lives, and *how* it's being used. Without this visibility, it's impossible to implement meaningful security measures.

Macie fits naturally alongside other tools you've explored for data security, like encryption and key management. While encryption protects your data, Macie provides insight into *which* data requires the most protection. You would use Amazon Macie when you need to identify and safeguard sensitive data, such as personally identifiable information (PII), financial data, or intellectual property, across large-scale AWS environments—especially in services like S3.

Data Discovery and Classification

The first step in protecting your data is knowing where it is. In AWS environments, data often sprawls across multiple buckets, services, and regions. Macie automates the process of scanning your Amazon S3 buckets to identify what data exists and classify it based on its content and sensitivity. For example, it

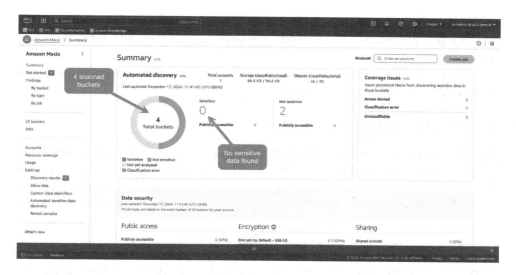

Figure 7.3: Macie dashboard.

can determine if a bucket contains credit card numbers, Social Security numbers, or other forms of PII.

What sets Macie apart is its ability to do this at scale. Instead of manually inspecting buckets or guessing where sensitive data might be, Macie provides a clear view of your data inventory and assigns sensitivity scores to help you prioritize areas that need attention.

In Figure 7.3 you can see the Dashboard of Macie after an initial scan.

As you can see in Figure 7.3, a total of four S3 buckets were scanned, and there was no sensitive data found in them. At the very bottom of the image, you can also see that all four buckets are set to encrypt by default.

Sensitive Data Identification

Once Macie has discovered and classified your data, it takes the next step: identifying specific types of sensitive data. It uses pre-built and customizable managed data identifiers to search for patterns that match common types of sensitive information, such as

- Names and addresses
- Credit card numbers
- Bank account details
- Personal health information (PHI)

For example, if your S3 buckets contain CSV files with employee records or logs with unencrypted credit card numbers, Macie will flag these findings, assign them a severity level, and provide actionable insights. This capability is invaluable for compliance with data privacy regulations like GDPR, CCPA, and HIPAA.

Macie not only tells you *where* sensitive data is, but also *how much* of it exists and whether it's being stored securely.

Automated Remediation

Identifying sensitive data is only half the battle—you also need to act on those findings. Macie integrates with AWS services like Amazon EventBridge and AWS Lambda to automate remediation tasks. For instance, if Macie detects unencrypted sensitive data in an S3 bucket, you can trigger an automatic workflow to

- Encrypt the data using AWS KMS.
- Restrict public access to the bucket.
- Notify security teams through Amazon SNS or other alerting tools.

This automated approach ensures that issues are addressed quickly, minimizing risks without requiring constant manual intervention. By combining Macie's insights with automated remediation, you can maintain a strong security posture and reduce the likelihood of data breaches.

So far, you've explored how Amazon Macie helps you discover and classify sensitive data, ensuring you know *what* you need to protect and *where* it's located. But discovering sensitive data is only part of the equation—once you've identified it, you need to ensure that it's properly protected, both *where it sits* and *as it moves*.

Introduction to Encryption

This leads the discussion to one of the fundamental tools for safeguarding data: *encryption*. If you've ever uploaded files to cloud storage services like iCloud, OneDrive, or Google Drive, you've benefited from encryption without even realizing it. Encryption ensures that if someone gains access to your files, they can't actually read the data unless they have the correct decryption key. AWS takes this concept further by providing encryption capabilities across its services, allowing you to protect data wherever it lives or moves in your environment.

Encryption is broken down into three areas:

- **Encryption at rest:** Protecting data stored on disks, buckets, and databases
- **Encryption in transit:** Safeguarding data as it travels between systems or over the network
- **Client-side encryption:** Encrypting data before it even reaches AWS storage

Each of these areas plays an important role in protecting your data at different stages of its lifecycle, and AWS provides tools and integrations that make encryption both secure and manageable. Let's start with encryption at rest.

Encryption at Rest

When you store data in the cloud, whether it's files, databases, or snapshots, it's like placing valuables in a safe. The question is, what if someone gets their hands on the safe? Encryption at rest ensures that even if someone gains unauthorized access to your storage, the data remains unreadable without the encryption keys. Think of it as a combination lock for your cloud storage, because if you have no key, you have no access.

This section looks at how AWS helps protect stored data with encryption options for services like EBS volumes, S3 buckets, and RDS databases.

EBS Volume Encryption

Elastic Block Store (EBS) provides persistent storage for your EC2 instances, much like virtual hard drives. EBS volume encryption ensures that all data stored on these virtual disks is encrypted automatically, including snapshots and any backups. This is especially important when running workloads that handle sensitive data, as it ensures your storage remains secure without requiring significant overhead or manual configurations.

S3 Bucket Encryption

Amazon S3 (Simple Storage Service) is often the go-to solution for storing objects like files, logs, and backups. With encryption options like server-side encryption (SSE) and client-side encryption, AWS ensures that your S3 buckets can meet strict security and compliance requirements.

RDS Encryption Options

Amazon RDS (Relational Database Service) offers encryption at rest for database instances, snapshots, and backups. Whether you're running MySQL, PostgreSQL, or Oracle databases, RDS encryption ensures that your data is protected without additional overhead.

Encryption in Transit

While encryption at rest protects data that's stored, encryption in transit secures your data as it moves from one place to another. If you're familiar with setting up secure connections, such as SSH or HTTPS, you've already worked with encryption in transit. You did this in Chapter 5 and earlier in this chapter with your EC2 instances and load balancer. In IT environments, data constantly flows between clients, servers, and applications, and ensuring that it's encrypted during transmission is critical to prevent eavesdropping or tampering.

The following sections look at how AWS implements encryption in transit through technologies like TLS, VPC traffic encryption, and API gateway encryption.

TLS Implementation

Transport Layer Security (TLS) is the backbone of secure communications on the Internet today, providing encrypted connections for applications like web servers, APIs, and messaging systems. In AWS, enabling TLS is a standard way to ensure that data remains secure as it travels between systems, such as between users and your ALB.

VPC Traffic Encryption

Virtual Private Cloud (VPC) traffic encryption secures data flowing between AWS services and instances within your network. Whether data is moving between EC2 instances, databases, or applications, encrypting VPC traffic ensures that internal communication remains private and protected.

API Gateway Encryption

The API Gateway serves as a front door for your applications, exposing endpoints that clients can access. Encrypting API traffic using TLS not only secures data transmission but also builds trust with users and ensures compliance with industry standards.

Client-Side Encryption

Client-side encryption ensures that your data is encrypted before it even reaches AWS storage services. By encrypting data locally, you maintain full control over encryption keys and processes, adding an extra layer of security against unauthorized access.

AWS provides tools like the AWS Encryption SDK and options for client-side encryption in S3 to make this process easier.

AWS Encryption SDK

The AWS Encryption SDK is a client-side library that simplifies the process of encrypting and decrypting data. It allows developers to implement encryption in their applications without needing to reinvent the wheel, providing support for encryption algorithms and key management.

S3 Client-Side Encryption

With S3 client-side encryption, you encrypt data locally before uploading it to an S3 bucket. This is especially useful when compliance or internal policies require that data be encrypted outside the cloud provider's control.

Best Practices

Before wrapping up the discussion of encryption, this section shares some best practices for managing encryption effectively across your AWS environment. These tips will help you ensure consistency, security, and compliance when protecting your data, whether it's at rest, in transit, or managed on the client side.

From there, you'll transition into the next key aspect of data protection—secrets management. This explains how AWS Secrets Manager helps you secure application credentials, API keys, and other sensitive secrets.

Now that you've explored encryption and its role in securing data at rest, in transit, and on the client side, there's one more critical piece to address: how you manage the secrets that protect this data. Encryption relies on keys, passwords, and credentials to remain secure, and if these secrets are mishandled, even the strongest encryption won't help.

This is where secrets management comes into play. AWS provides services like the AWS Secrets Manager to securely store, manage, and rotate sensitive information such as database credentials, API keys, and encryption keys. Proper secrets management ensures that your data remains protected while simplifying the often-complex task of managing credentials at scale.

Secrets Management with AWS Secrets Manager

AWS Secrets Manager is a fully managed service that securely stores and retrieves secrets such as database passwords, API keys, and other credentials. It not only stores secrets but also automates secret rotation, ensuring your credentials remain secure without requiring manual intervention.

Why does this matter? Imagine you've encrypted a database with KMS, but you're storing its access credentials in plain text. That's like locking a vault but leaving the key under the mat—effective secrets management, in contrast, ensures that the "keys" to your encrypted data are just as secure as the data itself.

Secrets Manager integrates seamlessly with AWS services like Amazon RDS, making it easy to rotate database credentials without downtime. By centralizing your secrets in a secure and auditable location, it reduces the risk of credential leaks and helps you meet compliance requirements.

Storing and Retrieving a Secret in AWS Secrets Manager

This section shows you how to store a database password in Secrets Manager using the AWS CLI and then retrieve it securely. This scenario is common when working with applications that need credentials to connect to a database.

This example shows you how to create a secret, retrieve it securely, and understand why this process matters.

To start, store the secret by running the following command:

```
[cloudshell-user@ip-10-140-27-250 ~]$ aws secretsmanager create-secret \
>     --name demo/db-password \
>     --description "RDS database password for my application" \
>     --secret-string '{"username":"admin", "password":"MyDataBasePassword"}'
{
    "ARN": "arn:aws:secretsmanager:us-west-2:387974667323:secret:demo/db-
password-AuzTR4",
    "Name": "demo/db-password",
    "VersionId": "64d65ba4-296b-4556-97b2-679e632e5b61"
}
[cloudshell-user@ip-10-140-27-250 ~]$
```

Here's what the command does:

- ■ --name demo/db-password: This is the name of your secret. Choose a name that makes sense for your environment, such as prod/db-password or app/db-password.

- ■ --description: This is a helpful note to describe the secret for future reference.

- ■ --secret-string: This stores the actual credentials as a JSON string. Replace admin and MyDataBasePassword with your real database username and password.

Note the ARN shown in your output, since it will be specific to your AWS account and environment. Do not use the ARN from the example; always use the ARN from your own output.

With the secret stored, you can now retrieve it securely. Use the following command, replacing the name with the secret you just created:

```
[cloudshell-user@ip-10-140-27-250 ~]$ aws secretsmanager get-secret-value \
>     --secret-id demo/db-password \
>     --query SecretString \
>     --output text
{"username":"admin", "password":"MyDataBasePassword"}
[cloudshell-user@ip-10-140-27-250 ~]$
```

When you run this command, the output displays the actual username and password you stored.

In practice, your applications can retrieve this secret programmatically. For example, if you're using Python, you can integrate AWS Secrets Manager with your application code like this. First create a file for the application code. In this case, I created something brief with Python:

```
[cloudshell-user@ip-10-140-27-250 ~]$ touch secrets.py
Add the code to the file:
[cloudshell-user@ip-10-140-27-250 ~]$ nano secrets.py
Here is the Python code I am using:
import boto3
import json

client = boto3.client('secretsmanager')
response = client.get_secret_value(SecretId="demo/db-password")
secret = json.loads(response['SecretString'])

print("Username:", secret['username'])
print("Password:", secret['password'])
```

Next, run the application and note the output. If you have any issues running this command, ensure that it is set as an executable. In my environment, I did not need to make any changes:

```
[cloudshell-user@ip-10-140-27-250 ~]$ python secrets.py
Username: admin
Password: MyDataBasePassword
[cloudshell-user@ip-10-140-27-250 ~]$
```

This approach pulls the credentials securely at runtime, eliminating the need to hardcode sensitive information in configuration files or environment variables. If the password is updated in Secrets Manager, the application will retrieve the new value automatically without requiring any redeployment. This is exactly what you want.

The next section shifts gears and looks at cryptographic best practices—exploring how to handle key lifecycle management, secure algorithm choices, and auditing to maintain a strong data protection strategy.

Cryptographic Best Practices

With all the tools and services discussed in this chapter—KMS, Macie, and Secrets Manager—how do you ensure you're using encryption and secrets management effectively? This section outlines some best practices for cryptographic security, helping you maintain a robust and scalable approach to data protection.

Key Lifecycle Management

Managing the lifecycle of encryption keys is critical to maintaining secure systems. Best practices include

- **Regular key rotation:** Periodically rotating keys reduces the impact of a compromised key. AWS KMS supports automatic key rotation for customer-managed keys.
- **Proper key storage:** Use centralized services like AWS KMS or Secrets Manager to store and manage keys securely.
- **Revocation and deletion:** When a key is no longer needed, ensure it is properly retired to prevent unauthorized access.

Algorithm Selection

Selecting the right cryptographic algorithms is essential for balancing security and performance. For most AWS services, AES-256 is the standard for symmetric encryption, providing a strong balance of security and efficiency. For asymmetric encryption, AWS supports RSA and ECC algorithms, which are commonly used for digital signatures and key exchanges. Always follow AWS recommendations and avoid outdated algorithms like SHA-1 or MD5.

Auditing and Monitoring

To ensure that encryption and secrets management processes remain secure over time, enable comprehensive monitoring and auditing:

- Use AWS CloudTrail to log all KMS and Secrets Manager activity, ensuring visibility into key usage and secret access.
- Monitor access patterns and detect anomalies using Amazon CloudWatch and AWS Config.
- Regularly review and update key policies, IAM roles, and access permissions to enforce the principle of least privilege.

These best practices help you maintain strong cryptographic controls while ensuring your security posture evolves with changing requirements.

Cleaning Up Your Resources

To ensure you don't incur unnecessary costs after completing the hands-on exercises in this chapter, it's important to clean up the resources you created. The following step-by-step guide deletes the resources in the reverse order of their creation. Follow these commands carefully, replacing placeholders with the actual values from your setup.

The first step is to remove the HTTPS listener from your ALB:

```
[cloudshell-user@ip-10-138-15-243 ~]$ aws elbv2 delete-listener --listener-
arn arn:aws:elasticloadbalancing:us-west-2:387974667323:listener/app/demo-
alb/563466163988716b/197c2b542ccb796a
```

Next, delete the ALB:

```
[cloudshell-user@ip-10-138-15-243 ~]$ aws elbv2 delete-load-balancer
--load-balancer-arn arn:aws:elasticloadbalancing:us-west-
2:387974667323:loadbalancer/app/demo-alb/563466163988716b
[cloudshell-user@ip-10-138-15-243 ~]$
```

Delete the target group:

```
[cloudshell-user@ip-10-138-15-243 ~]$ aws elbv2 delete-target-group --
target-group-arn arn:aws:elasticloadbalancing:us-west-
2:387974667323:targetgroup/ch7-demo-tg/ae4bb9d05b11b17b
[cloudshell-user@ip-10-138-15-243 ~]$
```

Delete the ACM certificate:

```
[cloudshell-user@ip-10-138-15-243 ~]$ aws acm delete-certificate --
certificate-arn arn:aws:acm:us-west-2:387974667323:certificate/
59c23fec-4fce-42ec-a0c4-d65a46510d1d
[cloudshell-user@ip-10-138-15-243 ~]$
```

Finally, you can delete the CloudFormation template to remove the remaining resources. Once you've done all this, you have successfully removed the resources that could incur charges.

Conclusion

This chapter explored the essential principles and techniques for securing data on AWS, focusing on data security and cryptography. Starting with the three states of data—at rest, in transit, and in use—it laid the groundwork for understanding how AWS services apply encryption to safeguard sensitive information at every stage of its lifecycle.

The chapter dove into the role of cryptography within AWS, showcasing how services like AWS Key Management Service (KMS) and CloudHSM enable secure key management while meeting compliance requirements. You learned how to create and manage Customer Master Keys (CMKs), enforce encryption policies, and implement least privilege access controls, ensuring that encryption remains robust and well-governed.

AWS Certificate Manager (ACM) was introduced as a key service for securing data in transit. The chapter demonstrated how to provision SSL/TLS certificates, deploy them to Application Load Balancers (ALBs), and automate renewals, ensuring the continuity of secure communications for Internet-facing applications.

The chapter also highlighted the power of Amazon Macie, which uses machine learning to discover, classify, and protect sensitive data stored in Amazon S3. By integrating Macie with other AWS services, you can automate remediation workflows, ensuring that your data remains protected consistently and efficiently.

The chapter concluded with a hands-on look at AWS Secrets Manager, a service that simplifies the secure storage, retrieval, and rotation of credentials. Centralizing sensitive information reduces the risk of mismanaged keys or exposed credentials, enhancing the security of your encrypted data.

Throughout this journey, I emphasized best practices, such as key rotation, policy enforcement, and automated monitoring, equipping you with the tools and techniques needed to maintain a strong data protection strategy on AWS.

But data security is only one piece of the puzzle. Even with encryption and secrets management in place, you need visibility into what's happening across your environment. The next chapter delves into monitoring and logging, exploring how tools like Amazon CloudWatch, AWS CloudTrail, and AWS Config can provide insights, detect anomalies, and help ensure compliance. These tools are essential for maintaining an auditable, transparent, and secure AWS environment. Get ready to move forward and see how monitoring and logging tie it all together!

References

Amazon Web Services, "AWS Key Management Service," `https://aws.amazon.com/kms/`

Amazon Web Services, "Data Encryption—Introduction to AWS Security," `https://docs.aws.amazon.com/whitepapers/latest/introduction-aws-security/data-encryption.html`

Data Security and Cryptography on AWS, `https://community.aws/content/2fKWqLT3hKm4WnfpdAd4chSRKA3/data-security-and-cryptography-on-aws?lang=en`

What is AWS Secrets Manager?, `https://docs.aws.amazon.com/secretsmanager/latest/userguide/intro.html`

Monitoring, Logging, and Compliance on AWS

"In God we trust; all others must bring data."
—W. Edwards Deming

Welcome to Chapter 8. So far, you've explored some security fundamentals, including learning how to manage identities with IAM and Identity Center, as well as techniques for infrastructure protection. This chapter focuses on the tools and practices that give you visibility into your AWS environment, ensure compliance with industry standards, and provide the insights needed to make informed decisions. In this chapter, you go through a final assembly or capstone so to speak, pulling together CloudWatch, CloudTrail, and other log streams into a powerful, unified security monitoring system.

Overview

Imagine driving a car without a dashboard. There's no speedometer, no fuel gauge, and no warning lights. You'd have no way to know if something was wrong until it was too late. The same applies to your AWS infrastructure. Monitoring and logging are your dashboard and black-box recorder. They give you visibility into what's happening across your environment, alert you to issues, and help you demonstrate compliance.

This chapter explores the essential AWS tools for monitoring and logging, including CloudWatch, CloudTrail, and other services that support security and compliance.

In this chapter, I aim to:

- Help you learn the tools available to monitor AWS resources and applications
- Show you how to log and audit activity
- Help you set up practical alerts and dashboards
- Explain how monitoring and logging tie into compliance frameworks like PCI DSS and HIPAA

By learning these tools and techniques, you'll have the visibility required to forecast costs, identify unwanted behavior, and troubleshoot issues when they arise. Logging and monitoring is an area that adds so much value and yet is often overlooked or minimized when building out an infrastructure.

Core Concepts of Monitoring and Logging

Before diving into AWS services, I want to clarify two key concepts:

- *Monitoring:* Keeping track of the health and performance of your AWS resources. This includes gathering metrics, setting up alarms, and visualizing data to detect anomalies.
- *Logging:* Recording events and activities for later review. Logs answer questions like, "Who did what, where, and when?"

AWS provides tools to achieve both. At a high level:

- Amazon CloudWatch handles monitoring and alerting.
- AWS CloudTrail provides logs for auditing and governance.
- Other services, like Config, S3 Access Logs, and VPC Flow Logs, help fill in the gaps.

With that said, I set this chapter up with a CloudFormation template that will create two EC2 instances for you to test with. Use the following template to begin. After the template is installed, you'll do a few additional bits of configuration before testing, but that will come a bit later in the chapter.

For now, if you're following along, just create a new stack with the following template. You can also get the template on GitHub at `https://github.com/8ca rroll/Securing-the-Cloud-with-Brandon-Carroll/`. Find the corresponding chapter folder and you'll find all the resources there, including the command list for all the examples I use in this chapter. In all the examples in this book, be sure to replace the placeholders and example values with your account ID, resource IDs, and ARNs.

```
AWSTemplateFormatVersion: '2010-09-09'
Description: 'Load Testing Setup with Target and Test Instances'

Parameters:
  LatestAmiId:
    Description: Latest Amazon Linux 2 AMI ID in the current region
    Type: 'AWS::SSM::Parameter::Value<AWS::EC2::Image::Id>'
    Default: '/aws/service/ami-amazon-linux-latest/amzn2-ami-hvm-x86_64-gp2'

Resources:
  # VPC and related resources
  VPC:
    Type: AWS::EC2::VPC
    Properties:
      CidrBlock: 10.0.0.0/16
      EnableDnsSupport: true
      EnableDnsHostnames: true
      Tags:
        - Key: Name
          Value: LoadTesting-VPC

  InternetGateway:
    Type: AWS::EC2::InternetGateway
    Properties:
      Tags:
        - Key: Name
          Value: LoadTesting-IGW

  VPCGatewayAttachment:
    Type: AWS::EC2::VPCGatewayAttachment
    Properties:
      VpcId: !Ref VPC
      InternetGatewayId: !Ref InternetGateway

  PublicSubnet:
    Type: AWS::EC2::Subnet
    Properties:
      VpcId: !Ref VPC
      CidrBlock: 10.0.1.0/24
      MapPublicIpOnLaunch: true
      Tags:
        - Key: Name
          Value: LoadTesting-PublicSubnet

  PublicRouteTable:
    Type: AWS::EC2::RouteTable
    Properties:
      VpcId: !Ref VPC
      Tags:
        - Key: Name
          Value: LoadTesting-PublicRouteTable

  PublicRoute:
    Type: AWS::EC2::Route
    Properties:
```

```
        RouteTableId: !Ref PublicRouteTable
        DestinationCidrBlock: 0.0.0.0/0
        GatewayId: !Ref InternetGateway

  SubnetRouteTableAssociation:
    Type: AWS::EC2::SubnetRouteTableAssociation
    Properties:
      SubnetId: !Ref PublicSubnet
      RouteTableId: !Ref PublicRouteTable

  # Security Group for Load Testing Instance
  LoadTestSecurityGroup:
    Type: AWS::EC2::SecurityGroup
    Properties:
      GroupDescription: Security group for load testing instance
      VpcId: !Ref VPC
      SecurityGroupIngress:
        - IpProtocol: tcp
          FromPort: 443
          ToPort: 443
          CidrIp: 0.0.0.0/0
          Description: Allow HTTPS from anywhere
        - IpProtocol: tcp
          FromPort: 80
          ToPort: 80
          CidrIp: 0.0.0.0/0
          Description: Allow HTTP from anywhere
        - IpProtocol: tcp
          FromPort: 22
          ToPort: 22
          CidrIp: 0.0.0.0/0
          Description: Allow SSH for management

  # Security Group for Target Instance
  TargetSecurityGroup:
    Type: AWS::EC2::SecurityGroup
    Properties:
      GroupDescription: Security group for target instance
      VpcId: !Ref VPC
      SecurityGroupIngress:
        - IpProtocol: tcp
          FromPort: 80
          ToPort: 80
          CidrIp: 0.0.0.0/0
          Description: Allow HTTP from anywhere
        - IpProtocol: tcp
          FromPort: 443
          ToPort: 443
          CidrIp: 0.0.0.0/0
          Description: Allow HTTPS from anywhere
        - IpProtocol: tcp
          FromPort: 22
          ToPort: 22
          CidrIp: 0.0.0.0/0
          Description: Allow SSH for management
```

```yaml
# IAM Role for SSM and CloudWatch
SSMRole:
  Type: AWS::IAM::Role
  Properties:
    AssumeRolePolicyDocument:
      Version: '2012-10-17'
      Statement:
        - Effect: Allow
          Principal:
            Service: ec2.amazonaws.com
          Action: sts:AssumeRole
    ManagedPolicyArns:
      - arn:aws:iam::aws:policy/AmazonSSMManagedInstanceCore
      - arn:aws:iam::aws:policy/CloudWatchAgentServerPolicy
    Path: /

SSMInstanceProfile:
  Type: AWS::IAM::InstanceProfile
  Properties:
    Path: /
    Roles:
      - !Ref SSMRole

# Target EC2 Instance
TargetInstance:
  Type: AWS::EC2::Instance
  Properties:
    ImageId: !Ref LatestAmiId
    InstanceType: t2.micro
    NetworkInterfaces:
      - DeviceIndex: 0
        AssociatePublicIpAddress: true
        SubnetId: !Ref PublicSubnet
        GroupSet:
          - !Ref TargetSecurityGroup
        DeleteOnTermination: true
    IamInstanceProfile: !Ref SSMInstanceProfile
    UserData:
      Fn::Base64: !Sub |
        #!/bin/bash
        yum update -y
        amazon-linux-extras install -y nginx1
        systemctl enable nginx
        systemctl start nginx
        yum install -y amazon-cloudwatch-agent
        systemctl enable amazon-cloudwatch-agent
        systemctl start amazon-cloudwatch-agent
    Tags:
      - Key: Name
        Value: Target-Instance

# Load Testing EC2 Instance
LoadTestInstance:
  Type: AWS::EC2::Instance
  Properties:
```

```
            ImageId: !Ref LatestAmiId
            InstanceType: t2.micro
            NetworkInterfaces:
              - DeviceIndex: 0
                AssociatePublicIpAddress: true
                SubnetId: !Ref PublicSubnet
                GroupSet:
                  - !Ref LoadTestSecurityGroup
                DeleteOnTermination: true
            IamInstanceProfile: !Ref SSMInstanceProfile
            UserData:
              Fn::Base64: !Sub |
                #!/bin/bash
                yum update -y
                yum install -y java-11-amazon-corretto unzip
                cd /home/ec2-user
                wget https://archive.apache.org/dist/jmeter/binaries/
apache-jmeter-5.6.3.zip
                unzip apache-jmeter-5.6.3.zip
                chown -R ec2-user:ec2-user apache-jmeter-5.6.3
                echo 'export JVM_ARGS="-Xms256m -Xmx512m -XX:MaxMetaspaceSize=128m"'
>> /home/ec2-user/.bashrc
            Tags:
              - Key: Name
                Value: LoadTest-Instance

Outputs:
  TargetInstanceId:
    Description: ID of the target EC2 instance
    Value: !Ref TargetInstance

  TargetInstancePrivateIP:
    Description: Private IP address of the target instance
    Value: !GetAtt TargetInstance.PrivateIp

  TargetInstancePublicIP:
    Description: Public IP address of the target instance
    Value: !GetAtt TargetInstance.PublicIp

  LoadTestInstanceId:
    Description: ID of the load testing instance
    Value: !Ref LoadTestInstance

  LoadTestInstancePrivateIP:
    Description: Private IP address of the load testing instance
    Value: !GetAtt LoadTestInstance.PrivateIp

  LoadTestInstancePublicIP:
    Description: Public IP address of the load testing instance
    Value: !GetAtt LoadTestInstance.PublicIp

  LoadTestSecurityGroupId:
    Description: ID of the Load Testing security group
    Value: !Ref LoadTestSecurityGroup
```

```
TargetSecurityGroupId:
  Description: ID of the Target security group
  Value: !Ref TargetSecurityGroup
```

Now that you have some test machines and the core concepts of monitoring and logging down, you'll explore each of these with examples and practical demonstrations in the following sections.

Monitoring with Amazon CloudWatch

Amazon CloudWatch is AWS's monitoring and observability service. It allows you to collect and analyze metrics, set up alarms, and visualize data using dashboards.

At its core, CloudWatch operates through four key components: metrics, alarms, logs, and dashboards. *Metrics* are numerical data points that measure the performance of resources, such as CPU usage or disk I/O, providing valuable insights into resource behavior. *Alarms* allow you to set predefined thresholds on these metrics, triggering alerts or automated actions when those thresholds are breached. *Logs* capture event and system-level data, offering detailed visibility into application and infrastructure activities, which can be stored and analyzed within CloudWatch Logs. Finally, *dashboards* present these metrics and logs in customizable, visual formats, enabling you to quickly assess the health and performance of your AWS environment at a glance. Together, these components empower you to proactively monitor, troubleshoot, and optimize your cloud infrastructure.

Now that you've learned about the key components of CloudWatch, you will put them into action with a practical example. Monitoring the CPU usage of an EC2 instance is one of the most common and essential use cases for CloudWatch. By tracking CPU performance, you can ensure your instances are operating efficiently, identify potential bottlenecks, and take proactive measures before they impact your workloads. In the following walkthrough, I guide you step by step through setting up CloudWatch to monitor CPU usage, configure alarms, and visualize the data using dashboards.

Monitoring EC2 CPU Usage with CloudWatch

Monitoring CPU usage is one of the most effective ways to ensure your EC2 instances are running efficiently and reliably. High CPU utilization can indicate performance bottlenecks, overloaded resources, or poorly optimized workloads. In this demonstration, I guide you through setting up Amazon CloudWatch to monitor CPU usage on an EC2 instance, create an alarm that triggers when CPU usage exceeds a specific threshold, and configure notifications to alert you when action is needed.

The goal is to not only set up monitoring but also to understand why each step is necessary and how the commands interact. By the end of this walk-through, you'll have a fully functional CPU monitoring and alerting system for your EC2 instance, and you'll know how to interpret and act on the insights it provides. Let's get started.

CloudWatch automatically collects basic metrics for EC2 instances, such as CPU utilization, disk reads/writes, and network traffic. These metrics provide insight into the performance and health of your instance.

Okay, so you are going to go back to CloudShell in the us-west-region. (This is the region I am using and should match most of my examples.) To list the available EC2 metrics in CloudWatch, run the aws cloudwatch list-metrics command. Make sure you follow the case that I use in the example, because it is case-sensitive:

```
[cloudshell-user@ip-10-142-80-191 ~]$ aws cloudwatch list-metrics --namespace AWS/
EC2
{
    "Metrics": [
        {
            "Namespace": "AWS/EC2",
            "MetricName": "CPUSurplusCreditsCharged",
            "Dimensions": [
                {
                    "Name": "InstanceId",
                    "Value": "i-07e253c0cbac07900"
                }
            ]
        },
        {
            "Namespace": "AWS/EC2",
            "MetricName": "EBSReadBytes",
            "Dimensions": [
                {
                    "Name": "InstanceId",
                    "Value": "i-069f08258d60557a2"
                }
            ]
        },
<< Remainder of the output omitted>

:
```

In this command, aws cloudwatch specifies that you're interacting with the AWS CloudWatch service. The list-metrics subcommand retrieves a list of all available metrics within a specific namespace. The --namespace AWS/EC2 option filters the output to display only EC2-related metrics. Without specifying a namespace, CloudWatch would return metrics across all AWS services, making it difficult to focus on EC2-specific data. The output of this command will include several metrics, such as CPU Utilization, and each metric will have associated dimensions like `InstanceId`, which tie the metric to a specific EC2 instance. If your instance isn't generating metrics, you may need to make sure that detailed monitoring is enabled on it.

Before you create your CPU alarm, you need to set up an SNS topic to receive notifications. Let's create that first:

```
[cloudshell-user@ip-10-142-87-21 ~]$ aws sns create-topic --name high-cpu-alert
{
    "TopicArn": "arn:aws:sns:us-west-2:387974667323:high-cpu-alert"
}
[cloudshell-user@ip-10-142-87-21 ~]$
```

This command creates an SNS topic and returns a Topic ARN. Note this ARN, as you'll need it for your alarm configuration. Be sure to replace it with your own email address. Now, subscribe your email to receive notifications:

```
[cloudshell-user@ip-10-142-87-21 ~]$ aws sns subscribe \
>      --topic-arn arn:aws:sns:us-west-2:387974667323:high-cpu-alert \
>      --protocol email \
>      --notification-endpoint awsuser@gameonnetworks.com
{
    "SubscriptionArn": "pending confirmation"
}
[cloudshell-user@ip-10-142-87-21 ~]$
```

You'll receive a confirmation email like the one shown in Figure 8.1. Make sure to click the link to verify your subscription.

Figure 8.1: Subscription email confirmation.

Now you're ready to create your CPU alarm based on the instance you want to monitor. For this you need the Instance ID. Armed with that information, use the following command:

```
[cloudshell-user@ip-10-142-87-21 ~]$ aws cloudwatch put-metric-alarm \
>       --alarm-name high-cpu-usage \
>       --metric-name CPUUtilization \
>       --namespace AWS/EC2 \
>       --statistic Average \
>       --period 300 \
>       --threshold 80 \
>       --comparison-operator GreaterThanThreshold \
>       --dimensions Name=InstanceId,Value=i-07e253c0cbac07900 \
>       --evaluation-periods 2 \
>       --alarm-actions arn:aws:sns:us-west-2:387974667323:high-cpu-alert \
>       --unit Percent
[cloudshell-user@ip-10-142-87-21 ~]$
```

This list highlights some of the important parameters for effective monitoring:

- --alarm-name: This is your unique identifier for the alarm. Choose something descriptive that helps you quickly identify the alarm's purpose.

- --metric-name and --namespace: These parameters specify what you're monitoring. CPU utilization is a standard metric in the AWS/EC2 namespace.

- --statistic and --period: The statistic "Average" over a period of 300 seconds (5 minutes) means CloudWatch will calculate the average CPU usage over each five-minute interval.

- --threshold and --comparison-operator: When the CPU usage goes above 80 percent (the threshold), the alarm will trigger because you're using the GreaterThanThreshold operator.

- --evaluation-periods: The value of 2 means the threshold must be breached for two consecutive periods (10 minutes total) before triggering the alarm. This helps avoid false alarms from brief spikes.

- --alarm-actions: This is where you specify your SNS topic ARN, determining where notifications will be sent when the alarm triggers.

To verify that your alarm was created successfully, run the following command:

```
[cloudshell-user@ip-10-142-87-21 ~]$ aws cloudwatch describe-alarms --alarm-names
high-cpu-usage
{
    "MetricAlarms": [
        {
            "AlarmName": "high-cpu-usage",
            "AlarmArn": "arn:aws:cloudwatch:us-west-2:387974667323:alarm:high-cpu-
usage",
```

```
              "AlarmConfigurationUpdatedTimestamp": "2024-12-
26T20:27:29.662000+00:00",
              "ActionsEnabled": true,
              "OKActions": [],
              "AlarmActions": [
                  "arn:aws:sns:us-west-2:387974667323:high-cpu-alert"
              ],
              "InsufficientDataActions": [],
              "StateValue": "OK",
              "StateReason": "Threshold Crossed: 2 datapoints [2.962487361729163
(26/12/24 20:23:00), 2.9233232246592076 (26/12/24 20:18:00)] were not greater than
the threshold (80.0).",
              "StateReasonData": "{\"version\":\"1.0\",\"queryDate\":\"2024-12-
26T20:28:51.467+0000\",\"startDate\":\"2024-12-
26T20:18:00.000+0000\",\"unit\":\"Percent\",\"statistic\":\"Average\",\"
period\":300,\"recentDatapoints\":[2.9233232246592076,2.962487361729163],\"
threshold\":80.0,\"evaluatedDatapoints\":[{\"timestamp\":\" 2024-12-26T20:
23:00.000+0000\",\"sampleCount\":4.0,\"value\":2.962487361729163}]}",
              "StateUpdatedTimestamp": "2024-12-26T20:28:51.469000+00:00",
              "MetricName": "CPUUtilization",
              "Namespace": "AWS/EC2",
              "Statistic": "Average",
              "Dimensions": [
                  {
                      "Name": "InstanceId",
                      "Value": "i-07e253c0cbac07900"
                  }
              ],
              "Period": 300,
              "Unit": "Percent",
              "EvaluationPeriods": 2,
              "Threshold": 80.0,
              "ComparisonOperator": "GreaterThanThreshold",
              "StateTransitionedTimestamp": "2024-12-26T20:28:51.469000+00:00"
          }
      ],
      "CompositeAlarms": []
}
(END)
```

Creating Meaningful Dashboards

Now that you have your alarm set up, you'll create a dashboard to visualize your CPU metrics. Dashboards are incredibly valuable for at-a-glance monitoring of your infrastructure.

In the following command, you will create a dashboard. Under normal circumstances, you would create the dashboard from the AWS Console. However, you are going to use the CLI for these examples. This is because I want you to become familiar with this method as you transition to creating your entire infrastructure in code, as you see later in this book. Additionally, you will need to specify the instance ID of any instance in the region you want to monitor with this dashboard.

```
[cloudshell-user@ip-10-140-17-0 ~]$ aws cloudwatch put-dashboard \
>      --dashboard-name "EC2-Monitoring" \
>      --dashboard-body '{
>         "widgets": [
>             {
>                 "type": "metric",
>                 "x": 0,
>                 "y": 0,
>                 "width": 12,
>                 "height": 6,
>                 "properties": {
>                     "metrics": [
>                         [ "AWS/EC2", "CPUUtilization", "InstanceId",
"i-07e253c0cbac07900" ]
>                     ],
>                     "period": 300,
>                     "stat": "Average",
>                     "region": "us-west-2",
>                     "title": "EC2 CPU Usage"
>                 }
>             }
>         ]
>     }'

{
    "DashboardValidationMessages": []
}
[cloudshell-user@ip-10-140-17-0 ~]$
[cloudshell-user@ip-10-140-17-0 ~]$
```

This dashboard configuration creates a single widget showing CPU utilization, but you can expand it to include other metrics like memory usage, disk I/O, or network traffic. The width and height parameters, 12 and 6, as shown in the previous command, control the size of the widget as seen on the dashboard page, and you can add multiple widgets by including additional entries in the widgets array.

Testing Your Monitoring Setup

To ensure your monitoring is working correctly, I'll generate some CPU load on the instance. Here's a simple way to test it.

First, connect to the LoadTest-Instance using SSM. Then update YUM and Java:

```
h-4.2$ sudo yum update -y
Loaded plugins: extras_suggestions, langpacks, priorities, update-motd
amzn2-core        | 3.6 kB  00:00:00
No packages marked for update
sh-4.2$ sudo yum install -y java-11-amazon-corretto wget unzip
Loaded plugins: extras_suggestions, langpacks, priorities, update-motd
Package 1:java-11-amazon-corretto-11.0.25+9-1.amzn2.
x86_64 already installed and latest version
```

```
Package wget-1.14-18.amzn2.1.x86_64 already installed and latest version
Package unzip-6.0-57.amzn2.0.1.x86_64 already installed and latest version
Nothing to do
```

Verify the Java version to ensure compatibility. The minimum version to run Apache JMeter is Java 8:

```
sh-4.2$ java -version
openjdk version "11.0.25" 2024-10-15 LTS
OpenJDK Runtime Environment Corretto-11.0.25.9.1 (build 11.0.25+9-LTS)
OpenJDK 64-Bit Server VM Corretto-11.0.25.9.1 (build 11.0.25+9-LTS, mixed mode)
sh-4.2$ cd /home/ssm-user
```

Next, download Apache JMeter. Apache JMeter is an open-source testing tool designed to measure and analyze the performance of applications and services, including those hosted on AWS. It enables you to simulate concurrent user traffic to test the scalability, reliability, and security of your infrastructure under various load conditions:

```
sh-4.2$ wget https://archive.apache.org/dist/jmeter/binaries/
apache-jmeter-5.6.3.zip
--2024-12-27 22:37:05--
https://archive.apache.org/dist/jmeter/binaries/apache-jmeter-5.6.3.zip
Resolving archive.apache.org (archive.apache.org)... 65.108.204.189, 2a01:4f9:
1a:a084::2
Connecting to archive.apache.org (archive.apache.
org)|65.108.204.189|:443... connected.
HTTP request sent, awaiting response... 200 OK
Length: 90631635 (86M) [application/zip]
Saving to: 'apache-jmeter-5.6.3.zip'

100%[=============================================
==================================================
=================================================>] 90,631,635  7.81MB/s   in 13s

2024-12-27 22:37:18 (6.76 MB/s) - 'apache-jmeter-
5.6.3.zip' saved [90631635/90631635]
```

Next, unzip the package:

```
h-4.2$ unzip apache-jmeter-5.6.3.zip
Archive:  apache-jmeter-5.6.3.zip
   creating: apache-jmeter-5.6.3/
  inflating: apache-jmeter-5.6.3/LICENSE
   creating: apache-jmeter-5.6.3/licenses/
   creating: apache-jmeter-5.6.3/licenses/flot-axislabels/
   creating: apache-jmeter-5.6.3/licenses/flot-axislabels/flot-axislabels-0.8.3/
  inflating: apache-jmeter-5.6.3/licenses/flot-axislabels/flot-axislabels-0.8.3/
LICENSE
   <<OUTPUT OMITTED>>
```

Now, adjust the permissions:

```
sh-4.2$ sudo chown -R ssm-user:ssm-user apache-jmeter-5.6.3
```

The next thing to do would be to check the version of jmeter. Note that when I check it, I get a memory error. Also note that you may have installed it in a different directory than I did, in which case you will need to ensure you are in the proper directory:

```
h-4.2$ /home/ssm-user/apache-jmeter-5.6.3/bin/jmeter -v
OpenJDK 64-Bit Server VM warning: INFO: os::commit_memory
(0x00000000c0000000, 1073741824, 0) failed; error='Not enough space' (errno=12)
#
# There is insufficient memory for the Java Runtime Environment to continue.
# Native memory allocation (mmap) failed to map 1073741824 bytes
for committing reserved memory.
# An error report file with more information is saved as:
# /home/ssm-user/hs_err_pid19757.log
```

If you get an error like this, edit the configuration file with the following command:

```
sudo vi /home/ssm-user/apache-jmeter-5.6.3/bin/jmeter
```

In the file, look for the HEAP line:

```
: "${HEAP:="-Xms1g -Xmx1g -XX:MaxMetaspaceSize=256m"}"
```

And replace it with this:

```
: "${HEAP:="-Xms256m -Xmx512m -XX:MaxMetaspaceSize=128m"}"
```

Save the file with :wq. Then check jmeter again:

```
h-4.2$ /home/ssm-user/apache-jmeter-5.6.3/bin/jmeter -v
WARN StatusConsoleListener The use of package scanning to locate
plugins is deprecated and will be removed in a future release
WARN StatusConsoleListener The use of package scanning to locate
plugins is deprecated and will be removed in a future release
WARN StatusConsoleListener The use of package scanning to locate
plugins is deprecated and will be removed in a future release
WARN StatusConsoleListener The use of package scanning to locate
plugins is deprecated and will be removed in a future release
Dec 27, 2024 10:40:15 PM java.util.prefs.FileSystemPreferences$1 run
INFO: Created user preferences directory.
```

```
Copyright (c) 1999-2024 The Apache Software Foundation
```

Now, create a test plan:

```
sh-4.2$ cat > /home/ssm-user/apache-jmeter-5.6.3/bin/test-plan.jmx << 'EOF'
> <?xml version="1.0" encoding="UTF-8"?>
> <jmeterTestPlan version="1.2" properties="5.0" jmeter="5.6.3">
>   <hashTree>
>     <TestPlan guiclass="TestPlanGui" testclass="TestPlan" testname="
Load Test Plan">
>       <elementProp name="TestPlan.user_defined_variables" elementType="
Arguments">
>         <collectionProp name="Arguments.arguments"/>
>       </elementProp>
>     </TestPlan>
>     <hashTree>
>       <ThreadGroup guiclass="ThreadGroupGui" testclass=" ThreadGroup"
testname="Thread Group">
>         <elementProp name="ThreadGroup.main_controller" elementType="
LoopController">
>           <boolProp name="LoopController.continue_forever">false</boolProp>
>           <stringProp name="LoopController.loops">$${__P(duration,300)}
</stringProp>
>         </elementProp>
>         <stringProp name="ThreadGroup.num_threads">$${__P(threads,10)}
</stringProp>
>         <stringProp name="ThreadGroup.ramp_time">$${__P(rampup,30)}
</stringProp>
>       </ThreadGroup>
>       <hashTree>
>         <HTTPSamplerProxy guiclass="HttpTestSampleGui"
testclass="HTTPSamplerProxy">
>           <stringProp name="HTTPSampler.domain">$${__P(target)}</stringProp>
>           <stringProp name="HTTPSampler.port">80</stringProp>
>           <stringProp name="HTTPSampler.protocol">http</stringProp>
>           <stringProp name="HTTPSampler.path">/</stringProp>
>           <stringProp name="HTTPSampler.method">GET</stringProp>
>         </HTTPSamplerProxy>
>       </hashTree>
>     </hashTree>
>   </hashTree>
> </jmeterTestPlan>
> EOF
```

Finally, run the test:

```
sh-4.2$ sudo /home/ssm-user/apache-jmeter-5.6.3/bin/jmeter
 -n -t /home/ssm-user/apache-jmeter-5.6.3/bin/test-plan.jmx \
>     -Jthreads=10 \
>     -Jrampup=30 \
>     -Jduration=300 \
>     -Jtarget=10.0.1.115 \
>     -l /home/ssm-user/apache-jmeter-5.6.3/bin/results.jtl
WARN StatusConsoleListener The use of package scanning to locate
plugins is deprecated and will be removed in a future release
```

```
WARN StatusConsoleListener The use of package scanning to locate
plugins is deprecated and will be removed in a future release
WARN StatusConsoleListener The use of package scanning to locate
plugins is deprecated and will be removed in a future release
WARN StatusConsoleListener The use of package scanning to locate
plugins is deprecated and will be removed in a future release
Dec 27, 2024 10:40:49 PM java.util.prefs.FileSystemPreferences$1 run
INFO: Created user preferences directory.
Creating summariser <summary>
Created the tree successfully using /home/ssm-user/apache-jmeter-5.6.3/bin/
test-plan.jmx
Starting standalone test @ 2024 Dec 27 22:40:49 UTC (1735339249960)
Waiting for possible Shutdown/StopTestNow/HeapDump/ThreadDump
message on port 4445
Warning: Nashorn engine is planned to be removed from a future JDK release
summary =        0 in 00:00:00 = ******/s Avg:       0 Min:
9223372036854775807 Max: -9223372036854775808 Err:       0 (0.00%)
Tidying up ...       @ 2024 Dec 27 22:40:50 UTC (1735339250920)
... end of run
sh-4.2$
```

In these steps, you are creating an XML-based JMeter test plan file that defines a load test, specifying elements such as the Test Plan, Thread Group, and HTTP Request sampler with configurable parameters like the number of threads, ramp-up period, and loop count. Then, you run this test plan in non-GUI mode using command-line options to override specific properties (like threads, duration, ramp-up, and target), and the results are logged to a file for later performance analysis.

The purpose of doing this is to simulate a realistic load on your AWS environment so that you can evaluate its performance, responsiveness, and scalability under stress conditions. By running a JMeter test plan, you also verify that your monitoring and logging configurations, such as those implemented with CloudWatch, are capturing the proper metrics and triggering alerts as expected. Next, let's look at the dashboard you created and see the load.

Accessing Your CloudWatch Dashboard

After creating your dashboard, you can view it either through the AWS Management Console or by using the AWS CLI. To view your dashboard metrics in real time, back in CloudShell, use this command:

```
[cloudshell-user@ip-10-142-87-21 ~]$ aws cloudwatch get-dashboard \
>     --dashboard-name "EC2-Monitoring"

{
    "DashboardArn": "arn:aws:cloudwatch::387974667323:dashboard/EC2-Monitoring",
    "DashboardBody": "{\"widgets\":[{\"type\":\"metric\",\"x\":0,\"y\":0,\"width\":
12,\"height\":6,\ "properties\":{\"metrics\":[[\"AWS/EC2\",\"CPUUtilization\",\
"InstanceId\",\"i-07e253c0cbac07900\"]],\"period\":300,\"stat\":\"Average\",\
"region\":\" us-east-1\",\"title\":\"EC2 CPU Usage\"}}]}",
```

```
        "DashboardName": "EC2-Monitoring"
}
[cloudshell-user@ip-10-142-87-21 ~]$
[cloudshell-user@ip-10-142-87-21 ~]$
```

What a mess, right? While the CLI provides the raw dashboard configuration, it's probably better used for configurations that you might automate and not for actually viewing the dashboards. For this, the AWS Management Console offers a more user-friendly visualization experience. Let's go view the dashboard there instead. To access your dashboard in the console, follow these steps:

1. Open the CloudWatch console.
2. Select Dashboards from the left navigation pane.
3. Click on the dashboard named EC2-Monitoring.

You can see this process in Figure 8.2.
Once you're viewing your dashboard, you can:

■ Adjust the time range using the time picker at the top of the dashboard.

■ Zoom in on specific time periods by clicking and dragging across the graph.

■ Export the data by clicking the actions menu on any widget.

To enhance your monitoring, consider adding these essential EC2 metrics to your dashboard:

■ Memory utilization

■ Network in/out

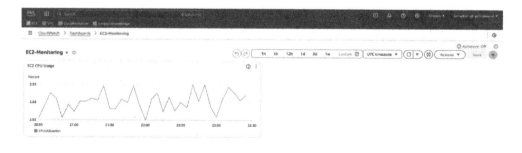

Figure 8.2: Viewing a custom CloudWatch dashboard.

- Disk read/write operations
- Status checks

Adding these metrics is valuable because they provide insight into key aspects of your instances' performance. Memory utilization lets you know if an instance is reaching its capacity; network metrics reveal data flow and potential bottlenecks; disk operations help diagnose I/O performance issues; and status checks confirm that the instance is healthy. By including these metrics, you can quickly identify issues and make informed decisions to optimize your environment.

You can add these metrics using the AWS Console's visual editor or by modifying your dashboard-body JSON in the CLI command you used earlier.

CloudWatch also has automatic dashboards. You get to these the same way as the custom dashboard; however, instead of the Custom Dashboard tab, you select Automatic Dashboards and then EC2, as shown in Figure 8.3.

Figure 8.4 shows the automatic EC2 dashboard.

At this point, you've built a solid foundation for monitoring EC2 instances using Amazon CloudWatch. But AWS monitoring doesn't stop at EC2—it extends across networking, security, and compliance. To build a truly robust monitoring strategy, it's essential to include VPC traffic monitoring, WAF insights, and IAM activity tracking.

The next section steps beyond EC2 and sets up monitoring for these other key areas.

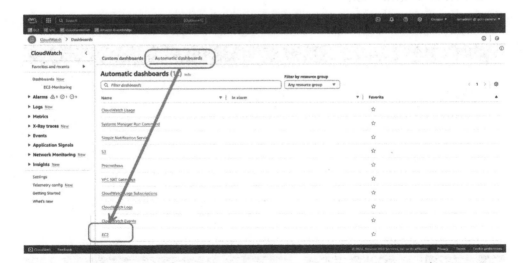

Figure 8.3: Viewing the automatic CloudWatch dashboards.

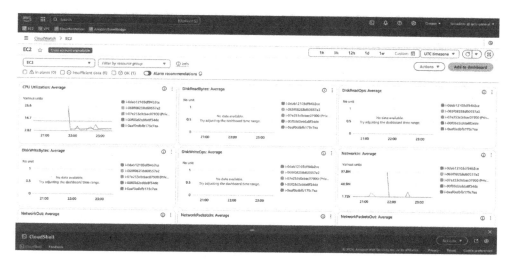

Figure 8.4: Viewing the EC2 automatic dashboard.

Monitoring Network Traffic with VPC Flow Logs

VPC Flow Logs capture detailed information about the IP traffic to and from network interfaces in your VPC. This visibility helps troubleshoot connectivity issues, detect unauthorized access attempts, and ensure compliance with security policies.

Enabling VPC Flow Logs

To enable VPC Flow Logs and send them to CloudWatch Logs, start by creating a role. Go to IAM Console → Roles → Create Role. Select Custom Trust Policy. Then paste the following trust policy JSON:

```
{
  "Version": "2012-10-17",
  "Statement": [
    {
      "Effect": "Allow",
      "Principal": {
        "Service": "vpc-flow-logs.amazonaws.com"
      },
      "Action": "sts:AssumeRole"
    }
  ]
}
```

This can be seen in Figure 8.5.

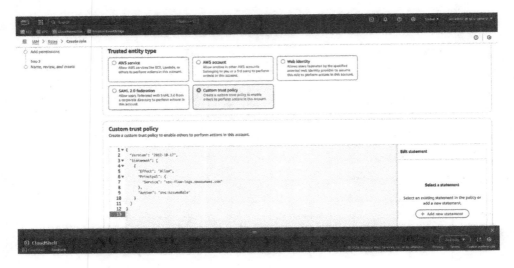

Figure 8.5: Custom trust policy.

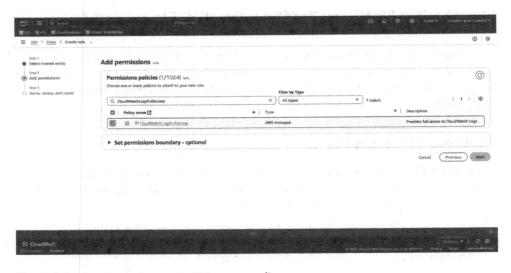

Figure 8.6: CloudWatchLogsFullAccess policy.

Click next and then attach the CloudWatchLogsFullAccess policy, as shown in Figure 8.6.

Give the policy a name, such as CloudWatchLogsFullAccess, and then create it. You can give it whatever name you prefer. Just be sure to note the ARN since it's needed for the next command. To then enable VPC Flow Logs and send them to CloudWatch Logs, use the following command, replacing the VPC value with your own VPC and the logs permission ARN with your own:

```
[cloudshell-user@ip-10-136-106-53 ~]$ aws ec2 create-flow-logs \
>     --resource-type VPC \
>     --resource-ids vpc-0488a892d43711307 \
>     --traffic-type ALL \
>     --log-destination-type cloud-watch-logs \
>     --log-group-name vpc-flow-logs \
>     --deliver-logs-permission-arn arn:aws:iam::387974667323:
role/vpc-flow-logs-role
{
    "ClientToken": "XecCg3GZXM0Z+xHz/UJFIjayQN1KS5Ipp+MEPAS/qPk=",
    "FlowLogIds": [
        "fl-0cd9909dcd7340821"
    ],
    "Unsuccessful": []
}
[cloudshell-user@ip-10-136-106-53 ~]$
```

Here is how this command breaks down:

- --resource-type specifies the type of resource you're monitoring (VPC in this case).

- --resource-ids is the ID of your VPC. Replace vpc-xxxxxxxx with your VPC ID.

- --traffic-type captures all traffic: accepted, rejected, and general flow.

- --log-destination-type specifies where the logs will be stored.

- --log-group-name names the CloudWatch Log Group where the VPC logs will be sent.

One thing to note is that there are other log destination types for VPC Flow Logs besides CloudWatch Logs. You can choose from the following:

- **Amazon S3**: You can configure VPC Flow Logs to deliver logs to an S3 bucket. This is useful for long-term storage, archival, and advanced analysis. You specify the ARN of the S3 bucket as the log destination, and optionally, you can include a subfolder path for better organization.

- **Amazon Kinesis Data Firehose**: Flow logs can also be sent to a Kinesis Data Firehose delivery stream. This allows you to process flow log data in near real time and deliver it to destinations such as Amazon S3, Amazon Redshift, or third-party tools like Splunk. This option is ideal for scenarios requiring real-time analytics or integration with external systems.

These options provide flexibility based on your use case, whether it involves real-time processing, long-term storage, or integration with external analytics tools. For now, this chapter sticks with CloudWatch Logs.

After running this command, the logs will begin flowing into the specified CloudWatch Log Group.

Analyzing VPC Flow Logs with CloudWatch Logs Insights

With your VPC Flow Logs stored in CloudWatch, you can query them for insights. For example, to detect rejected traffic:

```
[cloudshell-user@ip-10-136-106-53 ~]$ aws logs start-query \
>    --log-group-name vpc-flow-logs \
>    --start-time $(date --date="10 minutes ago" +%s) \
>    --end-time $(date +%s) \
>    --query-string 'fields @timestamp, @message | filter @message like /REJECT/'

{
    "queryId": "3816683e-2783-4922-83b2-7a9bed3e83c1"
}
[cloudshell-user@ip-10-136-106-53 ~]$
```

Next, use the query ID to view the data:

```
[cloudshell-user@ip-10-136-106-53 ~]$ aws logs get-query-results --
query-id 3816683e-2783-4922-83b2-7a9bed3e83c1
{
    "queryLanguage": "CWLI",
    "results": [
        [
            {
                "field": "@timestamp",
                "value": "2024-12-28 00:20:06.000"
            },
            {
                "field": "@message",
                "value": "2 387974667323 eni-03fe9840ffffafbcd
35.86.65.156 10.0.1.254 0 0 1 1 84 1735345206 1735345226 REJECT OK"
            },
            {
                "field": "@ptr",
                "value":
"CmsKLgoaMzg3OTc0NjY3MzIzOnZwYy1mbG93LWxvZ3MQBSIOCPbw9NTAMhDv1o7VwDISNRoYAgZa3Q
bfAAAACaq53MMABnb0P8AAAALyIAEowI2C1cAyMPD1idXAMjgpQJYtSPcgUIMYGAAgARAoGAE="
            }
        ],
        [
            {
                "field": "@timestamp",
                "value": "2024-12-28 00:19:58.000"
            },
:<<Output Omitted>>
```

The query extracts log entries showing rejected traffic, which can point to misconfigured security groups or potential intrusion attempts. This is what you are seeing in the previous output. Focus on the value "2 387974667323 eni-03fe9840ffffafbcd 35.86.65.156 10.0.1.254 0 0 1 1 84 1735345206 1735345226 REJECT OK". This represents a single VPC Flow Log record. Here's how each field breaks down:

- **Version (2)**: This indicates the version of the flow log format being used. In this case, it is version 2.

- **Account ID (387974667323)**: The AWS account ID associated with the network interface for which the traffic is being logged.

- **Interface ID (eni-03fe9840ffffafbcd)**: The ID of the Elastic Network Interface (ENI) that handled the traffic.

- **Source IP Address (35.86.65.156)**: The IP address from which the traffic originated.

- **Destination IP Address (10.0.1.254)**: The IP address to which the traffic was directed.

- **Source Port (0)**: The port number on the source device (zero indicates no specific port was used).

- **Destination Port (0)**: The port number on the destination device (zero indicates no specific port was used).

- **Protocol (1)**: The protocol number used for the traffic, where 1 corresponds to ICMP (Internet Control Message Protocol).

- **Packets Transferred (1)**: The total number of packets transferred during this flow.

- **Bytes Transferred (84)**: The total amount of data (in bytes) transferred during this flow.

- **Start Time (1735345206)**: The timestamp (in UNIX epoch format) when the flow started.

- **End Time (1735345226)**: The timestamp (in UNIX epoch format) when the flow ended.

- **Action (REJECT)**: Indicates whether the traffic was accepted or rejected by security group or network ACL rules; in this case, it was rejected.

- **Log Status (OK)**: Indicates whether the log entry was successfully captured; OK means it was successfully logged.

This record provides detailed information about a specific network flow, helping you analyze traffic patterns, troubleshoot connectivity issues, and ensure security compliance within your VPC environment.

Setting Alarms for Network Anomalies

When monitoring your network, it's important to detect unusual patterns or sudden spikes in outbound traffic. These spikes can indicate potential issues such as:

- **Data exfiltration:** Malicious activity attempting to send sensitive data out of your environment

- **Misconfigured applications:** Services generating excessive outbound traffic due to bugs or inefficiencies

- **Compromised instances:** Instances acting as bots or being used in Distributed Denial of Service (DDoS) attacks

By setting up an alarm in Amazon CloudWatch, you can ensure you're notified when outbound traffic exceeds a predefined threshold. Here's how to do it. First, set up an SNS topic:

```
[cloudshell-user@ip-10-136-106-53 ~]$ SNS_TOPIC=$(aws sns create-topic --
name network-anomalies-alert --query 'TopicArn' --output text) {

[cloudshell-user@ip-10-136-106-53 ~]$
```

Note the TopicArn, as you'll need it for the alarm configuration. Next, subscribe an email address to the SNS topic so you'll receive notifications. This example uses the variable you created in the previous step. This way, you can perform the exact configuration I am using and it will work for your environment as well:

```
[cloudshell-user@ip-10-136-43-25 ~]$ aws sns subscribe \
>       --topic-arn $SNS_TOPIC \
>       --protocol email \
>       --notification-endpoint brandon.carroll@gameonnetworks.com
{
    "SubscriptionArn": "pending confirmation"
}
[cloudshell-user@ip-10-136-43-25 ~]$
```

After running this, check your inbox for a confirmation email from AWS SNS. Click the confirmation link to activate your subscription.

Now that the SNS topic is ready, create an alarm that monitors outbound network traffic (NetworkPacketsOut) and triggers notifications when the threshold is exceeded:

```
[cloudshell-user@ip-10-136-106-53 ~]$ aws cloudwatch put-metric-alarm \
>       --alarm-name unusual-vpc-traffic \
>       --metric-name NetworkPacketsOut \
>       --namespace AWS/EC2 \
>       --statistic Average \
```

```
>      --period 300 \
>      --threshold 100000 \
>      --comparison-operator GreaterThanThreshold \
>      --evaluation-periods 1 \
>      --alarm-actions $SNS_TOPIC
[cloudshell-user@ip-10-136-106-53 ~]$
```

Here's how that command breaks down:

- --alarm-name: A unique name for the alarm (unusual-vpc-traffic) is best to help you identify its purpose.

- --metric-name: NetworkPacketsOut measures the number of packets sent from the instance.

- --namespace: The AWS/EC2 namespace focuses the alarm on EC2-related metrics.

- --statistic: Average calculates the average packet count over the defined period.

- --period: Data is evaluated every five minutes (300 seconds).

- --threshold: The alarm triggers if the average packet count exceeds 100,000.

- --comparison-operator: GreaterThanThreshold means the alarm triggers if the metric exceeds the threshold.

- --evaluation-periods: The alarm evaluates a single five-minute period before triggering.

- --alarm-actions: This command specifies the SNS topic ARN to notify (network-anomalies-alert).

These parameters were chosen to ensure the alarm is effective and responsive. The period of 300 seconds (five minutes) allows for timely detection of traffic anomalies without overwhelming you with alerts from brief, insignificant spikes. We all know how annoying that can be. Also, the threshold of 100,000 packets is a baseline value, but it should be fine-tuned based on your environment's normal traffic patterns to minimize false positives. The evaluation period of 1 ensures that a single five-minute spike is enough to trigger the alarm, enabling real-time responsiveness to potential issues.

When the outbound traffic exceeds the defined threshold, several actions occur. The alarm state transitions to ALARM in CloudWatch, signaling that an anomaly has been detected. Simultaneously, an SNS notification is sent to the endpoints subscribed to the topic, such as email addresses, Lambda functions, or incident management tools. Once notified, you can take appropriate action by investigating VPC Flow Logs, checking instance health, reviewing recent changes, and applying corrective measures as needed.

You can ensure that the alarm was created correctly by describing it with the following command:

```
[cloudshell-user@ip-10-136-106-53 ~]$ aws cloudwatch describe-alarms --
alarm-names unusual-vpc-traffic
{
    "MetricAlarms": [
        {
            "AlarmName": "unusual-vpc-traffic",
            "AlarmArn": "arn:aws:cloudwatch:us-west-
2:387974667323:alarm:unusual-vpc-traffic",
            "AlarmConfigurationUpdatedTimestamp": "2024-12-
28T00:37:01.751000+00:00",
            "ActionsEnabled": true,
            "OKActions": [],
            "AlarmActions": [
                "arn:aws:sns:us-west-2:387974667323:network-anomalies-alert"
            ],
            "InsufficientDataActions": [],
            "StateValue": "INSUFFICIENT_DATA",
            "StateReason": "Unchecked: Initial alarm creation",
            "StateUpdatedTimestamp": "2024-12-28T00:37:01.751000+00:00",
            "MetricName": "NetworkPacketsOut",
            "Namespace": "AWS/EC2",
            "Statistic": "Average",
            "Dimensions": [],
            "Period": 300,
            "EvaluationPeriods": 1,
            "Threshold": 100000.0,
            "ComparisonOperator": "GreaterThanThreshold",
            "StateTransitionedTimestamp": "2024-12-28T00:37:01.751000+00:00"
        }
    ],
    "CompositeAlarms": []
}
(END)
```

The `AlarmActions` indicate that you are sending the alerts to the correct SNS topic. You can ensure everything is configured properly by manually triggering the alarm state:

```
[cloudshell-user@ip-10-136-106-53 ~]$ aws cloudwatch set-alarm-state \
>       --alarm-name unusual-vpc-traffic \
>       --state-value ALARM \
>       --state-reason "Testing alarm notifications"
[cloudshell-user@ip-10-136-106-53 ~]$
[cloudshell-user@ip-10-136-106-53 ~]$
```

You can see the notification email in Figure 8.7.

The last thing to do here is to reset the alarm state now that you are done testing. Alarms in CloudWatch automatically transition back to the OK state when the underlying metric returns to a value within the defined threshold.

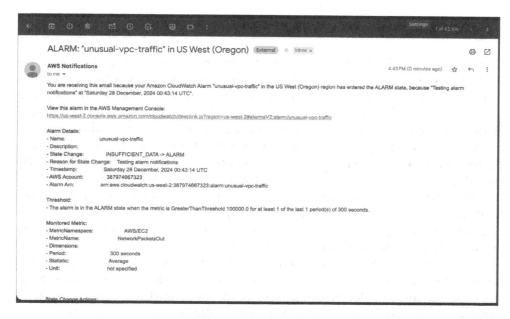

Figure 8.7: Manually triggered test notification email.

This behavior ensures that alarms are self-healing and reflect the current state of your monitored resource without requiring manual intervention. However, you should manually reset it because you're just testing:

```
[cloudshell-user@ip-10-136-106-53 ~]$ aws cloudwatch set-alarm-state \
>     --alarm-name unusual-vpc-traffic \
>     --state-value OK \
>     --state-reason "Resetting alarm after test"

[cloudshell-user@ip-10-136-106-53 ~]$
[cloudshell-user@ip-10-136-106-53 ~]$
```

One last thing to mention here is that the threshold (100,000 packets) may not align with your specific workload. You should monitor alarm activity over time and adjust the threshold as needed.

Monitoring network anomalies provides critical insight into potential threats and misconfigurations at the infrastructure level. By setting up alarms for unusual outbound traffic, you gain the ability to detect and respond to events like data exfiltration, compromised instances, or misconfigured applications. However, while network monitoring tells you what is happening, it doesn't always tell you who is responsible or how it happened. To fully understand the context behind these anomalies, you need visibility into who performed certain actions, what permissions were used, and when these activities occurred. This level of insight is achieved through IAM activity monitoring, which ensures you have a clear audit trail of user and role actions across your AWS environment.

Monitoring IAM Activity with CloudTrail

As discussed in Chapters 3 and 4, Identity and Access Management (IAM) is the foundation of security and access control in AWS. Every API call, whether it's modifying security groups, spinning up instances, or accessing sensitive data, is tied to an IAM role or user. You've configured a few of them so far. Unauthorized IAM activity, like policy changes, excessive permissions, or unauthorized user creation, can pose significant risks to your environment. AWS CloudTrail captures all API activity across your account, providing a detailed audit trail. By pairing CloudTrail logs with CloudWatch alarms, you can detect suspicious IAM events, such as `DeleteUser` or `AttachUserPolicy`, and take immediate action. This section guides you through setting up CloudTrail for IAM monitoring, creating meaningful alarms, and ensuring you have the tools to identify and respond to unauthorized activity effectively.

CloudTrail automatically logs management events, but to retain logs longer and enable deeper analysis, it's a good practice to store them in an S3 bucket. Start by creating an S3 bucket with a unique name, dedicated to storing CloudTrail logs. I'm doing that in the following code. Notice a location constraint in my command. You only need to do this if you are creating a bucket in a region other than `us-east-1`:

```
[cloudshell-user@ip-10-136-106-53 ~]$ aws s3api create-bucket \
>     --bucket cloudtrail-iam-logs \
>     --region us-west-2 \
>     --create-bucket-configuration LocationConstraint=us-west-2

{
    "Location": "http://cloudtrail-iam-logs.s3.amazonaws.com/"
}
[cloudshell-user@ip-10-136-106-53 ~]$
[cloudshell-user@ip-10-136-106-53 ~]$
```

Here is how this command breaks down:

- `--bucket cloudtrail-iam-logs`: Names the bucket where CloudTrail Logs will be stored.

- `--region us-west-2`: Ensures the bucket is created in the same region as your trail.

- `--create-bucket-configuration`: Specifies the location constraint explicitly (required for certain regions).

Now, make sure the bucket has proper permissions for CloudTrail to write logs. Apply the following bucket policy using your unique bucket name where you see mine:

```
[cloudshell-user@ip-10-136-106-53 ~]$ aws s3api put-bucket-policy \
>     --bucket cloudtrail-iam-logs \
```

```
>     --policy '{
>         "Version": "2012-10-17",
>         "Statement": [
>             {
>                 "Sid": "AWSCloudTrailAclCheck20150319",
>                 "Effect": "Allow",
>                 "Principal": {
>                     "Service": "cloudtrail.amazonaws.com"
>                 },
>                 "Action": "s3:GetBucketAcl",
>                 "Resource": "arn:aws:s3:::cloudtrail-iam-logs"
>             },
>             {
>                 "Sid": "AWSCloudTrailWrite20150319",
>                 "Effect": "Allow",
>                 "Principal": {
>                     "Service": "cloudtrail.amazonaws.com"
>                 },
>                 "Action": "s3:PutObject",
>                 "Resource": "arn:aws:s3:::cloudtrail-iam-logs/AWSLogs/*",
>                 "Condition": {
>                     "StringEquals": {
>                         "s3:x-amz-acl": "bucket-owner-full-control"
>                     }
>                 }
>             }
>         ]
>     }'
[cloudshell-user@ip-10-136-106-53 ~]$
[cloudshell-user@ip-10-136-106-53 ~]$
```

This policy grants CloudTrail permissions to write logs to the bucket. Using your unique bucket name, verify the bucket policy with the following command:

```
[cloudshell-user@ip-10-136-106-53 ~]$ aws s3api get-bucket-policy
--bucket cloudtrail-iam-logs
{
    "Policy": "{\"Version\":\"2012-10-17\",\"Statement\":[{\"Sid\":\"AWSCloudTrailA
clCheck20150319\",\"Effect\":\" Allow\",\"Principal\":{\"Service\":\"cloudtrail.
amazonaws.com\"},\"Action\":\"s3: GetBucketAcl\",\"Resource\":\"arn:aws:s3:::
cloudtrail-iam-logs\"}, {\"Sid\":\"AWSCloudTrailWrite20150319\",\"Effect\":\"
Allow\", \"Principal\":{\"Service\":\"cloudtrail.amazonaws.com\"},\"
Action\": \"s3:PutObject\",\"Resource\":\"arn:aws:s3:::cloudtrail-iam-logs/
AWSLogs/*\",\"Condition\":{\"StringEquals\":{\"s3:x-amz-acl\":\" bucket-
owner-full-control\"}}}]}"
}
[cloudshell-user@ip-10-136-106-53 ~]$
```

With the S3 bucket ready, create a CloudTrail trail to store IAM activity logs:

```
[cloudshell-user@ip-10-136-106-53 ~]$ aws cloudtrail create-trail \
>     --name iam-activity-trail \
>     --s3-bucket-name cloudtrail-iam-logs \
>     --is-multi-region-trail
```

```
{
    "Name": "iam-activity-trail",
    "S3BucketName": "cloudtrail-iam-logs",
    "IncludeGlobalServiceEvents": true,
    "IsMultiRegionTrail": true,
    "TrailARN": "arn:aws:cloudtrail:us-west-2:387974667323:trail/
iam-activity-trail",
    "LogFileValidationEnabled": false,
    "IsOrganizationTrail": false
}
[cloudshell-user@ip-10-136-106-53 ~]$
[cloudshell-user@ip-10-136-106-53 ~]$
```

Here's how that command breaks down:

- `--name iam-activity-trail`: Creates a trail named `iam-activity-trail`.

- `--s3-bucket-name cloudtrail-iam-logs`: Directs logs to the S3 bucket you just created.

- `--is-multi-region-trail`: Ensures events from all AWS regions are captured.

Now, start logging events to the trail:

```
[cloudshell-user@ip-10-136-106-53 ~]$ aws cloudtrail start-logging --
name iam-activity-trail
[cloudshell-user@ip-10-136-106-53 ~]$
```

Verify that logging is active:

```
[cloudshell-user@ip-10-136-106-53 ~]$ aws cloudtrail get-trail-status --
name iam-activity-trail
{
    "IsLogging": true,
    "StartLoggingTime": "2024-12-28T01:22:24.734000+00:00",
    "LatestDeliveryAttemptTime": "",
    "LatestNotificationAttemptTime": "",
    "LatestNotificationAttemptSucceeded": "",
    "LatestDeliveryAttemptSucceeded": "",
    "TimeLoggingStarted": "2024-12-28T01:22:24Z",
    "TimeLoggingStopped": ""
}
[cloudshell-user@ip-10-136-106-53 ~]$
```

Now that this is all in place, you can set up CloudWatch for real-time monitoring. To enable real-time analysis and alarms, CloudTrail Logs need to be sent to CloudWatch Logs. First, create a CloudWatch Log Group:

```
[cloudshell-user@ip-10-136-106-53 ~]$ aws logs create-log-group --
log-group-name cloudtrail-iam-logs
[cloudshell-user@ip-10-136-106-53 ~]$
```

CloudTrail requires an IAM role to send logs to CloudWatch. Start by creating a role with a trust policy:

```
[cloudshell-user@ip-10-136-106-53 ~]$ aws iam create-role \
>      --role-name CloudTrail_CloudWatchLogs_Role \
>      --assume-role-policy-document '{
>          "Version": "2012-10-17",
>          "Statement": [
>              {
>                  "Effect": "Allow",
>                  "Principal": {
>                      "Service": "cloudtrail.amazonaws.com"
>                  },
>                  "Action": "sts:AssumeRole"
>              }
>          ]
>      }'
{
    "Role": {
        "Path": "/",
        "RoleName": "CloudTrail_CloudWatchLogs_Role",
        "RoleId": "AROAVUVIXTQ525HFG4SZJ",
        "Arn": "arn:aws:iam::387974667323:role/CloudTrail_CloudWatchLogs_Role",
        "CreateDate": "2024-12-28T01:28:38+00:00",
        "AssumeRolePolicyDocument": {
            "Version": "2012-10-17",
            "Statement": [
                {
                    "Effect": "Allow",
                    "Principal": {
                        "Service": "cloudtrail.amazonaws.com"
                    },
                    "Action": "sts:AssumeRole"
                }
            ]
        }
    }
}
[cloudshell-user@ip-10-136-106-53 ~]$
```

Attach the necessary policy to this role:

```
[cloudshell-user@ip-10-136-106-53 ~]$ aws iam attach-role-policy \
>      --role-name CloudTrail_CloudWatchLogs_Role \
>      --policy-arn arn:aws:iam::aws:policy/AWSCloudTrail_FullAccess
[cloudshell-user@ip-10-136-106-53 ~]$
```

Next, create an inline policy to allow CloudTrail to send logs to CloudWatch using the command I use here, modified with your resource information of course:

```
[cloudshell-user@ip-10-136-106-53 ~]$ aws iam put-role-policy \
>      --role-name CloudTrail_CloudWatchLogs_Role \
>      --policy-name CloudWatchLogsPolicy \
```

```
>        --policy-document '{
>            "Version": "2012-10-17",
>            "Statement": [
>                {
>                    "Effect": "Allow",
>                    "Action": [
>                        "logs:CreateLogStream",
>                        "logs:PutLogEvents"
>                    ],
>                    "Resource": "arn:aws:cloudtrail:us-west-2:387974667323:trail/
iam-activity-trail:*"
>                }
>            ]
>        }'
[cloudshell-user@ip-10-136-106-53 ~]$
```

Verify the role was created successfully:

```
[cloudshell-user@ip-10-136-106-53 ~]$ aws iam get-role --
role-name CloudTrail_CloudWatchLogs_Role
{
    "Role": {
        "Path": "/",
        "RoleName": "CloudTrail_CloudWatchLogs_Role",
        "RoleId": "AROAVUVIXTQ525HFG4SZJ",
        "Arn": "arn:aws:iam::387974667323:role/
CloudTrail_CloudWatchLogs_Role",
        "CreateDate": "2024-12-28T01:28:38+00:00",
        "AssumeRolePolicyDocument": {
            "Version": "2012-10-17",
            "Statement": [
                {
                    "Effect": "Allow",
                    "Principal": {
                        "Service": "cloudtrail.amazonaws.com"
                    },
                    "Action": "sts:AssumeRole"
                }
            ]
        },
        "MaxSessionDuration": 3600,
        "RoleLastUsed": {}
    }
}
(END)
```

With the S3 bucket, IAM role, and CloudWatch Log Group ready, and a multiregion CloudTrail trail, you can enable CloudWatch Logs integration with the trail:

```
[cloudshell-user@ip-10-142-65-159 ~]$ aws cloudtrail update-trail \
--name iam-activity-trail \
--cloud-watch-logs-log-group-arn arn:aws:cloudtrail:us-west-2:387974667323
:trail/iam-activity-trail \
```

```
--cloud-watch-logs-role-arn arn:aws:iam::387974667323:role/
CloudTrail_CloudWatchLogs_Role
[cloudshell-user@ip-10-142-65-159 ~]$
```

Next, start logging:

```
[cloudshell-user@ip-10-142-65-159 ~]$ aws cloudtrail start-logging --
name iam-activity-trail
[cloudshell-user@ip-10-142-65-159 ~]$
```

Now, verify that logging is active:

```
[cloudshell-user@ip-10-142-65-159 ~]$ aws cloudtrail get-trail-status --
name iam-activity-trail
{
    "IsLogging": true,
    "LatestDeliveryTime": "2024-12-28T02:24:32.446000+00:00",
    "StartLoggingTime": "2024-12-28T01:22:24.734000+00:00",
    "LatestCloudWatchLogsDeliveryTime": "2024-12-28T02:24:22.145000+00:00",
    "LatestDeliveryAttemptTime": "2024-12-28T02:24:32Z",
    "LatestNotificationAttemptTime": "",
    "LatestNotificationAttemptSucceeded": "",
    "LatestDeliveryAttemptSucceeded": "2024-12-28T02:24:32Z",
    "TimeLoggingStarted": "2024-12-28T01:22:24Z",
    "TimeLoggingStopped": ""
}
[cloudshell-user@ip-10-142-65-159 ~]$
```

Now that CloudTrail Logs are streaming into CloudWatch, create a metric filter to monitor IAM actions like DeleteUser or AttachUserPolicy:

```
[cloudshell-user@ip-10-142-65-159 ~]$ aws logs put-metric-filter \
>     --log-group-name cloudtrail-iam-logs \
>     --filter-name iam-suspicious-activity \
>     --filter-pattern '{ ($.eventName = "DeleteUser") || ($.
eventName = "AttachUserPolicy") }' \
>     --metric-transformations metricName=SuspiciousIAMActivity,metricNamespace=
CloudTrailMetrics,metricValue=1

[cloudshell-user@ip-10-142-65-159 ~]$
[cloudshell-user@ip-10-142-65-159 ~]$
```

To get notified when suspicious IAM activity occurs, you can create a CloudWatch alarm. First create an SNS topic. You can use the same method you used previously, or you can chose not to create a variable and just note the ARN, as shown next. Just be sure to replace the ARN here with your ARN. Again, in all examples, be sure to replace the values I use with your own:

```
[cloudshell-user@ip-10-142-65-159 ~]$ aws sns create-topic --name iam-alerts
{
    "TopicArn": "arn:aws:sns:us-west-2:387974667323:iam-alerts"
}
[cloudshell-user@ip-10-142-65-159 ~]$
```

Note the topic ARN and then subscribe:

```
[cloudshell-user@ip-10-142-65-159 ~]$ aws sns subscribe \
>      --topic-arn arn:aws:sns:us-west-2:387974667323:iam-alerts \
>      --protocol email \
>      --notification-endpoint brandon.carroll@gameonnetworks.com
{
    "SubscriptionArn": "pending confirmation"
}
[cloudshell-user@ip-10-142-65-159 ~]$
```

Also, you've done this before, but make sure to confirm the subscription by clicking the link in the email. Now, create the CloudWatch alarm:

```
[cloudshell-user@ip-10-142-65-159 ~]$ aws cloudwatch put-metric-alarm \
>      --alarm-name iam-suspicious-activity-alarm \
>      --metric-name SuspiciousIAMActivity \
>      --namespace CloudTrailMetrics \
>      --statistic Sum \
>      --period 300 \
>      --threshold 1 \
>      --comparison-operator GreaterThanOrEqualToThreshold \
>      --evaluation-periods 1 \
>      --alarm-actions arn:aws:sns:us-west-2:387974667323:iam-alerts
[cloudshell-user@ip-10-142-65-159 ~]$
```

Verify that the alarm is created properly:

```
[cloudshell-user@ip-10-142-65-159 ~]$ aws cloudwatch describe-alarms --
alarm-names iam-suspicious-activity-alarm
{
    "MetricAlarms": [
        {
            "AlarmName": "iam-suspicious-activity-alarm",
            "AlarmArn": "arn:aws:cloudwatch:us-west-2:387974667323:alarm:
iam-suspicious-activity-alarm",
            "AlarmConfigurationUpdatedTimestamp": "2024-12-
28T02:35:56.762000+00:00",
            "ActionsEnabled": true,
            "OKActions": [],
            "AlarmActions": [
                "arn:aws:sns:us-west-2:387974667323:iam-alerts"
            ],
            "InsufficientDataActions": [],
            "StateValue": "INSUFFICIENT_DATA",
            "StateReason": "Unchecked: Initial alarm creation",
            "StateUpdatedTimestamp": "2024-12-28T02:35:56.762000+00:00",
            "MetricName": "SuspiciousIAMActivity",
            "Namespace": "CloudTrailMetrics",
            "Statistic": "Sum",
            "Dimensions": [],
            "Period": 300,
```

```
            "EvaluationPeriods": 1,
            "Threshold": 1.0,
            "ComparisonOperator": "GreaterThanOrEqualToThreshold",
            "StateTransitionedTimestamp": "2024-12-28T02:35:56.762000+00:00"
        }
    ],
    "CompositeAlarms": []
}
[cloudshell-user@ip-10-142-65-159 ~]$
```

Finally, manually trigger the alarm for testing:

```
[cloudshell-user@ip-10-142-65-159 ~]$ aws cloudwatch set-alarm-state \
>    --alarm-name iam-suspicious-activity-alarm \
>    --state-value ALARM \
>    --state-reason "Testing IAM alarm"
[cloudshell-user@ip-10-142-65-159 ~]$
```

You can now check the state of the alarm:

```
[cloudshell-user@ip-10-142-65-159 ~]$ aws cloudwatch describe-alarms --
alarm-names iam-suspicious-activity-alarm
{
    "MetricAlarms": [
        {
            "AlarmName": "iam-suspicious-activity-alarm",
            "AlarmArn": "arn:aws:cloudwatch:us-west-2:387974667323:alarm:
iam-suspicious-activity-alarm",
            "AlarmConfigurationUpdatedTimestamp": "2024-12-
28T02:35:56.762000+00:00",
            "ActionsEnabled": true,
            "OKActions": [],
            "AlarmActions": [
                "arn:aws:sns:us-west-2:387974667323:iam-alerts"
            ],
            "InsufficientDataActions": [],
            "StateValue": "ALARM",
            "StateReason": "Testing IAM alarm",
            "StateUpdatedTimestamp": "2024-12-28T02:43:46.356000+00:00",
            "MetricName": "SuspiciousIAMActivity",
            "Namespace": "CloudTrailMetrics",
            "Statistic": "Sum",
            "Dimensions": [],
            "Period": 300,
            "EvaluationPeriods": 1,
            "Threshold": 1.0,
            "ComparisonOperator": "GreaterThanOrEqualToThreshold",
            "StateTransitionedTimestamp": "2024-12-28T02:43:46.356000+00:00"
        }
    ],
    "CompositeAlarms": []
}
[cloudshell-user@ip-10-142-65-159 ~]$
```

Reset the state after you've verified it:

```
[cloudshell-user@ip-10-142-65-159 ~]$ aws cloudwatch set-alarm-state \
>       --alarm-name iam-suspicious-activity-alarm \
>       --state-value OK \
>       --state-reason "Resetting IAM alarm after test"
[cloudshell-user@ip-10-142-65-159 ~]$
```

With this setup, you now have full visibility into IAM activity, real-time monitoring for suspicious events, and notifications delivered through SNS. Unauthorized IAM actions like modifying policies or deleting users will trigger alarms, allowing you to respond quickly and keep your AWS environment secure.

By combining the CloudTrail Logs, CloudWatch alarms, and SNS notifications, you start to get deep visibility into IAM activity across your AWS account. Another area where you can gain more visibility is in your WAF configuration, which is covered next.

Monitoring AWS WAF Activity with CloudWatch and CloudTrail

An earlier chapter covered Web Application Firewall (WAF); however, one thing you did not learn at the time was how to monitor what it's doing. You already know that WAF serves as the frontline defense for your AWS-hosted web applications, protecting them from common threats like SQL injection, cross-site scripting (XSS), and other malicious attacks. While WAF rules and managed rule groups provide robust protection, understanding how these rules are triggered, analyzing blocked requests, and identifying patterns of malicious activity are aspects of maintaining an effective security posture that can too easily be overlooked.

This section explores how to monitor AWS WAF using CloudWatch and CloudTrail, create alarms for suspicious activity, and analyze logs to fine-tune your rules. By the end, you'll have practical insights into configuring WAF monitoring and responding proactively to threats.

Enabling WAF Logging

Before you start monitoring, you need to enable AWS WAF logging. WAF Logs can be sent to an Amazon S3 bucket, Amazon Kinesis Data Firehose, or CloudWatch Logs. For real-time analysis and easy querying, you'll configure WAF to log activity to CloudWatch Logs.

Start by creating a CloudWatch Log Group for WAF:

```
[cloudshell-user@ip-10-140-19-76 ~]$ aws logs create-log-group --
log-group-name aws-waf-logs-waf
[cloudshell-user@ip-10-140-19-76 ~]$
```

In this command, note that WAF requires a specific naming convention for CloudWatch Log Groups. The log group name must start with the prefix aws-waf-logs- to be valid for WAF logging. This log group will serve as the destination for WAF Logs, allowing you to query and analyze activity efficiently.

Next, create an IAM role that allows AWS WAF to write logs to the log group:

```
[cloudshell-user@ip-10-140-19-76 ~]$ aws iam create-role \
>     --role-name WAF_CloudWatchLogs_Role \
>     --assume-role-policy-document '{
>         "Version": "2012-10-17",
>         "Statement": [
>             {
>                 "Effect": "Allow",
>                 "Principal": {
>                     "Service": "waf.amazonaws.com"
>                 },
>                 "Action": "sts:AssumeRole"
>             }
>         ]
>     }'
{
    "Role": {
        "Path": "/",
        "RoleName": "WAF_CloudWatchLogs_Role",
        "RoleId": "AROAVUVIXTQ52BKZLKIIF",
        "Arn": "arn:aws:iam::387974667323:role/WAF_CloudWatchLogs_Role",
        "CreateDate": "2024-12-28T15:39:45+00:00",
        "AssumeRolePolicyDocument": {
            "Version": "2012-10-17",
            "Statement": [
                {
                    "Effect": "Allow",
                    "Principal": {
                        "Service": "waf.amazonaws.com"
                    },
                    "Action": "sts:AssumeRole"
                }
            ]
        }
    }
}
(END)
```

Attach the necessary policy to this role:

```
[cloudshell-user@ip-10-140-19-76 ~]$ aws iam attach-role-policy \
>     --role-name WAF_CloudWatchLogs_Role \
>     --policy-arn arn:aws:iam::aws:policy/CloudWatchFullAccessV2
[cloudshell-user@ip-10-140-19-76 ~]$
```

Additionally, add an inline policy to allow specific permissions for logging:

```
[cloudshell-user@ip-10-140-19-76 ~]$ aws iam put-role-policy \
>     --role-name WAF_CloudWatchLogs_Role \
>     --policy-name WAFLogsPolicy \
>     --policy-document '{
>         "Version": "2012-10-17",
```

```
>           "Statement": [
>               {
>                   "Effect": "Allow",
>                   "Action": [
>                       "logs:CreateLogStream",
>                       "logs:PutLogEvents"
>                   ],
>                   "Resource": "arn:aws:logs:us-west-
2:387974667323:log-group:aws-waf-logs:*"
>               }
>           ]
>       }'
[cloudshell-user@ip-10-140-19-76 ~]$
```

Now, enable logging on your WAF web ACL and point it to the log group.
You can use the WAF ARN from Chapter 5:

```
[cloudshell-user@ip-10-140-19-76 ~]$ aws wafv2 put-logging-configuration \
>   --logging-configuration '{
>       "ResourceArn": "arn:aws:wafv2:us-west-2:387974667323:regional/
webacl/ALBSecurityWebACL/26355319-25f8-47e7-900a-428811bd848b",
>       "LogDestinationConfigs": ["arn:aws:logs:us-west-2:387974667323:log-
group:aws-waf-logs-waf"],
>       "LoggingFilter": {
>           "DefaultBehavior": "KEEP",
>           "Filters": [
>               {
>                   "Behavior": "KEEP",
>                   "Requirement": "MEETS_ANY",
>                   "Conditions": [
>                       {
>                           "ActionCondition": {
>                               "Action": "BLOCK"
>                           }
>                       }
>                   ]
>               }
>           ]
>       }
>   }'
{
    "LoggingConfiguration": {
        "ResourceArn": "arn:aws:wafv2:us-west-2:387974667323:regional/
webacl/ALBSecurityWebACL/26355319-25f8-47e7-900a-428811bd848b",
        "LogDestinationConfigs": [
            "arn:aws:logs:us-west-2:387974667323:log-group:aws-waf-logs-waf"
        ],
        "ManagedByFirewallManager": false,
        "LoggingFilter": {
            "Filters": [
                {
                    "Behavior": "KEEP",
                    "Requirement": "MEETS_ANY",
                    "Conditions": [
```

```
                         {
                             "ActionCondition": {
                                 "Action": "BLOCK"
                             }
                         }
                     ]
                 }
             ],
             "DefaultBehavior": "KEEP"
         },
         "LogType": "WAF_LOGS",
         "LogScope": "CUSTOMER"
     }
}
(END)
```

Now verify the configuration:

```
[cloudshell-user@ip-10-140-19-76 ~]$ aws wafv2 get-logging-configuration \
>     --resource-arn arn:aws:wafv2:us-west-2:387974667323:regional/webacl/
ALBSecurity  WebACL/26355319-25f8-47e7-900a-428811bd848b
{
    "LoggingConfiguration": {
        "ResourceArn": "arn:aws:wafv2:us-west-2:387974667323:regional
/webacl/ALBSecurityWebACL/26355319-25f8-47e7-900a-428811bd848b",
        "LogDestinationConfigs": [
            "arn:aws:logs:us-west-2:387974667323:log-group:aws-waf-logs-waf"
        ],
        "ManagedByFirewallManager": false,
        "LoggingFilter": {
            "Filters": [
                {
                    "Behavior": "KEEP",
                    "Requirement": "MEETS_ANY",
                    "Conditions": [
                        {
                            "ActionCondition": {
                                "Action": "BLOCK"
                            }
                        }
                    ]
                }
            ],
            "DefaultBehavior": "KEEP"
        },
        "LogType": "WAF_LOGS",
        "LogScope": "CUSTOMER"
    }
}
(END)
```

With logging enabled, WAF will now send activity logs to the specified CloudWatch Log Group. The next section discusses how to analyze WAF Logs with CloudWatch Logs Insights.

Analyzing WAF Logs with CloudWatch Logs Insights

Once your AWS WAF Logs are streaming into CloudWatch Logs, you'll need a way to make sense of all that data. This is where CloudWatch Logs Insights comes into play. Logs Insights is an interactive query tool built into CloudWatch that allows you to search, analyze, and visualize your log data in real time. Think of it like a search engine specifically for your AWS logs.

At its core, CloudWatch Logs Insights works by letting you run queries against your logs. You can filter specific patterns, aggregate data, and even visualize results with graphs, all within the AWS Management Console. A benefit of Logs Insights is that it scales with your data. So, whether you're searching a few hundred log entries or millions of them, the queries are fast and efficient.

The syntax for CloudWatch Logs Insights is straightforward. You write queries using a mix of fields, filters, and aggregations to pinpoint the data you care about. For example:

- You can *filter* logs to show only blocked WAF requests.

- You can *group data* by IP address to identify repeated offenders.

- You can *sort results* by timestamps to see the most recent activity.

Let's jump into an example to make this concrete. To detect recent blocked requests from your WAF, run the following command:

```
[cloudshell-user@ip-10-140-19-76 ~]$ aws logs start-query \
>     --log-group-name aws-waf-logs-waf \
>     --start-time $(date --date="10 minutes ago" +%s) \
>     --end-time $(date +%s) \
>     --query-string 'fields @timestamp, httpRequest.clientIp,
httpRequest.uri, ruleGroupList | filter action = "BLOCK"'
{
    "queryId": "f47c2883-47de-4b42-ae5e-5812480665e9"
}
[cloudshell-user@ip-10-140-19-76 ~]$
```

Here's what each part of this query means:

- `fields @timestamp, httpRequest.clientIp, httpRequest.uri, ruleGroupList`: Specifies the data fields you want to see in the results—timestamp, client IP, requested URI, and the rule group that triggered the block.

- `filter action = "BLOCK"`: Filters the logs to only include entries where the WAF action was `BLOCK`.

The output will provide a query ID. This will get you a list of blocked requests, showing when they happened, which IP address made the request, the specific URL requested, and which WAF rule group took action. Once the query starts, CloudWatch returns a query ID. Copy that ID and use it to retrieve the results:

```
[cloudshell-user@ip-10-140-19-76 ~]$ aws logs get-query-results --query-id
   f47c2883-47de-4b42-ae5e-5812480665e9
{
    "queryLanguage": "CWLI",
    "results": [],
    "statistics": {
        "recordsMatched": 0.0,
        "recordsScanned": 0.0,
        "estimatedRecordsSkipped": 0.0,
        "bytesScanned": 0.0,
        "estimatedBytesSkipped": 0.0,
        "logGroupsScanned": 1.0
    },
    "status": "Complete"
}
[cloudshell-user@ip-10-140-19-76 ~]$
```

In this output, there were no matches to the query. You can see what a match would look like here:

```
{
    "results": [
        [
            {"field": "@timestamp", "value": "2024-12-28 12:45:00"},
            {"field": "httpRequest.clientIp", "value": "192.168.10.25"},
            {"field": "httpRequest.uri", "value": "/login"},
            {"field": "ruleGroupList", "value": "[SQLInjectionRuleGroup]"}
        ]
    ]
}
```

In the previous example:

- The blocked request happened at 12:45 PM.
- The client IP was 192.168.10.25.
- The request was for the /login endpoint.
- The SQLInjectionRuleGroup was the rule responsible for blocking it.

From this data, you could conclude that someone attempted an SQL injection attack on your login page. With this insight, you can now take further steps, such as blocking the offending IP or reviewing the WAF rules for additional protections.

CloudWatch Logs Insights isn't limited to simple queries; it can also perform aggregations and group data. For example, you can count how many times each IP address triggered a block. You can create a new query for that:

```
[cloudshell-user@ip-10-140-19-76 ~]$ aws logs start-query \
>     --log-group-name aws-waf-logs-securingtheawscloud \
>     --start-time $(date --date="10 minutes ago" +%s) \
>     --end-time $(date +%s) \
```

```
>       --query-string 'fields httpRequest.clientIp | filter action = "BLOCK" |
stats count(*) as BlockCount by httpRequest.clientIp'
{
    "queryId": "7fc8036e-e126-4e7a-989b-356fea273849"
}
[cloudshell-user@ip-10-140-19-76 ~]$
```

This query:

- Filters for blocked requests (action = "BLOCK")
- Groups the results by httpRequest.clientIp
- Counts how many times each IP address triggered a block (count(*) as BlockCount)

Also, notice that the log group begins with aws-waf-logs. This is a requirement. The output might look like this:

```
[cloudshell-user@ip-10-140-19-76 ~]$ aws logs get-query-results --query-id
 7fc8036e-e126-4e7a-989b-356fea273849
{
    "queryLanguage": "CWLI",
    "results": [
        [
          {"field": "httpRequest.clientIp", "value": "192.168.10.25"},
          {"field": "BlockCount", "value": "5"}
        ],
        [
          {"field": "httpRequest.clientIp", "value": "203.0.113.17"},
          {"field": "BlockCount", "value": "3"}
        ]
    ],
    "statistics": {
        "recordsMatched": 1.0,
        "recordsScanned": 12342.0,
        "estimatedRecordsSkipped": 0.0,
        "bytesScanned": 234234.0,
        "estimatedBytesSkipped": 0.0,
        "logGroupsScanned": 1.0
    },
    "status": "Complete"
}
[cloudshell-user@ip-10-140-19-76 ~]$
```

From this data, you can see that 192.168.10.25 triggered five blocks, while 203.0.113.17 triggered three blocks. Armed with this information, you might decide to temporarily block these IPs at the firewall level or investigate further.

Before I close out this section, let's talk about how to create alarms for suspicious WAF activity.

Creating Alarms for Suspicious WAF Activity

Logs are great for investigations, but you also need real-time alerts when something looks suspicious. In this section, you set up an alarm in CloudWatch to notify you whenever the number of blocked WAF requests exceeds a predefined threshold.

First, create a metric filter that will turn log data into measurable metrics:

```
[cloudshell-user@ip-10-140-19-76 ~]$ aws logs put-metric-filter \
>     --log-group-name aws-waf-logs-waf \
>     --filter-name waf-blocked-requests \
>     --filter-pattern '{ ($.action = "BLOCK") }' \
>     --metric-transformations
metricName=BlockedRequests,metricNamespace=WAFMetrics,metricValue=1
[cloudshell-user@ip-10-140-19-76 ~]$
```

This filter looks for action = "BLOCK" in the WAF Logs, converts each matching log entry into a metric called BlockedRequests in the WAFMetrics namespace, and assigns a value of 1 to each blocked request. Verify the filter:

```
[cloudshell-user@ip-10-140-19-76 ~]$ aws logs describe-metric-filters --
log-group-name aws-waf-logs-waf
{
    "metricFilters": [
        {
            "filterName": "waf-blocked-requests",
            "filterPattern": "{ ($.action = \"BLOCK\") }",
            "metricTransformations": [
                {
                    "metricName": "BlockedRequests",
                    "metricNamespace": "WAFMetrics",
                    "metricValue": "1"
                }
            ],
            "creationTime": 1735404323455,
            "logGroupName": "aws-waf-logs-waf",
            "applyOnTransformedLogs": false
        }
    ]
}
(END)
```

Since everything looks good with the filter, create an SNS topic for WAF alerts. You've done this a few times now, so this should be nothing new:

```
[cloudshell-user@ip-10-140-19-76 ~]$ aws sns create-topic --
name waf-alerts
{
    "TopicArn": "arn:aws:sns:us-west-2:387974667323:waf-alerts"
}
[cloudshell-user@ip-10-140-19-76 ~]$
```

Subscribe to the topic:

```
[cloudshell-user@ip-10-140-19-76 ~]$ aws sns subscribe \
>      --topic-arn arn:aws:sns:us-west-2:387974667323:waf-alerts \
>      --protocol email \
>      --notification-endpoint brandon.carroll@gameonnetworks.com
{
    "SubscriptionArn": "pending confirmation"
}
[cloudshell-user@ip-10-140-19-76 ~]$
```

Confirm the subscription via email, then create the alarm:

```
[cloudshell-user@ip-10-140-19-76 ~]$ aws cloudwatch put-metric-alarm \
>      --alarm-name waf-blocked-requests-alarm \
>      --metric-name BlockedRequests \
>      --namespace WAFMetrics \
>      --statistic Sum \
>      --period 300 \
>      --threshold 10 \
>      --comparison-operator GreaterThanThreshold \
>      --evaluation-periods 1 \
>      --alarm-actions arn:aws:sns:us-west-2:387974667323:waf-alerts
[cloudshell-user@ip-10-140-19-76 ~]$
```

In this example, the alarm triggers if there are more than 10 blocked requests in a five-minute period and notifications are sent to the waf-alerts SNS topic. Now verify the alarm:

```
[cloudshell-user@ip-10-140-19-76 ~]$ aws cloudwatch describe-
alarms --alarm-names waf-blocked-requests-alarm
{
    "MetricAlarms": [
        {
            "AlarmName": "waf-blocked-requests-alarm",
            "AlarmArn": "arn:aws:cloudwatch:us-west-2:387974667323:
alarm:waf-blocked-requests-alarm",
            "AlarmConfigurationUpdatedTimestamp": "2024-12-
28T16:52:30.143000+00:00",
            "ActionsEnabled": true,
            "OKActions": [],
            "AlarmActions": [
                "arn:aws:sns:us-west-2:387974667323:waf-alerts"
            ],
            "InsufficientDataActions": [],
            "StateValue": "INSUFFICIENT_DATA",
            "StateReason": "Unchecked: Initial alarm creation",
            "StateUpdatedTimestamp": "2024-12-28T16:52:30.143000+00:00",
            "MetricName": "BlockedRequests",
            "Namespace": "WAFMetrics",
            "Statistic": "Sum",
            "Dimensions": [],
            "Period": 300,
            "EvaluationPeriods": 1,
```

```
            "Threshold": 10.0,
            "ComparisonOperator": "GreaterThanThreshold",
            "StateTransitionedTimestamp": "2024-12-28T16:
52:30.143000+00:00"
        }
    ],
    "CompositeAlarms": []
}
(END)
```

With the alarm verified, you can manually trigger it:

```
[cloudshell-user@ip-10-140-19-76 ~]$ aws cloudwatch set-alarm-state  \
>       --alarm-name waf-blocked-requests-alarm \
>       --state-value ALARM \
>       --state-reason "Testing WAF alarm"
[cloudshell-user@ip-10-140-19-76 ~]$
```

Once the alarm is triggered, verify the email. An example of what this looks like is shown in Figure 8.8.

Finally, reset the alarm:

```
[cloudshell-user@ip-10-140-19-76 ~]$ aws cloudwatch set-alarm-state  \
>       --alarm-name waf-blocked-requests-alarm \
>       --state-value OK \
>       --state-reason "Resetting WAF alarm after test"
[cloudshell-user@ip-10-140-19-76 ~]$
```

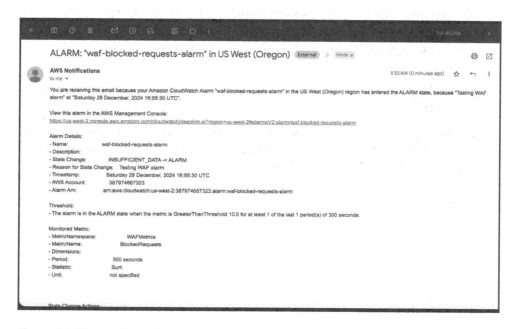

Figure 8.8: Triggered WAF alarm.

By combining WAF Logs, CloudWatch Logs Insights, and CloudWatch alarms, you've built a powerful monitoring and alerting system for your web applications. You can now detect and respond to malicious requests, analyze attack patterns, and fine-tune your WAF rules for better protection.

The next section explores how to tie these monitoring tools together into a cohesive security dashboard for centralized visibility and reporting.

Centralized Security Dashboard Setup

Earlier in this chapter, you created a CloudWatch dashboard to monitor specific metrics like EC2 CPU utilization and network anomalies. That initial dashboard provided a foundational view of critical performance indicators and alerting thresholds. However, a Centralized Security dashboard takes this concept further by tying together multiple AWS monitoring and logging services—CloudWatch, CloudTrail, VPC Flow Logs, AWS Config, and more—into a unified, security-focused view. This type of dashboard isn't just about tracking CPU or network activity; it's about gaining a holistic view of your AWS environment's security posture.

A centralized dashboard enables you to:

- See EC2 instance health, VPC network activity, IAM changes, and WAF events all in one place

- Correlate logs and metrics from different services to spot patterns or inconsistencies

- Provide a clear overview of compliance-related events and configuration changes

- Quickly identify the root cause of an issue by cross-referencing multiple data points

In this section, you build on the earlier dashboard by integrating additional layers of monitoring. Here's an example JSON configuration for an expanded security-focused dashboard (you can get this in the GitHub repo):

```
{
  "widgets": [
    {
      "type": "metric",
      "x": 0,
      "y": 0,
      "width": 6,
      "height": 6,
      "properties": {
        "metrics": [
```

```
            ["AWS/EC2", "CPUUtilization", "InstanceId",
    "i-0123456789abcdef0"]
        ],
        "region": "us-west-2",
        "stat": "Average",
        "period": 300,
        "title": "EC2 CPU Utilization"
      }
    },
    {
      "type": "log",
      "x": 6,
      "y": 0,
      "width": 6,
      "height": 6,
      "properties": {
        "query": "fields @timestamp, @message |
    filter @message like /REJECT/",
        "region": "us-west-2",
        "title": "Rejected VPC Traffic"
      }
    },
    {
      "type": "metric",
      "x": 0,
      "y": 6,
      "width": 6,
      "height": 6,
      "properties": {
        "metrics": [
            ["CloudTrailMetrics", "SuspiciousIAMActivity"]
        ],
        "region": "us-west-2",
        "stat": "Sum",
        "period": 300,
        "title": "Suspicious IAM Activity"
      }
    },
    {
      "type": "log",
      "x": 6,
      "y": 6,
      "width": 6,
      "height": 6,
      "properties": {
        "query": "fields @timestamp, @message |
    filter @message like /Blocked/",
        "region": "us-west-2",
        "title": "Blocked WAF Requests"
      }
    }
  ]
}
```

Here's how this enhanced dashboard improves on the initial setup:

■ The EC2 CPU Utilization widget remains, providing baseline performance visibility.

■ VPC Flow Logs (Rejected Traffic) tracks rejected network traffic, helping detect unauthorized access attempts.

■ Suspicious IAM activity displays aggregated IAM-related alerts, such as `DeleteUser` or `AttachUserPolicy` events, sourced from CloudTrail.

■ WAF Blocked Requests surfaces insights into blocked HTTP/S requests that may indicate ongoing attacks or misconfigurations.

To update this widget, first, take the JSON and save it to a file on your CloudShell. I used the touch command to create the file, then nano to edit it:

```
[cloudshell-user@ip-10-130-56-121 ~]$ touch security-dashboard.json
[cloudshell-user@ip-10-130-56-121 ~]$ nano security-dashboard.json
```

Once the file has been created, you can update the existing dashboard with the new JSON. To do this, use the following command:

```
[cloudshell-user@ip-10-130-56-121 ~]$ aws cloudwatch put-dashboard \
>      --dashboard-name "EC2-Monitoring" \
>      --dashboard-body file://security-dashboard.json

{
    "DashboardValidationMessages": []
}
[cloudshell-user@ip-10-130-56-121 ~]$
[cloudshell-user@ip-10-130-56-121 ~]$
```

After running the command, verify the updated widgets by running

```
[cloudshell-user@ip-10-130-56-121 ~]$ aws cloudwatch get-dashboard \
>      --dashboard-name "EC2-Monitoring"
{
    "DashboardArn": "arn:aws:cloudwatch::387974667323:dashboard/EC2-Monitoring",
    "DashboardBody": "{\"widgets\":[{\"type\":\"metric\",\"x\":0,\"y\":0,\"width\":
6,\"height\":6,\ "properties\":{\"metrics\":[[\"AWS/EC2\",\"CPUUtilization\",\
"InstanceId\",\" i-0123456789abcdef0\"]],\"region\":\"us-west-2\",\"stat\":\
"Average\",\" period\":300,\"title\":\"EC2 CPU Utilization\"}},{\"type\":\"log\",\
"x\":6,\"y \":0,\"width\":6,\"height\":6,\"properties\":{\"query\":\"fields
@timestamp, @message | filter @message like /REJECT/\",\"region\":\"us-west-2\",\
"title\": \"Rejected VPC Traffic\"}},{\"type\":\"metric\",\"x\":0,\"y\":6,\
"width\":6,\" height\":6,\"properties\":{\"metrics\":[[\"CloudTrailMetrics\",\
" SuspiciousIAMActivity\"]],\"region\":\"us-west-2\",\"stat\":\"Sum\",\
"period\":300,\"title\":\"Suspicious IAM Activity\"}},{\"type\":\"log\",\"x\":
6,\"y\":6,\"width\":6,\"height\":6,\"properties\":{\"query\":\"fields @timestamp,
@message | filter @message like /Blocked/\",\"region\":\" us-west-2\",\"title\":\
```

```
"Blocked WAF Requests\"}}]}",
    "DashboardName": "EC2-Monitoring"
}
[cloudshell-user@ip-10-130-56-121 ~]$
```

This looks correct, but it doesn't look good, so let's actually view it in the AWS Console:

1. Log in to the AWS Management Console.
2. Navigate to CloudWatch by searching for it in the top search bar.
3. In the CloudWatch Console, select Dashboards from the left-side navigation menu.
4. Locate and click on the dashboard named EC2-Monitoring.
5. Review the widgets and ensure they reflect the updated configuration.

You can see the updated dashboard in Figure 8.9.

At this point in time, there is no data showing on my widgets, but over time they will populate as I see more network activity.

Why This Centralized Dashboard Matters

Earlier, you focused on individual metrics and alerts. Now, you're bringing them together into one cohesive, security-focused visualization. This approach allows you to move beyond isolated monitoring and start correlating data across multiple AWS services.

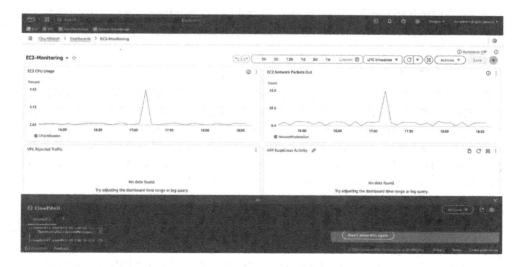

Figure 8.9: Updated security dashboard.

For example:

- A spike in blocked WAF requests can be cross-referenced with unusual outbound VPC traffic and recent IAM policy changes to build a clearer picture of a potential breach.
- During a security audit, you can quickly validate resource access logs from CloudTrail against real-time activity in CloudWatch.

By building on the earlier dashboard and expanding it with cross-service integration, you're creating a Security Operations Center (SOC)-like view tailored to AWS environments.

If you've followed along throughout this chapter, you already have most of the components configured. As mentioned in the onset of this chapter, this section serves as a final assembly, pulling together CloudWatch, CloudTrail, and other log streams into a powerful, unified security monitoring system.

This section discusses how these tools align with compliance frameworks like PCI DSS and HIPAA to solidify your monitoring strategy.

Compliance Framework Examples

AWS monitoring and logging tools play a critical role in achieving compliance with industry frameworks like PCI DSS (Payment Card Industry Data Security Standard) and HIPAA (Health Insurance Portability and Accountability Act). These frameworks have specific requirements around auditing, visibility, and security controls, and AWS services are designed to align with these standards. Among these tools, AWS Config stands out as an essential service for tracking resource configurations and ensuring compliance with predefined policies.

PCI DSS Compliance

AWS Config evaluates your AWS resources against PCI DSS requirements, ensuring critical configurations are in place and maintained. For example, you can enable a Config rule to verify that S3 buckets are encrypted and publicly accessible buckets are flagged for review. AWS CloudTrail complements this by providing a detailed audit trail of API activity, while Amazon CloudWatch sets up alarms for unauthorized changes to sensitive resources.

HIPAA Compliance

AWS Config simplifies HIPAA compliance by continuously monitoring configurations to ensure that resources handling protected health information (PHI) adhere to best practices. For instance, a Config rule can validate that all EBS volumes storing sensitive data have encryption enabled. Alongside this, AWS CloudTrail Logs access to PHI-related resources, and CloudWatch monitors for unauthorized activity. By integrating these tools, you create a robust monitoring and compliance strategy tailored to HIPAA requirements.

Use Cases in Compliance

Here are a few practical examples of how AWS Config enhances compliance:

- *Access auditing (PCI DSS):* AWS Config can verify that all IAM users have multifactor authentication (MFA) enabled, while CloudTrail Logs access patterns.

- *Change monitoring (HIPAA):* Config can track and alert on changes to security group rules, such as open ports, to ensure they don't expose PHI unintentionally.

- *Incident alerts (PCI DSS and HIPAA):* Config integrates with CloudWatch to trigger alarms when a rule violation occurs, such as an unencrypted database instance.

While AWS services like CloudTrail and CloudWatch provide visibility into activity and performance, AWS Config adds a layer of configuration compliance and remediation. By defining Config rules aligned with frameworks like PCI DSS and HIPAA, you can automate the detection of misconfigurations and take proactive steps to maintain compliance. When combined, these tools form a powerful compliance framework that simplifies audits, strengthens your security posture, and ensures regulatory requirements are consistently met.

Example AWS Config Rule for Compliance Monitoring

To make AWS Config's role in compliance a bit more real, let's walk through a simple example of an AWS Config rule that ensures all S3 buckets are encrypted. This is a common requirement in PCI DSS and HIPAA frameworks.

AWS provides managed rules that simplify compliance checks. For S3 bucket encryption, you'll use the `s3-bucket-server-side-encryption-enabled` rule. You're going to enable Config, and just let it go. This is a starting point, but the details of Config are outside of the scope of this book:

1. Open the AWS Config Console.

2. Choose 1-click setup.

3. Click Confirm.

4. Click Rules.

5. Click Add Rule.

6. Find the `cloudtrail-s3-bucket-public-access-prohibited` rule and select it. This can be seen in Figure 8.10.

7. Click Next.

8. Click Save.

This rule will automatically check if your S3 buckets have encryption enabled and flag any non-compliant resources. Alternatively, you could enable a conformance pack. Conformance packs create several rules around certain use cases. For example, in Figure 8.11, I am adding a conformance pack for PCI DSS. This will create the rules for you automatically.

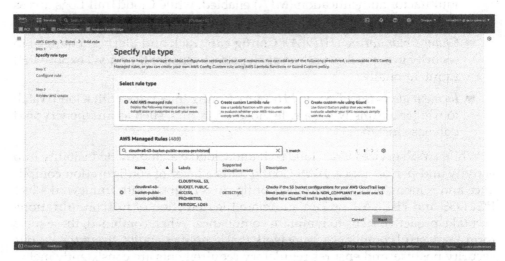

Figure 8.10: Adding the `cloudtrail-s3-bucket-public-access-prohibited` rule to Config.

Figure 8.11: PCS DSS conformance pack.

Best Practices for Monitoring and Logging in AWS Environments

With config enabled, this section discusses some best practices for monitoring and logging.

Enable CloudTrail Across All Regions

One of the foundational steps in AWS monitoring is enabling AWS CloudTrail across all regions, including global service events. CloudTrail acts as an audit log for all API calls made within your AWS account, offering a historical view of activities performed by users, roles, and AWS services. Without enabling it in all regions, you risk missing critical activity logs, especially if an attacker or misconfigured service operates in a region you don't actively use. Additionally, enabling global service events ensures that you capture actions related to services like IAM, which span across regions. Once CloudTrail is enabled comprehensively, the next logical step is to centralize these logs to simplify analysis and management.

Enabling AWS CloudTrail across all regions should generally be considered a best practice. It ensures comprehensive visibility into API activity across your AWS account, including regions you may not actively use. This is important because attackers or misconfigurations could exploit unmonitored regions to perform unauthorized actions without detection. By enabling multiregion trails, you centralize log collection into a single location, such as an S3 bucket or CloudWatch Logs, simplifying management and analysis. Additionally, capturing global service events (e.g., IAM and STS activity) ensures that critical account-wide actions are logged, helping you meet compliance requirements and troubleshoot security incidents effectively.

However, there might be specific scenarios where enabling CloudTrail in all regions is not necessary. For example, if your organization operates in a single region and has strict policies preventing the use of other regions, a single-region trail might suffice to reduce costs and simplify configuration. That said, even in such cases, enabling multiregion trails is often recommended as a safeguard against accidental or unauthorized activity in unused regions. Ultimately, you want to align this with your organization's security policies, compliance requirements, and operational needs.

Centralize Logs in Amazon S3 or CloudWatch Logs

Centralizing logs from multiple AWS services in a single location, such as Amazon S3 or CloudWatch Logs, streamlines log management and analysis. By aggregating data from EC2 instances, VPC Flow Logs, CloudTrail, and

WAF Logs, you can more easily identify patterns, detect anomalies, and troubleshoot issues across your environment. Amazon S3 offers long-term, cost-effective storage for logs, while CloudWatch Logs enables real-time querying and integration with monitoring tools. With your logs centralized, the next step is to ensure you're alerted to important events without being overwhelmed by false positives.

Set Meaningful Alarms

CloudWatch alarms are a powerful tool for alerting you to potential issues, but poorly configured alarms can result in either missed incidents or constant false positives. It's essential to set meaningful thresholds based on baseline operational metrics to ensure alarms are only triggered when actionable thresholds are crossed. For example, an alarm for CPU utilization on an EC2 instance should account for typical workload patterns. Additionally, consider using evaluation periods to reduce noise from temporary spikes. Once alarms are effectively configured, the next step is to make the most of your log data with advanced querying capabilities.

Leverage CloudWatch Logs Insights

CloudWatch Logs Insights is a powerful tool for analyzing large volumes of log data with flexible, on-the-fly querying capabilities. It allows you to search, filter, and visualize log data to identify trends, troubleshoot performance issues, and detect anomalies in real time. For example, you can query rejected VPC traffic logs or look for specific IAM events like DeleteUser. CloudWatch Logs Insights helps turn raw log data into actionable insights with minimal overhead. With logs being actively analyzed, it's equally important to monitor the IAM activity that often underpins critical changes.

Monitor IAM Activity Closely

IAM activity logs, captured by CloudTrail and analyzed in CloudWatch, are critical for identifying unauthorized access or privilege escalation attempts. Actions like DeleteUser, AttachUserPolicy, or CreateAccessKey are highly sensitive and should trigger alerts when detected. Regular monitoring of IAM activity helps ensure that no unauthorized changes slip through unnoticed. Additionally, enabling alarms for these activities allows immediate escalation and investigation. While IAM monitoring helps detect threats related to identity, regularly reviewing dashboards ensures you always have a clear, visual overview of your AWS environment.

Review Dashboards Regularly

Dashboards in CloudWatch provide a centralized, visual representation of key metrics and log insights. However, dashboards are only as valuable as their design and regular review. Ensure your dashboards display essential metrics such as CPU utilization, network anomalies, IAM activity, and WAF blocked requests. Regularly review and refine your dashboards based on evolving business needs and incident trends. By doing so, you can quickly identify patterns and spot anomalies before they become critical issues. With dashboards in place, it's crucial to maintain tight access controls for all monitoring and logging configurations.

Implement Least Privilege Access

Access to AWS monitoring and logging tools, including CloudWatch, CloudTrail, and AWS Config, should follow the principle of least privilege. Only authorized personnel should have permission to modify alarms, delete logs, or alter monitoring configurations. Use IAM roles and policies to enforce fine-grained access control and regularly review IAM permissions to avoid over-provisioning. By restricting access to only those who need it, you minimize the risk of accidental or malicious changes. Beyond access control, compliance validation through AWS Config further enhances your monitoring strategy.

Enable AWS Config Rules

AWS Config continuously monitors and evaluates your AWS resource configurations against predefined rules and compliance requirements. You can set up AWS Config rules to ensure resources, such as EC2 instances and security groups, comply with your organization's security policies. For example, a rule can check if CloudTrail is enabled in all regions or if specific ports are restricted in security groups. AWS Config integrates seamlessly with CloudWatch for alerting, allowing you to address misconfigurations proactively. Alongside configuration compliance, regularly rotating IAM credentials adds another layer of security.

Regularly Rotate IAM Credentials and Keys

Long-lived IAM access keys are a common security risk, as they can be exposed or compromised over time. AWS recommends regular rotation of IAM credentials and access keys to reduce the risk associated with credential leaks. Automating key rotation policies ensures credentials are consistently updated without relying on manual intervention. Additionally, monitor CloudTrail for key usage patterns to detect anomalies. With credential rotation policies in place, periodic audits become essential to ensure all systems and configurations align with security best practices.

Conduct Periodic Audits

Monitoring and logging setups are not "set it and forget it" systems—they require periodic audits to ensure they are functioning as intended. Review CloudTrail Logs, CloudWatch alarms, IAM access patterns, and AWS Config compliance reports regularly. Audits help identify gaps, outdated configurations, or potential misconfigurations. Additionally, periodic reviews can validate whether alarm thresholds remain effective as workloads evolve. These audits not only keep your environment secure but also prepare your organization for external compliance assessments.

By following these best practices, you'll build a robust foundation for monitoring and logging in AWS. From enabling CloudTrail in all regions to leveraging CloudWatch Logs Insights and implementing IAM credential rotation, these strategies ensure better visibility, faster response times, and stronger compliance alignment.

Cleaning Up Your Resources

If you've followed along with the examples in this chapter, it's important to clean up the resources you created to avoid unnecessary costs and maintain a clean AWS environment. You should have a bit of an understanding of pricing so that this cleanup process makes more sense to you.

AWS monitoring and logging tools come with associated costs, which vary based on usage. For example, Amazon CloudWatch charges for metrics, dashboards, alarms, and log storage. CloudTrail includes free management event logging for the last 90 days, but additional trails or extended log retention in S3 incur charges. Similarly, enabling services like VPC Flow Logs or WAF logging can generate significant data volumes, impacting CloudWatch Logs or S3 storage costs. To control expenses, regularly review your usage patterns, set appropriate retention policies for logs, and clean up unused resources. By understanding these pricing factors, you can balance effective monitoring with cost efficiency.

With that said, the following sections cover the list of items you should clean up.

CloudFormation Stack

Delete the CloudFormation stack used to create the EC2 instances, security groups, and IAM roles for testing:

```
aws cloudformation delete-stack --stack-name <stack-name>
```

CloudWatch Dashboards

Remove any custom CloudWatch dashboards you created (e.g., EC2-Monitoring):

```
aws cloudwatch delete-dashboards --dashboard-names EC2-Monitoring
```

CloudWatch Alarms

Delete all alarms created for monitoring CPU usage, network anomalies, IAM suspicious activity, and WAF blocked requests:

```
aws cloudwatch delete-alarms --alarm-names high-cpu-usage unusual-vpc-
traffic iam-suspicious-activity-alarm waf-blocked-requests-alarm
```

SNS Topics and Subscriptions

Unsubscribe email addresses from SNS topics and delete the topics (e.g., high-cpu-alert, network-anomalies-alert, iam-alerts, and waf-alerts):

```
aws sns unsubscribe --subscription-arn <subscription-arn>
aws sns delete-topic --topic-arn <topic-arn>
```

S3 Buckets

Empty and delete any S3 buckets created for storing CloudTrail Logs (e.g., cloudtrail-iam-logs):

```
aws s3 rm s3://cloudtrail-iam-logs --recursive
aws s3api delete-bucket --bucket cloudtrail-iam-logs
```

CloudTrail Trails

Stop logging and delete any CloudTrail trails you created (e.g., iam-activity-trail):

```
aws cloudtrail stop-logging --name iam-activity-trail
aws cloudtrail delete-trail --name iam-activity-trail
```

IAM Roles and Policies

Detach policies and delete IAM roles created for CloudTrail, VPC Flow Logs, or WAF logging:

```
aws iam detach-role-policy --role-name <role-name> --
policy-arn <policy-arn>
aws iam delete-role --role-name <role-name>
```

VPC Flow Logs

Delete VPC Flow Logs configured for your VPC:

```
aws ec2 delete-flow-logs --flow-log-id <flow-log-id>
```

CloudWatch Log Groups

Delete log groups used for VPC Flow Logs, WAF Logs, or CloudTrail Logs:

```
aws logs delete-log-group --log-group-name vpc-flow-logs
aws logs delete-log-group --log-group-name aws-waf-logs-waf
aws logs delete-log-group --log-group-name cloudtrail-iam-logs
```

Conclusion

This chapter explored how AWS monitoring and logging tools like CloudWatch, CloudTrail, and Config work together to provide visibility, accountability, and compliance across your cloud environment. By implementing monitoring alarms, analyzing logs, and creating dashboards, you can proactively identify and address potential security issues before they escalate.

As you continue building your AWS security posture, the next step is preparing for resilience and recovery. Chapter 9, "Resilience and Recovery Strategies," dives into AWS tools designed for incident response and disaster recovery. You'll learn how to build robust systems that can withstand failures and recover quickly when the unexpected happens.

Let's keep building!

References

AWS CloudWatch Logs Documentation, https://docs.aws.amazon.com/cloudwatch/

AWS CloudTrail Logs Documentation, https://docs.aws.amazon.com/cloudtrail/

AWS Command Line Interface Documentation, https://docs.aws.amazon.com/cli/

AWS Config Documentation, https://docs.aws.amazon.com/config/

Resilience and Recovery Strategies

"The greatest glory in living lies not in never falling, but in rising every time we fall."

— Nelson Mandela

Resilience and recovery strategies are pivotal for organizations running workloads on AWS. As a cloud security professional, you might wonder why resilience planning and the inevitable recovery efforts that follow disruptions matter to your day-to-day responsibilities. In short, resilience ensures that systems remain secure and operational in the face of various failures, and recovery is about returning to normal operations quickly and safely when those failures happen. This chapter aims to give you a high-level overview of resilience and recovery strategies so that you can start to think of them through the lens of a security professional. While the build-out of these strategies may not be the direct responsibility of a security professional, having a basic understanding will certainly help.

Why Resilience and Recovery Matter to Cloud Security Professionals

Resilience and recovery strategies play an essential role in protecting the availability, integrity, and confidentiality of your cloud environment. As a cloud security professional, you need more than just strong preventive controls. You also need to ensure that your systems can bounce back from disruptions and meet regulatory standards. Many compliance frameworks explicitly require business continuity plans and well-defined recovery objectives, such as Recovery Point Objective (RPO) and Recovery Time Objective (RTO), which you learn more about later in this chapter. Meeting these benchmarks means that, no matter what happens, whether it be a sudden data center outage, a security incident, or even a natural disaster, your organization can maintain operations and keep its data secure.

At the heart of this responsibility is data protection. Security isn't limited to preventing unauthorized access. It also involves making sure information stays available when users need it most. That's where strategies like immutable backups, versioning, and multiregional replication come into play. These practices prepare you to respond effectively to incidents like ransomware attacks or accidental deletions, minimizing disruption and safeguarding critical data.

Finally, even though AWS builds resilience into its services, you retain control over configuration decisions like backup policies, replication setups, and failover strategies. This is the shared responsibility model in action. AWS handles the underlying infrastructure, but you design and implement your own disaster recovery plan. By combining AWS's platforms with well-structured resilience and recovery processes, you ensure your security posture remains strong under all circumstances.

What's Involved in Resilience and Recovery

Resilience and recovery start with understanding how you'll protect and retrieve your data when things go wrong. The overall process can be seen in Figure 9.1. Let's talk through what this involves.

First, resilience and recovery start with identifying the right backup frequency, whether it's daily, hourly, or continuous, and figuring out how long to keep those backups on hand. Security enters the conversation immediately through measures like data encryption (often leveraging AWS KMS), strict access controls, and secure storage practices. On top of that, most organizations adopt one of several disaster recovery patterns. You might opt for a *pilot light* setup, which keeps a minimal core of your environment running, a *warm standby*, with a scaled-down but always-ready copy in another region, or a fully duplicated *multisite* approach. Each pattern has its own tradeoffs in terms of complexity, cost, and speed of recovery.

Each of these disaster recovery strategies serves different needs based on your organization's goals for downtime (RTO) and data loss (RPO). Let's take a quick look at what each entails:

- **Pilot light:** A cost-effective approach where only critical components are kept running in a secondary region. This strategy minimizes costs but requires more time to scale up during a disaster. It's ideal for applications that can tolerate some downtime but need rapid data recovery.

- **Warm standby:** Builds on pilot light by maintaining a smaller-scale version of your production environment that's always running and ready to handle traffic at reduced capacity. This approach strikes a balance between cost and recovery speed, making it suitable for business-critical systems.

- **Multisite active/active:** Involves running fully operational environments in multiple regions simultaneously. This ensures near-zero downtime but comes with higher costs and complexity. It's best suited for mission-critical services like financial or healthcare applications that demand high availability.

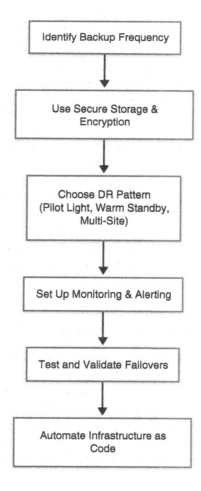

Figure 9.1: The main building blocks of resilience and recovery.

You explore these strategies in more detail later in this chapter when you learn how they align with RTO and RPO metrics in the "Establishing Key Metrics and Choosing a Strategy" section. Additionally, practical examples of implementing these approaches using AWS services are covered in sections like "Building a Resilient Architecture with CloudFormation."

Monitoring and alerting are also vital pieces of the puzzle. If you're not detecting issues promptly, your recovery times are going to suffer. That's where AWS services like Amazon CloudWatch and AWS Config come into play, giving you eyes on your environment so you can act quickly. Testing your plan isn't optional either. Just like you wouldn't trust a new feature without a test run, you'll want to verify that backups are restorable, that failovers happen smoothly, and that automation tools like AWS CloudFormation and Terraform (covered in Chapter 12) can reliably rebuild your infrastructure.

Automation tools like AWS CloudFormation and Terraform play a crucial role in disaster recovery because they allow you to define and deploy your infrastructure as code. This means that instead of manually re-creating resources during an outage—a time-consuming and error-prone process— you can quickly and consistently rebuild your environment with pre-tested templates. For example, if your primary region becomes unavailable, you can use these tools to deploy identical infrastructure in your secondary region within minutes.

You learn how to use AWS CloudFormation for building resilient architectures later in this chapter, in the "Building a Resilient Architecture with CloudFormation" section. Additionally, Chapter 12 dives deeper into Terraform and its role in managing multicloud environments. By leveraging these tools, you ensure that your recovery processes are both efficient and repeatable, reducing downtime and minimizing human error during critical moments.

In a resilient environment, each component, ranging from backups, testing, monitoring, and automation, works together to minimize downtime and keep data secure.

Establishing Key Metrics and Choosing a Strategy

Now that you've explored the basic elements of resilience, backups, monitoring, and various DR patterns, it's time to define the metrics that drive every recovery plan: RTO and RPO. These two numbers help you balance cost, complexity, and downtime. Once you understand how RTO and RPO tie into each of AWS's four main DR approaches, you'll have the foundation to give your input on which strategy best fits your workloads. The next section looks at how these concepts come together, beginning with the simplest disaster recovery method, backup and restore.

Understanding Recovery Objectives

Before diving into specific strategies, you need to understand two critical metrics that shape every resilience strategy:

- **Recovery Time Objective (RTO):** Represents the maximum acceptable downtime. If your application fails at 2:00 p.m., and your RTO is one hour, you need to be operational by 3:00 p.m.

- **Recovery Point Objective (RPO):** Defines the maximum acceptable data loss measured in time. An RPO of 15 minutes means your backup systems must never contain data more than 15 minutes old.

RPO is not just about ensuring that your backups are recent; it's also about determining how much data your business can afford to lose if a disaster occurs. For example, an RPO of 15 minutes means that, in the worst-case scenario, you could lose up to 15 minutes of data created before the outage. This metric directly influences how frequently backups or data replication processes need to occur.

It's important to note that RPO also reflects the duration of time during which data generated by your systems may not be recoverable. For instance, if a database writes new transactions every second but is only backed up every 15 minutes, any transactions within that 15-minute window could be permanently lost in a disaster.

To put this into perspective:

- A low RPO (e.g., seconds) is critical for businesses like financial institutions or e-commerce platforms where even minor data loss could result in significant financial or reputational damage.

- A higher RPO (e.g., hours) might be acceptable for workloads like internal reporting systems where losing some data has minimal impact.

This chapter explores how RPO ties into AWS disaster recovery strategies in the section, "Establishing Key Metrics and Choosing a Strategy." Additionally, when the chapter discusses AWS services like Amazon RDS, DynamoDB Global Tables, and S3 Cross-Region Replication, you'll see practical examples of how to achieve specific RPO targets.

AWS offers four main approaches to disaster recovery, each balancing cost with recovery speed:

STRATEGY	RTO	RPO	COST	USE CASE
Backup and restore	Hours	Hours	$	Noncritical workloads
Pilot light	Tens of minutes	Minutes	$$	Important applications
Warm standby	Minutes	Minutes	$$$	Business critical systems
Multisite active/active	Seconds	Seconds	$$$$	Mission critical services

This table highlights the four main disaster recovery approaches AWS offers, each balancing cost against recovery speed:

- **Backup and restore:** The simplest and most cost-effective strategy, suitable for noncritical workloads. However, it has the longest Recovery Time Objective (RTO) and Recovery Point Objective (RPO), as restoring backups and rebuilding infrastructure can take hours.

- **Pilot light:** A step up from backup and restore, this approach ensures critical components are always running in a secondary region. While it reduces RTO to tens of minutes and RPO to minutes, it requires scaling up additional resources during a disaster.

- **Warm standby:** Maintains a scaled-down but functional copy of your production environment in another region. This ensures faster recovery (RTO/RPO in minutes) but comes at a higher cost compared to pilot light.

- **Multisite active/active:** The most robust strategy, running fully operational environments in multiple regions simultaneously. It delivers near-zero RTO and RPO, but is also the most expensive and complex to implement.

Each approach comes with tradeoffs in cost, complexity, and recovery speed. Choosing the right strategy depends on your workload's requirements and business priorities. The chapter dives deeper into these approaches in the "Establishing Key Metrics and Choosing a Strategy" section, where they are aligned with RTO and RPO metrics.

Building a Resilient Architecture with CloudFormation

To better understand the resilience and recovery concepts, you'll set up a sample environment using AWS CloudFormation. This will include EC2 instances, IAM roles, and networking components.

If you're following along, create a new stack with the following template. You can also find the template on GitHub: https://github.com/8carroll/Securing-the-Cloud-with-Brandon-Carroll/blob/main/Chapter9.yaml. In my example, I am using the us-west-2 region. Be sure to use that region or make the needed changes before deploying the template. In addition, for all the examples, you'll find the commands to copy and paste in the respective chapter folder in the GitHub repo. Be sure to replace all account IDs, resource IDs, and ARNs with the ones from your account:

```
AWSTemplateFormatVersion: '2010-09-09'
Description: 'Environment for testing AWS resilience strategies'

Parameters:
  LatestAMI:
    Type: AWS::SSM::Parameter::Value<String>
```

```
      Description: The latest Amazon Linux 2 AMI ID
      Default: /aws/service/ami-amazon-linux-latest/amzn2-ami-hvm-x86_64-gp2

Resources:
  # VPC and Network Configuration
  VPC:
    Type: AWS::EC2::VPC
    Properties:
      CidrBlock: 10.0.0.0/16
      EnableDnsHostnames: true
      EnableDnsSupport: true
      Tags:
        - Key: Name
          Value: Monitoring-Demo-VPC

  InternetGateway:
    Type: AWS::EC2::InternetGateway
    Properties:
      Tags:
        - Key: Name
          Value: Monitoring-Demo-IGW

  AttachGateway:
    Type: AWS::EC2::VPCGatewayAttachment
    Properties:
      VpcId: !Ref VPC
      InternetGatewayId: !Ref InternetGateway

  PublicSubnet:
    Type: AWS::EC2::Subnet
    Properties:
      VpcId: !Ref VPC
      CidrBlock: 10.0.1.0/24
      MapPublicIpOnLaunch: true
      AvailabilityZone: !Select [ 0, !GetAZs "" ]
      Tags:
        - Key: Name
          Value: Public-Subnet

  PublicRouteTable:
    Type: AWS::EC2::RouteTable
    Properties:
      VpcId: !Ref VPC
      Tags:
        - Key: Name
          Value: Public-Route-Table

  PublicRoute:
    Type: AWS::EC2::Route
    DependsOn: AttachGateway
    Properties:
      RouteTableId: !Ref PublicRouteTable
      DestinationCidrBlock: 0.0.0.0/0
      GatewayId: !Ref InternetGateway
```

```
PublicSubnetRouteTableAssociation:
  Type: AWS::EC2::SubnetRouteTableAssociation
  Properties:
    SubnetId: !Ref PublicSubnet
    RouteTableId: !Ref PublicRouteTable

# Security Groups
WebServerSecurityGroup:
  Type: AWS::EC2::SecurityGroup
  Properties:
    GroupDescription: Allow web and SSM traffic
    VpcId: !Ref VPC
    SecurityGroupIngress:
      - IpProtocol: tcp
        FromPort: 80
        ToPort: 80
        CidrIp: 0.0.0.0/0
      - IpProtocol: tcp
        FromPort: 443
        ToPort: 443
        CidrIp: 0.0.0.0/0

# IAM Role for SSM and CloudWatch Agent Permissions
SSMInstanceRole:
  Type: AWS::IAM::Role
  Properties:
    AssumeRolePolicyDocument:
      Version: '2012-10-17'
      Statement:
        - Effect: Allow
          Principal:
            Service: ec2.amazonaws.com
          Action: sts:AssumeRole
    ManagedPolicyArns:
      - arn:aws:iam::aws:policy/AmazonSSMManagedInstanceCore
      - arn:aws:iam::aws:policy/CloudWatchAgentServerPolicy

SSMInstanceProfile:
  Type: AWS::IAM::InstanceProfile
  Properties:
    Path: /
    Roles:
      - !Ref SSMInstanceRole

# EC2 Instance for the Web Server
WebServer:
  Type: AWS::EC2::Instance
  Properties:
    ImageId: !Ref LatestAMI
    InstanceType: t2.micro
    SubnetId: !Ref PublicSubnet
    SecurityGroupIds:
      - !Ref WebServerSecurityGroup
    IamInstanceProfile: !Ref SSMInstanceProfile
```

```
    UserData:
      Fn::Base64: !Sub |
        #!/bin/bash
        yum update -y && amazon-linux-extras enable nginx1 && yum install -y
nginx &&  systemctl enable nginx && systemctl start nginx && yum install -y
amazon-cloudwatch-agent  && systemctl enable amazon-cloudwatch-agent &&
systemctl start amazon-cloudwatch-agent
      Tags:
        - Key: Name
          Value: Web-Server

Outputs:
  WebServerPublicIP:
    Description: Public IP of the web server instance.
    Value: !GetAtt WebServer.PublicIp
```

After deploying the stack, verify the resources in the AWS Management Console. Ensure the EC2 instances are running and accessible. You should be able to connect to them with Session Manager.

Now that you have the test environment and a basic understanding of recovery objectives, you can consider an example of the simplest disaster recovery approach: a backup and restore strategy.

Implementing a Backup and Restore Strategy

The backup and restore strategy is foundational in disaster recovery because it focuses on regularly backing up data and restoring it when a disaster occurs. This approach inherently has a higher Recovery Time Objective (RTO) and Recovery Point Objective (RPO) compared to other strategies. The reason for this is simple: during a disaster, you must first retrieve your backups, redeploy infrastructure, and then restore data before resuming operations. These steps take time, which increases downtime (RTO) and the potential for data loss (RPO).

However, this strategy is also the most cost-effective and straightforward because it doesn't require maintaining live or partially active environments in a secondary region. Instead, you only pay for storage costs (e.g., Amazon S3 or S3 Glacier) and occasional testing of your restoration processes. This makes it ideal for noncritical workloads, where downtime or data loss is acceptable within certain limits.

For example:

▪ A payroll system might use backup and restore if it only needs to be operational once every two weeks.

▪ Internal reporting systems could tolerate longer recovery times since they are not customer-facing.

Additionally, backup and restore is easy to implement because it leverages AWS services like AWS Backup, Amazon S3, and Amazon RDS snapshots. These services automate backup processes, ensuring that data is consistently protected without requiring complex configurations. This simplicity makes it a great starting point for organizations new to disaster recovery planning.

While this strategy is cost-effective, its limitations make it unsuitable for workloads requiring near-zero downtime or minimal data loss. For such cases, more advanced strategies like pilot light or warm standby are better suited.

Before you create your backup plan, it's important to understand the role of backup vaults and plans in AWS Backup:

- A *backup vault* is an encrypted repository where AWS stores recovery points created during backup jobs. Vaults provide centralized management for organizing and securing your data. In this example, you'll create two vaults: one (`primary-backup`) in the primary region (`us-west-2`) and another (`secondary-backup`) in the secondary region (`us-east-1`). These vaults ensure that you have geographically dispersed copies of your data for disaster recovery.

- A *backup plan*, on the other hand, is a policy that automates how and when resources are backed up. It includes rules specifying the schedule (e.g., daily at 5:00 a.m. UTC), target vaults, retention periods, and even cross-region copy actions. In this case, you'll create a plan named `cross-region-backup`, which backs up resources daily to `primary-backup` and then copies those backups to `secondary-backup`.

When determining your own backup strategy:

- **Consider workload criticality:** Critical systems may need frequent backups with cross-region copies.

- **Align schedules with compliance requirements:** Ensure that retention periods meet regulatory obligations.

- **Optimize costs:** Use lifecycle policies to transition older backups to cold storage or delete them after they're no longer needed.

By combining these elements, you can ensure that your data is secure, compliant, and recoverable during disasters.

Before you create your backup plan, you need to create backup vaults in the primary and secondary regions. For this example, the primary region is `us-west-2` and the secondary region is `us-east-1`. Use the `aws backup create-backup-vault` command to accomplish this:

```
[cloudshell-user@ip-10-136-108-221 ~]$ aws backup create-backup-vault \
>     --backup-vault-name primary-backup \
>     --region us-west-2
{
    "BackupVaultName": "primary-backup",
    "BackupVaultArn": "arn:aws:backup:us-west-2:387974667323:backup-
vault:primary-backup",
    "CreationDate": "2025-01-08T00:30:43.976000+00:00"
}
```

```
[cloudshell-user@ip-10-136-108-221 ~]$ aws backup create-backup-vault \
>     --backup-vault-name secondary-backup \
>     --region us-east-1
{
    "BackupVaultName": "secondary-backup",
    "BackupVaultArn": "arn:aws:backup:us-east-1:387974667323:backup-
vault:secondary- backup",
    "CreationDate": "2025-01-08T00:30:57.081000+00:00"
}
[cloudshell-user@ip-10-136-108-221 ~]$
```

Now you need to create a cross-region backup plan, and to do this, you need to gather your account ID. In the `aws backup create-backup-plan` command, I am creating a cross-region backup plan in my account with us-east-1 "secondary-backup" as the destination backup vault:

```
[cloudshell-user@ip-10-136-108-221 ~]$ aws backup create-backup-plan \
>     --cli-input-json '{
>         "BackupPlan": {
>             "BackupPlanName": "cross-region-backup",
>             "Rules": [{
>                 "RuleName": "daily-cross-region",
>                 "TargetBackupVaultName": "primary-backup",
>                 "ScheduleExpression": "cron(0 5 ? * * *)",
>                 "StartWindowMinutes": 60,
>                 "CopyActions": [{
>                     "DestinationBackupVaultArn": "arn:aws:backup:us-east-
1:387974667323:backup-vault:secondary-backup"
>                 }]
>             }]
>         }
>     }'
{
    "BackupPlanId": "4547d26c-2796-4cc0-8d7f-79bc9d897c51",
    "BackupPlanArn": "arn:aws:backup:us-west-2:387974667323:backup-
plan:4547d26c-2796-4cc0-8d7f-79bc9d897c51",
    "CreationDate": "2025-01-08T00:34:38.367000+00:00",
    "VersionId": "ZDA2NWZkMTUtNjUyOC00MDBmLTgyYzYtNWQ3MTNjNzAwNjQw"
}
[cloudshell-user@ip-10-136-108-221 ~]$
```

Let's examine each component of this command in detail. The BackupPlanName parameter serves as a unique identifier for the backup plan, making it easy to manage and reference. The RuleName parameter creates a distinct label for this specific backup rule within the plan. By using ScheduleExpression with a cron expression, you schedule the backup to execute automatically at 5:00 a.m. UTC each day. The StartWindowMinutes parameter allocates AWS Backup a 60-minute window to initiate the backup process, providing flexibility for resource availability. Finally, the CopyActions parameter defines the destination for the backup copy, specifically targeting the designated disaster recovery region.

To verify your backup plan was created successfully, use the `get-backup-plan` command:

```
[cloudshell-user@ip-10-136-108-221 ~]$ aws backup get-backup-plan \
>     --backup-plan-id $(aws backup list-backup-plans --query
'BackupPlansList[?BackupPlanName==`cross-region-backup`].BackupPlanId' --output
text)
{
    "BackupPlan": {
        "BackupPlanName": "cross-region-backup",
        "Rules": [
            {
                "RuleName": "daily-cross-region",
                "TargetBackupVaultName": "primary-backup",
                "ScheduleExpression": "cron(0 5 ? * * *)",
                "StartWindowMinutes": 60,
                "CompletionWindowMinutes": 10080,
                "RuleId": "407cb1b6-9299-4dd1-8a13-e76b8f875709",
                "CopyActions": [
                    {
                        "DestinationBackupVaultArn": "arn:aws:backup:us-
east-1:387974667323:backup-vault:secondary-backup"
                    }
                ],
                "ScheduleExpressionTimezone": "Etc/UTC"
            }
        ]
    },
    "BackupPlanId": "4547d26c-2796-4cc0-8d7f-79bc9d897c51",
    "BackupPlanArn": "arn:aws:backup:us-west-2:387974667323:backup-
plan:4547d26c-2796-4cc0-8d7f-79bc9d897c51",
    "VersionId": "ZDA2NWZkMTUtNjUyOC00MDBmLTgyYzYtNWQ3MTNjNzAwNjQw",
    "CreationDate": "2025-01-08T00:34:38.367000+00:00"
}
(END)
```

The next step is to assign resources to the backup plan. To do this, you need to note the backup plan ID from the previous output, your account ID, and the instance ID for the EC2 instance you want to be a part of the plan. You'll also need an IAM role ARN that AWS Backup can use to access and manage your resources. Typically, this role is `AWSBackupDefaultServiceRole`, which comes with all the necessary permissions.

First check to see if the role exists:

```
[cloudshell-user@ip-10-132-55-250 ~]$ aws iam get-role --role-name
AWSBackupDefaultServiceRole

An error occurred (NoSuchEntity) when calling the GetRole operation: The role
with name  AWSBackupDefaultServiceRole cannot be found.
[cloudshell-user@ip-10-132-55-250 ~]$
```

As you can see from the output, the role does not exist. Therefore, you need to create it manually.

You need to create a trust policy document. You can find this in the GitHub repo, called trust-policy.json:

```
{
  "Version": "2012-10-17",
  "Statement": [
    {
      "Effect": "Allow",
      "Principal": {
        "Service": "backup.amazonaws.com"
      },
      "Action": "sts:AssumeRole"
    }
  ]
}
```

Create and save this file in CloudShell:

```
[cloudshell-user@ip-10-132-55-250 ~]$  touch trust-policy.json
[cloudshell-user@ip-10-132-55-250 ~]$ nano touch trust-policy.json
<< Paste the Policy into the doc and save>
```

Then run the following command to create the role and attach the trust policy:

```
[cloudshell-user@ip-10-132-55-250 ~]$ aws iam create-role \
>      --role-name AWSBackupDefaultServiceRole \
>      --assume-role-policy-document file://trust-policy.json
{
    "Role": {
        "Path": "/",
        "RoleName": "AWSBackupDefaultServiceRole",
        "RoleId": "AROAVUVIXTQ53RQ5IIQ57",
        "Arn": "arn:aws:iam::387974667323:role/AWSBackupDefaultServiceRole",
        "CreateDate": "2025-02-25T13:20:59+00:00",
        "AssumeRolePolicyDocument": {
            "Version": "2012-10-17",
            "Statement": [
                {
                    "Effect": "Allow",
                    "Principal": {
                        "Service": "lambda.amazonaws.com"
                    },
                    "Action": "sts:AssumeRole"
                }
            ]
        }
    }
}
(END)
```

Next, attach the managed policies that grant AWS Backup permissions:

```
[cloudshell-user@ip-10-132-55-250 ~]$ aws iam attach-role-policy \
>      --role-name AWSBackupDefaultServiceRole \
>      --policy-arn arn:aws:iam::aws:policy/service-role/
```

```
AWSBackupServiceRolePolicyForBackup
[cloudshell-user@ip-10-132-55-250 ~]$ aws iam attach-role-policy \
>       --role-name AWSBackupDefaultServiceRole \
>       --policy-arn arn:aws:iam::aws:policy/service-role/AWSBackupServiceRolePolicy
ForRestores
[cloudshell-user@ip-10-132-55-250 ~]$
```

Now check whether the role exists one more time:

```
[cloudshell-user@ip-10-132-55-250 ~]$ aws iam get-role --role-name
AWSBackupDefaultServiceRole
{
    "Role": {
        "Path": "/",
        "RoleName": "AWSBackupDefaultServiceRole",
        "RoleId": "AROAVUVIXTQ53RQ5IIQ57",
        "Arn": "arn:aws:iam::387974667323:role/AWSBackupDefaultServiceRole",
        "CreateDate": "2025-02-25T13:20:59+00:00",
        "AssumeRolePolicyDocument": {
            "Version": "2012-10-17",
            "Statement": [
                {
                    "Effect": "Allow",
                    "Principal": {
                        "Service": "lambda.amazonaws.com"
                    },
                    "Action": "sts:AssumeRole"
                }
            ]
        },
        "MaxSessionDuration": 3600,
        "RoleLastUsed": {}
    }
}
(END)
```

> **note** This is one area where the AWS Console helps simplify your configuration. Had
> you done this on the AWS Console, it would have created the role for you during the
> backup creation. This is great for doing things one time, but as you start thinking about
> doing this over and over, you can see where at some point turning these commands
> into code that you can run will increase your ability to scale this to multiple regions.

With that said, now that this role is created, note its ARN (e.g., `arn:aws:iam::`
`ACCOUNT _ ID:role/service-role/AWSBackupDefaultServiceRole`) for use in
subsequent steps.

Now that you have all the required information (backup plan ID, account ID,
instance ID, and IAM role ARN), run the following command to assign an EC2
instance to your backup plan:

```
[cloudshell-user@ip-10-130-34-133 ~]$ aws backup create-backup-selection \
>       --backup-plan-id 4547d26c-2796-4cc0-8d7f-79bc9d897c51 \
>       --backup-selection '{
```

```
>          "SelectionName": "ec2-backup-selection",
>          "IamRoleArn": "arn:aws:iam::387974667323:role/service-role/
AWSBackupDefaultServiceRole",
>          "Resources": [
>              "arn:aws:ec2:us-west-2:387974667323:instance/i-05a2bedf9c2e1844d"
>          ]
>      }'
{
    "SelectionId": "d5e77900-4137-41a7-921f-7ca700f0b083",
    "BackupPlanId": "4547d26c-2796-4cc0-8d7f-79bc9d897c51",
    "CreationDate": "2025-01-08T13:34:33.477000+00:00"
}
[cloudshell-user@ip-10-130-34-133 ~]$
```

Here's what each parameter does:

- SelectionName: Specifies a unique name for this resource selection (ec2-backup-selection) for easy identification within the backup plan.

- IamRoleArn: Defines the IAM role that AWS Backup will use to access and manage resources.

- Resources: Lists ARNs of resources included in the backup plan. In this example, you target a specific EC2 instance (i-05a2bedf9c2e1844d), which serves as a web server hosting critical application components.

By assigning this web server to the backup plan, you ensure that its configuration and attached EBS volumes are protected against data loss or downtime.

Now that you've assigned the resource, you should verify it with the following command:

```
[cloudshell-user@ip-10-130-34-133 ~]$ aws backup list-backup-selections --
backup-plan-id 4547d26c-2796-4cc0-8d7f-79bc9d897c51
{
    "BackupSelectionsList": [
        {
            "SelectionId": "d5e77900-4137-41a7-921f-7ca700f0b083",
            "SelectionName": "ec2-backup-selection",
            "BackupPlanId": "4547d26c-2796-4cc0-8d7f-79bc9d897c51",
            "CreationDate": "2025-01-08T13:34:33.477000+00:00",
            "IamRoleArn": "arn:aws:iam::387974667323:role/service-role/
AWSBackupDefaultServiceRole"
        }
    ]
}
[cloudshell-user@ip-10-130-34-133 ~]$
```

The aws backup list-backup-selections command retrieves all resource selections associated with a specific backup plan. By specifying the --backup-plan-id parameter (in this case, 4547d26c-2796-4cc0-8d7f-79bc9d897c51), you ensure that you are querying the correct backup plan created earlier.

This command is used to verify that the EC2 instance (or other resources) has been successfully assigned to the backup plan and that all configurations are correct.

The output includes details such as the SelectionId, a unique identifier for the resource selection; the SelectionName, which helps identify this selection within the backup plan; and the IamRoleArn, which confirms that AWS Backup is using the correct IAM role (AWSBackupDefaultServiceRole) to manage these resources. Verifying these details ensures that critical resources are included in the backup plan and that AWS Backup has the necessary permissions to protect them. This step is crucial for confirming that your disaster recovery strategy is properly configured and ready to safeguard your resources.

> **note** This backup and restore strategy provides a foundational approach to disaster recovery. It ensures that your data is protected and can be restored in the event of a failure. However, it's important to note that this is not a "set it and forget it" solution. Regular testing is essential to verify that backups are restorable and that your infrastructure can be rebuilt reliably using tools like AWS CloudFormation and Terraform. Without testing, even the best-designed plans may fail when they're needed most.

Restoring backups involves retrieving data from your backup vaults and redeploying infrastructure in your recovery region. For example, in this scenario, you would use AWS Backup to restore your EC2 instances and attached volumes, then ensure that your applications are fully operational in the disaster recovery region. This process highlights why RTOs for backup and restore strategies are often measured in hours—it takes time to retrieve data and rebuild systems.

For workloads requiring faster recovery times, more advanced strategies such as pilot light, warm standby, and multisite active/active come into play. Each strategy involves tradeoffs between cost, complexity, and recovery speed. As a security professional, your role is to ensure that any chosen strategy aligns with security best practices, regulatory requirements, and organizational priorities. While you may not be responsible for implementing every aspect of these solutions, understanding their implications allows you to ask the right questions and contribute to informed decision-making.

By combining robust backup solutions with regular testing and collaboration across teams, you can build resilience into your AWS environment. This ensures that when disaster strikes, your organization is prepared to recover quickly while maintaining security and compliance standards.

With a grasp of how resilience strategies fit into the larger picture, the next section moves on to where resilience and recovery overlap with security-related responsibilities. It also looks at how different roles in an organization collaborate to ensure these strategies are both effective and secure.

Where Resilience and Recovery Intersect with Security Tasks

Security teams and resilience teams work hand in hand. While your security focus is often on preventing and detecting threats, resilience tasks make sure that when incidents or breaches happen, you can restore normal operations quickly and securely. For example:

- **IAM and backup policies:** Setting strict permissions around backup vaults, ensuring that only authorized roles can create, modify, or delete backups.

- **Immutable storage:** Combining versioned S3 buckets and cross-region replication for an added layer of safety.

- **Forensic readiness:** Keeping backup copies for analysis after an incident. A well-defined resilience plan includes retaining logs and images that can be used for root-cause investigations.

Responsibilities and Collaboration

Resilience and recovery initiatives are often driven by specialized teams such as Business Continuity or Disaster Recovery groups, but cloud security professionals play a key role in making sure these efforts are secure and compliant. For example, you may define encryption and backup retention policies, verify that failover mechanisms uphold security best practices, and confirm that multiregion replication is properly protected. You'll also work closely with operations teams or Site Reliability Engineers (SREs) to align on Identity and Access Management (IAM) rules and ensure infrastructure designs support your security requirements.

Coordination doesn't stop there. Development teams might need to adjust code or configurations for high availability and swift recovery, all under your watchful eye to maintain security principles. Meanwhile, upper management and compliance officers will turn to you for updates on risks and assurance that regulations and industry standards are met. By fostering collaboration across these various stakeholders, you ensure that your resilience and recovery strategies are robust, efficient, and seamlessly integrated with the broader security posture.

Cleaning Up Your Resources

To ensure that you don't leave unnecessary resources running after completing this chapter, it's important to clean up the environment you created. This will help avoid incurring unexpected costs and maintain a tidy AWS account. Follow these steps to remove the resources associated with your backup and recovery setup.

Delete the Backup Selection

The first step is to remove the resource selection from your backup plan. Use the following command, replacing `BackupPlanId` and `SelectionId` with the values from your setup:

```
[cloudshell-user@ip-10-140-21-243 ~]$ aws backup delete-backup-selection \
>     --backup-plan-id 4547d26c-2796-4cc0-8d7f-79bc9d897c51 \
>     --selection-id d5e77900-4137-41a7-921f-7ca700f0b083
[cloudshell-user@ip-10-140-21-243 ~]$
```

Delete the Backup Plan

Once all resource selections are removed, delete the backup plan itself:

```
[cloudshell-user@ip-10-140-21-243 ~]$ aws backup delete-backup-plan \
>     --backup-plan-id 4547d26c-2796-4cc0-8d7f-79bc9d897c51
{
    "BackupPlanId": "4547d26c-2796-4cc0-8d7f-79bc9d897c51",
    "BackupPlanArn": "arn:aws:backup:us-west-2:387974667323:backup-
plan:4547d26c-2796-4cc0-8d7f-79bc9d897c51",
    "DeletionDate": "2025-02-25T22:45:54.591000+00:00",
    "VersionId": "ZDA2NWZkMTUtNjUyOC00MDBmLTgyYzYtNWQ3MTNjNzAwNjQw"
}
[cloudshell-user@ip-10-140-21-243 ~]$
```

Delete the Backup Vaults and Template

If you no longer need the backup vaults created in us-west-2 and us-east-1, delete them. Ensure there are no recovery points in the vaults before proceeding. Issue this command to delete the primary value in us-west-2:

```
[cloudshell-user@ip-10-140-21-243 ~]$ aws backup delete-backup-vault \
>     --backup-vault-name primary-backup
```

Then switch to us-east-1 and issue this command to delete the secondary-backup vault:

```
[cloudshell-user@ip-10-132-51-33 ~]$ aws backup delete-backup-vault \
>     --backup-vault-name secondary-backup
[cloudshell-user@ip-10-132-51-33 ~]$
```

Finally, delete the CloudFormation template. You can do this from the AWS Console if this is how you loaded it.

Conclusion

Resilience and recovery strategies are crucial for maintaining continuity and safeguarding data within AWS environments. By understanding how to design and implement backup solutions, plan for failovers, and orchestrate disaster recovery, you establish a reliable security foundation. While the finer points of pilot light, warm standby, and multisite active/active might lie outside the scope of a cloud security professional's direct responsibilities, having a working knowledge of these methods ensures the right questions get asked—and that any selected strategy meets security requirements.

Resilience and recovery strategies are crucial for maintaining continuity and safeguarding data within AWS environments. The backup and restore strategy you implemented in this chapter provides a solid foundation for protecting resources during disasters. However, for workloads requiring faster recovery times or stricter RTO/RPO requirements, more advanced strategies like pilot light, warm standby, and multisite active/active come into play.

These advanced strategies build on the principles of backup and restore but require close collaboration between security teams, operations teams, and disaster recovery specialists to implement effectively. As a cloud security professional, your role is to ensure that any chosen strategy aligns with security requirements, regulatory obligations, and best practices. For example, you might define encryption policies for replicated data, verify IAM permissions for failover processes, or confirm that multiregional replication meets compliance standards.

It's also important to recognize that disaster recovery is not a "set it and forget it" solution. Regular testing of backups, failovers, and infrastructure rebuilds is essential to ensure your plans work as intended when disaster strikes. By combining robust backup solutions with advanced strategies like pilot light or warm standby—alongside continuous testing—you can build a resilient environment capable of minimizing downtime and protecting critical data.

With this understanding of resilience strategies, you'll now turn your attention to how security teams can streamline these efforts using operational best practices and automation. Chapter 10, "Security Operations and Automation," explores how GitOps practices can enable consistent enforcement of security policies while accelerating incident response.

References

AWS Resilience Hub, https://aws.amazon.com/resilience

Disaster Recovery of Workloads on AWS: Recovery in the Cloud, https://docs.aws.amazon.com/whitepapers/latest/disaster-recovery-work loads-on-aws/disaster-recovery-options-in-the-cloud.html

Security Operations and Automation

"Automation is not about replacing humans; it's about amplifying their capabilities to operate at cloud scale."

—Werner Vogels, CTO of Amazon

In your journey through securing your cloud resources on AWS, you've built a solid foundation of identity management, infrastructure protection, threat detection, and data security. This chapter explores how to operationalize these controls through automation, enabling security to function at cloud scale. This chapter also bridges the gap between individual security controls and a comprehensive, automated security framework that can protect your environment 24/7.

The Evolution of Security Operations

Traditional security operations centered on manual reviews, human analysts, and reactive responses. However, the scale and speed of cloud computing have changed the way we assess security operations. When a single AWS account can spawn thousands of resources across multiple regions in minutes, human-centered security operations simply can't keep up with the pace. The reality is the requirements have changed. What are those requirements?

- **Real-time threat detection and response:** Developers can't wait for daily or weekly security scans anymore. When someone's poking around where they shouldn't be in your AWS account, you need to know immediately. Whether it's unusual API calls or someone trying to access sensitive S3 buckets, immediate alerts are required.

- **Automated remediation of security issues:** Manually fixing security issues doesn't scale. If someone accidentally exposes an RDS instance to the Internet or misconfigures an IAM role, you want systems that can automatically detect and fix these issues.

- **Continuous compliance monitoring:** Compliance isn't always received well, and it's often overlooked. Traditionally, manual compliance checks have been time-consuming and prone to human error. Setting up a means of automated monitoring of your organization's compliance can protect your organization and also take away some of the stigma that comes with the idea of compliance overall.

- **Integration with existing security tools:** Most teams already have security tools they trust and use daily. The key is making these work smoothly with AWS services.

- **Scalable incident management:** As your AWS footprint grows, you'll have more resources to protect. No security team can manually review every alert.

Before you get started, I have to say this again. I know you're probably catching on by now, but all the commands and code I enter in my environment, and thus use for the examples in this book, can be found in my GitHub repo at https://github.com/8carroll/Securing-the-Cloud-with-Brandon-Carroll. All the resources you need are in the Chapter 10 folder. Make sure you replace any of the IDs, ARNs, and so on with your own account information.

With that said, you can start with the following CloudFormation template that will set you up for testing later.

Save the following template as chapter10.yaml (it's also in GitHub):

```
AWSTemplateFormatVersion: '2010-09-09'
Description: >
  Chapter 10 Test Environment for Security Automation.
  This template creates a VPC, a public subnet (with an Internet Gateway,
route table, and association),
  a security group for the instance, an IAM role and instance profile for
SSM access, and a test EC2 instance
  using the latest Amazon Linux 2 AMI. The Outputs include the InstanceId
and Public IP for testing.

Parameters:
  VpcCIDR:
    Type: String
    Default: 10.0.0.0/16
    Description: CIDR block for the VPC.
  PublicSubnetCIDR:
    Type: String
    Default: 10.0.1.0/24
    Description: CIDR block for the public subnet.
```

```
      InstanceType:
        Type: String
        Default: t2.micro
        Description: EC2 instance type for the test instance.
      SSMParameterAMI:
        Type: AWS::SSM::Parameter::Value<AWS::EC2::Image::Id>
        Default: /aws/service/ami-amazon-linux-latest/amzn2-ami-hvm-x86_64-gp2
        Description: SSM parameter to retrieve the latest Amazon Linux 2 AMI.

Resources:
  TestVPC:
    Type: AWS::EC2::VPC
    Properties:
      CidrBlock: !Ref VpcCIDR
      EnableDnsSupport: true
      EnableDnsHostnames: true
      Tags:
        - Key: Name
          Value: Chapter10-VPC

  TestInternetGateway:
    Type: AWS::EC2::InternetGateway
    Properties:
      Tags:
        - Key: Name
          Value: Chapter10-IGW

  VPCGatewayAttachment:
    Type: AWS::EC2::VPCGatewayAttachment
    Properties:
      VpcId: !Ref TestVPC
      InternetGatewayId: !Ref TestInternetGateway

  PublicSubnet:
    Type: AWS::EC2::Subnet
    Properties:
      VpcId: !Ref TestVPC
      CidrBlock: !Ref PublicSubnetCIDR
      MapPublicIpOnLaunch: true
      AvailabilityZone: !Select [ 0, !GetAZs "" ]
      Tags:
        - Key: Name
          Value: Chapter10-Public-Subnet

  PublicRouteTable:
    Type: AWS::EC2::RouteTable
    Properties:
      VpcId: !Ref TestVPC
      Tags:
        - Key: Name
          Value: Chapter10-Public-RouteTable

  PublicRoute:
    Type: AWS::EC2::Route
    DependsOn: VPCGatewayAttachment
```

```yaml
      Properties:
        RouteTableId: !Ref PublicRouteTable
        DestinationCidrBlock: 0.0.0.0/0
        GatewayId: !Ref TestInternetGateway

  SubnetRouteTableAssociation:
    Type: AWS::EC2::SubnetRouteTableAssociation
    Properties:
      SubnetId: !Ref PublicSubnet
      RouteTableId: !Ref PublicRouteTable

  TestSecurityGroup:
    Type: AWS::EC2::SecurityGroup
    Properties:
      GroupDescription: Security group for Chapter 10 test instance
      VpcId: !Ref TestVPC
      SecurityGroupIngress:
        - IpProtocol: tcp
          FromPort: 22
          ToPort: 22
          CidrIp: 0.0.0.0/0
      Tags:
        - Key: Name
          Value: Chapter10-SG

  SSMInstanceRole:
    Type: AWS::IAM::Role
    Properties:
      AssumeRolePolicyDocument:
        Version: '2012-10-17'
        Statement:
          - Effect: Allow
            Principal:
              Service: ec2.amazonaws.com
            Action: sts:AssumeRole
      ManagedPolicyArns:
        - arn:aws:iam::aws:policy/AmazonSSMManagedInstanceCore
    Metadata:
      Comment: "Role for EC2 instances to use SSM Session Manager."

  SSMInstanceProfile:
    Type: AWS::IAM::InstanceProfile
    Properties:
      Path: /
      Roles:
        - !Ref SSMInstanceRole

  TestInstance:
    Type: AWS::EC2::Instance
    Properties:
      ImageId: !Ref SSMParameterAMI
      InstanceType: !Ref InstanceType
      SubnetId: !Ref PublicSubnet
      IamInstanceProfile: !Ref SSMInstanceProfile
      SecurityGroupIds:
```

```
        - !Ref TestSecurityGroup
      Tags:
        - Key: Name
          Value: Chapter10-TestInstance

Outputs:
  VPCId:
    Description: ID of the test VPC.
    Value: !Ref TestVPC
  PublicSubnetId:
    Description: ID of the public subnet.
    Value: !Ref PublicSubnet
  TestSecurityGroupId:
    Description: ID of the test security group.
    Value: !Ref TestSecurityGroup
  TestInternetGatewayId:
    Description: ID of the test Internet Gateway.
    Value: !Ref TestInternetGateway
  InstanceId:
    Description: ID of the test EC2 instance.
    Value: !Ref TestInstance
  InstancePublicIP:
    Description: Public IP address of the test instance.
    Value: !GetAtt TestInstance.PublicIp
  LatestAMIOutput:
    Description: Latest Amazon Linux 2 AMI ID.
    Value: !Ref SSMParameterAMI
```

Then, deploy the stack as follows:

```
aws cloudformation create-stack --stack-name chapter10 --template-body
file://chapter10.yaml --capabilities CAPABILITY_NAMED_IAM
aws cloudformation wait stack-create-complete --stack-name chapter10
```

Once the stack creation is complete, note the outputs (especially `InstanceId` and `InstancePublicIP`).

With the stack deployed, you're ready to dig into this topic!

Building Automated Security Controls

Imagine you're running multiple EC2 instances processing sensitive financial data. You need a system that automatically isolates potentially compromised instances to prevent lateral movement in case of a security breach. You'll build a simple, automated response system that triggers when GuardDuty detects suspicious activity. The basic flow of this automation can be seen in Figure 10.1.

GuardDuty severity scores range from 0 to 8.9 for low, 9.0 to 6.9 for medium, and 7.0 to 10 for high severity. These scores are determined based on the type

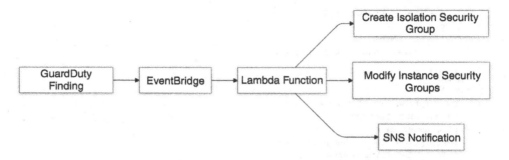

Figure 10.1: Basic automation flow.

of threat detected, its potential impact, and the confidence level of the detection algorithm. The Lambda function:

1. Creates a new security group specifically for isolation.

2. Moves the suspicious instance to this isolation group.

3. Alerts the security team via SNS.

The following Lambda function implements this workflow. I explain each piece of the code in the code comments. You can also download the code from the Chapter 10 folder in my GitHub repo at https://github.com/8carroll/ Securing-the-Cloud-with-Brandon-Carroll.

```python
import boto3
import json
import logging

logger = logging.getLogger()
logger.setLevel(logging.INFO)

def lambda_handler(event, context):
    try:
        # Initialize AWS clients
        ec2 = boto3.client('ec2')
        sns = boto3.client('sns')

        # Extract event details
        finding = event['detail']
        instance_id = finding['resource']['instanceDetails']['instanceId']

        if finding['severity'] >= 7:
            try:
                # Create an isolation security group
                sg_response = ec2.create_security_group(
                    GroupName=f'ISOLATION-{instance_id}',
                    Description='Automated isolation security group'
                )
                group_id = sg_response['GroupId']
```

```
            logger.info(f"Created isolation security group {group_id}
for instance {instance_id}")
        except Exception as e:
            logger.error(f"Error creating security group for instance
{instance_id}: {e}")
            raise

        try:
            # Apply the isolation security group
            ec2.modify_instance_attribute(
                InstanceId=instance_id,
                Groups=[group_id]
            )
            logger.info(f"Modified instance {instance_id} to use security
group {group_id}")
        except Exception as e:
            logger.error(f"Error modifying instance {instance_id}
attributes: {e}")
            raise

        try:
            # Notify security team via SNS
            sns.publish(
                TopicArn='arn:aws:sns:region:account:SecurityAlerts',
                Message=f'High severity finding detected. Instance
{instance_id} isolated.'
            )
            logger.info(f"Published SNS notification for instance {instance_
id}")
        except Exception as e:
            logger.error(f"Error publishing SNS notification for instance
{instance_id}: {e}")
            raise

    return {
        'statusCode': 200,
        'body': 'Security automation completed'
    }

except Exception as err:
    logger.error(f"Unhandled exception: {err}")
    return {
        'statusCode': 500,
        'body': json.dumps({'error': str(err)})
```

I come back to the code in a bit. But first, before you deploy this code, there are a few steps you need to do to make things work. You'll need to:

1. Set up an SNS topic for security alerts.

2. Configure appropriate IAM permissions for the Lambda function.

3. Deploy a Lambda function with the previous code.

4. Create an EventBridge rule that watches for GuardDuty findings.

In the end, this automation helps you respond to security incidents 24/7, even when your team is offline. The isolated instance can then be investigated during business hours so that other resources in your environment won't be impacted. Let's walk through setting up this automated instance isolation solution step by step using the AWS CLI. Start with the SNS topic, since you'll need its ARN for later steps:

```
[cloudshell-user@ip-10-138-24-182 ~]$ aws sns create-topic --name SecurityAlerts
{
    "TopicArn": "arn:aws:sns:us-west-2:387974667323:SecurityAlerts"
}
[cloudshell-user@ip-10-138-24-182 ~]$
```

Note the topic ARN since you will need it for the next step.
Topic ARN:_____
Next, subscribe to the topic. You can see the following result when I subscribe to the SNS topic that I just created. You can follow along using the same command; just be sure to replace the topic ARN and email address with your own values.

```
[cloudshell-user@ip-10-138-24-182 ~]$ aws sns subscribe \
>     --topic-arn arn:aws:sns:us-west-2:387974667323:SecurityAlerts \
>     --protocol email \
>     --notification-endpoint
brandon.carroll+sns@example.com
{
    "SubscriptionArn": "pending confirmation"
}
[cloudshell-user@ip-10-138-24-182 ~]$
```

Notice that the subscription is pending. You'll next need to check your email and confirm the subscription by clicking the Confirm Subscription link in the email. The email will resemble Figure 10.2.

Now you'll create the IAM role and policies the Lambda function needs. In CloudShell, create a file called `trust-policy.json` using the `touch trust-policy.json` command.

Then use nano to edit the file using the `nano trust-policy.json` command.

Then add the following code to the file. You can find the code on my GitHub repo at `https://github.com/8carroll/Securing-the-Cloud-with-Brandon-Carroll`, in the Chapter 10 folder.

Figure 10.2: SNS confirmation email.

```
{
  "Version": "2012-10-17",
  "Statement": [
    {
      "Effect": "Allow",
      "Principal": {
        "Service": "lambda.amazonaws.com"
      },
      "Action": "sts:AssumeRole"
    }
  ]
}
```

Alternatively, you can use `cat` to insert the code into a file, which is what I've done in the following output:

```
[cloudshell-user@ip-10-138-24-182 ~]$ cat << 'EOF' > trust-policy.json
> {
>   "Version": "2012-10-17",
>   "Statement": [
>     {
>       "Effect": "Allow",
>       "Principal": {
>         "Service": "lambda.amazonaws.com"
>       },
>       "Action": "sts:AssumeRole"
>     }
>   ]
> }
> EOF
[cloudshell-user@ip-10-138-24-182 ~]$
```

Either method will work, so choose the method you are most comfortable with. Once you have the trust policy file created, create an IAM role using the `aws iam create-role` command. You can see my input and the resulting output here:

```
[cloudshell-user@ip-10-138-24-182 ~]$ aws iam create-role \
>     --role-name SecurityAutomationRole \
>     --assume-role-policy-document file://trust-policy.json
{
    "Role": {
        "Path": "/",
        "RoleName": "SecurityAutomationRole",
        "RoleId": "AROAVUVIXTQ5RP3F2QUTZ",
        "Arn": "arn:aws:iam::387974667323:role/SecurityAutomationRole",
        "CreateDate": "2025-01-23T15:39:59+00:00",
        "AssumeRolePolicyDocument": {
            "Version": "2012-10-17",
            "Statement": [
                {
                    "Effect": "Allow",
                    "Principal": {
                        "Service": "lambda.amazonaws.com"
```

```
                    },
                    "Action": "sts:AssumeRole"
                }
            ]
        }
    }
}
(END)
```

Save the ARN from the output because you'll need it when you create the Lambda.

Role ARN: _____

Now, create the policy that grants necessary permissions:

Using the same method as you did for the trust policy, create a `lambda-policy.json` file with the following code.

> **tip** As you go through this code, note the resource you are giving access to. You might be saying, "This is a security book, so why is this policy so permissive?" and the answer is pretty simple. When you initially build something, I recommend doing it this way so you are not troubleshooting restrictive security controls. I can't tell you how many times I've worked the opposite way and ended up troubleshooting the wrong thing. Doing it this way lets you ensure it works, then you tighten it up. If it breaks, you know exactly what to look at.

```json
{
    "Version": "2012-10-17",
    "Statement": [
        {
            "Effect": "Allow",
            "Action": [
                "ec2:CreateSecurityGroup",
                "ec2:ModifyInstanceAttribute",
                "ec2:DescribeInstances",
                "sns:Publish",
                "logs:CreateLogGroup",
                "logs:CreateLogStream",
                "logs:PutLogEvents"
            ],
            "Resource": "*"
        }
    ]
}
```

You can also find this code in the Chapter 10 folder in my GitHub repo at https://github.com/8carroll/Securing-the-Cloud-with-Brandon-Carroll. Next, create the role and attach the policy with the `aws iam put-role-policy` command. You can see my output here:

```
[cloudshell-user@ip-10-138-24-182 ~]$ aws iam put-role-policy \
>     --role-name SecurityAutomationRole \
```

```
>        --policy-name SecurityAutomationPolicy \
>        --policy-document file://lambda-policy.json
[cloudshell-user@ip-10-138-24-182 ~]$
```

Now that the role has been created, you can create the Lambda. To do this, you need that code that I showed you earlier in this chapter, called lambda_function.py. If you didn't get that file, you can grab it from my GitHub repo in the Chapter 10 folder. Once you have it, zip it. An alternative is to cat the text into a file. If you are following along and deploying this using CloudShell, this may be the easiest way to get the code in there, unless you want to touch the file, use nano to paste it in, save it, and then zip it. Here, you can see the input and output from me, where I cat the file, then paste the code in, then use Ctrl+D to save it. After that, I zip the file.

```
[cloudshell-user@ip-10-132-34-55 ~]$ cat > lambda_function.py

import boto3
import json
import os

def lambda_handler(event, context):
    # Initialize AWS clients
    ec2 = boto3.client('ec2')
    sns = boto3.client('sns')

    # Retrieve SNS Topic ARN from an environment variable
    sns_topic_arn = os.environ.get('SNS_TOPIC_ARN')
    if not sns_topic_arn:
        raise ValueError("SNS_TOPIC_ARN environment variable is not set")

    # Extract event details
    finding = event['detail']
    instance_id = finding['resource']['instanceDetails']['instanceId']

    # Implement automated response
    if finding['severity'] >= 7:
        # Create an isolation security group
        response = ec2.create_security_group(
            GroupName=f'ISOLATION-{instance_id}',
            Description='Automated isolation security group'
        )

        # Apply the isolation security group
        ec2.modify_instance_attribute(
            InstanceId=instance_id,
            Groups=[response['GroupId']]
        )

        # Notify security team
        sns.publish(
            TopicArn=sns_topic_arn,
            Message=f'High severity finding detected. Instance {instance_id}
isolated.'
```

```
        )

    return {
        'statusCode': 200,
        'body': 'Security automation completed'
    }

CTRL+D
```

```
[cloudshell-user@ip-10-132-34-55 ~]$ zip function.zip lambda_function.py
  adding: lambda_function.py (deflated 54%)
[cloudshell-user@ip-10-132-34-55 ~]$
```

Now create the Lambda function. Lambda is a serverless compute service that lets you run your code without having to manage servers. With Lambda, you write your code, upload it, and AWS takes care of provisioning and scaling the resources needed to run your function. You only pay for the compute time your code actually uses, down to the millisecond.

Here's how AWS Lambda operates:

- **Triggers:** Lambda functions can be triggered by various AWS services or external events. For example, a new file uploaded to an S3 bucket, a message on an SQS queue, or, as in this example, a security finding delivered by Amazon EventBridge.

- **Code execution:** Once it's triggered, Lambda runs your code inside a lightweight, isolated environment. You specify the code (like lambda_function.lambda_handler) and the runtime (such as Python 3.9) when creating the function.

- **Scalability:** Lambda automatically scales your function in response to the number of incoming events. If there are many triggers, Lambda can run multiple instances of your function in parallel.

- **Resource management:** You don't need to worry about maintaining or patching the underlying infrastructure. AWS handles that for you.

- **Environment variables:** Lambda supports environment variables, which allows you to pass configuration settings (like the SNS topic ARN in this case) into your function without hardcoding them.

Now that you have an understanding of Lambda, create the function using the aws lambda create-function command. For this command, you will give it a name, select the runtime, identify the role (this is the one you created earlier) and the handler, define the zip file where the code is, set the timeout, and then define the SNS topic you created as an environment variable. Save the function ARN from the output because you will need it later.

```
[cloudshell-user@ip-10-132-34-55 ~]$ aws lambda create-function \
>     --function-name InstanceIsolationAutomation \
```

```
>       --runtime python3.9 \
>       --role
arn:aws:iam::387974667323:role/SecurityAutomationRole \
>       --handler lambda_function.lambda_handler \
>       --zip-file fileb://function.zip \
>       --timeout 30 \
>       --environment Variables={SNS_TOPIC_ARN=arn:aws:sns:us-west-
2:387974667323:SecurityAlerts}

{
    "FunctionName": "InstanceIsolationAutomation",
    "FunctionArn": "arn:aws:lambda:us-west-2:387974667323:function:
InstanceIsolationAutomation",
    "Runtime": "python3.9",
    "Role": "arn:aws:iam::387974667323:role/SecurityAutomationRole",
    "Handler": "lambda_function.lambda_handler",
    "CodeSize": 679,
    "Description": "",
    "Timeout": 30,
    "MemorySize": 128,
    "LastModified": "2025-01-24T21:09:07.408+0000",
    "CodeSha256": "s6r4m1h48RONyaohSsKcuIlm7p4/mRF35VY0yuX5ym4=",
    "Version": "$LATEST",
    "Environment": {
        "Variables": {
            "SNS_TOPIC_ARN": "arn:aws:sns:us-west-2:387974667323:SecurityAlerts"
        }
    },
    "TracingConfig": {
        "Mode": "PassThrough"
    },
    "RevisionId": "add34da5-2584-4b89-ab9f-24ac27b6b871",
    "State": "Pending",
    "StateReason": "The function is being created.",
    "StateReasonCode": "Creating",
    "PackageType": "Zip",
    "Architectures": [
        "x86_64"
    ],
    "EphemeralStorage": {
        "Size": 512
    },
    "SnapStart": {
        "ApplyOn": "None",
        "OptimizationStatus": "Off"
    },
    "RuntimeVersionConfig": {
        "RuntimeVersionArn": "arn:aws:lambda:us-west-2::runtime:57e9dce4a928fd5b7
bc1015238a5bc8a9146f096d69571fa4219ed8a2e76bfdf"
    },
    "LoggingConfig": {
        "LogFormat": "Text",
        "LogGroup": "/aws/lambda/InstanceIsolationAutomation"
    }
}
(END)
```

Function ARN: _____

At this point, you need to create the EventBridge rule. To do this, you are going to create a file pattern that looks for high-severity findings. I create this file in the following code snippet:

```
[cloudshell-user@ip-10-132-34-55 ~]$ cat << 'EOF' > event-pattern.json
> {
>   "source": ["aws.guardduty"],
>   "detail-type": ["GuardDuty Finding"],
>   "detail": {
>     "severity": [7, 8, 9, 10]
>   }
> }
> EOF
[cloudshell-user@ip-10-132-34-55 ~]$
```

Next, create an EventBridge rule. Use the `aws events put-rule` command and give it two values—the name and the event pattern file name. Save the RuleArn from the output for later.

```
[cloudshell-user@ip-10-132-34-55 ~]$ aws events put-rule \
>     --name GuardDutyHighSeverityFindings \
>     --event-pattern file://event-pattern.json
{
    "RuleArn": "arn:aws:events:us-west-2:387974667323:rule/GuardDutyHighSeverity
Findings"
}
[cloudshell-user@ip-10-132-34-55 ~]$
```

RuleArn:_____

Now you need to add permission for EventBridge to invoke Lambda using the `aws lambda add-permission` command. This requires a function name, statement ID, action, principal, and source ARN from the rule you just created.

```
[cloudshell-user@ip-10-132-34-55 ~]$ aws lambda add-permission \
>     --function-name InstanceIsolationAutomation \
>     --statement-id EventBridgeInvoke \
>     --action lambda:InvokeFunction \
>     --principal events.amazonaws.com \
>     --source-arn arn:aws:events:us-west-2:387974667323:rule/GuardDutyHighSeverity
Findings
{
    "Statement": "{\"Sid\":\"EventBridgeInvoke\",\"Effect\":\"Allow\",\"Principal\"
:{\"Service\":\" events.amazonaws.com\"},\"Action\":\"lambda:InvokeFunction\",\
"Resource\":\" arn:aws:lambda:us-west-2:387974667323:function:InstanceIsolation
Automation\", \"Condition\":{\"ArnLike\":{\"AWS:SourceArn\":\"arn:aws:events:us-
west- 2:387974667323:rule/GuardDutyHighSeverityFindings\"}}}"
}
[cloudshell-user@ip-10-132-34-55 ~]$
```

Finally, add the Lambda function as a target for the EventBridge rule. You should have saved the function ARN earlier; you will need it for the `aws events put-targets` command to work. In this command, you also need to specify the name of the rule you created earlier and provide an ID for the target. The `Id` parameter is a unique identifier for this specific target within the rule. It can be any string or number you choose, but it must be unique within this rule. In this example, I use "1" as a simple identifier to represent this target. This ID allows AWS to distinguish between multiple targets associated with a single EventBridge rule.

```
[cloudshell-user@ip-10-132-34-55 ~]$ aws events put-targets \
>       --rule GuardDutyHighSeverityFindings \
>       --targets "Id"="1","Arn"="arn:aws:lambda:us-west-
2:387974667323:function:InstanceIsolationAutomation"
{
    "FailedEntryCount": 0,
    "FailedEntries": []
}
[cloudshell-user@ip-10-132-34-55 ~]$
```

Your automated instance isolation system is now ready. When GuardDuty detects high-severity findings, it will:

1. Trigger the Lambda function through EventBridge.
2. Create an isolation security group.
3. Move the suspicious instance to that group.
4. Send you an email notification.

Now that the automation is in place, let's see it in action. GuardDuty will generate a finding if it detects suspicious activity (like unusual API calls or port scans). If you want to simulate a high-severity event without waiting for a real incident, you can let GuardDuty create the events for you. Here's how to do it.

First, get your GuardDuty Detector ID using the following AWS CLI command:

```
[cloudshell-user@ip-10-144-114-129 ~]$ aws guardduty list-detectors
{
    "DetectorIds": [
        "24c9ba318e0b9a9c48065c18cf0a9790"
    ]
}
```

Grab your unique detector ID and then issue the following command:

```
[cloudshell-user@ip-10-144-114-129 ~]$ aws guardduty create-sample-
findings --detector-id 24c9ba318e0b9a9c48065c18cf0a9790
[cloudshell-user@ip-10-144-114-129 ~]$
```

At this point, you will see several events in GuardDuty. You can see this in Figure 10.3.

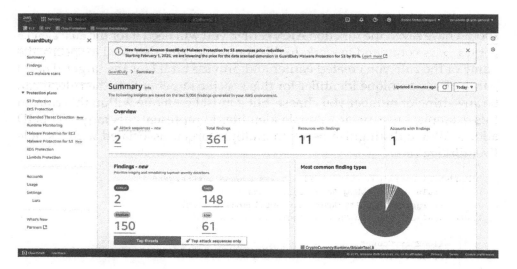

Figure 10.3: GuardDuty-generated events.

Figure 10.4: EventBridge rule invoked.

After a few minutes, navigate to Amazon EventBridge --> Rules --> GuardDutyHighSeverityFindings. Once you're in the rule, select the Monitoring tab and you should see an invocation. This can be seen in Figure 10.4.

Finally, navigate to the Lambda Function at Lambda --> Functions --> InstanceIsolationAutomation and note the invocation there. This can be seen in Figure 10.5.

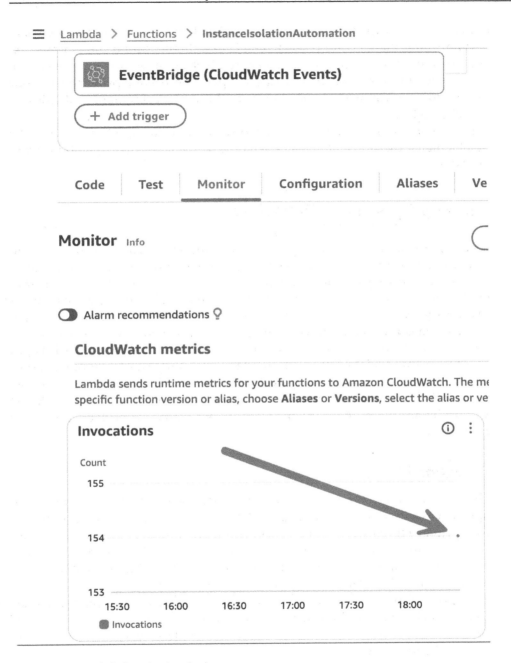

Figure 10.5: Lambda function invoked.

By walking through deployment, testing the automation with a sample GuardDuty finding, and finally cleaning up the environment, you've come full circle on the use case. This example demonstrates how an EC2 instance suspected of high-severity threats is automatically isolated, preventing lateral movement and notifying the security team, which is exactly the kind of 24/7 protection you need in a cloud-scale environment. You'll clean up your resources later in the chapter, but for now, you're ready to apply these same principles in your production environment or move on to building out even more sophisticated security orchestration.

Now that you have a bit of automated security running, let's back up, get a bit of a bigger picture, and break down how modern security operations work on AWS.

Security Operations Workflow

Security operations on AWS require a systematic approach that combines continuous monitoring, automated response, and structured recovery procedures. Rather than treating security as a series of isolated tasks, modern cloud security implements a workflow where detection, response, and recovery work together seamlessly. By leveraging AWS's native security services and automation capabilities, you can build a robust security operations workflow that scales with your infrastructure and responds to threats in real time. This workflow isn't just about detecting threats; rather, it's about creating a repeatable, automated process that maintains your security posture while reducing manual intervention. So now that you know the dream, let's examine each phase of this workflow and understand how AWS services can work together to protect your cloud environment.

Detection Phase

The detection phase forms your first line of defense in AWS, combining multiple services to create comprehensive threat monitoring. GuardDuty serves as your primary threat detection service, continuously analyzing VPC Flow Logs, DNS logs, and CloudTrail events for suspicious activities. When GuardDuty identifies potential threats, such as cryptocurrency mining on EC2 instances or compromised credentials, it generates detailed findings.

Security Hub acts as your central command center, aggregating these findings from GuardDuty and other security services. It normalizes this security data into a standardized format and enables you to track your security posture across all your AWS accounts.

CloudWatch provides the metrics and logging infrastructure needed to detect anomalies in your environment. By setting up CloudWatch alarms, you can monitor for specific patterns that might indicate security issues, such as unusual API call volumes or failed authentication attempts.

CloudTrail records every API call made in your AWS accounts, providing a detailed audit trail of all actions. This audit trail becomes crucial for security analysis and forensics when investigating potential security incidents.

Response Phase

When a security issue is detected, your response mechanisms spring into action. EventBridge (formerly CloudWatch Events) serves as the orchestrator, watching for security findings and triggering automated responses based on predefined rules. For example, when GuardDuty detects a compromised EC2 instance, EventBridge can automatically trigger a Lambda function to isolate that instance.

Lambda functions act as your automated responders, executing predefined remediation actions. These functions can perform tasks like revoking IAM credentials, updating security groups, or isolating resources from the network. The key is to automate these responses to reduce the time between detection and remediation.

Systems Manager allows you to execute predefined security playbooks across your AWS infrastructure. These playbooks can include patching systems, updating configurations, or running security scans. Step Functions takes this automation further by orchestrating complex, multistep remediation workflows that might involve multiple AWS services and approval steps.

Recovery Phase

The recovery phase focuses on returning your environment to a known-good state after a security incident. This starts with automated backup restoration, where you can use AWS Backup to restore resources to a point before the security incident occurred.

Infrastructure redeployment leverages Infrastructure as Code (IaC) through CloudFormation or CDK to rebuild compromised environments in a clean, verified state. This ensures that your recovered infrastructure matches your security baselines and compliance requirements.

Security control validation involves verifying that all security controls are properly restored and functioning. This includes checking that security groups, NACLs, and IAM policies are correctly configured. AWS Config can help verify that your restored resources comply with your security policies.

Finally, incident documentation captures the entire incident lifecycle, including what was detected, how it was remediated, and what recovery actions were taken. This documentation becomes valuable for improving your security posture and preparing for future incidents.

Understanding Security Automation Components

The instance isolation Lambda function you created is one example of security automation, but it's part of a larger security operations framework. This section explains how these pieces fit together in a playbook.

Security playbooks are the documented procedures and automated responses that define how your system handles security events. These playbooks can be implemented in several ways:

- **Lambda functions:** Like the instance isolation example, these are serverless functions that execute specific security actions.

- **Systems manager automation documents:** These are for more complex workflows involving multiple AWS services.

- **Step functions:** These orchestrate multiple Lambda functions and other AWS services in a specific sequence that you define.

Where Automation Lives

Security automations in AWS typically reside in:

- Lambda functions for immediate responses
- Systems Manager for operational procedures
- Step Functions for complex workflows
- EventBridge rules for event routing

For example, the instance isolation playbook is implemented through:

- An EventBridge rule that watches for high-severity GuardDuty findings
- A Lambda function that contains the isolation logic
- SNS for notifications

Implementing Different Types of Playbooks

Now that you understand where your automation code lives, let's look at how to implement different types of Security playbooks. Each playbook needs:

- Trigger conditions (like the GuardDuty finding severity check)
- Response actions (like the instance isolation)
- Documentation and testing procedures

Implementing Security Playbooks

Security playbooks in AWS are standardized procedures that guide your response to security incidents. They transform abstract security concepts into concrete, repeatable actions that your team can execute consistently.

Playbook Components

A security playbook in AWS needs several interconnected components that work together to detect, evaluate, and respond to security events. Let's examine each component and understand how it functions.

Trigger Conditions

Trigger conditions define exactly when a playbook should execute. These conditions monitor specific AWS events or metrics that indicate a potential security issue. Here's a practical example:

```
def evaluate_trigger(finding):
    return (
        finding['source'] == 'aws.guardduty' and
        finding['severity'] >= 7 and
        finding['type'].startswith('Recon')
    )
```

This trigger evaluates GuardDuty findings and activates when it detects high-severity reconnaissance activity. The severity threshold of 7 ensures you're only responding to significant threats, while filtering out lower-priority alerts.

Response Actions

When a trigger condition is met, your playbook needs to execute specific remediation steps. These actions typically involve AWS API calls to modify your infrastructure's security posture:

```
def execute_response(finding):
    ec2 = boto3.client('ec2')
    instance_id = finding['resource']['instanceId']

    # Create isolation security group
    sg_response = ec2.create_security_group(
        GroupName=f'ISOLATE-{instance_id}',
        Description='Isolation Security Group'
    )

    # Apply isolation
    ec2.modify_instance_attribute(
        InstanceId=instance_id,
        Groups=[sg_response['GroupId']]
    )
```

This response creates a new security group and moves the affected instance into it, effectively isolating it from other resources. This automated response happens within seconds of detecting the threat, much faster than manual intervention.

Workflow Implementation

The complete workflow ties together detection, evaluation, and response in a coordinated sequence:

```
def security_incident_workflow(event, context):
    # 1. Initial Assessment
    finding = parse_finding(event)

    # 2. Enrichment
    enriched_data = enrich_finding(finding)

    # 3. Risk Evaluation
    risk_score = calculate_risk(enriched_data)

    # 4. Response Selection
    if risk_score > CRITICAL_THRESHOLD:
        execute_critical_response(enriched_data)
    elif risk_score > HIGH_THRESHOLD:
        execute_high_priority_response(enriched_data)
    else:
        execute_standard_response(enriched_data)

    # 5. Documentation
    document_incident(enriched_data, risk_score)
```

This workflow demonstrates how a playbook processes security events through multiple stages, from initial detection to final documentation. The risk-based response selection ensures proportional actions based on the threat severity.

Testing Your Framework

Testing your playbooks is crucial for ensuring they work as intended:

```
def generate_test_event():
    """
```

This generates a sample security event.

This sample mimics an EventBridge event that might be triggered by a high-severity security incident.

In production, you can view real events in the EventBridge console by selecting the relevant rule, or by checking the CloudWatch logs for events from services like Security Hub or GuardDuty.

```
            """
        return {
            "detail": {
                "severity": 8,
                "resource": {
                    "instanceDetails": {
                        "instanceId": "i-0123456789abcdef0"
                    }
                },
                "additionalInfo": {
                    "description": "Simulated high severity security event for
testing."
                }
            }
        }
    }
def test_security_playbook():
    # 1. Setup test environment
    test_resources = create_test_resources()

    # 2. Simulate security event
    event = generate_test_event()

    # 3. Execute playbook
    response = execute_playbook(event)

    # 4. Validate response
    assert response['containment_status'] == 'successful'
    assert response['notification_sent'] == True

    # 5. Cleanup
    cleanup_test_resources(test_resources)
```

This testing framework validates your playbook's effectiveness without impacting production resources. Regular testing ensures your security responses remain reliable as your environment evolves.

Additionally, enabling logging for your Lambda functions is helpful for diagnosing execution details during testing. You can also run tests directly in the AWS Lambda console to view real-time log output and verify that your function performs as expected.

By implementing these components together, you create an automated security response system that can detect and respond to threats 24/7, maintaining your security posture—even when your team is offline.

Understanding Security Orchestration

The GuardDuty instance isolation workflow you built earlier demonstrates a basic security orchestration pattern. This section breaks down how this orchestration works and explores other common security automation patterns.

Anatomy of Security Orchestration

The GuardDuty example demonstrates the core components of security orchestration:

- **Event source (GuardDuty):** Generates security findings.
- **Event router (EventBridge):** Routes events to appropriate responses.
- **Response logic (Lambda):** Contains the automation code.
- **Response actions:** These are the specific security controls executed to mitigate threats. In the example, these actions are implemented by the Lambda function, which performs tasks such as creating an isolation security group, moving the suspicious instance into that group, and notifying the security team. While Lambda executes the logic, the actions themselves represent the tangible changes made to your AWS environment in response to a threat.
- **Notification (SNS):** Keeps security teams informed.

Additional Orchestration Patterns

The following sections explain other common security orchestration workflows.

Credential Exposure Response

When GuardDuty detects potentially compromised IAM credentials, this workflow automatically:

- Disables the affected IAM user to prevent further unauthorized access
- Revokes any active sessions using AWS STS
- Generates new credentials for the legitimate user
- Notifies the security team through SNS

This process is shown in Figure 10.6. This rapid response helps minimize the impact of credential theft or exposure.

S3 Data Protection

When AWS Config detects an S3 bucket with insecure settings, this workflow automatically:

- Enables default encryption on the bucket using AWS KMS
- Removes any public access settings that might expose data

- Updates the bucket policy to enforce secure access controls
- Alerts the security team about the remediation actions

This process is shown in Figure 10.7. This automation helps prevent data breaches from misconfigured S3 buckets.

Network Security Response

When suspicious network activity is detected by GuardDuty in VPC Flow Logs, this workflow:

- Updates Network ACLs to block malicious traffic
- Modifies security groups to restrict access
- Adds the suspicious IP addresses to AWS WAF rules
- Notifies the security team about the network threats

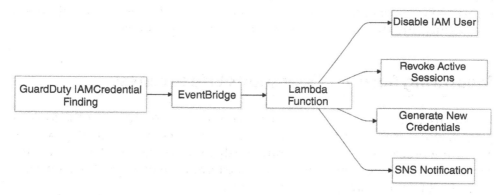

Figure 10.6: GuardDuty IAM credential finding.

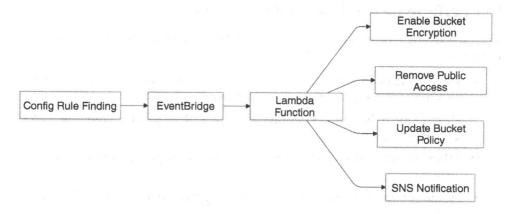

Figure 10.7: S3 data protection.

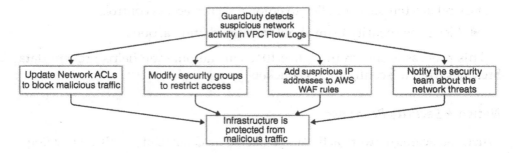

Figure 10.8: Network security response.

This process is shown in Figure 10.8. This multilayered response helps protect your infrastructure from network-based attacks.

These orchestration patterns demonstrate how AWS services can work together to provide automated, real-time security responses that protect your environment even when your team is offline. That being said, the next section discusses how to measure the effectiveness of your security operations.

Measuring Security Operations Effectiveness

For security operations to be effective, you need more than just the tools at your disposal. You need a way to measure the impact they are having, as well as putting processes in place to continuously improve their performance. This section explores one way to implement meaningful metrics that demonstrate the value of your security automation efforts.

Key Performance Indicators (KPIs)

The effectiveness of security operations can be measured through several critical metrics:

- **Mean Time to Detect (MTTD):** This measures how quickly your automated systems identify potential security threats.
- **Mean Time to Respond (MTTR):** This tracks the speed of your automated response mechanisms.
- **False Positive Rate:** This indicates the accuracy of your detection systems.
- **Incident Response Rate:** This shows the percentage of successfully handled security events.

One way to display these metrics is through the use of CloudWatch dashboards. You can create a CloudWatch dashboard to track these metrics. You can find the text for this command in the Chapter 10 folder, SecurityOperationsMetrics. txt file in my GitHub repo at https://github.com/8carroll/Securing-the-Cloud-with-Brandon-Carroll. (I do want to mention, however, that this is just an example. My demo environment doesn't have much to see, and likely as you get started, yours won't either.)

```
[cloudshell-user@ip-10-138-3-141 ~]$ aws cloudwatch put-dashboard \
>     --dashboard-name SecurityOperationsMetrics \
>     --dashboard-body '{
>       "widgets": [
>         {
>           "type": "metric",
>           "properties": {
>             "metrics": [
>               ["SecurityMetrics", "MTTD", "Environment", "Production"],
>               ["SecurityMetrics", "MTTR", "Environment", "Production"]
>             ],
>             "period": 300,
>             "stat": "Average",
>             "region": "us-west-2",
>             "title": "Response Metrics"
>           }
>         }
>       ]
>     }'
{
    "DashboardValidationMessages": []
}
[cloudshell-user@ip-10-138-3-141 ~]$
```

Cleaning Up Your Resources

Once you've finished testing, it's a good idea to tear down any resources you no longer need. This cleanup not only prevents unnecessary charges but also limits the surface area for potential configuration drift.

To remove these resources, start by deleting the EventBridge rule using this command:

```
[cloudshell-user@ip-10-144-114-129 ~]$ aws events delete-rule --name
GuardDutyHighSeverityFindings
[cloudshell-user@ip-10-144-114-129 ~]$
```

Then, remove the Lambda function with the following command:

```
[cloudshell-user@ip-10-144-114-129 ~]$ aws lambda delete-function --function-
name InstanceIsolationAutomation
[cloudshell-user@ip-10-144-114-129 ~]$
```

Next, detach or remove the IAM policies and roles by running the following command:

```
[cloudshell-user@ip-10-144-114-129 ~]$ aws iam delete-role-policy --role-
name SecurityAutomationRole --policy-name SecurityAutomationPolicy
[cloudshell-user@ip-10-144-114-129 ~]$
[cloudshell-user@ip-10-144-114-129 ~]$ aws iam delete-role --role-name Security
AutomationRole
```

Unsubscribe from the SNS topic with the following command, replacing the ARN with your own:

```
[cloudshell-user@ip-10-144-114-129 ~]$ aws sns unsubscribe --subscription-arn
arn:aws:sns:us-west-2:387974667323:SecurityAlerts:7f86bcd0-940b-498d-82bd-
5146a0d05ebd
```

Delete the topic using the following command:

```
[cloudshell-user@ip-10-144-114-129 ~]$ aws sns delete-topic --topic-
arn arn:aws:sns:us-west-2:387974667323:SecurityAlerts
```

Finally, if you deployed your environment through CloudFormation, remove everything with the following commands:

```
[cloudshell-user@ip-10-144-114-129 ~]$ aws cloudformation delete-stack --stack-name
chapter10
[cloudshell-user@ip-10-144-114-129 ~]$ aws cloudformation wait stack-delete-
complete --stack-name chapter10
[cloudshell-user@ip-10-144-114-129 ~]$
```

This ensures that you won't incur unnecessary charges or leave unused resources behind.

Operational Metrics that Matter

When measuring the effectiveness of your AWS security operations, I recommend focusing on the key areas covered in this table:

Number of GuardDuty Findings by Severity Level	Tracking GuardDuty findings by severity level helps identify patterns in security threats and measure the effectiveness of your security controls, while also indicating if your security posture is improving or degrading over time.
Percentage of Automated Responses to Security Events	The percentage of automated responses to security events demonstrates your organization's ability to respond to threats continuously without human intervention, with higher automation rates typically leading to faster incident resolution.

Compliance Percentage with AWS Security Best Practices	Monitoring compliance with AWS security best practices provides an objective measure of your security posture and helps identify configuration drift before it becomes a security issue, while also satisfying auditor requirements.
Number of Unauthorized Access Attempts	Finally, tracking unauthorized access attempts helps identify potential credential compromise or brute-force attacks, validates the effectiveness of your IAM policies and security groups, and provides early warning of potential security incidents.

These metrics should be reviewed on a regular basis to help understand trends, identify areas needing improvement, validate security control effectiveness, and guide your future security automation investments. Along the line of future security automation investments, let's talk about the continuous improvement process.

Continuous Improvement Process

To maintain effective security operations in AWS, establish a continuous improvement process that evolves with your environment. Start by defining clear objectives for your security automation—which specific threats you want to address and what successful remediation looks like. Choose KPIs that directly align with these security goals, such as response times to high-severity GuardDuty findings or the percentage of successful automated remediations. Implement automated data collection through CloudWatch metrics and Security Hub findings to ensure accurate and consistent measurement. Schedule regular reviews of these metrics with your security team to identify trends and areas needing improvement. Share these results with stakeholders to demonstrate the value of your security automation and justify further investments. I also recommend using the insights gained from these measurements to refine your automation strategy, whether that means adjusting EventBridge rules, updating Lambda functions, or creating new security playbooks to address the latest threats.

So now you are getting a sense of the processes behind security operations and automation. The next section discusses one final topic related to the resilience of your security operations.

Building Resilient Security Operations

Building resilient security operations in AWS requires a multilayered approach that builds upon the resilience principles discussed in Chapter 9. Start with basic resilient security monitoring by implementing GuardDuty across all regions and configuring Security Hub as your centralized security command center. While the book focused on single-region deployments through Chapter 8, true resilience requires expanding your security controls across multiple regions and availability zones.

When implementing redundant security controls, deploy your security automation components across multiple availability zones. Configure EventBridge rules with multiple targets to ensure critical security alerts have redundant notification paths. Just as you've seen with the automated responses using Lambda functions, each layer of security automation should have built-in redundancy.

For automated recovery procedures, implement AWS Backup to maintain copies of critical security configurations and automation components. Use Systems Manager automation runbooks to define recovery procedures that can automatically restore security controls if primary systems fail. Configure AWS Config rules to continuously validate that security controls remain properly configured across your environment.

The key to resilient security operations lies in extending the detection, monitoring, and response capabilities you've built throughout this book across regions. By implementing redundant monitoring across regions, maintaining automated response capabilities that can operate independently, and regularly testing your security automation through game days and failure scenarios, you create a security operation that remains effective even during disruptions. Remember that security resilience isn't just about technical controls—it requires well-documented procedures, cross-trained teams, and regular validation of your recovery capabilities. Most importantly, measure your security operations effectiveness through CloudWatch metrics and Security Hub benchmarks to ensure your controls remain effective and identify areas needing improvement before incidents occur.

Conclusion

Security operations and automation represent the cornerstone of modern AWS cloud security. Throughout this chapter, you've explored how to transform individual security controls into a comprehensive, automated security framework that operates at cloud scale. By implementing automated security playbooks, orchestrating security services, measuring operational effectiveness, and building resilient operations, you've learned to create a security program that can protect your AWS environment continuously and efficiently.

Some key takeaways from this chapter include:

- Security automation is essential for operating at cloud scale.
- Well-designed playbooks ensure consistent security responses.

- Orchestrated security services provide comprehensive protection.
- Measuring security operations drives continuous improvement.
- Resilient security operations maintain effectiveness during disruptions.

Remember that security automation isn't about replacing security teams. Security automation is about empowering security teams to operate more effectively and focus on the more complex security challenges rather than routine tasks.

In Chapter 11, you'll explore how to bridge the gap between security operations and modern development practices. You'll learn how to implement security as code, enabling your organization to build security directly into the development process. This approach ensures that security controls are version-controlled, tested, and deployed alongside your infrastructure, creating a truly integrated security program.

The skills you've learned in this chapter about security automation serve as a foundation as you dive into the developer's approach to AWS security. You'll see how the automated controls you've built can be transformed into code, making them more maintainable, testable, and scalable.

References

Amazon CloudWatch Documentation, https://docs.aws.amazon.com/cloudwatch/

Amazon EventBridge Documentation, https://docs.aws.amazon.com/eventbridge/

Amazon GuardDuty Documentation, https://docs.aws.amazon.com/guardduty/

Amazon Simple Notification Service Documentation, https://docs.aws.amazon.com/sns/

AWS Config Documentation, https://docs.aws.amazon.com/config/

CHAPTER

11

Applying the Developer Mindset to AWS Security

"In God we trust; all others must bring data."
—W. Edwards Deming

Throughout this book, you've explored AWS security from various angles—from fundamental concepts to specific services and operational strategies. This chapter shifts gears to examine security through a developer's lens. This perspective isn't really about writing code. It's more about treating security as a programmable, version-controlled, automated component of your infrastructure. By adopting a developer's mindset, you can leverage tools and practices that are used in software development to enhance your security posture.

This chapter explores the philosophy of Security as Code (SaC) and introduces GitOps principles, setting the foundation for the detailed implementation strategies covered in Chapter 12. While this chapter emphasizes a developer's mindset, it's also about embracing a DevSecOps philosophy that integrates robust security practices into every stage of the development lifecycle. By blending agile development techniques with proactive security measures, you can ensure that security isn't an afterthought but a shared responsibility woven into your entire infrastructure workflow.

Understanding the Developer Mindset

The traditional security approach often involves manual configurations, point-and-click interfaces, and reactive measures. As you saw in Chapter 10, this approach quickly becomes unsustainable when managing security at cloud scale. Think about how you automated instance isolation with Lambda functions. That was just the beginning of treating security as code.

While traditional security operations centered on manual reviews and human analysts, the scale and speed of cloud computing have fundamentally changed this approach. When a single AWS account can spin up thousands of resources across multiple regions in minutes, human-centered security operations simply can't keep up with the pace.

You need real-time threat detection and response. You can't wait for daily or weekly security scans to take place anymore. I've mentioned this before, but when someone's in your account and they are accessing areas of your account or resources they shouldn't be, you need to know immediately. Whether it's unusual API calls or someone trying to access sensitive S3 buckets, immediate alerts are required.

This is where the developer mindset comes in. Developers have long understood that code provides consistency, repeatability, and validation. When you apply this mindset to security, you shift your security controls into programmable, testable components that can be version-controlled, reviewed, and automatically deployed. Instead of clicking through the AWS Console to configure security groups or IAM policies, you define these configurations as code, making them versionable, testable, and repeatable.

Security operations on AWS require a systematic approach that combines continuous monitoring, automated responses, and structured recovery procedures. Rather than treating security as a series of isolated tasks, modern cloud security implements a workflow where detection, response, and recovery work together seamlessly. By using AWS's native security services and automation capabilities, you can build a security operations workflow that scales with your infrastructure and responds to threats in near real time. This workflow isn't just about detecting threats; it's about creating a repeatable, automated process that maintains your security posture while reducing manual intervention.

Remember those security playbooks you created in Chapter 10? Now imagine those playbooks as code, stored in version control, automatically tested with each change, and deployed consistently across your entire AWS infrastructure. This is what you gain when you adopt a developer's mindset. For example, if someone accidentally exposes an RDS instance to the Internet or misconfigures an IAM role, you want systems that can automatically detect and fix these issues. By thinking like a developer, you can create these automated remediation systems in a maintainable, testable way. When adjustments need to be made, you can do so in code and push the change everywhere it needs to be in a matter of minutes.

The Security as Code Philosophy

Security as Code (SaC) represents a fundamental shift in how developers approach security in cloud environments. Rather than treating security as a separate concern, SaC integrates security directly into the development and deployment pipeline, as shown in Figure 11.1.

This means expressing security controls, policies, and configurations as code, making them

- Versionable
- Testable
- Repeatable
- Reviewable

I mention pipelines a bit in this chapter, but I want to make sure that I define what a pipeline is. A *pipeline* is an automated sequence of steps that takes code or configurations from development to deployment in a structured and repeatable manner. In the context of Infrastructure as Code (IaC), a pipeline ensures that each change to your infrastructure definitions goes through a series of stages, such as validation, testing, and deployment, before being applied to your AWS environment. These stages often include automated security scans, compliance checks, and integration tests to catch issues early and ensure that only secure and compliant changes are deployed. Pipelines not only streamline the deployment process but also enforce consistency and reduce the risk of human error by automating repetitive tasks. For AWS environments, tools like AWS CodePipeline and third-party CI/CD tools can be used to implement these workflows effectively.

The transformation of security into code brings several fundamental principles that reshape how developers approach AWS security. When security controls are expressed as code, they become an integral part of the application rather than an afterthought. The next section looks at the key benefits this provides.

Figure 11.1: Security as Code workflow.

Automated Policy Enforcement

Security policies can be automatically enforced across all AWS environments, ensuring that every resource deployment adheres to organizational standards. For instance, when a developer attempts to create an S3 bucket, automated checks can verify encryption settings, access policies, and versioning configurations.

Early Detection and Prevention

By integrating security directly into the development cycle, vulnerabilities are identified and addressed during the development phase. This approach saves time and resources.

Standardization Through Automation

Security automation eliminates the inconsistencies that often arise from manual configurations. When security controls are coded, they can be consistently applied across all AWS resources, reducing the risk of misconfigurations that could lead to security vulnerabilities.

Collaborative Security Model

The SaC approach transforms security from a specialized function into a shared responsibility. Developers, operations teams, and security professionals collaborate through the same code-based workflows, using familiar tools and processes.

Continuous Validation

With security expressed as code, you can continuously validate your security posture through

- Automated security testing
- Policy compliance checks
- Configuration validation
- Real-time monitoring and alerts

To bring these concepts to life, I highlight some tools and AWS services that enable continuous validation of your security posture. For automated security testing, Amazon Inspector scans workloads such as EC2 instances and container images for vulnerabilities and unintended network exposure. AWS

Config ensures policy compliance by continuously evaluating resource configurations against desired baselines. For configuration validation, CloudFormation Guard can validate your IaC templates against custom policy rules before deployment. Finally, Amazon GuardDuty provides real-time monitoring and alerts by detecting malicious activity or unauthorized behavior in your AWS environment. These tools work together to automate and enhance your security practices, ensuring consistency and scalability across your infrastructure.

This approach ensures that security remains an active, evolving component of your AWS infrastructure rather than a static set of controls. By treating security as code, you create a feedback loop where security improvements can be rapidly tested, deployed, and validated across your entire infrastructure.

Now that you understand the SaC philosophy and hopefully see how it builds on the automation work from Chapter 10, the next section explores one of its most crucial components: version control.

The Role of Version Control

Version control serves as the cornerstone of modern security practices in AWS environments, transforming how you can manage and secure your infrastructure. As shown in Figure 11.2, version control enables a structured workflow for managing security changes. Each modification to security configurations follows a defined path through development, validation, and production phases, ensuring that changes are properly reviewed and tested before being applied to your AWS infrastructure. When you store security configurations, policies, and infrastructure code in version control systems, you gain several critical security advantages that align with a developer-focused approach.

Complete Audit History

Every change to security configurations and infrastructure code is tracked with detailed metadata, including who made the change, when it occurred, and why it was implemented. This tracking creates an immutable record that satisfies compliance requirements and aids in security investigations.

Collaborative Security Review

Through pull requests and code review processes, security changes undergo thorough examination before implementation. This collaborative approach ensures that multiple team members validate security configurations, reducing the risk of misconfigurations or security gaps.

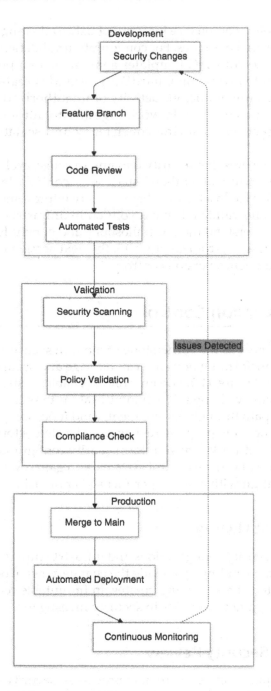

Figure 11.2: Version control security workflow.

Branch-Based Security Testing

Using feature branches allows teams to test security changes in isolation before merging them into production. This practice enables

- Security policy validation
- Compliance checking
- Configuration testing
- Impact assessment

Rollback Capabilities

In the event of a security incident or misconfiguration, version control provides the ability to quickly revert to a known good state. This capability significantly reduces the mean time to recovery and minimizes the impact of security issues.

While version control provides the ability to roll back to a known good state, it is not always as simple as clicking a button. Rolling back requires careful planning and preparation to ensure the process is effective and minimizes disruption. To perform a rollback, you would typically identify the specific commit or version in your repository that represents the last known secure configuration. Once identified, you would revert the infrastructure code in your version control system to this state and redeploy it through your pipeline. For example, in Git, this might involve using commands like `git revert` or `git checkout` to restore previous commits.

However, there are challenges to consider. Infrastructure changes often have dependencies or stateful components that cannot be easily undone without impacting running services. For instance, rolling back an IAM policy could unintentionally disrupt application access if not carefully managed. Similarly, infrastructure resources such as databases or storage buckets may have accumulated new data since the last deployment, making a full rollback impractical without data loss.

To address these challenges, it's critical to plan for rollbacks as part of your overall deployment strategy. This includes maintaining detailed documentation of changes, testing rollback procedures in staging environments, and implementing safeguards such as automated backups for stateful resources. Additionally, tools like AWS CloudFormation and Terraform can help by enabling you to define IaC and manage rollbacks more systematically through their change-management features. By treating rollbacks as a deliberate and well-tested process rather than an ad hoc reaction, you can ensure that they are reliable and minimally disruptive in the event of a security incident or misconfiguration.

Infrastructure Versioning

When managing AWS resources through IaC, version control becomes essential for tracking changes to security groups, IAM policies, and network configurations. This approach ensures that infrastructure security remains consistent and reproducible.

Security Policy Evolution

Version control allows security policies to evolve while maintaining a clear history of changes. Teams can track policy modifications over time, understand the reasoning behind security decisions, and ensure that security controls adapt to new threats while maintaining compliance.

By treating security configurations as code and leveraging version control, you create a more robust, traceable, and collaborative security posture. This approach not only improves security management but also aligns with modern DevSecOps practices, making security an integral part of our AWS infrastructure management.

Now that you understand how version control supports your security practices, you can explore how to secure the IaC process itself.

The Peer Review

The peer review is one of the most significant benefits of incorporating version control into your security workflows. By leveraging pull requests and code reviews, teams can collaboratively examine proposed changes to security configurations, policies, or infrastructure code before they are merged into production. This process ensures that multiple sets of eyes validate the changes, reducing the likelihood of misconfigurations or introducing vulnerabilities.

During peer reviews, team members can

- Identify potential security risks or compliance issues early.
- Share knowledge and best practices, fostering a culture of continuous learning.
- Ensure adherence to organizational security standards and coding guidelines.

For example, when updating an IAM policy stored in version control, a peer review might catch overly permissive permissions that could otherwise expose sensitive resources. This collaborative approach not only improves the quality of security implementations but also aligns with DevSecOps principles by integrating security into the development lifecycle.

Infrastructure as Code Security

Before diving into securing Infrastructure as Code (IaC), take a moment to understand what IaC is and how it works. IaC is the process of dynamically managing and provisioning infrastructure through code instead of through manual processes to simplify app development, configuration, and runtime.

Introduction to IaC

Terraform is one of the most widely used IaC tools, thanks to its extensive provider library. Its declarative approach supports provisioning infrastructure from all major clouds, including AWS, Google Cloud, and Azure. It's not a native AWS service, so you'll need to install the binaries to use it. You can read more about that at `https://developer.hashicorp.com/terraform/tutorials/aws-get-started/install-cli`.

AWS CloudFormation is the AWS-native IaC service, and I use it just as much. In fact, you will likely find more CloudFormation template examples that you can use in your environment than Terraform examples, although there are a lot out there. You write CloudFormation templates in YAML or JSON, and you can find a huge repository of examples at `https://github.com/aws-samples/startup-kit-templates`.

This section talks about each of them in a bit more detail.

I want you to think back to the AWS CLI commands that you have used in this book. Each command expressed what you wanted to do and included all the values—some required, some not—that you provided to create or update a resource. IaC does the same thing, but it's written as code and executed later, somewhere in your pipeline. IaC is written as declarative code. In other words, you declare what the state of the resources should be. These examples cover the two popular approaches to IaC. First, here is a snippet of CloudFormation code:

```
# CloudFormation Example
Resources:
  MyS3Bucket:
    Type: 'AWS::S3::Bucket'
    Properties:
      BucketName: my-secure-bucket
      BucketEncryption:
        ServerSideEncryptionConfiguration:
          - ServerSideEncryptionByDefault:
              SSEAlgorithm: AES256
```

This YAML code defines a resource of type S3 bucket. The `Properties` section specifies the bucket name and enables server-side encryption using the AES-256 algorithm. CloudFormation will handle the actual creation and configuration of the bucket based on this declaration. I should also mention that CloudFormation can be written in JSON as well. (I tend to go back and forth between the two, depending on the example I start from.)

The following Terraform example accomplishes the same goal as the previous CloudFormation example; however, it uses different syntax:

```
# Terraform Example
resource "aws_s3_bucket" "secure_bucket" {
  bucket = "my-secure-bucket"

  server_side_encryption_configuration {
    rule {
      apply_server_side_encryption_by_default {
        sse_algorithm = "AES256"
      }
    }
  }
}
```

This HCL (HashiCorp Configuration Language) code (it looks a bit like JSON, but it's not) creates an S3 bucket with the same security configuration. The resource block defines the bucket and its encryption settings, which Terraform will use to create and configure the bucket in AWS.

Both examples demonstrate the declarative approach to IaC, where you specify the desired end state rather than the steps to create it. Although the examples in this chapter are simple, both tools can manage complex infrastructure deployments with multiple interconnected resources. To learn more about IaC and its implementation in AWS, visit AWS's comprehensive guide at aws.amazon.com/what-is/iac.

Now that you understand how to write basic IaC, let's explore how to secure these infrastructure definitions.

Securing Your IaC Implementation

IaC is not actually the infrastructure. It's the code that's going to be the infrastructure once you push it through a pipeline (more on that in the next chapter) and it gets deployed. So even before you deploy the infrastructure, you can check to make sure that there are no security issues with what you plan to deploy using that code. To do this, you scan the code preemptively, before deploying it. By preemptively scanning your IaC, you can identify misconfigurations and compliance issues before they are deployed.

Continuous Integration (CI) and Continuous Deployment (CD) are foundational practices in modern software development, designed to streamline and automate the process of building, testing, and deploying applications. CI involves frequently merging code changes into a shared repository, where automated tests validate the code to catch errors early in the development process. Once the code passes these tests, CD takes over, automating the packaging and deployment of the application to staging or production environments. This approach minimizes manual intervention, reduces deployment risks, and enables teams to release updates quickly and reliably. Together, CI/CD ensures that software changes are integrated smoothly and delivered efficiently, fostering a faster feedback loop and improving overall quality.

In the area of Continuous Integration and Continuous Deployment (CI/CD), IaC scans act as an important checkpoint, making sure that infrastructure deployments are secure by design and facilitating rapid and safe iterations of infrastructure changes.

To implement secure IaC practices, you

- Automate policies and configuration checks to save time and reduce the risk of human error. Manually reviewing each IaC template for over 100 policies can create security gaps. Automating this process ensures continuous governance and strengthens the security posture.

- Embed security into everyday processes by integrating IaC security into CI/CD pipelines. This ensures that every pull request and commit is validated with security checks, preventing misconfigurations and maintaining the security integrity of the environment.

When implementing IaC security, several powerful, and often free, scanning tools can help identify vulnerabilities and misconfigurations before they reach production. Tools like Checkov, Snyk, cfn-nag, and Terrascan analyze your infrastructure code for common security issues, compliance violations, and best practice deviations. These tools can be integrated directly into your development workflow, scanning your infrastructure code during the development process and as part of your CI/CD pipeline.

Figure 11.3 shows how these tools fit into your security workflow.

These scanning tools operate at multiple stages of your development process. During local development, they can run pre-commit scans to catch issues before code is committed. In the CI/CD pipeline, they perform automated scans as part of the build process, preventing insecure configurations from being deployed. Each tool has its strengths. Checkov excels at policy enforcement, Snyk provides comprehensive vulnerability scanning, and Terrascan offers strong compliance-checking capabilities. There are many others to explore or you can write your own.

Consider this example of implementing security checks in your IaC using Python:

```
# Example security validation function
def validate_s3_security(bucket_config):
    security_issues = []
```

```
if not bucket_config.get('encryption_enabled'):
    security_issues.append("S3 bucket must have encryption enabled")

if bucket_config.get('public_access'):
    security_issues.append("S3 bucket must not be publicly accessible")

return security_issues
```

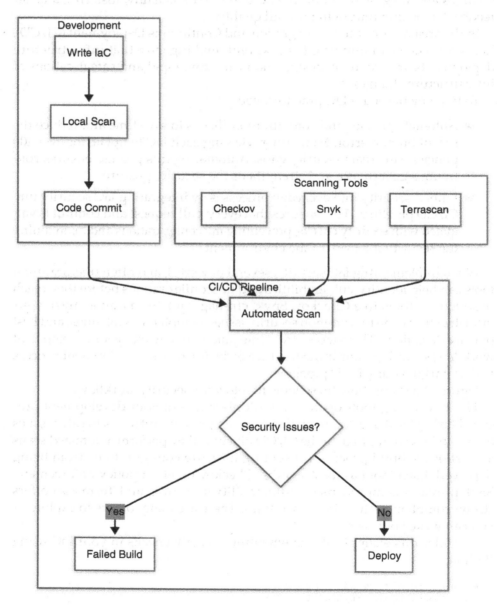

Figure 11.3: IaC security scanning workflow.

This Python function demonstrates a simple security validation check for S3 buckets, aligning with the security practices discussed in Chapter 7 about data security. Here's how it works.

The `validate _ s3 _ security` function takes a bucket configuration as input and checks for two critical security requirements:

- Encryption check:
  - It verifies if the bucket has encryption enabled.
  - If `encryption _ enabled` is FALSE or not present, it adds an error message to the `security _ issues` list.
  - This aligns with the requirement that all sensitive data in S3 must be encrypted.
- Public access check:
  - It checks if the bucket has public access enabled.
  - If `public _ access` is TRUE, it adds an error message to the `security _ issues` list.
  - This helps prevent accidental data exposure through public bucket access.

The function returns a list of any security issues found, which can be used by automation tools to

- Prevent deployments that don't meet security standards
- Generate compliance reports
- Trigger automated remediation workflows

This would typically be executed in your CI/CD pipeline as part of the pre-deployment validation stage, not as a Lambda function. It could be integrated into a CI/CD pipeline as a custom validation step during the build phase. When a developer commits IaC changes to the version-controlled repository, the CI/CD tool—such as AWS CodePipeline paired with CodeBuild or GitHub Actions—automatically initiates a build process. During this stage, the pipeline executes a series of tasks including building, testing, and validating your infrastructure definitions. This is often done by the pipeline initializing a container to run the code in. Your security validation function is invoked as a script or command-line call that processes your IaC files (for example, in JSON or YAML format) and checks them for common security misconfigurations.

The output from this script is used to determine whether the IaC changes meet your predefined security standards. If security issues are found, the script returns errors that cause the pipeline to fail, halting the deployment process until the issues are resolved. Conversely, if no issues are found, the pipeline continues toward further testing and ultimately deploying the changes. This setup not only automates the security scanning process but also enforces a robust quality gate that prevents insecure configurations from reaching production while maintaining clear, version-controlled records of all changes.

It's a security scanning function that would run alongside other IaC security checks before your infrastructure changes are deployed. When the container instance completes, it can then be released and terminated.

The function would be part of your pipeline's security scanning step, similar to how tools like Checkov, Snyk, and Terrascan operate. These tools typically operate during the build or testing stages of a CI/CD pipeline. For example, Checkov can run as a pre-commit hook on a developer's local machine or as part of a pipeline in tools like AWS CodePipeline, GitHub Actions, and Jenkins.

Similarly, `cfn-nag` is tailored for AWS CloudFormation templates and can be integrated into pipelines as an action within AWS `CodePipeline` or executed locally. It identifies security risks such as overly permissive IAM roles or unencrypted resources. Tools like Snyk and Terrascan also provide static analysis for IaC, with Snyk focusing on vulnerabilities in dependencies and Terrascan excelling at compliance checks. These tools typically output detailed reports highlighting issues and recommendations for remediation.

These scans happen during the build and test phase of your CI/CD pipeline to catch security issues before they reach production.

A typical workflow would be as follows:

1. Developer commits IaC changes.
2. CI/CD pipeline triggers.
3. Security scanning tools run (including this validation).
4. If security issues are found, the pipeline fails.
5. If no issues are found, continue with deployment.

For AWS environments, you would typically implement this using tools like AWS CodePipeline or GitHub Actions, with the security scanning happening after the build stage but before any deployment to AWS resources takes place.

By integrating security checks directly into the development process and "shifting left" (integrating security checks early in development), developers can spot and fix security problems early on, before the code goes live.

Now that you've explored how to secure IaC, you'll turn your attention in the next section to the broader concept of continuous security. While IaC security focuses on the definition and deployment of infrastructure, continuous security encompasses the ongoing monitoring, validation, and enforcement of security controls throughout the entire lifecycle of your AWS environment.

Embracing Continuous Security

The dynamic nature of cloud environments demands a shift from periodic security assessments to continuous security monitoring and enforcement. This approach ensures that security controls evolve alongside your infrastructure, providing real-time protection against emerging threats.

Looking at Figure 11.4, you can see how continuous security operates as an interconnected system. The process begins in the SaC phase, where security requirements like "all S3 buckets must be encrypted" are transformed into IaC templates using tools like CloudFormation or Terraform. These templates then undergo automated testing to verify that they meet security requirements before moving forward.

The continuous validation phase takes these templates through security scanning using tools like Checkov and Snyk to identify vulnerabilities, while policy checks confirm compliance with security standards. Only after passing these validations does the code proceed to deployment. Once deployed, the monitoring phase kicks in, with the security hub continuously watching the infrastructure while tracking compliance status against established security baselines. When issues are detected, they trigger updates to security policies, creating a feedback loop that continuously improves your security posture. This cyclical approach ensures your security controls evolve and strengthen over time, rather than remaining static.

For example, if the security hub detects an unencrypted S3 bucket, this triggers an update to the security policies, which then updates the IaC templates to enforce encryption, creating a self-improving security system. The key difference from traditional security approaches is that everything is defined, validated, and enforced through code, making security controls consistent, repeatable, and automatically enforced across your AWS infrastructure.

To implement this continuous security approach through IaC, you define your security checks within your templates. This configuration creates an AWS Config rule that continuously monitors S3 buckets for encryption compliance. Instead of using manual checks or CLI commands, you define your compliance requirements as code, making them version-controlled and automatically enforced.

You can extend this approach to implement automated policy enforcement through IaC templates that define security guardrails:

```
# Terraform example
resource "aws_organizations_policy" "security_controls" {
  content = jsonencode({
    Version = "2012-10-17"
    Statement = [
      {
        Effect = "Deny"
```

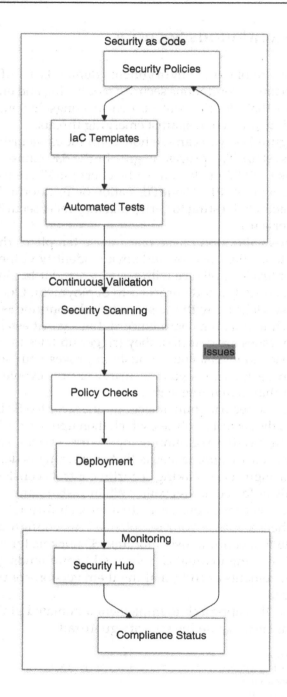

Figure 11.4: Continuous security through IaC.

```
        Action = ["s3:PutBucketPublicAccess"]
        Resource = "*"
      }
    ]
  })
}
```

When security issues are detected, automated remediation can be triggered through event-driven architectures defined in your IaC. This creates a self-healing infrastructure where security controls are not just monitored but automatically enforced and remediated when needed.

The key to successful continuous security is treating it as an integral part of your IaC practices. By defining security controls, compliance requirements, and remediation procedures as code, you create a repeatable and verifiable security posture that evolves with your infrastructure.

Conclusion

This chapter explored how adopting a developer's mindset transforms AWS security from a static set of controls into a dynamic, programmable component of your infrastructure. By treating security as code and embracing version control practices, you can establish a foundation for more consistent, maintainable, and automated security operations. The chapter also discussed how this approach aligns with DevSecOps, blending development and security into one continuous workflow that addresses governance and compliance without slowing down innovation.

The chapter began by examining the Security as Code (SaC) philosophy and identified how version-controlled security policies and Infrastructure as Code (IaC) accelerate misconfiguration detection. By integrating compliance checks and governance requirements into the same processes developers use daily, you can ensure your deployments respect organizational standards and regulatory obligations. Automated scanning tools, such as Checkov and Terrascan, highlight possible violations before changes reach production, resulting in a more proactive and transparent security culture.

If you want to see these concepts in action, you can try deploying a simple CloudFormation or Terraform example from my GitHub repository. This sample demonstrates how an IaC template can enforce encryption and access-control best practices while running security scans that confirm compliance before anything is actually deployed. By observing these checks firsthand, you will gain practical insight into how DevSecOps ties security, governance, and compliance together in a developer-friendly manner.

In Chapter 12, you'll put these concepts into practice by implementing GitOps for AWS infrastructure. You'll learn how to establish GitOps workflows, create infrastructure pipelines, and maintain security controls through version-controlled repositories. This hands-on implementation will show you how to transform the principles you've learned into a comprehensive GitOps practice that unifies development and enhances your AWS security posture.

Reference

AWS Getting Started with IaC, https:// aws.amazon.com/what-is/iac/

Implementing GitOps for AWS Infrastructure

"GitOps is not just about managing code; it's about creating a single source of truth that brings together development practices and infrastructure security in perfect harmony."

—Unknown

The previous chapter explored how adopting a developer's mindset transforms AWS security from a static set of controls into dynamic, programmable components. This chapter takes that foundation and implements GitOps practices specifically for AWS infrastructure security. It demonstrates how to use Git, your single source of truth for AWS infrastructure, focusing on practical implementation using AWS Network Firewall as the primary example. However, since this chapter uses Terraform as the IaC, the actual source of truth for the network is the Terraform state file, but you can store it in Git! Chapter 5 introduced AWS Network Firewall. You are going to re-create that firewall in this chapter and manage firewall rules and policies through GitOps practices, ensuring consistent, auditable, and automated security controls.

Before you jump in, make sure you head over to the GitHub repo at `https://github.com/8carroll/Securing-the-Cloud-with-Brandon-Carroll`, navigate to the Chapter 12 folder, and grab the resources. It includes all the commands you need, but make sure you change the account ID, resource IDs, and ARNs to match your environment.

Understanding GitOps Implementation in AWS

GitOps extends beyond traditional version control, serving as a methodology that treats infrastructure configurations as code, with Git repositories acting as the definitive source of truth for your entire AWS environment.

This approach brings several benefits to AWS security operations. When infrastructure changes are managed through Git, organizations gain automated compliance capabilities where every modification is automatically tracked, reviewed, and validated before deployment, creating a comprehensive audit trail that satisfies compliance requirements while ensuring consistent security standards.

Additionally, maintaining infrastructure state in Git enables rapid recovery capabilities—during security incidents, teams can quickly recover from failures by simply redeploying the last known good configuration, significantly reducing mean time to recovery (MTTR). These capabilities work together to create a more resilient and compliant security posture that can adapt quickly to incidents while maintaining proper governance.

AWS does offer several tools that can be used to deploy a GitOps pipeline. These include AWS CodeCommit, AWS CodePipeline, AWS CodeBuild, and AWS CodeDeploy, along with Amazon CodeCatalyst, to name a few. In fact, if you look on aws.amazon.com under Products --> Developer Tools, you will find several other tools that are in the same realm. However, it's hard to do anything with GitOps or Git and not think about GitHub. So in this chapter, I show you how to set your pipeline up using GitHub Actions.

While AWS's native tools provide deep integration with AWS services, GitHub is widely used for version control and collaborative development. Its widespread adoption, extensive feature set, and security capabilities make it one of the most commonly used choices for implementing GitOps practices. Additionally, GitHub Actions provides some pretty cool automation capabilities that integrate easily with AWS, allowing developers to build sophisticated deployment pipelines.

This approach not only demonstrates how to integrate third-party tools with AWS securely, but also aligns with common industry practices where organizations often use a mix of cloud-native and external tools to build their security pipelines. By using GitHub, you'll learn patterns that can be applied regardless of which Git platform you ultimately choose for your organization.

Let's examine the implementation strategy. First, let's look at the basic components of the GitOps implementation, showing how GitHub repositories connect to AWS through GitHub Actions; see Figure 12.1.

In Figure 12.1, you get the basic sense of what you will accomplish. You spent a lot of time configuring the AWS resources using the AWS CLI. The AWS Console looks way better, but the point of all of that was to prepare you to write your config as code.

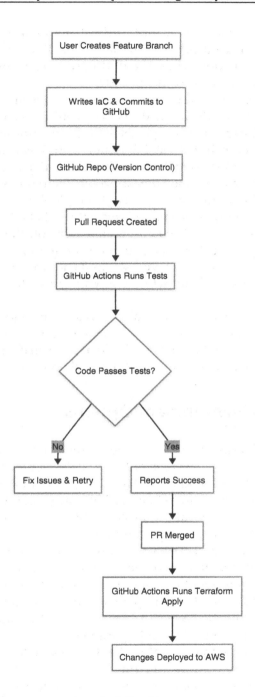

Figure 12.1: Basic GitOps components and relationships.

You will now describe your security infrastructure as code. This example uses Terraform, the HashiCorp Markup language. But you can use CDK and Python or CloudFormation. They are all different forms of expressing what your infrastructure should look like in code.

So what is the goal here? You want to write the code and commit it to your GitHub repository. This will handle the version control. But rather than commit to the main branch, which really represents the production environment, you'll commit to a feature branch. The GitHub Action workflow runs when you create a pull request. This performs any tests you build. You don't deploy to production at this point, but you run a bunch of tests to see if it looks as if it would deploy correctly. This could be running security checks, looking at the guardrails, or just seeing if the Terraform is formatted correctly. If that all checks out, you can then merge the pull request. If you do that, it kicks off the action again, only this time it actually deploys to AWS, authenticating with an OpenID Connect (OIDC) authentication connection you set up. That's the high level.

Let's now look at the GitHub Action that will run with the pull request and merge to main.

For your convenience, you can find all the code examples used in this chapter in my GitHub repository at `https://github.com/8carroll/Securing-the-Cloud-with-Brandon-Carroll` in the Chapter 12 folder. You can clone the repo, fork the repo, copy and paste from the repo, or type it all yourself.

Development Environment Options

When it comes to development environments, there are compelling options for both local and cloud-based development. A local development environment that includes VS Code, AWS Toolkit, and Amazon Q Developer creates a powerful workspace. This includes comprehensive IDE integration with AWS services, the ability to work offline, local testing capabilities, pre-commit hook support, and integration with local security scanning tools.

On the other hand, cloud-based IDEs provide a consistent, preconfigured development environment that's accessible through any web browser. This means you don't have to worry about local software installations, version conflicts, or system compatibility issues. For example, when using GitHub Codespaces, often the necessary tools like the AWS CLI, Terraform, and Git are preinstalled and configured, allowing you to start coding immediately.

Whatever you choose to use in this chapter, be sure to focus mostly on the infrastructure you are configuring and don't get lost in the endless task of tweaking your development environment. I use Codespaces as well as a local VS Code installation in the examples.

To begin, navigate to `https://github.com/8carroll/Securing-the-Cloud-with-Brandon-Carroll` and fork the repository to your own GitHub account by clicking Fork. This creates your own copy of the repository where you can safely experiment with the code.

As shown in Figure 12.2, you'll find the Fork button in the top-right corner of the repository interface.

You'll find the Code button in the repository interface of your forked version, where you can access the Codespaces tab and create a new codespace on the main branch.

This approach provides several benefits:

- You maintain your own version of the code.
- You can make changes without affecting the original repository.
- You can practice proper GitOps workflows by creating pull requests.
- You have full control over your own repository settings.
- You can experiment with different configurations safely.

This is in line with best practices. Now that you have the code forked into your own account, you can continue setting up your environment. As shown in Figure 12.3, you'll find the Code button in your repository's interface, where you can access the Codespaces tab.

Figure 12.2: GitHub repository Fork button.

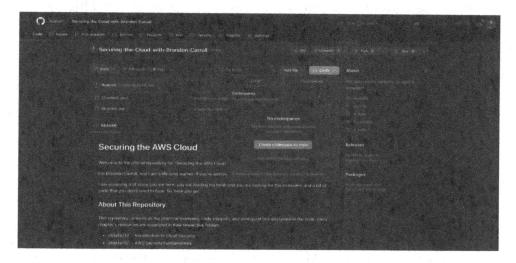

Figure 12.3: GitHub Codespaces access button.

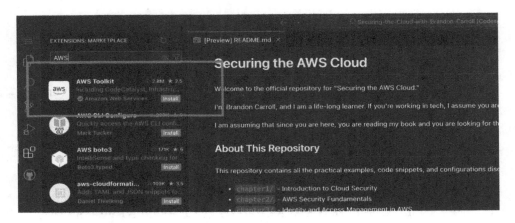

Figure 12.4: Installing the AWS Toolkit.

When you create a new codespace, GitHub launches a cloud-based VS Code environment preconfigured with many of the tools needed for working with AWS infrastructure development. This environment comes with Git preconfigured and authenticated to your GitHub account, enabling seamless version control operations. Once installed, you can confirm the AWS Toolkit is active by opening the Extensions view (Ctrl+Shift+X) to see it listed as installed, or by checking for the AWS Explorer icon in the Activity Bar, which indicates it's running. If the AWS Toolkit is not installed, you can find the extension by clicking on Extensions in the left menu bar, then searching for AWS, as shown in Figure 12.4. Once you find the extension, click Install.

Once the installation is complete, you will see two pop-up messages in the bottom-right corner of the browser window. One pop-up is informational, and the other one is prompting you to install Amazon Q Developer. I highly recommend using Amazon Q Developer to improve your code.

Amazon Q Developer leverages advanced AI to perform real-time code reviews that quickly identify code quality issues and potential security vulnerabilities, ensuring that best practices are followed.

For network security professionals, this means that misconfigurations in Infrastructure as Code are promptly flagged, allowing for rapid remediation before threats can materialize. By integrating seamlessly with your development environment, Amazon Q Developer not only improves code completion and logic guidance but also reinforces secure coding practices—ultimately strengthening your overall network security posture.

If you plan to use Amazon Q Developer, you'll need to set up an AWS Builder ID. You can do this by following the AWS documentation on creating your Builder ID at `https://docs.aws.amazon.com/signin/latest/userguide/create-aws _ builder _ id.html`, which provides step-by-step instructions for the setup. Once it's configured, your Builder ID will enable you to authenticate seamlessly with Amazon Q Developer and enjoy its full range of benefits.

There's a wealth of benefits you'll gain from using Amazon Q Developer, such as code completion, assistance figuring out the logic, and so on. You can read more about that at `https://aws.amazon.com/q/developer`.

Configuring AWS Authentication for GitHub Actions

With a development environment set up, you need to establish secure communication between GitHub and AWS. While traditional approaches might use long-term access keys, you'll implement OpenID Connect (OIDC) authentication following AWS security best practices. This method eliminates the need to store sensitive credentials while maintaining strict access controls. If you think back to what you've already learned in this book, you already know this is the way you should be doing things.

First, you are going to create the OIDC provider. You'll need the following information:

- **Provider URL:** `https://token.actions.githubusercontent.com`
- **Audience or client ID:** `sts.amazonaws.com`

A thumbprint is a unique identifier derived from the certificate of an OpenID Connect (OIDC) identity provider. Specifically, it is the SHA-1 hash of the X.509 certificate used by the identity provider to secure its communications. This thumbprint is used by AWS Identity and Access Management (IAM) to verify the authenticity of the identity provider during OIDC-based authentication. By ensuring that the thumbprint matches the certificate presented by the provider, AWS can trust that the identity provider is legitimate and authorized to interact with your AWS account. If you'd like to learn more about how to obtain the thumbprint for an OIDC provider, you can read about that at `https://docs.aws.amazon.com/IAM/latest/UserGuide/id_roles_providers_create_oidc_verify-thumbprint.html`.

To enable the OIDC provider on AWS, navigate to IAM --> Identity Providers and click Add Provider. You will then enter the required information, as shown in Figure 12.5.

1. Select OpenID Connect.
2. Enter the Provider URL.
3. Enter the Audience.
4. Click Add Provider.

The next step is to assign a role. In Figure 12.6, you can see an Assign Role button. Clicking that will give you the option to create a new role or select an existing role. For this example, I am going to create a new role called `GitHubActionsRole`.

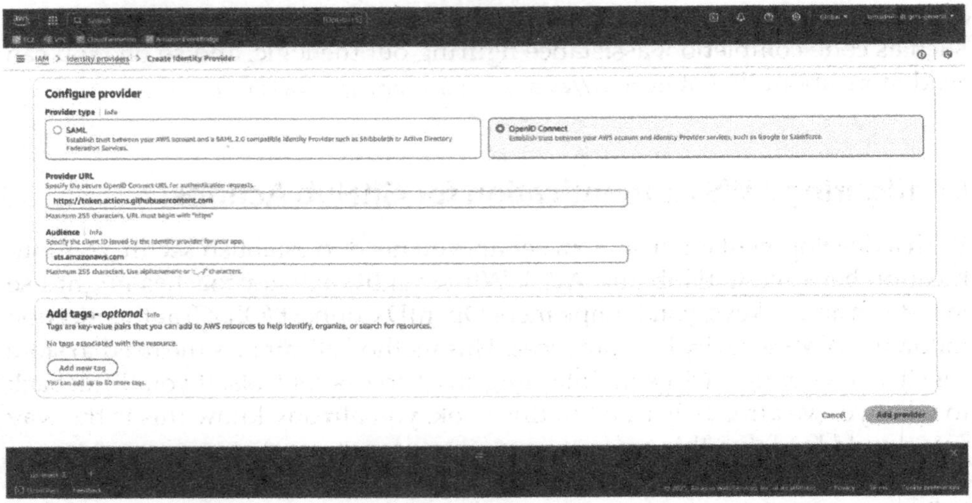

Figure 12.5: Creating the OIDC provider.

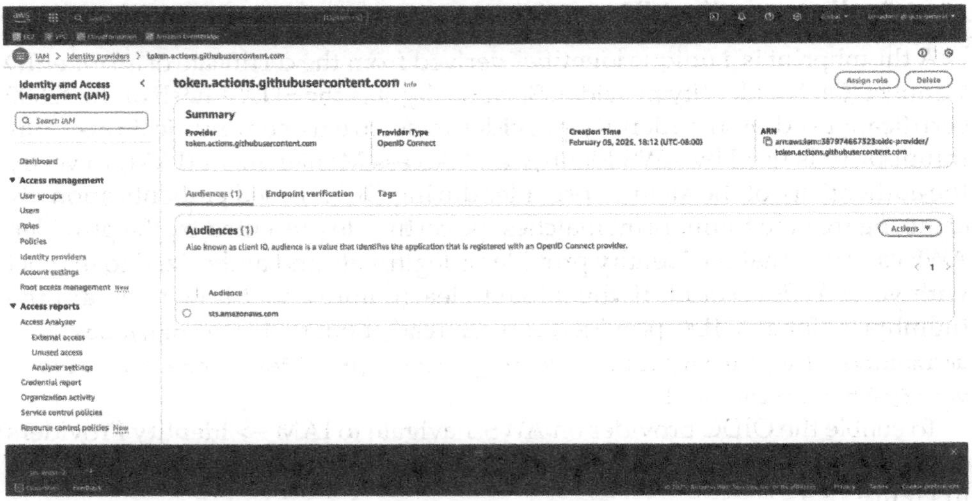

Figure 12.6: Creating the role.

On the Select Trusted Entity page, select Web Identity, select the audience, and then enter your GitHub organization, GitHub repository, and branch. You can see an example of this in Figure 12.6.

On the Permissions Policies page shown in Figure 12.7, select the permissions you want to allow. Since I will be using this role for a lot of infrastructure configuration, I've selected Administrator. Under normal circumstances, you would apply the principle of least privilege here.

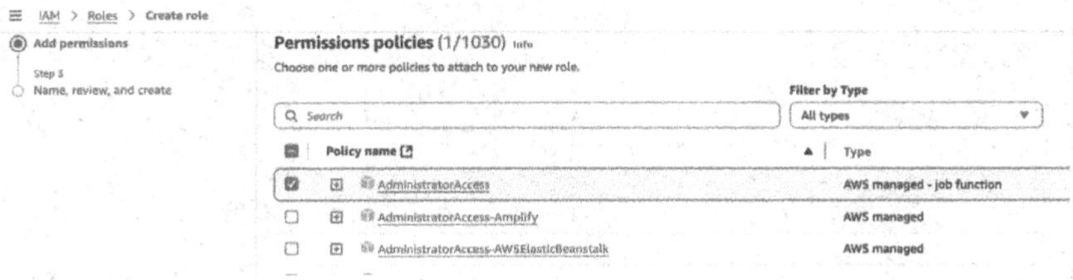

Figure 12.7: Permissions policies for GitHubActionsRole.

To follow the principle of least privilege when assigning roles for GitHub Actions, you can create roles with permissions tailored specifically to the actions required by your workflows. For example, if your workflow involves storing Terraform state files in S3, you can create a role with `s3:GetObject` and `s3:PutObject` permissions scoped to the specific bucket. If you're using DynamoDB for state locking, a role with `dynamodb:GetItem`, `dynamodb:PutItem`, and `dynamodb:DeleteItem` permissions limited to the relevant table is sufficient. For workflows managing AWS Network Firewall rules, you can grant permissions like `network-firewall:UpdateFirewallPolicy` and `network-firewall:UpdateRuleGroup`, scoped to specific resources. These minimal permission sets ensure that your workflows operate securely without granting unnecessary access, reducing the risk of accidental or malicious misuse.

Finally on the Name, Review, and Create page, give the policy a name and click Create Role. At this point in time, you have a new role for GitHub to access your AWS account. Note the role ARN.

Now navigate back to the GitHub repo and select Settings --> Secrets and Variables --> Actions --> New Repository Secret, as shown in Figure 12.8.

Name the secret AWS _ IAM _ ROLE and enter the ARN in the secret field. With the authentication part done, you can finish a little prep work in your AWS environment.

Preparing for the Terraform Backend

You need to think about how Terraform maintains the state of your configuration. Normally, it's maintained in Terraform state files locally, but when you work in the cloud—and when others can potentially be modifying the config as well— you need to store the state files in a central location and configure a locking method. To do this, I'll create an S3 bucket to store the Terraform State files and DynamoDB for locking. This needs to be created before you set up the GitHub Actions. In the following example, you can see that I am creating an S3 bucket called `terraformstatebucketsecuringtheawscloud` in `us-west-2`.

Figure 12.8: Adding the role ARN to GitHub.

To ensure the security of your Terraform state files, it's critical to enable encryption for the S3 bucket where these files are stored. Terraform state files often contain sensitive information, such as resource configurations and secrets, making encryption a necessary safeguard. You can configure server-side encryption by default for the S3 bucket using AWS-managed keys (SSE-S3) or AWS Key Management Service (SSE-KMS) for more control over encryption keys. For example, you can add the encrypt = true parameter in your Terraform backend configuration to enable encryption. Additionally, enabling bucket policies to enforce encryption ensures that all objects uploaded to the bucket are encrypted, providing an extra layer of protection against unauthorized access.

```
[cloudshell-user@ip-10-132-54-246 ~]$ aws s3api create-bucket \
>     --bucket terraformstatebucketsecuringtheawscloud \
>     --region us-west-2 \
>     --create-bucket-configuration LocationConstraint=us-west-2
{
    "Location": "http://terraformstatebucketsecuringtheawscloud.s3.amazonaws.com/"
}
[cloudshell-user@ip-10-132-54-246 ~]$
```

Next, you'll set up versioning for the S3 bucket. Enabling versioning for an S3 bucket provides a critical layer of protection by allowing you to recover from unintended overwrites, accidental deletions, or application failures. When versioning is enabled, Amazon S3 keeps multiple versions of an object, so if an object is overwritten, the previous version remains accessible, and if an object is deleted, a delete marker is added instead of permanent removal. This ensures that you can restore previous versions when needed, making versioning particularly valuable for preserving important data and maintaining reliability in cloud-based workflows. Since I didn't include that when I created the bucket, I can enable it with the following command:

```
[cloudshell-user@ip-10-138-5-235 ~]$ aws s3api put-bucket-versioning \
>     --bucket terraformstatebucketsecuringtheawscloud \
>     --versioning-configuration Status=Enabled
[cloudshell-user@ip-10-138-5-235 ~]$
```

Now that you have created the S3 bucket, you can verify its configuration. First, check that the bucket exists and is accessible:

```
[cloudshell-user@ip-10-138-5-235 ~]$ aws s3api head-bucket --bucket
terraformstatebucketsecuringtheawscloud
{
    "BucketRegion": "us-west-2",
    "AccessPointAlias": false
}
[cloudshell-user@ip-10-138-5-235 ~]$
```

Next, verify the bucket's public access settings:

```
[cloudshell-user@ip-10-138-5-235 ~]$ aws s3api get-public-access-block --bucket
terraformstatebucketsecuringtheawscloud
{
    "PublicAccessBlockConfiguration": {
        "BlockPublicAcls": true,
        "IgnorePublicAcls": true,
        "BlockPublicPolicy": true,
        "RestrictPublicBuckets": true
    }
}
[cloudshell-user@ip-10-138-5-235 ~]$
```

The output shows that the bucket has the appropriate security configurations:

- Located in the us-west-2 region
- Public access blocking enabled for all settings
- Access point alias disabled

One last thing you need to do here is configure state locking with DynamoDB. State locking is a safety feature that prevents multiple users or processes from simultaneously modifying your infrastructure, which could lead to conflicts or corruption of your Terraform state. When you implement state locking with DynamoDB, Terraform automatically creates a lock entry in a DynamoDB table before making any changes to your infrastructure. If another user or process attempts to modify the infrastructure while it's locked, they'll have to wait until the first operation completes and releases the lock. The cost for this feature is affordable since DynamoDB uses a pay-per-request pricing model, meaning you only pay for the actual lock operations you perform. These operations are typically infrequent and brief, resulting in minimal costs. Realistically, the cost is often just pennies per month for small- to medium-sized teams. To implement state locking, you'll need to create a DynamoDB table with a primary key called LockID and configure your Terraform backend to use this table. This small investment in infrastructure safety can prevent costly mistakes and ensure your infrastructure changes are applied consistently and reliably.

You can implement state locking with the following command:

```
[cloudshell-user@ip-10-138-5-235 ~]$ aws dynamodb create-table \
>     --table-name terraform_state_lock \
>     --billing-mode PAY_PER_REQUEST \
>     --attribute-definitions AttributeName=LockID,AttributeType=S \
>     --key-schema AttributeName=LockID,KeyType=HASH
{
    "TableDescription": {
        "AttributeDefinitions": [
            {
                "AttributeName": "LockID",
                "AttributeType": "S"
            }
        ],
        "TableName": "terraform_state_lock",
        "KeySchema": [
            {
                "AttributeName": "LockID",
                "KeyType": "HASH"
            }
        ],
        "TableStatus": "CREATING",
        "CreationDateTime": "2025-02-05T16:27:59.145000+00:00",
        "ProvisionedThroughput": {
            "NumberOfDecreasesToday": 0,
            "ReadCapacityUnits": 0,
            "WriteCapacityUnits": 0
        },
        "TableSizeBytes": 0,
        "ItemCount": 0,
        "TableArn": "arn:aws:dynamodb:us-west-2:387974667323:table/
terraform_state_lock",
        "TableId": "aeaa31f0-ec39-408b-b47d-e4cfa88fcb15",
        "BillingModeSummary": {
            "BillingMode": "PAY_PER_REQUEST"
        },
        "DeletionProtectionEnabled": false
    }
}
(END)
```

Next, return to the GitHub repository and add another secret called TF_ STATE_BUCKET, entering the ARN for the S3 bucket you just created. The Secret value should be the ARN of the bucket. Based on what I named the bucket in this example, the ARN will be arn:aws:s3:::terraformstatebucketsecuringt heawscloud. (You'll need to replace that bucket name with the name you used if you're following along.)

At this point you've set up OIDC for authentication and created a dedicated S3 bucket for Terraform state files along with state locking, as well as set up your secrets in GitHub. You still need to:

- Implement your GitHub Actions workflow structure with conditional steps.
- Create the Terraform configuration files in the chapter12/infrastructure directory.
- Add a backend.tf file to configure the S3 backend with state locking.
- Implement Network Firewall rules using Terraform resources.
- Add automated testing for your Network Firewall configuration.

Creating the GitHub Actions Workflow

Now that you have configured the authentication and storage, this section walks you through the GitHub Actions workflow. This workflow will automate the deployment of your AWS Network Firewall rules while maintaining security and compliance checks throughout the process. So, what is GitHub Actions?

GitHub Actions is an automation platform integrated directly into GitHub repositories that enables continuous integration and continuous deployment (CI/CD) workflows. In this context, you're using GitHub Actions to automate the deployment and management of AWS Network Firewall rules through Infrastructure as Code (IaC). When you define your workflow, GitHub Actions automatically triggers specific tasks when certain events occur, such as pushing code to the main branch or creating pull requests. The implementation uses OpenID Connect (OIDC) for secure authentication between GitHub and AWS, eliminating the need for long-term access credentials. The workflow you've created validates Terraform configurations, plans the changes, and automatically applies them when code is merged to the main branch, ensuring that your network security rules are consistently and reliably deployed across your AWS infrastructure. This GitOps approach not only automates your security infrastructure deployment but also provides version control, audit trails, and collaborative review processes for all changes to your network security posture.

When you forked the repo, a workflow came with it. Your repo should have a structure similar to the following:

```
├── .github
│   └── workflows
│       └── network-firewall.yml
├── README.md
├── chapter12
│   ├── infrastructure
│   │   ├── .DS_Store
│   │   ├── backend.tf
│   │   ├── firewall-rules.tf
│   │   ├── network_firewall.tf
│   │   ├── provider.tf
│   │   └── variables.tf
```

The GitHub Action sits at the top level of the repository, in the `.github\workflows` directory. Here, I call it `network-firewall.yml`. The workflow runs in two scenarios:

- **On a push to the main branch:** This ensures that changes merged into `main` are deployed.

- **On a pull request to `main`:** This runs a Terraform plan to preview changes before merging.

The workflow only applies to changes in the `chapter12/infrastructure/` directory:

```
on:
  push:
    branches: [ main ]
    paths:
      - 'chapter12/infrastructure/**'
  pull_request:
    branches: [ main ]
    paths:
      - 'chapter12/infrastructure/**'
```

Here are the environment variables:

```
env:
  TF_VERSION: 1.6.0
  AWS_REGION: us-west-2
```

The Job: terraform runs on Ubuntu Linux (`ubuntu-latest`) and has IAM permissions set as follows:

```
permissions:
  id-token: write
  contents: read
```

id-token: write allows OIDC authentication to AWS, enabling secure access without the need to store long-term credentials.

contents: read grants the ability to read the contents of the repository.

Check out the repository:

```
- name: Checkout code
  uses: actions/checkout@v4
```

This pulls the latest code from GitHub into the runner. A GitHub Actions runner is a virtual machine or container that executes the steps defined in your workflow. It provides the environment where your code is checked out, commands are run, and tasks like configuring AWS credentials or deploying infrastructure are performed. Runners can be GitHub-hosted, offering preconfigured environments for popular operating systems like Ubuntu, Windows, and macOS, or self-hosted, allowing you to customize the environment to meet specific requirements.

Configure the AWS credentials as follows:

```
- name: Configure AWS Credentials
  uses: aws-actions/configure-aws-credentials@v4
  with:
    role-to-assume: arn:aws:iam::387974667323:role/GitHubActionsRoleAllRepos
    role-session-name: samplerolesession
    aws-region: ${{ env.AWS_REGION }}
```

The AWS credentials:

- Use OIDC authentication to assume the IAM role GitHubActionsRoleAllRepos in AWS.

- Avoid storing static AWS credentials (secure access via GitHub OIDC).

- Use the AWS _ REGION from the environment variables.

Next, set up Terraform:

```
- name: Setup Terraform
  uses: hashicorp/setup-terraform@v3
  with:
    terraform_version: ${{ env.TF_VERSION }}
```

This installs Terraform v1.6.0 (as defined in env.TF _ VERSION). Before you initialize terraform, make sure you add that variable in GitHub.

Now initialize Terraform:

```
- name: Terraform Init
  working-directory: ./chapter12/infrastructure
  run: terraform init -backend-config="bucket=${{ secrets.TF_STATE_BUCKET }}"
```

The Terraform init command is executed in the chapter12/infrastructure directory. The backend is configured to remotely store state in an S3 bucket. The bucket name is stored as a GitHub Secret.

Next, check the Terraform formatting:

```
- name: Terraform Format
  working-directory: ./chapter12/infrastructure
  run: terraform fmt -check
```

The workflow verifies that the Terraform code is correctly formatted using `terraform fmt -check`. The workflow will fail if the Terraform code formatting is incorrect.

Now, validate the Terraform configuration:

```
- name: Terraform Validate
  working-directory: ./chapter12/infrastructure
  run: terraform validate
```

This runs `terraform validate` to ensure that Terraform files are correctly structured.

Now, plan changes on the PRs. This refers to the process of running a Terraform plan as part of your pull request (PR) workflow. This step generates an execution plan that clearly outlines which parts of your infrastructure will be created, updated, or destroyed if the changes in the PR were to be merged. In doing so, it provides reviewers with a detailed preview of the proposed changes, allowing them to verify that the modifications align with the intended configuration before any actual deployment occurs. This safeguard helps prevent unintended alterations to your production environment, ensuring that only validated and approved changes are applied.

```
- name: Terraform Plan
  working-directory: ./chapter12/infrastructure
  run: terraform plan -no-color
  if: github.event_name == 'pull_request'
```

The trigger for this action is a pull request. The Terraform plan is then executed to show the changes that will be applied without actually making the modifications. This allows reviewers to validate the correctness of the infrastructure changes.

Apply changes on push to `main`:

```
- name: Terraform Apply
  working-directory: ./chapter12/infrastructure
  run: terraform apply -auto-approve
  if: github.event_name == 'push'
```

The `terraform apply -auto-approve` command is used to deploy infrastructure changes; this command only runs if the GitHub event is a push to the main branch. The changes are applied automatically, without the need for manual approval. While this is easy to do when testing, if you do this manually, it's not a best practice. However, when you have a pipeline involved and checks in place, you will use this to make sure it proceeds to the checks without manual intervention.

If you're wondering about the Checkov rules, there are far too many to discuss in this book. What I will say is that the defaults are based on best practices. They don't fit everyone, so be sure to look through the documentation and the rules that are enabled. They also have a tendency to change from time to time since they are based on current best practices.

Now that you have an idea of how the workflow is intended to function, the next section looks at what the Terraform files are going to do.

Terraform for IaC

For this GitOps example, you're going to create and maintain AWS Network Firewall. The Terraform code that exists in the repo already simply builds a firewall. If you did not delete the firewall you created in Chapter 5, you should do that first. This configuration assumes that you are starting from scratch.

If you want to use Terraform to manage an existing firewall, you must import it first. You can find out more about importing existing resources in the Terraform documentation at https://www.terraform.io/cli/import/usage.

Again, referring back to the directory structure, you should have at least five files in Chapter 12's infrastructure folder. Let's walk through what each of these files does.

```
├── chapter12
│   ├── infrastructure
│   │   ├── backend.tf
│   │   ├── firewall-rules.tf
│   │   ├── network_firewall.tf
│   │   ├── provider.tf
│   │   └── variables.tf
```

Let's start with the backend.tf file:

```
################################
# TERRAFORM BACKEND (S3 + DDB)
################################
terraform {
  backend "s3" {
    bucket         = "terraformstatebucketsecuringtheawscloud"
    key            = "network-firewall/terraform.tfstate"
    region         = "us-west-2"
    encrypt        = true
    dynamodb_table = "terraform_state_lock"
  }
}
```

This file sets up the Terraform backend to store state files remotely in an S3 bucket. It includes configurations for state locking using DynamoDB, preventing simultaneous updates from multiple users. This ensures that Terraform operations are consistent and safe in a team environment.

At this point in the chapter, you've already spent significant time discussing and implementing Terraform configurations, so I'll just briefly revisit how Terraform works to ensure clarity. Terraform operates as an Infrastructure as Code tool that allows you to define your desired infrastructure state in configuration files. It then compares this desired state with the current state of your infrastructure and calculates the necessary changes to align the two. These changes are applied through a series of commands (`terraform init`, `terraform plan`, and `terraform apply`), ensuring that your infrastructure is created, updated, or destroyed in a predictable and controlled manner. The process is powered by a state file, which acts as a record of your current infrastructure and is critical for tracking changes over time.

In a collaborative cloud environment like the one you're building here, Terraform's ability to store state files remotely (e.g., in an S3 bucket) and implement locking mechanisms (e.g., via DynamoDB) ensures consistency and prevents conflicts when multiple users or processes are working on the same infrastructure. This approach aligns perfectly with GitOps principles, allowing you to manage infrastructure as code while maintaining security, reliability, and traceability across your AWS environment.

Here's the `provider.tf` file:

```
##########################
# PROVIDER CONFIGURATION
##########################
provider "aws" {
  region = var.aws_region
}
```

This file configures the AWS provider that Terraform uses to deploy resources. It specifies the AWS region where all resources will be created. This ensures that Terraform has the correct credentials and settings to interact with AWS infrastructure.

Here's the `variables.tf` file:

```
##########################
# VARIABLES
##########################
variable "aws_region" {
  default = "us-west-2"
}

variable "s3_bucket_name" {
  default = "terraformstatebucketsecuringtheawscloud"
}
```

```
variable "dynamodb_table_name" {
  default = "terraform_state_lock"
}

variable "vpc_cidr" {
  default = "10.0.0.0/16"
}

variable "subnet_cidrs" {
  type    = list(string)
  default = ["10.0.1.0/24", "10.0.2.0/24"]
}

variable "availability_zones" {
  type    = list(string)
  default = ["us-west-2a", "us-west-2b"]
}
```

This file defines input variables that allow for flexible and reusable Terraform configurations. It includes variables for AWS region, S3 bucket name, VPC CIDR blocks, subnet CIDRs, and availability zones, ensuring that deployments can be customized without modifying the core Terraform code.

Here's the `vpc.tf` file:

```
#########################
# VPC CONFIGURATION
#########################
resource "aws_vpc" "main" {
  cidr_block           = var.vpc_cidr
  enable_dns_support   = true
  enable_dns_hostnames = true
  tags                 = { Name = "NetworkFirewallVPC" }
}

resource "aws_subnet" "firewall" {
  count             = length(var.subnet_cidrs)
  vpc_id            = aws_vpc.main.id
  cidr_block        = var.subnet_cidrs[count.index]
  availability_zone = element(var.availability_zones, count.index)
  tags              = { Name = "NetworkFirewallSubnet-${count.index}" }
}

resource "aws_internet_gateway" "gw" {
  vpc_id = aws_vpc.main.id
  tags   = { Name = "MainIGW" }
}

resource "aws_route_table" "public" {
  vpc_id = aws_vpc.main.id
  tags   = { Name = "PublicRouteTable" }
}

resource "aws_route" "internet_access" {
```

```
   route_table_id          = aws_route_table.public.id
   destination_cidr_block = "0.0.0.0/0"
   gateway_id              = aws_internet_gateway.gw.id
}

resource "aws_route_table_association" "subnet_assoc" {
   count            = length(var.subnet_cidrs)
   subnet_id        = aws_subnet.firewall[count.index].id
   route_table_id = aws_route_table.public.id
}
```

This file provisions the network infrastructure, including the VPC, subnets, Internet Gateway, route tables, and routes. The VPC provides an isolated cloud network, while the subnets segment the network into different availability zones. The Internet Gateway and route table configurations ensure external connectivity where required.

Here's the `firewall-rules.tf` file:

```
#########################
# FIREWALL RULE GROUPS
#########################
resource "aws_networkfirewall_rule_group" "allow_basic_traffic" {
   capacity = 100
   name     = "allow-basic-traffic"
   type     = "STATEFUL"

   rule_group {
     rules_source {
       stateful_rule {
         action = "PASS"
         header {
           destination       = "ANY"
           destination_port = "ANY"
           protocol          = "TCP"
           direction         = "ANY"
           source_port       = "ANY"
           source            = "ANY"
         }
         rule_option { keyword = "sid:1" }
       }
     }
   }
}
```

This file defines the AWS Network Firewall rule groups. It includes stateful rules that determine how traffic is allowed or denied. The rules specify actions for TCP, UDP, and ICMP traffic, ensuring that only authorized communication occurs within the network.

Here's the `firewall-policy.tf` file:

```
#########################
# FIREWALL POLICY
#########################
```

```
resource "aws_networkfirewall_firewall_policy" "main" {
  name = "network-firewall-policy"

  firewall_policy {
    stateless_default_actions          = ["aws:pass"]
    stateless_fragment_default_actions = ["aws:pass"]
    stateful_rule_group_reference {
      resource_arn = aws_networkfirewall_rule_group.allow_basic_traffic.arn
    }
  }
}
```

This file creates the firewall policy, which ties together the rule groups and determines how traffic is processed. It includes configurations for stateless and stateful filtering and references the rule groups that dictate allowed and blocked traffic.

Here's the `network-firewall.tf` file:

```
##########################
# FIREWALL INSTANCE
##########################
resource "aws_networkfirewall_firewall" "main" {
  name                 = "SecureInfraFirewall"
  firewall_policy_arn  = aws_networkfirewall_firewall_policy.main.arn
  vpc_id               = aws_vpc.main.id

  subnet_mapping {
    subnet_id = aws_subnet.firewall[0].id
  }
}
```

This file deploys the AWS Network Firewall and associates it with the firewall policy. It also configures the firewall to use the appropriate VPC and subnet mappings, ensuring that the firewall operates within the intended network environment.

Here's the `outputs.tf` file:

```
##########################
# OUTPUTS
##########################
output "firewall_id" {
  value = aws_networkfirewall_firewall.main.id
}

output "firewall_policy_arn" {
  value = aws_networkfirewall_firewall_policy.main.arn
}

output "vpc_id" {
  value = aws_vpc.main.id
}

output "subnet_ids" {
  value = aws_subnet.firewall[*].id
}
```

This file defines Terraform outputs that display important resource details after deployment. It includes outputs such as the VPC ID, firewall ID, firewall policy ARN, and subnet IDs, making it easy to reference critical information for troubleshooting or integration with other infrastructure.

Now that you have an understanding of the files, you can look at the typical workflow. If you create these files on a local machine, you then need to:

1. Push these files to your repository.

2. Create a pull request to test the GitHub Actions workflow.

3. Review the Terraform plan output in the pull request.

4. Merge the changes to main to trigger the deployment to your AWS account.

This setup will establish the foundation for managing your Network Firewall rules through GitOps, allowing you to add more complex firewall rules and policies, as needed.

Now, just to make a few clarifications. When you fork my repository to implement this GitOps solution in your own AWS environment, you need to make several important modifications:

1. Update the trust policy:
    - You'll need to modify the trust policy for your IAM role to reference your forked repository instead of mine.
    - The token.actions.githubusercontent.com:sub condition needs to match your GitHub username and repository name.
    - For example, change repo:8carroll/Securing-the-Cloud-with-Brandon-Carroll to repo:your-username/their-repo-name.

2. Create GitHub secrets:
    - You need to create your own repository secrets in your forked repository.
    - AWS _ IAM _ ROLE is the ARN of your IAM role.
    - TF _ STATE _ BUCKET is your own S3 bucket name for the Terraform state.

3. Create AWS resources:
    - Create your own S3 bucket for the Terraform state.
    - Set up your own DynamoDB table for state locking.
    - Create your own OIDC provider in the AWS account.
    - Configure your own IAM role with appropriate permissions.

4. Configure the infrastructure:
    - Update any hardcoded AWS account IDs in the Terraform configurations.

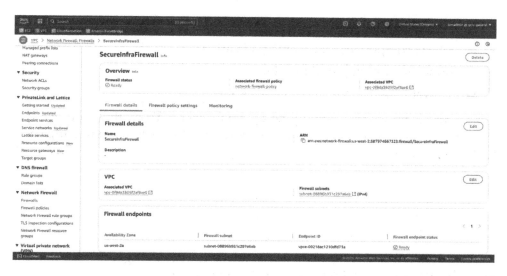

Figure 12.9: IaC deployed AWS network firewall.

- Modify region settings if you're using a different region.
- Update the VPC and subnet IDs to match your environment.

If you've done all of that as you've followed along, you should have a working firewall that shows "ready," as shown in the bottom-right corner of Figure 12.9.

Implementing Security Controls Through GitOps

When implementing Infrastructure as Code, it's crucial to include security scanning and validation steps in your pipeline. Here are some popular free tools you can add to your GitHub Actions workflow:

GitGuardian (free for public repositories):

- Scans for hardcoded secrets, credentials, and API keys
- Can be added as a GitHub Action step
- Prevents accidental exposure of sensitive information

Checkov (open source):

- Scans Terraform code for security misconfigurations
- Checks against hundreds of built-in policies
- Validates AWS security best practices

TFlint (open source):

- Lints Terraform code for potential errors
- Enforces AWS provider-specific rules
- Ensures consistent code quality

TerraScan (open source):

- Detects compliance and security violations
- Supports multiple cloud providers
- Integrates well with CI/CD pipelines

Let's modify the GitOps pipeline to use Checkov. To do that, you need to edit the `.github/workflows/network-firewall.yml` file. Add the following code before the `TFPLAN`:

```
- name: Run Checkov
    uses: bridgecrewio/checkov-action@master
    with:
      directory: ./chapter12/infrastructure
      framework: terraform
```

You can add this directly to the main branch. It will not trigger a run. Instead, you will add some new firewall rules to trigger the run.

First, in the GitHub interface, create a new feature branch called `AddingFirewallRules`, as shown in Figure 12.10.

> **note** A *feature branch* is an isolated branch created from the main branch specifically for developing a new feature or change. This approach allows you to work on the feature independently, testing and refining your code without impacting the stability of your main branch. Once the feature is complete and has undergone a thorough review, the branch is merged back into the main branch to incorporate the validated changes into production.

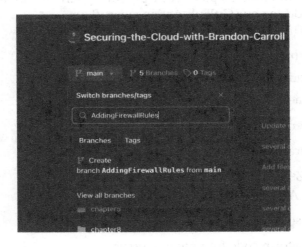

Figure 12.10: Adding firewall rules.

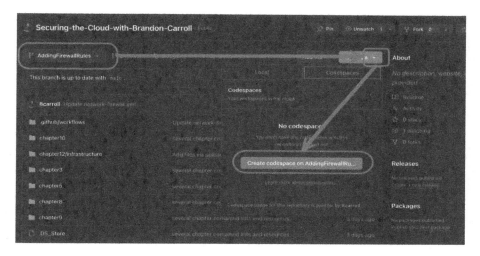

Figure 12.11: Creating a codespace on a feature branch.

Next, you can create a new codespace on that branch, as shown in Figure 12.11. Replace the contents of the `firewall-rules.tf` file in the `chapter12/infrastructure` directory with the following:

```
#########################
# FIREWALL RULE GROUPS
#########################
resource "aws_networkfirewall_rule_group" "allow_basic_traffic" {
  capacity = 100
  name     = "allow-basic-traffic"
  type     = "STATEFUL"

  rule_group {
    rules_source {
      stateful_rule {
        action = "PASS"
        header {
          destination      = "ANY"
          destination_port = "ANY"
          protocol         = "TCP"
          direction        = "ANY"
          source_port      = "ANY"
          source           = "ANY"
        }
        rule_option { keyword = "sid:1" }
      }

      stateful_rule {
        action = "PASS"
        header {
          destination      = "ANY"
          destination_port = "ANY"
          protocol         = "UDP"
```

```
        direction       = "ANY"
        source_port     = "ANY"
        source          = "ANY"
      }
      rule_option { keyword = "sid:2" }
    }

    stateful_rule {
      action = "PASS"
      header {
        destination     = "ANY"
        destination_port = "ANY"
        protocol        = "ICMP"
        direction       = "ANY"
        source_port     = "ANY"
        source          = "ANY"
      }
      rule_option { keyword = "sid:3" }
    }
  }
 }
}
```

Next, commit and push the changes:

```
@8carroll → /workspaces/Securing-the-Cloud-with-Brandon-
Carroll (AddingFirewallRules) $ git add chapter12/infrastructure/firewall-rules.tf
raffic detection"
@8carroll → /workspaces/Securing-the-Cloud-with-Brandon-Carroll
(AddingFirewallRules) $ git commit - m "Add security rules for malicious traffic
detection"
[AddingFirewallRules eb72201] Add security rules for malicious traffic detection
 1 file changed, 14 insertions(+)
@8carroll → /workspaces/Securing-the-Cloud-with-Brandon-Carroll
(AddingFirewallRules) $ git push origin AddingFirewallRules
Enumerating objects: 9, done.
Counting objects: 100% (9/9), done.
Delta compression using up to 2 threads
Compressing objects: 100% (4/4), done.
Writing objects: 100% (5/5), 1001 bytes | 1001.00 KiB/s, done.
Total 5 (delta 2), reused 0 (delta 0), pack-reused 0 (from 0)
remote: Resolving deltas: 100% (2/2), completed with 2 local objects.
To https://github.com/8carroll/Securing-the-Cloud-with-Brandon-Carroll
   feaabae..eb72201  AddingFirewallRules -> AddingFirewallRules
@8carroll → /workspaces/Securing-the-Cloud-with-Brandon-
Carroll (AddingFirewallRules) $
```

Return to the GitHub interface, and you should see a message to create a pull request, as shown in Figure 12.12.

When you click that Compare & Pull Request button, you are taken to the page to create the pull request. You can see this in Figure 12.13. Make sure you are going from your feature branch into main and then create the pull request.

The merge request will run its checks, as shown in Figure 12.14, and you can click on Details to see Checkov run as part of the pipeline now.

Figure 12.12: Compare & Pull Request button.

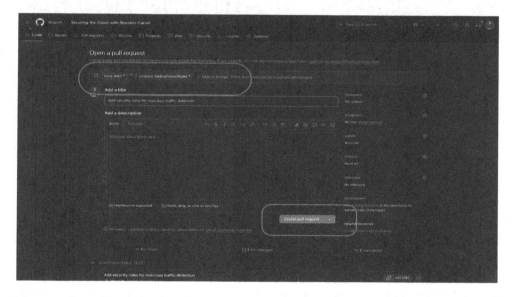

Figure 12.13: Create the pull request.

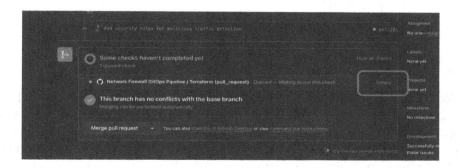

Figure 12.14: Workflow running.

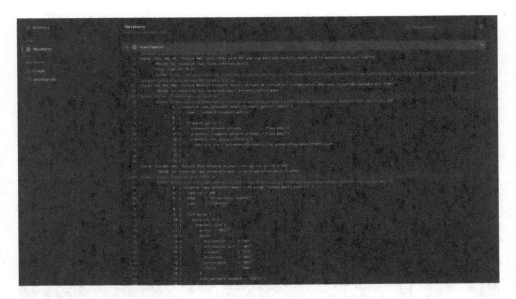

Figure 12.15: Checkov checks before deploy.

Looking at the details, you can see the checks that Checkov is looking at, with links to provide details about how to address the issues Checkov is finding. This is shown in Figure 12.15.

In this case, Checkov has identified several issues with the configuration. What you'll notice is that, even though you have a working firewall, you weren't following some security best practices, and Checkov knows it. Checkov has failed several checks, which will prevent the deployment from continuing. This is exactly why developers build pipelines and insert checks prior to deployment.

For now, on the left side, click on Workflow File, then the pencil to edit. Replace your Checkov configuration with the following code and commit it to the branch.

```
- name: Run Checkov
    uses: bridgecrewio/checkov-action@master
    with:
      directory: ./chapter12/infrastructure
      framework: terraform
      skip_check: CKV_AWS_346,CKV_AWS_345,CKV_AWS_344,CKV2_
AWS_11,CKV2_AWS_12,CKV2_AWS_63
```

Notice in the previous code that a check has been skipped. Why would you do this? Consider a situation where a default check is not aligned with your organization's policy. You can easily skip the check, while leaving it in the configuration so that you know what's going on. If policy changes and you need to start checking it again, the rule is already there. However, if you were to start seeing these fire off and you determine that you need to remediate, you

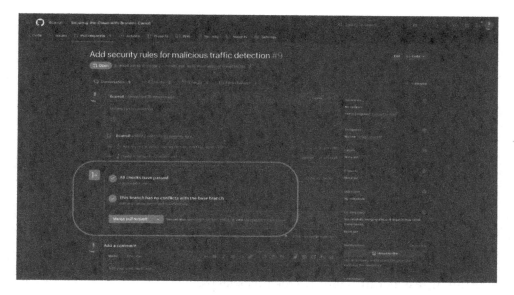

Figure 12.16: All the checks have passed.

should do so. I won't tell you whether you should or not. This should be an organization decision.

The workflow will run again. Check the details, and this time Checkov should pass. You can see this in Figure 12.16. You're now ready to merge to main so the infrastructure will get the update. Remember, at this point no infrastructure has been changed. AWS infrastructure is only changed when there is a change on the main branch in your repo.

Next, click on Merge Pull Request and confirm the merge. From there, you can click on Actions and watch the deployment succeed. You can also log in to your AWS account and view the rules in the firewall configuration.

Cleaning Up Your Resources

Now that you have explored the basics of a GitOps pipeline for security infrastructure, it's time to clean up. You'll notice a second GitHub Action in the workflow folder, called terraform-destroy.yml. This must be run manually. It will remove all the infrastructure you have created with Terraform. Open the file in the GitHub interface by clicking on the name, then click the View Runs button. From there, click Run Workflow and click Run Workflow again, as shown in Figure 12.17. You'll need to type **destroy** before you can click Run Workflow a second time.

This process will take some time, but when completed, your firewall will be deleted.

Figure 12.17: Workflow complete.

To completely clean up the AWS resources created during your GitOps setup, you'll need to remove the S3 bucket, DynamoDB table, IAM role, and OIDC provider separately, since these items persist even after destroying the main firewall infrastructure. Here are the quick steps:

- **S3 bucket:** First, empty the bucket by deleting all objects and their versions (if versioning is enabled), then delete the bucket using either the AWS Console or the AWS CLI (for example, using `aws s3 rb s3://your-bucket-name --force`).

- **DynamoDB table:** Delete the DynamoDB table used for state locking by navigating to the DynamoDB Console or running a command such as `aws dynamodb delete-table --table-name your-table-name`.

- **IAM role:** Detach any managed policies attached to the IAM role and then delete the role via the IAM Console or by calling `aws iam delete-role --role-name YourRoleName`.

- **OIDC provider:** Finally, remove the OIDC provider by going to IAM --> Identity Providers in the AWS Console or executing `aws iam delete-open-id-connect-provider --open-id-connect-provider-arn YourOIDCProviderARN`.

Following these steps will help you fully remove the auxiliary resources that were set up to support your Terraform state and GitOps workflow.

Conclusion

As you conclude both this chapter on GitOps and your journey through AWS cloud security, it's important to recognize how far you've come. You started with fundamental IAM concepts in Chapter 3, where you created users and learned about AWS security best practices. You then expanded those identity concepts with AWS IAM Identity Center in Chapter 4. Chapter 5 dove deep into infrastructure protection, implementing AWS Network Firewall, WAF, security groups, and NACLs.

Your journey continued through Chapter 6, where you explored threat detection using Amazon GuardDuty, and Chapter 7, where you implemented encryption strategies for both data at rest and in transit. Chapter 8 taught you the importance of monitoring your security posture through CloudWatch and CloudTrail, while Chapter 9 showed you how security and resilience go hand in hand in the cloud.

The final chapters of your journey—Chapters 10, 11, and 12—have transformed your approach from manual security implementations to automated, code-driven security practices. You've evolved from clicking through the AWS Console to writing Infrastructure as Code, and finally to implementing full GitOps practices with automated security checks.

Remember that cloud security is not a destination but a continuous journey of learning, adapting, and improving. The foundations covered in this book—from basic AWS security concepts to advanced automation practices—provide you with the tools to build secure, compliant, and efficient cloud environments.

Keep learning, keep practicing, and most importantly, keep building secure infrastructure. The future of cloud security depends on professionals like you who understand both the technical details and the bigger picture of securing cloud environments.

Thank you for joining me on this journey through AWS cloud security. It's your turn now to take these concepts, make them your own, and continue advancing the state of cloud security in your organizations.

Reference

Terraform Import, `https://developer.hashicorp.com/terraform/cli/import`

Index

Note: Page numbers followed by *f* refer to figures.